SHAKESPEARE, THE REFORMATION AND THE INTERPRETING SELF

EDINBURGH CRITICAL STUDIES IN SHAKESPEARE AND PHILOSOPHY
Series Editor: Kevin Curran

Edinburgh Critical Studies in Shakespeare and Philosophy takes seriously the speculative and world-making properties of Shakespeare's art. Maintaining a broad view of 'philosophy' that accommodates first-order questions of metaphysics, ethics, politics and aesthetics, the series also expands our understanding of philosophy to include the unique kinds of theoretical work carried out by performance and poetry itself. These scholarly monographs will reinvigorate Shakespeare studies by opening new interdisciplinary conversations among scholars, artists and students.

Published Titles
Rethinking Shakespeare's Political Philosophy: From Lear to Leviathan
Alex Schulman
Shakespeare in Hindsight: Counterfactual Thinking and Shakespearean Tragedy
Amir Khan
Second Death: Theatricalities of the Soul in Shakespeare's Drama
Donovan Sherman
Shakespeare's Fugitive Politics
Thomas P. Anderson
Is Shylock Jewish?: Citing Scripture and the Moral Agency of Shakespeare's Jews
Sara Coodin
Chaste Value: Economic Crisis, Female Chastity and the Production of Social Difference on Shakespeare's Stage
Katherine Gillen
Shakespearean Melancholy: Philosophy, Form and the Transformation of Comedy
J. F. Bernard
Shakespeare's Moral Compass
Neema Parvini
Shakespeare and the Fall of the Roman Republic: Selfhood, Stoicism and Civil War
Patrick Gray
Revenge Tragedy and Classical Philosophy on the Early Modern Stage
Christopher Crosbie
Shakespeare and the Truth-Teller: Confronting the Cynic Ideal
David Hershinow
Derrida Reads Shakespeare
Chiara Alfano
Conceiving Desire in Lyly and Shakespeare: Metaphor, Cognition and Eros
Gillian Knoll
Immateriality and Early Modern English Literature: Shakespeare, Donne, Herbert
James A. Knapp
Hazarding All: Shakespeare and the Drama of Consciousness
Sanford Budick
Touching at a Distance: Shakespeare's Theatre
Johannes Ungelenk
Hospitality in Shakespeare's Drama
Sophie Battell
Shakespeare, the Reformation and the Interpreting Self
Roberta Kwan

Forthcoming Titles
Making Publics in Shakespeare's Playhouse
Paul Yachnin
The Play and the Thing: A Phenomenology of Shakespearean Theatre
Matthew Wagner
Shakespeare, Levinas and Adaptation
Lisa Starks
Shakespeare's Theatre of Judgment: Seven Keywords
Kevin Curran

For further information please visit our website at: edinburghuniversitypress.com/series/ecsst

SHAKESPEARE, THE REFORMATION AND THE INTERPRETING SELF

♦ ♦ ♦

ROBERTA KWAN

EDINBURGH
University Press

Edinburgh University Press is one of the leading university presses in the UK. We publish academic books and journals in our selected subject areas across the humanities and social sciences, combining cutting-edge scholarship with high editorial and production values to produce academic works of lasting importance. For more information visit our website: edinburghuniversitypress.com

Edinburgh University Press Ltd
The Tun – Holyrood Road
12(2f) Jackson's Entry
Edinburgh EH8 8PJ

Typeset in 12/15 Adobe Sabon by
IDSUK (DataConnection) Ltd

A CIP record for this book is available from the British Library

ISBN 978 1 4744 6194 8 (hardback)
ISBN 978 1 4744 6196 2 (webready PDF)
ISBN 978 1 4744 6197 9 (epub)

CONTENTS

ACKNOWLEDGEMENTS

Generosity and gift are important ideas in this book. In writing it, I have been the recipient of numerous acts of generosity. Many people's gifts of their expertise, interest and time have helped improve my thinking and writing, and enabled me to complete the book.

I owe special thanks to Michelle Hamadache and Liam Semler. Thank you, Michelle and Liam, for your undertakings to read drafts of the whole manuscript, for each of your attentive engagements with it, and for being constant sources of encouragement. Many thanks also to Toby Davidson, Stephanie Russo and John Severn for your insightful feedback on parts of the book. Peter Bolt, Tony Cousins, Antonina Harbus, Peter Holbrook, Meredith Lake, Georgina Loveridge, Paul Sheehan and Richard Smith made valuable contributions at crucial points. Thank you to each of you.

I am grateful for the support and encouragement of Hsu-Ming Teo and other colleagues (past and present) in Macquarie University's then Department of English, now Discipline of Literature. This project has also been supported by a Macquarie University Faculty of Arts publication subsidy. Opportunities to present at Macquarie Departmental Seminars and the Early Modern Literature and Culture group at The University of Sydney benefited this book, as did lively class discussions with my 'Shakespeare and Modernity' students at The University of Sydney.

In 2019, after a prolonged period of unexpected disruption, an ADM Senior Research Fellowship gave me time to make headway on this project. Thank you, Annette Pierdziwol, for your warm support of the Fellows, and ADM staff for welcoming me in your office for the year.

It has been a great pleasure working with Edinburgh University Press. I would like to thank Michelle Houston and Kevin Curran for their enthusiasm for the project, the press's two reviewers, whose thoughtful, perceptive responses helped sharpen my thinking about the topic, and Michelle, Susannah Butler and Fiona Conn for being always understanding. Thanks also to the many others at EUP who have had a hand in this book, and to Christine Barton and Elske Janssen for their work in its production stage.

Earlier versions of small portions of Chapters 2, 3 and 4 were published in the *Journal of Language, Literature and Culture* and *English Studies*.

I feel very fortunate to have had the ongoing encouragement of my parents, Betty and Michael Kwan, and many friends and colleagues, including Emma Gleadhill, Ben Gray, Bree Hayward, Jessica King (dec.), Karen Lamb, Paul Lennox, Liz Reynolds, Justine Toh, Jimmy Van and Letitia Wigney. (I wish I could name everyone whose kind interest helped me keep plugging away.) Most of all, I am deeply grateful to Elizabeth Taylor who exemplified generosity and the hermeneutic virtue of sympathetic understanding in the many ways she helped me carry the extra load that comes with this sort of endeavour. I could not have written this book without Liz's gracious support. Finally, an off-script and heartfelt thanks to Joel the computer fixer, who expressed much enthusiasm for a stranger's book that he will likely never see, but which he generously rescued three paragraphs from its end.

SERIES EDITOR'S PREFACE

Picture Macbeth alone on stage, staring intently into empty space. 'Is this a dagger which I see before me?' he asks, grasping decisively at the air. On one hand, this is a quintessentially theatrical question. At once an object and a vector, the dagger describes the possibility of knowledge ('Is this a dagger') in specifically visual and spatial terms ('which I see before me'). At the same time, Macbeth is posing a quintessentially philosophical question, one that assumes knowledge to be both conditional and experiential, and that probes the relationship between certainty and perception as well as intention and action. It is from this shared ground of art and inquiry, of theatre and theory, that this series advances its basic premise: Shakespeare is philosophical.

It seems like a simple enough claim. But what does it mean exactly, beyond the parameters of this specific moment in *Macbeth*? Does it mean that Shakespeare had something we could think of as his own philosophy? Does it mean that he was influenced by particular philosophical schools, texts and thinkers? Does it mean, conversely, that modern philosophers have been influenced by him, that Shakespeare's plays and poems have been, and continue to be, resources for philosophical thought and speculation?

The answer is yes all around. These are all useful ways of conceiving a philosophical Shakespeare and all point to lines of inquiry that this series welcomes. But Shakespeare is philosophical in a much more fundamental way as well. Shakespeare is philosophical because the plays and poems actively create new worlds of knowledge and new scenes of ethical encounter. They ask big questions, make bold arguments and develop new vocabularies in order to think what might otherwise be unthinkable. Through both their scenarios and their imagery, the plays and poems engage the qualities of consciousness, the consequences of human action, the phenomenology of motive and attention, the conditions of personhood and the relationship among different orders of reality and experience. This is writing and dramaturgy, moreover, that consistently experiments with a broad range of conceptual crossings, between love and subjectivity, nature and politics, and temporality and form.

Edinburgh Critical Studies in Shakespeare and Philosophy takes seriously these speculative and world-making dimensions of Shakespeare's work. The series proceeds from a core conviction that art's capacity to think – to formulate, not just reflect, ideas – is what makes it urgent and valuable. Art matters because unlike other human activities it establishes its own frame of reference, reminding us that all acts of creation – biological, political, intellectual and amorous – are grounded in imagination. This is a far cry from business-as-usual in Shakespeare studies. Because historicism remains the methodological gold standard of the field, far more energy has been invested in exploring what Shakespeare once meant than in thinking rigorously about what Shakespeare continues to make possible. In response, Edinburgh Critical Studies in Shakespeare and Philosophy pushes back against the critical orthodoxies of historicism and cultural studies to clear a space for scholarship that confronts aspects of literature that can neither be reduced to nor adequately explained by particular historical contexts.

Shakespeare's creations are not just inheritances of a past culture, frozen artefacts whose original settings must be expertly reconstructed in order to be understood. The plays and poems are also living art, vital thought-worlds that struggle, across time, with foundational questions of metaphysics, ethics, politics and aesthetics. With this orientation in mind, Edinburgh Critical Studies in Shakespeare and Philosophy offers a series of scholarly monographs that will reinvigorate Shakespeare studies by opening new interdisciplinary conversations among scholars, artists and students.

Kevin Curran

TEXTUAL NOTE

Unless otherwise indicated, all biblical references come from *The Geneva Bible: 1560 Edition*. University of Wisconsin Press, 1969. Reprint, Peabody, MA: Hendrickson, 2007.

Unless otherwise indicated, the following editions have been used for quotations from Shakespeare's works:

All's Well That Ends Well. Edited by Suzanne Gossett and Helen Wilcox. The Arden Shakespeare Third Series. London: Bloomsbury, 2019.

Hamlet (Second Quarto Text). Edited by Ann Thompson and Neil Taylor. The Arden Shakespeare Third Series. London: A & C Black, 2006.

Measure for Measure. Edited by Brian Gibbons. The New Cambridge Shakespeare. Updated ed. Cambridge: Cambridge University Press, 2006.

Troilus and Cressida. Edited by David Bevington. The Arden Shakespeare Third Series. London: Bloomsbury, 1998.

Quotations from Shakespeare's other plays: *William Shakespeare: The Complete Works*. Edited by John Jowett, William Montgomery, Gary Taylor and Stanley Wells. 2nd ed. Oxford: Oxford University Press, 2005.

INTRODUCTION

REFORMATION: It is as it were the *Aequator*, or that *remarkable* Line, dividing betwixt *Eminent Prelates, Leaed Writers*, and *Benefactors to the Publick*, who lived *Before* or *After It*.

Thomas Fuller, *The History of the Worthies of England*[1]

What I am describing is the mode of the whole human experience of the world. I call this experience hermeneutical.

Hans-Georg Gadamer, *Philosophical Hermeneutics*[2]

Am I a coward?

Hamlet, II.ii.506

Hamlet needs to know. So does *Hamlet*'s audience. Is he a coward? Hamlet's problem represents one of countless occasions in Shakespeare's plays in which their characters' fortunes are bound up with their acts of interpretation. We could take up the words of the philosopher Hans-Georg Gadamer and describe these characters' 'experience of the world' as 'hermeneutical'. In turn, Shakespeare's characters and the worlds they occupy compel interpretations. Our experience of them is hermeneutical.

Describing his dramas this way brings Shakespeare close to the spirit of our time. We share with him, it seems, the assumption that to be human is to be an interpreter who seeks understanding, but does not always arrive at it. Understanding is at once the mode of being 'of human life itself' and 'always interpretation'.[3] So wrote Gadamer, whose groundbreaking work in the later twentieth century continues to demarcate the field of modern philosophical hermeneutics and whose influence is felt across the humanities today. Gadamer's insistence (alongside his teacher Martin Heidegger) that interpretation is basic to being – hermeneutics' 'so-called ontological turn' away from method – echoes through present-day conceptions of selfhood.[4] It seems a given, at least in the historical and cultural context out of which I write, that the modern self is what I call an 'interpreting self'. Otherwise put, we are always striving to know from within a 'hermeneutical *situation*', that is, 'a standpoint that limits the possibility of vision'. The entirety of our living embodies a tension. We are 'opened' toward knowing, yet inevitably delimited by our 'finitude and historicity'.[5]

Why does this modern account of human subjectivity seem to make sense of the desires, dilemmas and actions of Shakespeare's characters – his interpreting selves? What is it about Shakespeare's plays that continues to draw us to them to illuminate human experience? Why do these texts of the past feel relevant to our circumstances, our concerns, our deepest yearnings? This book explores these questions. My focus is the mid-career plays which many critics, following F. S. Boas, have termed Shakespeare's 'problem plays': *Hamlet*, *Troilus and Cressida*, *Measure for Measure* and *All's Well that Ends Well*.[6] While my emphasis so far has been on the modern, this book does not (primarily) offer a 'presentist' reading of these plays, in keeping with Ewan Fernie's account of presentism as a 'commitment to "the now"', to the present over the past, a priority which produces 'a strategy of interpreting texts in relation to current affairs'.[7] Instead, I turn first of all to seemingly distant ideas about human being and knowing to investigate the impression that the problem plays capture for us our own hermeneutical mode of experiencing the world.

These ideas were the theological concerns central to the culture-changing sixteenth-century Protestant Reformation or Reformations.[8] Theology – discourse about God and about humans and the universe in relation to God – permeated the culture of early modern England. As Arthur Marotti and Ken Jackson assert, no one in Shakespeare's time 'could imagine a theologically empty world'. To invert Marotti and Jackson's formula, one could say that early modern English people lived in a theologically full world. Of course, this description also characterises the milieu of generations prior to the playwright's. But, as Huston Diehl notes, Shakespeare and his contemporaries were the first to live in a post-Reformation, Protestant polity. In 2007, Brian Cummings commented that 'the shadow of the Reformation has been observed even across the face of Shakespeare studies, previously regarded as sacred ground for the secular spirit'. Since then, the 'shadow' has become increasingly palpable, and the myriad influences on Shakespeare's art of what Peter Marshall describes as the 'gradual yet profound cultural transformation' wrought by the Reformation in England is now a burgeoning field of enquiry.[9]

The Reformers contended for theological ideas and accompanying practices that not only divided the church, but also, by personalising understanding, played a pivotal role in (re)configuring how individuals know and individuals as knowers. This book explores keynotes of the Reformers' hermeneutics as they re-sound in the problem plays' representations of the interpreting self. The doctrines of *sola scriptura* and the priesthood of all believers gave rise to the Protestant interpreting self. Other ideas at the crux of the Reformers' theological programme shaped this subjectivity.

Within the framework of early modern Protestant hermeneutics, knowledge of God and self constitute the heart of human understanding, human fallenness corrupts and limits this understanding, and the reparative grace given by the divine other underwrites the possibility of human knowing, of reversal effected from beyond the self.

My endeavour in this book is to show how Shakespeare's engagement with the prevailing, theologically informed model of human subjectivity of his day both contributes to and complicates our sense that his plays elucidate human experience in the modern world. A perhaps unexpected tradition underlies this study. Throughout this book, I draw on an intellectual history that links modern hermeneutics back to the Reformers' theological hermeneutics. That is, the Reformers were significant, but now mostly forgotten, ancestors of the present-day interpreting self. They bequeathed the modern West a far-reaching, long-lasting 'hermeneutical legacy' (as Jens Zimmermann calls it).[10] Indeed, Gadamer himself locates Protestant hermeneutics in the substructure of modern philosophical hermeneutics. Early modern theological hermeneutics and modern philosophical hermeneutics both emphasise interpretation as ontology and, correspondingly, that ontology plays out in the self's interpretive postures, acts and experiences. Before Heidegger and Gadamer, hermeneutics had already experienced a kind of 'ontological turn'.

Gerald Bruns, for instance, proposes that Martin Luther's preparation of his first theological lectures during the winter semester of 1513–14 may represent the 'symbolic moment of transition between ancient and modern hermeneutics'. Luther gave his students a text of the Psalter printed with 'wide margins and lots of white space between the lines'. This was a radical and subversive, and 'modern', text.[11] Luther and his students would have been accustomed to the sight of the biblical text surrounded by the twelfth-century *Glossa Ordinaria*, comprised of a thick set of glosses on the biblical text drawn principally from the writings of the early Church Fathers. The *Glossa* became so influential that biblical scholars and teachers were more likely to read it than Scripture itself.[12]

Luther's text of the Psalter signals a refiguring of this relationship. As he literally opened up the space for his students to note his thoughts, and perhaps their own, Luther placed himself, and them, in the role of interpreter of knowledge. More than that, Luther opened himself (and his students) directly to the 'voice' of the other in the biblical excerpt. The understanding on offer in this hermeneutical situation was not so much propositional, but personal: 'what one understands (that is, enters into) is the mode of being or life of faith informed by the text'. For Luther, Scripture transforms one's self-understanding as one interprets it. In this, as Bruns observes, Luther followed Augustine's hermeneutics, as he (and his fellow Reformers) did in many aspects of their theology (a relationship I will expand on in the next chapter). Bruns also looks forward in time to Heidegger and Gadamer, figuring them as bearing a family resemblance to Luther. Heidegger mirrors Luther's posture of sitting under, rather than standing over, a text, while Gadamer is, in Bruns's assessment, somewhat of a 'secular Luther'. Both Luther and Gadamer prioritise 'the question of what it is to inhabit a given hermeneutical situation'.[13]

Inhabiting Hermeneutical Situations

What is it to inhabit a given hermeneutical situation, to be an interpreting self? This book's investigations take place at the intersection of three hermeneutical situations. The first involves the scenarios we encounter in *Hamlet*, *Troilus*, *Measure* and *All's Well*, each with their moving parts of characters' motives and desires, acts of ruthlessness and compassion, and circumstances marked by haplessness and happenstance. Shakespeare's own *mise en scène*, his belonging within a theologically full world reconstructed by the Reformation, constitutes the second hermeneutical situation. The third is our own context, broadly speaking. In it, modern philosophical hermeneutics has influenced the naturalised (and of course conflicting) accounts of human identity and knowing which (post)modern Western culture upholds. This convergence of past and present situates this book in, one could say, a fourth hermeneutical situation. What is it to inhabit this given hermeneutical situation? How do twenty-first-century interpreters bring together Shakespeare's plays, the theological works at the heart of his culture and the tradition of hermeneutics which connects these texts to our own times?

In their landmark article of the early twenty-first century, Jackson and Marotti remind postmodern interpreters of early modern religious cultures that we can neither bridge the gap to this historically distant world nor rationalise our difference from it. That is, 'the early modern era [is] a period that is and is not like our own'. As such, Jackson and Marotti argue, navigating hermeneutical situations like the one I have constructed for this book involves recognising the dialectic that we encounter in this space. Specifically, we should 'respond deeply to the interplay of defamiliarizing experiences and familiar knowledge', a response that involves 'reading with respect for the "other," as in an "other" culture'. As Jackson and Marotti show, when applied to reading the other culture of early modern religion, such an interpretive stance is both complicated and complicates the assumptions of a secular-religious binary that sets us entirely apart from this other culture.[14]

Gadamer employs the same dialectical language as Jackson and Marotti to clarify the nature of interpretive endeavours involving cultural artefacts of the past, or 'traditionary text[s]' as Gadamer calls them. For him, this 'hermeneutic work is based on a polarity of familiarity and strangeness' inherent in 'the language in which the text addresses us, the story that it tells us'. That is, 'hermeneutic work' unfolds 'in the play between [a] traditionary text's strangeness and familiarity to us, between being a historically intended, distanced object and belonging to a tradition'.[15] It is axiomatic that a traditionary text (or 'work of art') belongs to a tradition. A precondition of hermeneutics, according to Gadamer, is that this text's interpreters share its belonging: 'a person seeking to understand something [. . .] has, or acquires, a connection with the tradition from which the text speaks'.[16] Monica Vilhauer elaborates: 'not only is tradition our object of investigation in the human sciences, it is also something we are connected to and *belong* to as historical beings'.[17] One seeks understanding of (textual) traces of the past in what Gadamer terms the '*in-between*', in the interplay of a text's historical alterity and tradition's mediation of its proximity. My choice of 'seek' here gestures to the posture of interpreting selves working in this 'in-between'. For Gadamer, arriving at final, determinative knowledge cannot be the outcome of this undertaking. Instead, what ensues is that 'we understand in a *different* way, *if we understand at all*'.[18]

Understanding 'in a different way', understanding informed by a dialectic of strangeness and familiarity, encapsulates, to a significant degree, my aim in reading Shakespeare's plays as part of the theologically modulated hermeneutic tradition that emphasises interpretation as ontology. Here, the nature of the texts and tradition that comprise this book's hermeneutic work necessitate some recalibrating of Gadamer's model. On one hand, we continue to stress the currency of Shakespeare's historically distanced texts. They are familiar, rather than strange, to us. Or at least we perceive them to be. On the other hand, because the Reformation occupies a place in the history of the hermeneutical tradition to which both Shakespeare's texts and we as their twenty-first-century interpreters belong, this tradition itself embodies a dialectic of remoteness and immediacy. Indeed, Gadamer is quick to stress that, while tradition evokes familiarity by connecting historical texts and their modern interpreters, this resonance does not signal continuity ('as is the case with the unbroken stream of tradition').[19]

Rupture, rather than coherence, especially explains the ancestral branch of modern hermeneutics that informs this study. Its origins, the Reformers' texts, are now largely strange to us. Many of the culture-shaping ideas derived from these mainstream early modern works made their way into Shakespeare's plays, more than that, into the bloodstream of Western identity. They are significantly present in the background of our intuitions about human being and knowing. But we no longer recognise them. As such, the mapping of strange and familiar, early modern and (post)modern in the particular 'in-between' in which this book is located gives rise to a polyphony of resonance and dissonance. Some aspects of the early modern Protestant self who frames my engagements with Shakespeare's characters and their circumstances closely resembles models of subjectivity that are regularly brought to bear on readings of Shakespeare's plays. In other ways, the Reformers' self complicates our assumed hermeneutic paradigms as their ideas about human being and knowing cut sharply against the grain of our (post)modern narratives of selfhood.

We are in unison, I think, with the Reformers' emphasis on the 'human hermeneutical condition' (as Kevin Vanhoozer phrases it), on fallen humanity's desire to know and individuals' frequent experiences of epistemological and interpersonal frustration.[20] But modernity is less at home with other hermeneutical implications of the Reformers' theology. Their figuring of knowing as an inherently intersubjective phenomenon seems to strike an especially jangling chord in our present social and intellectual climate. As mentioned in my quick sketch of Luther's hermeneutics (via Bruns), Protestant hermeneutics posits that understanding, including self-understanding, takes place not when interpreting selves read themselves into a 'text' (written or otherwise), but when they open themselves to the much more confronting and personal experience of being read by the (textual) other.[21] That is, understanding is received (through revelatory acts of grace) more than it is acquired, a delineation of the autonomy of individuals that, it seems, threatens their very agency. As my engagements with some present-day critical responses will indicate, the perception that the Reformers stripped away the agency of the interpreting self has, not surprisingly, engendered a high level of unease and sometimes sheer disdain towards them and their ideas about revelation and grace.

This book keeps circling back to this question of human agency in its explorations of the 'in-between' of Shakespeare's plays and the hermeneutical tradition. With Jackson and Marotti's call to respect the otherness of temporally distant religious cultures in mind, I will show how my (inevitably partial) recovery of the hermeneutical tradition that includes Shakespeare and ourselves brings forth a different understanding of the Protestant interpreting self. This model cuts across prevailing outlooks on subjectivity and agency that cannot accommodate the Reformers' theology of divine revelation and rescue. In short, the Protestant interpreting self embodies a seeming paradox. This self, it appears, at once does not have and does have agency. Divine grace (re-)constitutes this fundamentally intersubjective self in relation to others, especially the divine other himself. Yet, the same grace empowers her to be a moral and ethical agent. She is given enough understanding of herself and God to (fallibly and fitfully) exercise her will to resist her tendency towards self-interested readings of self and others, and choose instead to interpret others in accordance with a paradigm of grace.

This model of selfhood, I suggest, refracts a different and sometimes penetrating light on Shakespeare's interpreting selves and, through them, the values and outlooks that characterise the modern self. Protestant hermeneutics offers a lens through which to look again at Shakespeare's problem plays, to understand them in a different way as they stage the human hermeneutical condition, heighten audiences' awareness of our own interpretive mode of being and prompt us to question what it is to inhabit a hermeneutical situation.

Shakespeare and Hermeneutics

Moving to Shakespeare's stage, it seems a matter of course that I firstly turn my attention to *Hamlet*. *Hamlet* is probably the Shakespearean drama (the drama, period, some may argue) that most strikingly represents and effects for audiences a consciousness of the self as an interpreting creature. Many scholars have agreed with Maynard Mack's description of *Hamlet*'s world as laden with 'questions, anguished, meditative, alarmed'.[22] Hamlet contributes to this tense mood even as it enshrouds him. 'Am I a coward?' he asks in the third of his famous soliloquies (II.ii.506). Theatregoers hear these words as one of many acts of self-interpretation. Throughout the play, Hamlet appears obsessed with understanding himself, moreover, with understanding per se.

'Hamlet' could be a metonym for humanity's hermeneutical condition. That is not to say that Shakespeare situates his audience as passive, objective observers of his self-reflexive, meaning-seeking hero. Hamlet's question entangles playgoers and readers in a complex interpretive web, compelling us to try to make sense of him. Is he a coward, or is his inaction a reasonable response to the ambiguities obfuscating the prior words of the ghost? Further, is Hamlet's question artless? Or is he stalling, avoiding real-world action by mimicking the travelling player who 'could force his soul so to his own conceit' (II.ii.488)? *Hamlet*'s audience feels the urgency to understand Hamlet. The hermeneutical situation Shakespeare constructs for his audience foregrounds our own anxieties around knowing by filtering our interpretive acts through the prism of Hamlet's fraught interpretations of himself and his society. Throughout the play, we retrace and revise our interpretation of Shakespeare's protagonist. Seeking to make sense of Hamlet makes us more aware of our status, and fallibility, as sense makers.

While it is almost impossible to leave *Hamlet* out of a book investigating humanity's hermeneutical condition, it is no surprise that *Troilus*, *Measure* and *All's Well* also make the list. 'Problem play', first used to describe the late-Victorian social realist dramas of Ibsen and Shaw, has been a contested and somewhat fluid category since Boas appropriated and redefined the term in 1896, applying it to these three plays and *Hamlet*.[23] To Boas, a quartet of common characteristics mark out the plays as befitting the 'problem' epithet. The dramas each depict profligate young men and degenerate societies 'ripe unto rottenness', present emotional and ethical dilemmas, confound their audiences and end unsatisfactorily, thus requiring theatregoers 'to interpret their enigmas as best we can'.[24] Despite objections, the problem play label has, to employ Paul Yachnin's aptly chosen term, 'stuck' – especially to *Troilus*, *Measure* and *All's Well*.[25] *Hamlet*'s inclusion in the group has provoked greater resistance. Boas acknowledges that *Hamlet*'s tragic ending sets it apart from the other plays. Nevertheless, he insists that *Hamlet* shares with the other three a 'general temper and atmosphere' – an 'untraditional, disturbing nature', as Susan Snyder puts it – such that none of the four plays can 'be strictly called comedies or tragedies'. While not everyone agrees, 'critical history' has, Snyder notes, found 'the basic grouping too useful to abandon'.[26]

The grouping is indeed useful for exploring Shakespeare's absorption of the turn to interpretation as ontology advanced by the Protestant Reformation. The common elements of the problem plays identified by Boas offer some preliminary clues as to why these plays may especially show the influence of Protestant hermeneutics. First, Boas's stress on the plays' attention to individual and societal corruption suggests the centrality to the moral imaginations of early modern English people of the biblical Fall narrative and accompanying pessimistic Protestant doctrine of human fallenness. This anthropological paradigm is a critical component of the Reformers' hermeneutics, problematising knowing and understanding in ways which, centuries later, echo in the emphasis on human finitude which we find in modern philosophical hermeneutics.

Many critics observe the problem plays' mutual pessimistic view of human nature. The characters seem unable to disentangle themselves from the moral frailties they embody – hubris and hypocrisy, for instance – or the fallen condition of their worlds. For Snyder, each problem play presents a 'bleak view of a hard-core depravity', especially in their characterisations of 'young men in crisis'. (On this point about Shakespeare's male protagonists, Snyder follows E. M. W. Tillyard, but Boas is in the background.)[27] Here I add that the plays also feature morally complex (mostly) young women, whose actions contribute to the 'bleak view' offered to audiences. Moreover, and of most interest to this study, *Hamlet*, *Troilus*, *Measure* and *All's Well* implicate their dubious, fallible characters in their interpretations of themselves, others and their environment, and of the moral and ethical issues (such as revenge and bed tricks) they encounter in worlds manifesting greater or lesser degrees of 'rottenness'.

According to Jean Howard, definitions of the problem play after Boas have 'centred largely on moral questions' that perplex characters and audiences alike.[28] Howard relies (probably too exclusively) on Ernest Schanzer's mid-twentieth-century account of Shakespeare's problem plays. For Schanzer, each play leaves theatregoers in a state of confusion by staging a central moral dilemma in such a way that offers no conclusive resolution.[29] (In what appears to be a case of confirmation bias, Schanzer argues that of Boas's four problem plays, only *Measure* fits this description, grouping it instead with *Julius Caesar* and *Antony and Cleopatra*.) Like Boas before them, Schanzer and Howard highlight the problem plays' effects on their audiences. The plays alert us, one could say, to our hermeneutical condition as, within the hermeneutical situation of the theatre, their characters' disorientation spills over into audiences' experiences and processes of sense making.

As Boas notes, the plays' jarring endings – either the seemingly forced comic conclusions of *Measure* and *All's Well* or *Hamlet*'s and *Troilus*'s ambiguous dénouements – especially amplify our puzzlement (and also, Boas suggests, our excitement and fascination).[30] Here, I return to the matter of genre, vividly figured by Rosalie Colie as 'tiny subcultures with their own habits, habitats, and structures of ideas as well as their own forms'.[31] Contemplations of these literary subcultures come packaged, of course, with larger questions about knowing and understanding. The problem plays' 'generic anomaly' is the starting point of many people's endeavours to pinpoint the plays' mutual 'problem'.[32] To Yachnin (with *Troilus*, *Measure* and *All's Well*, but not *Hamlet*, in view), the plays 'explode genre'.[33]

While the First Folio lists them as 'Comedies', *Measure*'s and *All's Well*'s dark tones, moral knottiness and the unsettled state in which they leave their audiences do not sit easily with the plays' 'elaborately comic shaping[s]'.[34] Many critics prefer to see them as 'tragicomedies', inspired to some extent by Giovanni Battista (Giambattista) Guarini's 1590 tragicomedy *Il pastor fido* (translated into English in 1602) and Guarini's defence of the new genre in *The Compendium of Tragicomic Poetry* (1601).[35] To Guarini, tragicomedies are at once tragic and comic in both form and effect, 'mingling [. . .] tragic and comic pleasure, which does not allow hearers to fall into excessive tragic melancholy or comic relaxation'.[36] As Verna Foster comments, the 'organic relationship between the tragic and the comic' Guarini delineates continues to underlie theoretical accounts of tragicomedy.[37]

Troilus is also, in Foster's opinion (and that of W. B. Yeats and Jan Kott), a tragicomedy.[38] But the play's history shows that it cannot be neatly classified. As Michael Neill observes, *Troilus* is exemplary of the 'generic instability' of early modern works.[39] When first published in two versions by the same printer in 1609, *Troilus*'s title page announced it as a history play. In one of these versions, a prefatory note 'to an euer reader' also insistently infers that this 'historie' is a comedy: 'it deserues such a labour, as well as the best commedy in Terrence or Plautus'.[40] Contrarily, the First Folio retitles it *The Tragedie of Troylus and Cressida*. As is well known, the play occupies a liminal space in the Folio, inserted (as a last-minute addition) between the 'Histories' and the 'Tragedies' and not listed in the 'Catalogve'. These early indications of editorial indecision adumbrate *Troilus*'s continuing status as an interpretive conundrum for its 'euer reader[s]'. Through the centuries, many readers have commented on *Troilus*'s singularity, its embodiment of, in David Bevington's words, 'a genre, or *mélange* of genres, all to itself'.[41]

What about *The Tragicall Historie of Hamlet, Prince of Denmark*, as it is titled (minus or plus the comma) in both Q1 (1603) and Q2 (1604/1605), but which had, by the First Folio, shed one generic category to become simply: *The Tragedie of Hamlet, Prince of Denmark*? This titular difference does not necessarily confuse *Hamlet*'s generic status. Instead, the play clouds the locus of its tragedy. Uncertainty lies at *Hamlet*'s core. Shakespeare's play, with its questioning mood and indeterminacy, compels playgoers to try to put our fingers on who and/or what may be responsible for the tragedy playing out before us, and also trips us up throughout this endeavour. Attending to *Hamlet*'s tragic 'habits' and 'habitats' does not ease the complications and difficulties around knowing which the play engenders. In this way, *Hamlet* is like the other problem plays, disrupting neat correlations of genre and meaning. As the action in these plays pivots on their characters' unknowing, or flawed knowing, or deceptive knowing, and invites their audiences to make judgements about these characters as interpreters of self and others, circumstances and cosmos, they also have the effect of shifting our interpretive gazes onto ourselves. The problem plays prompt their viewers and readers to question what it is to inhabit the hermeneutical situations in which we find ourselves.

The Reformation and Hermeneutics

This question, and the image of the interpreting self it contains, takes us back to the scene of Shakespeare's writing: to theological hermeneutics, to Luther and his students' reading of the Psalter sans the *Glossa Ordinaria*, and hence to one of the decisive pressure points that brought on the Protestant Reformation. Epistemological authority was the matter at issue. An evolving conception of interpretation as basic to human being, of all people as (in a sense) analogues of Luther and his students, developed from conflicts over who held the keys to the knowledge of ultimate concern to most people across the sixteenth-century Christian world.

What is this knowledge? Luther's fellow Reformer Jean Calvin explains in the famous, programmatic opening of *The Institution of Christian Religion* (*Institutes* henceforth): 'The whole summe in a maner of all our wisedome [. . .] consisteth in two partes, that is to say, the knowledge of God, and of our selues.'[42] With Heidegger's and Gadamer's notion of a 'hermeneutical circle [which] describes the ontological structure of understanding' in the background, Zimmermann characterises Calvin's (and his fellow Reformers') pairing of knowledge of God and self as a 'hermeneutical circle of self-knowledge' or 'existential hermeneutical circle of self and God'.[43] Where does one attain this interdependent, framing knowledge, this 'existential apprehension' of God and self that cultivates wisdom?[44] Who is authorised to determine what this knowledge is?

The controversy erupting around these questions played a large part in causing what Diarmaid MacCulloch calls 'the greatest fault-line to appear in Christian culture since the Latin and Greek halves of the Roman empire went their separate ways a thousand years before'.[45] As Gadamer describes it, the Reformers stood on one side of this 'fault-line' in 'defense of their own understanding of Scripture [as the primary and final source of knowledge of God and self] against the attack of the Tridentine theologians and their appeal to the indispensability of tradition'. Gadamer guides us from this theological controversy to its contribution to the reconfiguring of the relation of self and knowing. 'During the Reformation', Gadamer writes, 'Protestant hermeneutics developed from an insistence on understanding Scripture solely on its own basis (*sola scriptura*) as against the principle of tradition upheld by the Roman church.'[46] The Reformers' 'insistence', in opposition to Roman Catholicism's emphasis on 'tradition', occasioned vernacular translations of the Bible and 'the universal priesthood of all believers' – 'laymen' reading Scripture for themselves.[47] (It is worth noting that the sixteenth-century understanding of 'tradition' differs from Gadamer's use of the term in his hermeneutics.) In Chapter 1, I will expand on how the Reformers' notions of *sola scriptura* and the universal priesthood of all believers shaped a Protestant hermeneutics that was instrumental in starting a 'hermeneutic revolution', as Jean Grondin terms it.[48]

Along with this 'revolution', placing the Bible in the hands of the laity also brought about a hermeneutical complication not previously encountered. This was 'the difficulty involved with reading, that is, of bringing the scriptures to speak' without priestly mediation.[49] Ordinary readers struggled to make sense of what they were reading, a situation which, according to Gadamer, 'raised the art of understanding in its diverse dimensions to methodical self-awareness'. This 'modern' construction of subjectivity that implicates the self in understanding became a culture shifting overflow of 'the Reformation's theological turning against the tradition and toward the principle of scripture'.[50] Unfamiliar as it may be to us, this turn is impressed into our present-day assumption that we relate hermeneutically to all aspects of reality.

Gadamer identifies a further 'hermeneutical problem' resulting from 'the Reformation's return to scripture'. This 'problem' centred on the 'Christian message itself'. With the uncoupling of the biblical text from tradition, Scripture's readers encountered 'a new, uncanny radicality' which cut against the grain of humans' 'natural prior self-understanding', that is, against the prevailing pre-Reformation perspective on knowledge of ultimate concern. Specifically, as Gadamer puts it, the Reformers interpreted Scripture as teaching that 'not obedience to the law and the performing of meritorious works but faith alone – and that means faith in the incredible fact of God's becoming man and in the resurrection – promises justification'.[51] 'Justification by grace through faith alone' became the Reformation's catchcry, preached in opposition to Roman Catholicism's incorporation of meritorious human works in the economy of salvation. Vanhoozer, writing on the hermeneutical implications of the Reformers' understanding of the operation of divine grace, defines grace as 'the gift of God's beneficent presence and activity'.[52] For Luther and company, faith alone in grace alone, that is, faith in God's presence and activity, which culminated in Christ's revelatory and salvific incarnation and resurrection (and between these two events, his crucifixion), opens the door to knowledge of God. In turn, knowing God aids greater (but not full) self-understanding.

Together with their emphasis on the Fall's corruptive effects across every domain of human being, the Reformers' pivotal teaching on divine revelation and grace map the material dynamics of their theological hermeneutics: their conception of what it is to be an interpreting self. To summarise the connections which I will develop in Chapter 1, first, the Reformers harnessed their anthropology to their hermeneutics. For them, the Fall ensured that humans' interpretations of themselves, of others (including the divine other), and of the world and how to act in it will be circumscribed and impaired by both unknowing and self-interest. 'The vnderstanding minde is subiect to blindnes, and the hart to peruersnesse' is how Calvin describes the human condition.[53] Yet, second, divine grace underwrites the possibility, although not the certainty, of human understanding. Through divine 'beneficent presence and activity', through God's self-revelation in both Christ and Scripture and the transformative reversals he effects in minds and hearts, it is possible for human interpretive acts to yield knowledge. Further, as both the Fall which undermined knowing and the grace which makes knowing possible situate the self interpersonally in relationship with transcendent others – first, God, and then other people – such interpretive acts are also necessarily bound up with ethics. The interpreting self figured by the Reformers' theological hermeneutics is an intersubjective, rather than autonomous, knower – knowing and understanding (and failing to know and understand) in ways that are affected by and affect others.

A theologically resonant rendering of the interpreting self as fallen runs through *Hamlet*, *Troilus*, *Measure* and *All's Well*. 'Human fallenness' could well serve as a synonym for the 'hard-core depravity' which Snyder identifies with the plays' perspectives on human nature.[54] In each problem play, Shakespeare entangles his characters' impoverished epistemological and moral conditions in their responses to the existential, interpersonal, ethical and, not infrequently, theological problems and choices in the foreground of the hermeneutical situations in which they find themselves. These negotiations, it is worth adding, underscore the plays' relevance to modern audiences. Concomitantly, the problem plays each hint (some more loudly than others) at the possibility of hermeneutical assistance from a transcendent source akin to divine grace, however distant or parodic this assistance may be.

By contending that these plays are clothed with contemporary theological concerns, I am not suggesting that they are propositional vehicles for the Protestantism of Elizabethan and Jacobean England. Clearly, Shakespeare's plays are not propositional. Nor does my argument rest on Shakespeare's personal allegiance to Protestantism. In years gone by, much critical energy has been devoted to proving that Shakespeare was an orthodox Protestant, or a staunch Catholic, or a person of no religious belief. But, in Cummings's efficient summary, 'the materials for a spiritual autobiography of William Shakespeare are manifestly missing'. Like David Daniell, in this book I seek 'to come properly to Shakespeare through [his] Protestant inheritance' as a member of the first generation of English people to live in a Protestant polity.[55] While the settings of the problem plays are best described as a religious mixed bag – pre-Christian, Catholic and Protestant – Shakespeare's 'Protestant inheritance' comes out in these plays' representations of the self's open-ended, at times pressured and precarious, relationship to reality as its interpreter.

Interpreting Shakespeare and the Reformation

If this book is unconcerned about Shakespeare's confessional stance, the question remains about where it sits within the increasingly busy field of Shakespeare and religion. In 2017, Marotti and Jackson summarised the 'three basic approaches' taken by contemporary scholars. One approach is historicist and includes arguments for Shakespeare's 'supposed beliefs'; a second adduces early modern theatre, especially Shakespearean theatre, in support of a 'secularization thesis'; the third, the expansive domain of political theology, engages critical theory to read Shakespeare's works as the products of 'a significant ethical and religious thinker'.[56] Each approach contributes to the shape of my own, be it through points of agreement or difference. On historicism, as discussed, while the Reformation is integral to the critical paradigm I employ to interpret Shakespeare's problem plays, so too is the passageway from the past to the present opened up by the hermeneutic tradition. My investigations encompass both the plays' historical circumstances and our sense that these plays hold up a mirror to the modern-day self.

The second approach is of course inclusive of the once dominant and still influential voices of New Historicist scholars. On one hand, we must credit New Historicists of the later twentieth century for their significant role in animating a renewed enthusiasm in the interfaces between Shakespeare and early modern England's religio-cultural landscape. Daniel Swift, for example, notes the debt owed to Stephen Greenblatt by all scholars who have taken notice of Shakespeare's interest in contemporary issues around the sacraments.[57] Yet New Historicism established a trajectory for explorations of Shakespeare and religion whose seemingly ineluctable destination is a secularising theatre, brought into being by a playwright who drew on an emotionally plangent, evocative 'Catholic aesthetic' to resist and replace the hegemonic institutions and ideologies of early modern Protestant England.[58] As Michael Davies observes, in contrast to a warm and generative Catholic aesthetic, Greenblatt and many other critics characterise Protestantism as authoritarian and oppressive, austere and wanting imagination.[59]

By collapsing religion into politics and reading Protestantism as univocally harmful, New Historicism elides the lived experiences and wide-ranging emotional connections to Christianity of everyday people within an early modern British Protestantism which was, in Alec Ryrie's assessment, 'an *intense*, *dynamic*, and *broad-based* religious culture'.[60] This book follows a different path to New Historicism, one already taken by some scholars working within the turn to religion in Shakespeare and early modern literary studies of the last four or five decades. A willingness to 'take seriously religious beliefs, ideas, and history' energises this scholarship (to cite Jackson and Marotti's description of Debra Shuger's effect on the field).[61] In associating this book with that ethos, I also have in mind the challenge Davies identified earlier this century, namely, the need (and opportunity) to redress the lack of scholarship that 'reads Shakespeare [. . .] as a dramatist sensitive and indeed interior to the language and modes of thinking of the mainstream Protestantism of his time'.[62]

In contrast, the third approach to Shakespeare and religion invests the turn to religion with the interests and language of postmodern philosophy and theology. As described by Julia Reinhard Lupton, one of the leading exponents of this way of reading Shakespeare, the turn is a 'return to theory', a recentring of scholarly attention on 'the big questions and systematic frameworks of psychoanalysis, philosophy, theology, and politics'.[63] 'Return' signals a reversal of fortune for theology after its 'overt rejection' (William West's term) from the realm of theory.[64] Through the work of Lupton and others, early modern literary studies in the twenty-first century has embraced perhaps unexpected alliances between theology and theory. As West, repurposing a biblical motif, acutely puts it: 'the stone the builders refused looks more and more likely to be the capstone'.[65] To Lupton, '*religion is a form of thinking*' that affords a framework for considerations of what Hannah Arendt (and Kant) call 'thought-things': 'speculative questions, inherently unanswerable' that have occupied humans as thinkers irrespective of their situatedness in place and time. Theology offers a room in which one can sit and 'think with' or 'think alongside' Shakespeare and his plays about these enduring questions.[66]

The overlaps between this third approach and this book become evident in Lupton's 're-affiliat[ion]' of religious thinking with both 'the high tradition of formal theology, philosophy, and hermeneutics [and] ordinary acts of rumination'. For Lupton, both modes of religious thinking are directed, ultimately, to the question of how to live, that is, to living virtuously with others as 'an exemplary subjective possibility'.[67] This emphasis on community, on the self as an ethical, responsible actor, also comes to the surface throughout this study. Without doubt, the growing body of work on Shakespeare and political theology opens up space for this book in the critical landscape of early modern literature and religion. All the same, while at times this return to theory intersects with the ways in which I seek to bring together Shakespeare, theology and significant questions about human being, at other times a wide-angle lens is needed to see both approaches in the same frame.

Here, I revisit the issue of the relation of Shakespeare's plays to his own religious context – the question mark, one might say, over who, along with Shakespeare, is in the room as our theological thought partners. For Lupton, the necessary condition for the type and direction of thinking with Shakespeare she envisages is religion's decoupling from culture to stake a claim for its 'universality', as opposed to its 'universalism' – an orientation towards 'truth' rather than 'a species of ideology'.[68] To Lupton and Graham Hammill, religion has a twofold relation to culture: religious expression is localised and historicised, and yet, because of its transhistorical concerns and markers of identity, religion also 'aim[s] to transcend culture'.[69] Across place and time, religion's discourses find expression in transitory manifestations of 'universality' such as 'kinship with the poor, love of neighbor [and] creaturely community'. Although Lupton's (and company's) hermeneutics incorporates an 'awareness of Shakespeare's historical possibilities', it not only lightly touches on the religious thinking, hence culture, of the playwright's day, but is also wary of it, especially the Reformers' thinking.[70]

For instance, in her chapter on 'Paul Shakespeare', Lupton suggests that Luther's reading of Galatians 2 employs a form of 'Marcionism': the creation and exacerbation of binaries.[71] In Galatians 2, Paul narrates his clash with Peter over the latter's imposition of Jewish food laws on a Gentile congregation. As Lupton sees it, Luther's interpretation of this chapter represents a divisive Protestantism, which she contrasts with the reconciling impulse of Catholic theology. Luther, according to Lupton, sets Paul against Peter (whom Luther denounces) and reads the two apostles as metonyms for, respectively, Protestantism and Catholicism.[72] That is, for Lupton, the Reformers' thinking pulls against the 'pluralist, creaturely, and universal' inflections of both Shakespeare and 'universalist' religion, the latter exemplified by the multivocal Paul Lupton synthesises from Protestant, Catholic, Jewish and postmodern philosophical thought.[73]

But contrary to this reading of Luther, he does not associate the apostles with opposite sides of the Reformation divide; nor does he elevate Paul over Peter. Rather, Luther writes in his *Lectures on Galatians* that 'all the apostles had the same calling, the same commission, and the same Gospel. [. . .] there was parity among them throughout'. To Luther, Paul did not 'rebuke' Peter to 'put him to shame', but to preserve the truth.[74] Moreover, if Peter functions as a metonym for any group of people, this group is all humanity, or perhaps all believers. Luther aligns the apostle's 'sin' with David's, that of 'other saints', and his own and his readers' while, in the next breath, assuring them that, although 'sin is always present and the godly feel it [. . .] it is ignored and hidden in the sight of God, because Christ the Mediator stands between'. Luther then urges his readers that 'because you have taken hold of

Christ by faith [. . .] go and love God and your neighbor', an instance of the 'universalist' religious postures identified by Lupton that echoes throughout Luther's and his fellow Reformers' writings (including numerous times in these lectures).[75] Rather than separate Peter and Paul, Luther interprets the Galatians account of their conflict through the lens of the Reformers' theologies of human fallenness and divine grace and their issuing in (perhaps surprising) implications for living in the world with others. These ideas and ways of being were central to the religious thinking of Shakespeare's culture and inform this book's attempt to 'think with Shakespeare' (to borrow Lupton's inspiring image).

In Chapter 1, I explore the key events and ideas of the Reformation that gave rise to a sense of human existence as hermeneutic and a Protestant configuration of the interpreting self. In subsequent chapters, I read the problem plays alongside different facets of this model of subjectivity, as well as hermeneutical issues pertinent to each play which, in turn, foreground its relevance to our own milieu. My focus in Chapter 2 is the extent to which we consider Hamlet responsible for the hermeneutical tragedy that unfolds in *Hamlet*'s play-world. My reading offers an account of the interpreting self that sits somewhat at right angles to interpretations of Hamlet which absolutise either his freedom to chart his own destiny or his powerlessness in the face of determining forces. Such polarising responses to Shakespeare's character, I suggest, mirror modern-day tendencies to interpret others and their circumstances similarly.

It has often been observed that the cynical play-world which Shakespeare presents in *Troilus*, with its depiction of selves and societies fragmenting under the strain of characters' vainglory and hunger for recognition, feels uncomfortably close to our own. In Chapter 3, I argue that the Reformers' alertness to the possible deceptiveness of one's self-interpretations and the potential that this flawed knowledge has to corrode the self as a moral agent echo in *Troilus*'s critical stance towards its characters, and perhaps also through *Troilus* into the present day.

Chapter 4 (on *Measure*) engages with the current critical discontent engendered by the Reformers' elision of human merit from the economy of salvation and the implications of their discourse on divine mercy for two major themes in modern conceptions of selfhood: justice and individual agency. While some critics read *Measure*'s problematic Duke as an embodiment of the Reformers' theology, my contention is that their ideas about mercy critique him. Shakespeare's representation of his play-acting Duke parallels him with his Deputy – the hypocritical, egregious Angelo – even as *Measure*'s unsettling expressions of mercy turn the tables to ask uncomfortable questions about modernity's self-determining, self-justifying self.

The end-oriented hermeneutic suggested by *All's Well*'s title calls to mind the prominent eschatological hermeneutic which directed early modern English people's attention to the next life in a way that made them acutely aware of their epistemological limitations, relational incompleteness and ethical responsibilities in this one. Chapter 5 parallels this state of being with the experience Shakespeare engenders for his audience through his play's eschatological allusions and equivocal ending. I argue that our response to Shakespeare's play gestures to a 'desire for transcendence' which is 'secretly', but deeply, embedded in modern Western culture (as Gadamer puts it).[76] This desire is resonant with the hermeneutic tradition which informs my undertaking to understand in a different way both Shakespeare's problem plays and our sense of their abiding relevance.

Notes

1. Thomas Fuller, *The History of the Worthies of England* (London: J.G.W.L. and W.G., 1662), 39. Italics original.

2. Hans-Georg Gadamer, *Philosophical Hermeneutics*, ed. and trans. David E. Linge (Berkeley: University of California Press, 1976), 15.
3. Hans-Georg Gadamer, *Truth and Method*, trans. Joel Weinsheimer and Donald G. Marshall, 2nd, rev. ed. (London: Continuum, 2004), 250, 306.
4. Gerald L. Bruns, *Hermeneutics Ancient and Modern* (New Haven: Yale University Press, 1992), 2.
5. Gadamer, *Truth and Method*, 301; xxiii, xxvii. Italics original.
6. Frederick S. Boas, *Shakespeare and his Predecessors* (New York: C. Scribner's Sons, 1896), 345.
7. Ewan Fernie, 'Shakespeare and the Prospect of Presentism', *Shakespeare Survey* 58 (2005): 169, 174.
8. I will follow Diarmaid MacCulloch in using 'Reformation' as 'shorthand' for the multiple Protestant Reformations which took place on the Continent and in England. I will also use 'Reformers' to refer generally to the major players in the Protestant Reformation(s). Diarmaid MacCulloch, *Reformation: Europe's House Divided 1490–1700* (London: Penguin Books, 2004), xix.
9. Arthur F. Marotti and Ken Jackson, 'Religion, Secularity, and Shakespeare', in *The Shakespearean World*, ed. Jill L. Levenson and Robert Ormsby (Abingdon: Routledge, 2017), 544; Huston Diehl, 'Religion and Shakespearean Tragedy', in *The Cambridge Companion to Shakespearean Tragedy*, ed. Claire McEachern (Cambridge: Cambridge University Press, 2003), 86; Brian Cummings, 'The Protestant and Catholic Reformations', in *The Oxford Handbook of English Literature and Theology*, ed. Andrew Hass, David Jasper and Elisabeth Jay (Oxford: Oxford University Press, 2007), 80; Peter Marshall, '(Re)defining the English Reformation', *Journal of British Studies* 48, no. 3 (2009): 565.
10. Jens Zimmermann, *Recovering Theological Hermeneutics: An Incarnational-Trinitarian Theory of Interpretation* (Grand Rapids, MI: Baker Academic, 2004), 17.
11. Bruns, *Hermeneutics Ancient and Modern*, 139–40.
12. Alister E. McGrath, *The Intellectual Origins of the European Reformation*, 2nd ed. (Malden, MA: Blackwell, 2004), 123–4.

13. Bruns, *Hermeneutics Ancient and Modern*, 139–40, 147, 146, 145, 143, 158.
14. Ken Jackson and Arthur F. Marotti, 'The Turn to Religion in Early Modern English Studies', *Criticism* 46, no. 1 (2004): 182, 180, 179–180.
15. Gadamer, *Truth and Method*, 295.
16. Ibid. 299, 295.
17. Monica Vilhauer, *Gadamer's Ethics of Play: Hermeneutics and the Other* (Lanham, MD: Lexington Books, 2010), 53. Italics original.
18. Gadamer, *Truth and Method*, 295, 296. Italics original.
19. Ibid. 295.
20. Kevin J. Vanhoozer, 'Discourse on Matter: Hermeneutics and the "Miracle" of Understanding', in *Hermeneutics at the Crossroads*, ed. Kevin J. Vanhoozer, James K. A. Smith and Bruce Ellis Benson (Bloomington: Indiana University Press, 2006), 28–9.
21. Bruns, *Hermeneutics Ancient and Modern*, 146.
22. Maynard Mack, 'The World of *Hamlet*', *Yale Review* 41 (1952): 504.
23. Jean E. Howard, 'Shakespeare and Genre', in *A Companion to Shakespeare*, ed. David Scott Kastan (Malden, MA: Blackwell Publishers, 1999), 306; Boas, *Shakespeare and his Predecessors*, 345; See Michael Jamieson, 'The Problem Plays, 1920–1970: A Retrospective', in *Aspects of Shakespeare's 'Problem Plays'*, ed. Kenneth Muir and Stanley Wells (Cambridge: Cambridge University Press, 1982), 126–7.
24. Boas, *Shakespeare and his Predecessors*, 345.
25. Paul Yachnin, 'Shakespeare's Problem Plays and the Drama of His Time: *Troilus and Cressida*, *All's Well That Ends Well*, *Measure for Measure*', in *A Companion to Shakespeare's Works, Volume IV: The Poems, Problem Comedies, Late Plays*, ed. Richard Dutton and Jean E. Howard (Oxford: Blackwell Publishing, 2005), 46.
26. Boas, *Shakespeare and his Predecessors*, 345; Susan Snyder, 'Introduction', in *All's Well That Ends Well*, ed. Susan Snyder (Oxford: Oxford University Press, 1993), 16.

27. Snyder, 'Introduction', 18–19. See also E. M. W. Tillyard, *Shakespeare's Problem Plays* (London: Chatto & Windus, 1950), 6–8.
28. Howard, 'Shakespeare and Genre', 306.
29. Ernest Schanzer, *The Problem Plays of Shakespeare: A Study of Julius Caesar, Measure for Measure, Antony and Cleopatra* (London: Routledge and Kegan Paul, 1963), 6.
30. Boas, *Shakespeare and his Predecessors*, 345.
31. Rosalie L. Colie, *The Resources of Kind: Genre-Theory in the Renaissance*, ed. Barbara K. Lewalski (Berkeley: University of California Press, 1973), 116.
32. Snyder, 'Introduction', 18.
33. Yachnin, 'Shakespeare's Problem Plays', 46.
34. Snyder, 'Introduction', 18.
35. Arthur Kirsch, 'The Bitter and the Sweet of Tragicomedy: Shakespeare's *All's Well That Ends Well* and Montaigne', *Yale Review* 102, no. 2 (2014): 64.
36. Giambattista Guarini, 'The Compendium of Tragicomic Poetry', in *Literary Criticism: Plato to Dryden*, ed. and trans. Allan H. Gilbert (Detroit: Wayne State University Press, 1962), 512.
37. Verna A. Foster, *The Name and Nature of Tragicomedy* (2004; repr. Abingdon: Routledge, 2016), 11.
38. Ibid. 10n3; David Bevington, 'Introduction', in *Troilus and Cressida*, ed. David Bevington (London: Bloomsbury, 1998), 4.
39. Michael Neill, 'Shakespeare's Tragedies', in *The New Cambridge Companion to Shakespeare*, ed. Margreta De Grazia and Stanley Wells (Cambridge: Cambridge University Press, 2010), 134n5.
40. William Shakespeare, *The Famous Historie of Troylus and Cresseid* (London: G. Eld, 1609), 2v.
41. Bevington, 'Introduction', 4. Italics original.
42. Jean Calvin, *The Institution of Christian Religion*, trans. Thomas Norton (London: Arnold Hatfield, 1599), 1.1.1.
43. Hans-Georg Gadamer, *Gesammelte Werke*, 1 (Tubingen: Mohr Siebeck, 1985–95), 298–9, quoted in Jens Zimmermann, *Humanism and Religion: A Call for the Renewal of Western*

Culture (Oxford: Oxford University Press, 2012), 240; Zimmermann, *Recovering Theological Hermeneutics*, 30, 272.

44. John T. McNeill (ed.), *Calvin, Institutes of the Christian Religion*, trans. Ford Lewis Battles, 2 vols (Philadelphia: Westminster Press, 1960), 1.1.1n1.
45. MacCulloch, *Reformation*, xx.
46. Gadamer, *Truth and Method*, 175, xxx. 'Tridentine' denotes the Council of Trent (1545–63), the event which began the Roman Catholic Counter-Reformation.
47. Hans-Georg Gadamer, 'Hermeneutics as a Theoretical and Practical Task', in *The Gadamer Reader: A Boquet of the Later Writings*, ed. and trans. Richard E. Palmer (Evanston, IL: Northwestern University Press, 2007), 255.
48. Jean Grondin, *Introduction to Philosophical Hermeneutics*, trans. Joel Weinsheimer (New Haven: Yale University Press, 1994), 39.
49. Gadamer, 'Hermeneutics as a Theoretical and Practical Task', 255.
50. Ibid. 255.
51. Ibid. 258.
52. Kevin J. Vanhoozer, *Biblical Authority After Babel: Retrieving the Solas in the Spirit of Mere Protestant Christianity* (Grand Rapids, MI: Brazos Press, 2016), 53.
53. Calvin, *Institution of Christian Religion*, 2.1.9.
54. Snyder, 'Introduction,' 18.
55. Brian Cummings, 'Religion', in *The Oxford Handbook of Shakespeare*, ed. Arthur F. Kinney (Oxford: Oxford University Press, 2012), 666; David Daniell, 'Shakespeare and the Protestant Mind', *Shakespeare Survey* 54 (2001): 9.
56. Marotti and Jackson, 'Religion, Secularity, and Shakespeare', 542.
57. Daniel Swift, *Shakespeare's Common Prayers: The Book of Common Prayer and the Elizabethan Age* (Oxford: Oxford University Press, 2012), 152.
58. Marotti and Jackson, 'Religion, Secularity, and Shakespeare', 542; Michael Davies, 'Introduction: Shakespeare and Protestantism', *Shakespeare* 5, no. 1 (2009): 8.

59. Davies, 'Introduction', 8.
60. Alec Ryrie, *Being Protestant in Reformation Britain* (Oxford: Oxford University Press, 2013), 3. Italics original.
61. See also their list of other scholars who contributed to this approach by arguing for 'an ongoing, intimate relationship' between early modern drama and the 'religious culture(s) of the age', Jackson and Marotti, 'The Turn to Religion', 168, 172. Examples of more recent works reflective of this approach include: Jennifer Clement, *Reading Humility in Early Modern England* (Farnham: Ashgate, 2015); Brian Cummings, *Mortal Thoughts: Religion, Secularity and Identity in Shakespeare and Early Modern Culture* (Oxford: Oxford University Press, 2013); Thomas Fulton and Kristen Poole (eds), *The Bible on the Shakespearean Stage: Cultures of Interpretation in Reformation England* (Cambridge: Cambridge University Press, 2018); Hannibal Hamlin, *The Bible in Shakespeare* (Oxford: Oxford University Press, 2013).
62. Davies, 'Introduction', 9.
63. Julia Reinhard Lupton, 'The Religious Turn (to Theory) in Shakespeare Studies', *English Language Notes* 44, no. 1 (2006): 148.
64. William N. West, 'Humanism and the Resistance to Theology', in *The Return of Theory in Early Modern English Studies: Tarrying with the Subjunctive*, ed. Paul Cefalu and Bryan Reynolds (Basingstoke: Palgrave MacMillan, 2011), 167.
65. Ibid. 168.
66. Lupton, 'The Religious Turn', 147. Julia Reinhard Lupton, *Thinking with Shakespeare: Essays on Politics and Life* (Chicago: The University of Chicago Press, 2011), 23. Italics original.
67. Lupton, 'The Religious Turn', 147; Lupton, *Thinking with Shakespeare*, 17, 24.
68. Lupton, 'The Religious Turn', 146–7.
69. Graham Hammill and Julia Reinhard Lupton, 'Sovereigns, Citizens, and Saints: Political Theology and Renaissance Literature', *Religion & Literature* 38, no. 3 (2006): 1.
70. Lupton, 'The Religious Turn', 147; Lupton, *Thinking with Shakespeare*, 23.

71. Lupton, *Thinking with Shakespeare*, 223–4, 227.
72. Ibid. 223–4.
73. Ibid. 22.
74. Martin Luther, *Lectures on Galatians 1535: Chapters 1–4*, trans. Jaroslav Pelikan, ed. Jaroslav Pelikan and Walter A. Hansen (Saint Louis: Concordia Publishing House, 1963), 102, 116.
75. Ibid. 133.
76. Hans-Georg Gadamer, *Die Lektion des Jahrhunderts* (Münster: Lit Verlag, 2002), 139, quoted in and trans. Jens Zimmermann, 'The Ethics of Philosophical Hermeneutics and the Challenge of Religious Transcendence', *Philosophy Today* 51 (2007): 57n22.

CHAPTER 1

A HERMENEUTIC REVOLUTION

Call me a fool,
Trust not my reading nor my observations,
Which with experimental seal doth warrant
The tenor of my book.

Friar, *Much Ado About Nothing*, IV.i.166–9

Where does our effort to understand begin?

Hans-Georg Gadamer, 'Hermeneutics as Practical Philosophy'[1]

Luther's reforming acts laid the basis for a hermeneutic revolution.

Jean Grondin, *Introduction to Philosophical Hermeneutics*[2]

In acknowledging the inconclusiveness of his 'reading' and 'observations', *Much Ado*'s Friar serves as an emblem of Shakespeare's dramatic representations of the interpreting self. This book draws on an intellectual history that connects the Reformation to modern hermeneutics to argue that the sources of the Shakespearean selves (to borrow the title of Charles Taylor's well-known book) whom we moderns find so relevant to our own self-perceptions and experiences can be found, first of all, at the heart of the playwright's theologically full culture. Hans-Georg Gadamer, modern philosophical hermeneutics' leading light, asks about the origins of 'our effort to understand': 'Why are we interested in understanding a text or some experience of the world, including our doubts about patent self-interpretations?'[3] Jean Grondin, cited in my third epigraph, captures the basic consensus that the sixteenth-century Protestant Reformation must feature in responses to Gadamer's inquiry.

The Reformation was the most significant impetus behind a refiguring of how people know and ensuing sense that to be human is to understand through interpretation. This chapter examines how this 'hermeneutic revolution', with its emphasis on interpretation as ontology, developed out of Luther's 'reforming acts' and the theological ideas which both drove and emerged from these acts. But first, I will take us to the end of the story – to a sketch of Shakespeare's theologically full world and the interpreting self living within it. The weight of scholarly work done in recent years has (thankfully) relieved me of the need to contend for the relevance to Shakespeare of religion and the Reformation. Instead, I will highlight key aspects of the playwright and his contemporaries' hermeneutical experiences, experiences connected to the Reformation's role in relocating sense-making into the domain of individual being.

A crucial trigger for this change was the opportunity afforded to sixteenth-century English people to read and interpret the Bible in their own language. The Bible was, of course, widely believed to be the Word of God, divine revelation containing the answer to the problem of great concern to most early modern people: How does a person attain eternal salvation? Or, in the relational language used by the Reformers, how can human beings know and be known by God in both this life and the next? It is well recognised that the vernacular Bible became a bedrock of early modern English society. Defending vernacular translations, the influential Elizabethan clergyman and theologian William Whitaker set forth a Protestant mantra of his age: 'God hath commanded all [Christians] to read the scriptures: therefore all are bound to read the scriptures.' The image of post-Reformation English men and women – 'all maner of persons of what estate or condicion so euer they be' (as Archbishop Thomas Cranmer phrases it) – with their heads bent over the Bible is familiar to us. But as Thomas Fulton and Kristen Poole argue, much less discussion has been had about how English people were urged to 'not just *read* the Bible, but to *interpret* it'. The latter imperative is spelled out in the 1559 edition of *The Book of Common Prayer* (*BCP*) – a text as ubiquitous as the Bible across private and public spheres of thought and action in Shakespeare's England.[4]

One of the *BCP*'s best-known Collects (short prayers) was, and continues to be, read on the Second Sunday of Advent. The prayer asks God to enable each congregation member to 'hear' the Holy Scriptures and to 'read, mark, learn, and inwardly digest them'.[5] This is a prayer for understanding through active, personal engagement with the text. Moreover, the widespread availability of vernacular Bibles in England and elsewhere in Europe meant that, 'for the first time in centuries', lay Christians could not only read and interpret Scripture for themselves, but they could also, as R. Ward Holder observes, 'judge the fitness of their religious leaders' interpretations'. Ordinary people possessed a new-found hermeneutic agency. Employing it was, 'at least in theory', encouraged by some theologians, including Jean Calvin, whose theology became pre-eminently influential in the English church.[6]

Caroline Litzenberger cites one account of such engagement. In 1538, Thomas Cromwell directed every parish to put 'a Bible of the largest volume in English' in a convenient location where it could be seen and read.[7] Two years later – on Sunday, 18 April 1540 – the Visitation Act book of John Bell, Bishop of Worcester, records that: 'Humfrey Grynshill, a weaver from Stonehouse, "was redyng the byble in englyshe in Cryste Church in Gloucester"'. Unable to find evidence for purgatory in '"any part of the hole scriptur [. . .] but only hell and heven"', Grynshill declared that '"he wolde have no prayers sayde for his sowle when so ever he shall dye, nor any other suffragies of the churche"'.[8] Grynshill's reading, marking, learning and inward 'digesting' brought about a radical change in his understanding of how a person attains salvation. Commenting on Grynshill's decisive reading experience, Peter Marshall observes that Henry VIII 'had given a green light to DIY hermeneutics of this sort'. In David Daniell's assessment, the style of the early English Bibles may well have fostered interpretive postures such as Grynshill's. Beginning with William Tyndale's 1526 New Testament translation, the 'direct clear language of great simplicity and power' chosen for the vernacular text provided English people with a model of free enquiry in their own language, applicable both to religious questions such as Grynshill's and all matters of concern.[9]

Of course, early modern people's hermeneutic engagement with the vernacular Bible extended beyond acts of reading. They also listened to and embodied portions of Scripture, and interpretations of it. Through their mandatory attendance at church on Sundays and holy days, parishioners heard the Bible in the liturgy of the *BCP* and in the homilies, all, as the *BCP*'s Preface instructs, 'read and sung in the church in the English tongue, to the end that the congregation may be thereby edified'.[10] Cranmer and his assistants adopted Tyndale's 'direct clear language' to produce these formative religious texts comprising excerpts of Scripture (from the Great Bible of 1539), allusions to Scripture and the Reformers' interpretations of Scripture. Further, as Judith Maltby points out, the *BCP* is a 'performed and participatory text'. It invites all lay people – literate or otherwise – to immerse themselves in enacting a Protestant-shaped 'dynamic and relational' experience of communing with God.[11] For instance, the involvement of the congregation in the Sunday morning church service includes their singing of metrical psalms, kneeling to say the prayer of General Confession, standing to recite the Apostles' Creed, kneeling again to pray as they say the Lord's Prayer and respond in the preces, and participating in the Litany and of course the Lord's Supper.[12]

The real-life implementation of the last of these – the Protestant 'aspiration' that people frequently partake in the Lord's Supper – offers a perhaps unexpected insight into early modern people's hermeneutical engagement with the *BCP*. As Ryrie notes, most people chose to only receive communion one to three times annually, a practice inherited from the medieval church that Protestant ministers and theologians tried to, but could not, overturn.[13] The *BCP*'s prescribed form seemingly circumscribes and regulates participants' thoughts and actions. Yet, parishioners' resistance to more regular occasions of receiving the Lord's Supper suggests, as Daniel Swift argues, that decreeing people's involvement is the very point at which the *BCP* actually 'diffuses its single authority'. Here, 'individual will encounters regular form'.[14] Such encounters took place not only in the domain of public worship but also, perhaps especially so, when the prayer book was used for personal devotions.

Shakespeare and his contemporaries were encouraged to 'say Morning and Evening Prayer privately' on the days when they could not attend public worship.[15] As Swift shows from his study of the marginalia of Elizabethan and Jacobean prayer books, readers often appeared to view their relationships with the text as dialogical rather than monological, as involving 'creative manipulation' rather than 'mechanical repetition'. Annotations range in content and tone. Some are 'touching', some 'eccentric' and some, such as those made by an anonymous Elizabethan prayer book reader, 'almost blasphemous'. This person had translated some English verses into Latin, returned the 'Holy Ghost' to the text via its margins, and added a short Eucharistic prayer that nods to the real presence of Christ's body and blood in the sacrament.[16] These acts of writing and rewriting intimate the author's quiet defiance of the Protestant status quo.

To remain briefly within the private spaces of the household, it is worth noting the hermeneutical implications of early modern people's reading of two other forms of religious writing. The first is found within the Bible itself: the marginal glosses and annotations juxtaposed alongside the biblical text, published especially in editions produced for 'private study', as Thomas Dabbs describes them.[17] Dabbs is referring to the popular Geneva English Bible, the work of the Marian exiles and the version that features most often in Shakespeare's abundant biblical allusions.[18] The Geneva Bible was 'the most widely read book of any kind' between its first (New Testament only) edition in 1557 and the early decades of the seventeenth century.[19] More than 180 editions were published, some using black letter type, which was also used for vernacular texts aimed at a popular readership.[20]

From one perspective, the inclusion of extratextual commentary in the Geneva (and other) Bibles belies the foundational, momentous Reformation doctrines of *sola scriptura* and the priesthood of all believers, suggesting that Protestant Bible translators, editors and printers believed that they should direct, perhaps control, readers' interpretations of the text. As Vivienne Westbrook observes, these 'paratextual aids [. . .] were always inflected with the particular doctrinal stance' of the English Bibles' producers. At the same time, Fulton and Poole suggest that this material also functioned as an instructional tool, teaching people how to 'approach Scripture on their own'. The aids facilitated what Helen Wilcox identifies as 'the newly enfranchised practice of individual interpretation of the Bible in English [. . . that] underpins the public and interpretative role of the early modern audience' not only in church, but also in the theatre.[21]

Alongside the (glossed) Bible and the *BCP*, early modern English people embraced theological writings. Calvin was extremely well received. People turned to translations of Calvin's vast corpus – his sermons, catechism and commentaries, as well as his magnum opus, *The Institution of Christian Religion* – as aids to 'a communal grasp of the Scriptures'.[22] From his 'painstaking reconstruction of the publishing history', Andrew Pettegree concludes that the English 'apparently had an almost insatiable appetite for Calvin's works'. This deduction is perhaps unexpected, unthinkable even. Today, Calvin more often than not personifies the 'austere aesthetic' which Anthony Dawson, for example, associates with reformed thought.[23]

Is it possible that some, perhaps many, of the people who flocked to the Globe to watch Shakespeare's dramas also consumed Calvin's writings? Data compiled from surviving wills and inventories implies so, showing that Calvin tops the list of works collectively owned by English people.[24] Shakespeare's contemporaries (quite possibly Shakespeare himself) read ideas by Calvin and other Reformers, argued about them 'in a variety of private and semi-public settings', and heard them filtered through sermons, catechisms and other public discourses.[25] These ideas were instrumental in moving Shakespeare's theologically full world towards a perspective on the self as one who knows through interpretation. As will be seen, the Reformers' flagship theological contentions, formed within the cauldron of religious dispute and change, underlay recastings of, first, ordinary people's relation to the Bible and second, their understanding of the all-important question of how one can know and be known by God.

Renaissance Humanism and the Hermeneutic Revolution

Before expanding on the Reformers' pivotal ideas, it is important to note that there were, of course, multiple factors behind early modern English people's new relationship to the Bible. Mass printing meant that the Bible, along with a host of other (mostly religious) works, could be both disseminated and afforded as never before.[26] While the figures are debatable, literacy rates were increasing throughout the sixteenth century.[27] Growing cosmopolitanism and urbanisation, especially in London, multiplied 'possibilities for interchange'.[28] These interchanges frequently involved robust dialogue about 'sensitive religious matters'.[29] Most importantly, Renaissance humanism, enabled, like the Reformation, by these other factors, played a leading role in cultivating an appetite for change. As Peter Harrison sees it, Renaissance humanists provided 'some help' to the Reformers' realisation of 'a new approach to the biblical text' that in turn 'wrought a hermeneutical revolution'.[30]

The task of defining Renaissance humanism has provoked much disagreement. I will sidestep the debates belonging elsewhere by adopting Diarmaid MacCulloch's view that 'humanist identity [. . . .] represented a refocusing of old learning', a love of the words in 'ancient texts' which humanists believed could be invoked to improve their own societies. Similarly, Paul Oskar Kristeller characterises Renaissance humanism as a 'broad concern with the study and imitation of classical antiquity'; it was, in Alister McGrath's summary of Kristeller, an 'essentially cultural and educational' movement.[31] The 'battle-cry' *ad fontes*, back to the sources, encapsulates the humanist project.[32] Much has been written about the relationship of Renaissance humanism to the Reformation. Did the Reformation originate in humanism? Here, I draw upon McGrath's summary: it's 'complex', but humanism did not 'cause' the Reformation. Humanism was, however, 'unquestionably an essential catalyst' for the Reformation, and humanists were nearly all Christians who situated their actions 'within the context of the life and thought of the church'.[33]

My interest is in how the agenda and actions of the Renaissance humanists helped to both pave the way for early modern people to see themselves as readers and interpreters of the Bible (and all knowledge) and give shape to this self-understanding. One implication of *ad fontes* was that humanists eschewed medieval commentaries which mediated knowledge of ancient sources – religious and otherwise. Instead, they sought to immerse themselves in the original texts, including the New Testament and the works of the patristic writers.[34] Doing so required obtaining 'the best possible version' of these texts, which meant determining the accuracy of extant renderings.[35] For instance, humanists placed Jerome's fourth-century Latin Vulgate, the Bible of the Catholic church, under the spotlight and found it wanting. McGrath highlights the work of the Italian humanist Lorenzo Valla, who exposed significant errors in the Vulgate translation, thus questioning both its authority and theological ideas derived from it.[36]

Valla based his criticism on his reading of the Greek New Testament. He did indeed go back to the source. Valla's method is representative of humanism's insistence on 'direct study' of the ancient texts in their original language, a concern that inspired and accelerated humanists' productions of accurate versions of the Hebrew Old Testament and Greek New Testament.[37] The year 1517 saw the publication of the final of six volumes of the Spanish Catholic Complutensian Polyglot, comprised of the Hebrew and Greek texts printed alongside new Latin interpretations of these texts and the Latin Vulgate. But the feat of this 'ultimate Christian humanist enterprise' has been eclipsed by the 1516 Greek New Testament produced by the most famous Renaissance humanist, Desiderius Erasmus.[38] For the Reformers, it was 'nothing less than providential' that humanism's emphasis on *ad fontes* both engendered doubt about the credibility of the Vulgate and some of the religious knowledge it endorsed, and advanced the publication of Erasmus's Greek New Testament.[39] The latter, Erasmus's text, soon became 'a major influence on Protestantism', used in the production of many vernacular New Testaments, including Luther's and Tyndale's.[40]

Luther's and his fellow Protestants' reforming acts were built on the philological and literary expertise, and the publishing activity, of Renaissance humanists, a dependence that extended beyond the text of Scripture.[41] Humanist scholars also produced 'reliable editions' of the works of the Church Fathers, including Ambrose, Jerome and Augustine.[42] Editions of the writings of Augustine of Hippo by both Erasmus and the Amerbach brothers proved especially indispensable to the Reformers. MacCulloch describes Luther's actions as setting in motion an 'Augustinian revolution'.[43] Of all the patristic writings humanist scholarship had made freshly available, Luther judged Augustine's to be the most theologically sound. It was Augustine's teaching that Luther and other first-generation Reformers turned to as they sought to rectify the theology of the medieval church and recover the substance of the '*vera theologia*'.[44]

In particular, the Reformers appealed to Augustine's soteriology. MacCulloch argues that, contrary to the 'myth' promulgated first by Protestants and later by Catholics behind the mid-sixteenth-century Counter-Reformation, 'the old church was immensely strong, and that strength could only have been overcome by the explosive power of an idea', specifically, 'a new statement of Augustine's ideas on salvation'. For MacCulloch, if the medieval church was not on its last legs, then we should recognise that it was the Reformers' ideas which fuelled the radical changes they effected in people's thinking and in the church.[45] And at least on the critical question of salvation, these ideas rested considerably on the theology of a North African bishop living more than a millennium earlier.

In essence, Augustine's soteriology contrasts and connects human and divine natures, and human and divine agency. To Augustine, human beings are profoundly fallen, thus 'morally helpless' and unable to make even the smallest contribution to their own salvation, that is, to establishing a divine-human relationship of knowing and being known.[46] Nevertheless, this salvation is possible, effected solely by the action of a powerful, loving God who gives salvation as a 'gracious gift' to his elect.[47] As will be seen, the Reformers' recovery of both Augustine's pessimistic theological anthropology and his confidence in the efficacy of divine grace translated directly into their theological hermeneutics: their figuring of human knowing and humans as knowers. Here, it is worth pointing out that, like Luther, Calvin owed much of his thinking about the human condition and gratuitousness of God's grace to Augustine. Augustine features so regularly in Calvin's expositions of these two topics that, in John McNeill's assessment, the Reformer's thinking was at one with that of his theological forebear.[48] The hermeneutic revolution expedited by the Reformation was inseparable from the Augustinian revolution, made possible by Renaissance humanists' enthusiasm for the works of the Fathers, and their skill in producing trustworthy editions of these texts and developing methods to study them.

There is an irony in all of this. By placing Augustine's theology in the hands of the Reformers, Renaissance humanists undermined their own optimistic ambition to enlist 'old learning' to better society. The growing influence of the Reformers' reprising of Augustine's grim diagnosis of fallen humanity put a major dampener on the humanist programme of cultural and religious renewal.[49] McGrath suggests that in the Reformation's 'early phase', a 'productive misunderstanding' and mutual commitment to the principle of *ad fontes* smoothed over the 'profound differences' between humanists and Reformers.[50] But Luther and Erasmus's heated dispute of the mid-1520s over the issue of whether humans can and do play any part in choosing and contributing to their salvation (discussed later in this chapter) brought these differences into the open. Augustine's ideas about salvation became significant sticking points between humanists and Reformers.

I will show how these ideas came to bear on the subjectivity – the 'structure, operations, and interactions' (as L. E. Semler helpfully puts it) – of the early modern self.[51] As my sketch of Shakespeare's theologically full world suggests, this self was developing a growing consciousness of herself as an interpreter of vital knowledge contained in Scripture, and by derivation, all knowledge. More immediately, my focus is how what Luther said and did in the early decades of the sixteenth century 'laid the basis' for this reframing of selfhood that gave rise to the 'human hermeneutical condition'.[52] The answer lies in the Reformation's material and formal principles with which Luther is closely associated: justification by grace through faith alone and *sola scriptura*.

Luther's 'Reforming Acts'

By the late Middle Ages, the moral and legal concept of justification had become the primary metaphor in the Catholic Church's responses to the question overshadowing human existence: how does an individual secure God's saving grace? How can the self know and be known by God? Theologically, justification means being seen as righteous: not guilty in the eyes of a righteous (just) God. The Fall overturned human beings' originary righteous status before God, thus estranging God and humanity. Justification 'rectifies' – 'puts right' – this relational rupture.[53] All unrighteous or fallen people (all humanity) need justification to attain eternal salvation. But while nearly everyone desired justification, by Shakespeare's time the church had divided over the problem of how one is justified. Richard Hooker refers to this parting of ways in his

1586 sermon on Habakkuk (published in 1612) when he discusses 'that grand question, which hangeth yet in controversy between us and the Church of Rome, about the matter of Justifying Righteousness'.[54] This 'grand question' pivoted on the issue of human merit (and continues to do so). To Rome, people's good works function as a form of merit contributing to their righteousness. Protestants disagreed – adamantly. They insisted that justification results only from faith in Christ's merit. *Sola fides* was the Reformation's material principle.

In *Love's Labour's Lost*, Shakespeare alludes to the grand question. After prompting the Forester to praise her beauty, the Princess, in jest, pays him for acting as a 'glass' and then comments: 'See, see, my beauty will be saved by merit! / O heresy in fair, fit for these days' (IV.i.18, 21–2). In a parody of, from a Protestant perspective, the 'heretical' Roman Catholic view of justification, the Princess's 'merit' – the money she gives the Forester – 'saves' her beauty via his elicited flattery. Article eleven of the Thirty-Nine Articles of Religion (1563), the official Elizabethan statement of doctrine and practice, shows why the Princess's quip was a 'heresy': 'We are accompted righteous before God, only for the merite of our Lord & Saviour Jesus Christ, by faith, & not for our owne works or deseruynges.'[55] Only Christ's merit reckons a person righteous.

This is the perspective on the urgent matter of his eternal destiny which Shakespeare would have heard in church or if, for instance, he had attended a sermon at Paul's Cross. But imagine that Shakespeare was born a couple of generations earlier. If he had turned up at the Paul's Cross Lenten sermons in 1540, he would have walked into the thick of a deadly verbal brawl over the idea of justification by grace through faith alone, a 'cock-fight' as one of its combatants, the Reformer Robert Barnes, described it. Ralph Werrell outlines the unfolding drama. On the first Sunday in Lent (15 February), the preacher was Stephen Gardiner, Bishop of Winchester, a Catholic who had nevertheless accepted Henry VIII's separation from Rome.[56] Gardiner chose to preach against justification by faith as a Lutheran 'abuse of scripture' undermining Christian piety, and which he likened to succumbing to the devil's temptation of Christ in the wilderness.[57] Barnes followed two weeks later, refuting (and unwisely) personally attacking Gardiner. In a letter to John Æpinus, Barnes wrote that he was in the midst of a 'fierce controversy' with Gardiner, and that he (Barnes) 'vindicate[s] the efficacy of the blood of Jesus Christ my Lord; but hitherto I stand alone in doing it'.[58]

In fact, Barnes overstates his singularity. On the next two Lenten Sundays – 7 and 14 March – William Jerome and Thomas Gerrard preached on justification by faith. Both agreed entirely with Barnes. On 30 July 1540, all three were executed. Werrell argues that politics accounts more for their deaths than religion.[59] Nonetheless, the charge was heresy, and Barnes, Jerome and Gerrard found themselves, like *Love's Labour's Lost*'s princess, on the wrong side of the law – but for the opposite reason. How can the self know and be known by God? Not many years after the trio's executions, English people experienced a significant transformation in what they were to believe about this pressing concern. Justification by faith alone is, as McGrath puts it, one of the 'few ideas with the capacity to dismantle great institutions and invert the judgments of previous generations'.[60] How did the Reformers' material principle gain such a powerful hold over the church and culture of much of sixteenth-century Europe?

This question is tied up with the story of the once Roman Catholic monk whom Gardiner denounced as the Protestant Reformation's spearhead. As is well known, Luther was intensely invested in his salvation. 'From the depth of my heart [I] wanted to be saved', an aged Luther writes of himself as a young monk, then priest, then chair of biblical studies at the University of Wittenberg. Yet, although Luther lived 'as a monk without reproach [. . . he] could not believe' that his works of satisfaction – his fasting, praying, self-flagellating vigils, and Masses offered to the saints and Mary – were sufficient to attain this salvation by justifying him before a righteous God. In consequence, he 'hated the righteous God who punishes sinners' and 'raged with a fierce and troubled conscience'. Rereading one verse of Scripture was, in Luther's narrative, the catalyst for his epistemological, affective and ultimately spiritual turnround. In Romans 1: 17, Paul writes: 'For by it [the Gospel of Christ] the righteousnes of God is reueiled, from faith to faith: as it is written: The iuste shal liue by faith.' Luther had despairingly read 'the righteousness of God' as a threat of divine wrath: humans had been set up for failure and damnation as they could not meet God's harsh demands for 'the formal or active righteousness' that only serves to condemn them.[61]

But as Luther 'beat importunately upon Paul at that place', he 'began to understand' that humans do not earn righteousness, but rather receive it. That is, 'the righteousness of God [. . .] is a gift of God [. . .] the passive righteousness with which merciful God justifies us by faith'. How are fallen human beings justified? Luther realised that 'passive' not 'active' righteousness resolves this crux. He experienced this new understanding of justification as a personal metamorphosis, recalling that 'I felt that I was altogether born again and had entered paradise itself through open gates.'[62] Although he does not specify when this 'rebirth' took place, and its timing is now a matter of much debate, Luther's change of mind no doubt set 'this obscure German monk and professor from an obscure university' (as Carl Trueman describes him) and his theology of justification on a collision course with the authority and practices of the papacy and the church.[63]

Luther's own explication of justification by grace through faith alone underscores the doctrine's polemical force. In *The Freedom of a Christian*, a 'little treatise' he sent to Pope

Leo X in the autumn of 1520, Luther contends that if works of righteousness 'are done under the false impression that through them one is justified [. . . .] they are not free, and they blaspheme the grace of God since to justify and to save by faith belongs to the grace of God alone'.[64] These conclusions are a logical implication of Luther's theology of justification. They were also incendiary.

Justification by faith undermined Rome's 'complex edifice of salvation': Mary and the saints; the church, its sacraments and its priests; papal power; and purgatory.[65] On 15 June 1520, before receiving Luther's *Freedom of a Christian*, Pope Leo had already issued a papal bull – the *Exsurge Domine* – condemning Luther on the count of forty-one 'heretical or scandalous or false or offensive' propositions.[66] In the following year, Luther was first excommunicated and then ordered to the Diet of Worms, the imperial assembly alluded to in Act 4 of *Hamlet*. At Worms, Luther denied papal ambassador Johann Eck's demand that he either renounce or retract his 'heretical' writings. In May 1521, Emperor Charles V issued the Edict of Worms, making Luther a marked man and threatening punishment for anyone who disseminated his writings. But the match had been lit. Luther's insistence that a person becomes righteous before God only through faith in God's own gift of justification became a crucial plank in 'the first phase of Protestantism'.[67]

Clearly, Luther's attempts to reform the church's theology of salvation also represented a challenge to the religious authorities. Harrison suggests that the 'crisis of religion' sparked by Luther and his fellow Reformers was 'perhaps above all else, a crisis of authority'.[68] For, the Reformers insisted, in critical matters of theology (such as God's modus operandi in justifying people), the Bible, rather than the church, is the 'primary and final authority'.[69] This 'principle of scripture', as Gadamer calls it, became the Reformation's formal principle: *sola scriptura*.[70] As will be seen, primary and final, rather than 'only', are necessary boundary markers delimiting what the Reformers did and did not mean by *sola scriptura*. In addition to *sola scriptura*, the Reformers' 'radical doctrine' of the universal priesthood of all believers prised open the church's and the papacy's firm control over who could read, interpret and question interpretations of Scripture.[71] Together, *sola scriptura* and the priesthood of all believers represented significant threats to the church hierarchy and opened the door for ordinary people to read Scripture in ways that required 'new guidance'.[72] These doctrines fostered a hermeneutical connection between individuals and understanding.

Before elaborating, I must address a potential misconception. It is important not to portray the medieval church as having little or no regard for the Bible. As the Protestant historian Trueman observes, this reductionism can be a wont of modern Protestant historiography.[73] But Luther's own experience bears witness to the contrary. He, like all professors of theology, was tasked to explain, interpret and give instruction on Scripture, which he vowed to do when, in 1512, he was admitted as a '*doctor in biblia*' at Wittenberg. As Erik Herrmann points out, Luther's reforming acts were 'a conscientious expression' of these vows. Indeed, the Bible, albeit the Latin Vulgate, was the 'central, foundational' source of medieval theology.[74] Contrary to popular perception, the concept of *sola scriptura* did not originate with the Reformers.[75] But Luther's 'circumstances forced him to make [it] explicit'.[76]

Changes to the definition of 'tradition' provide a window on these circumstances. Until the thirteenth century, theologians understood tradition as 'a traditional interpretation of the Bible' that had its origins in the apostles' interpretive practices. This hermeneutic protected the church from heresy. Claims about new doctrines, such as those advanced by the second-century Gnostics, were assessed against normative interpretations of Scripture.[77] This conception of tradition complemented the historical church's teaching that the Bible is the ultimate, authoritative source of God's revelation of himself to his creation. But in the fourteenth and fifteenth centuries 'tradition' took on a new meaning as the late medieval church deemed 'unwritten apostolic traditions' on a par with Scripture.[78] These traditions, thought of as divine revelation '*in addition to Scripture*', were believed to have been received by the apostles and passed down through the ages within the church.[79] '*Partim-partim*, "partly-partly"' is the Council of Trent's encapsulation of their theology of divine revelation.[80] This situation compelled the Reformers to explicitly advocate for *sola scriptura*, especially as Rome saw itself as the gatekeeper of both forms of revelation.[81] It is little wonder that hostility ensued.

Luther's instrumental role in this upheaval can be traced to his own encounters with the Bible, which transformed his epistemology and soteriology, and his life. Scripture's primacy is Luther's point in his 'Explanations of the Ninety-five Theses' (1518), published ten months after he posted his famous 'Ninety-five Theses'. Luther contends that, rather than advocating for preaching about indulgences, 'it is the duty and intention of the pope to desire the Word of God to be preached above everything else, always, and everywhere, as he knows he has been commanded by Christ to do'.[82] These 'Explanations' were published after Pope Leo X had already communicated, via his Master of the Sacred Palace, Silvestro Mazzolini da Prierio (known as Prierias), his displeasure over the 'Ninety-five Theses'. Prierias's *In praesumptiosas Martini Lutheri Conclusiones, de potestate Papae, Dialogus*, published in spring 1518, unambiguously grants the Roman Church authority over Scripture.[83] For instance, Prierias writes that, on the matter of indulgences, anyone who contends that the 'Roman church cannot do what it *de facto* does, is a heretic'.[84] This tract convinced Luther that papal and scriptural authority could not be reconciled.[85]

Clear battle lines had been drawn, and remained in place as the Reformation evolved and the Counter-Reformation commenced. On 8 April 1546, the fourth session of the Council of Trent issued a 'Decree Concerning the Canonical Scriptures'. Trent's goal was 'to restrain petulant spirits' by forbidding anyone from 'wresting the sacred Scripture to his own senses [and] presume to interpret the said sacred Scripture contrary to that sense which holy mother Church [. . .] hath held and hold'. The church, the Decree states unambiguously, has the right to 'judge of the true sense and interpretation of the holy Scriptures'.[86] Calvin, by this time the Reformation's leading thinker, used even more forceful language to decry this epistemological and hermeneutical power structure as 'a most hurtfull error'. In Calvin's opinion, promulgators of this 'error' are 'robbers of Gods honour [who] seeke vnder colour of the Church to bring in an vnbridled tyrannie [and] care nothing with what absurdities they snare both themselues and other[s]'.[87] To the Reformers, Rome had exchanged the roles of church and Scripture. In Whitaker's words, 'the church is subject to the scripture; therefore it ought not to judge of scripture'. Interpreting Scripture, Whitaker maintains, is not the special right of 'any certain see, or succession of men'.[88]

Instead, the Reformers argued for Scripture's 'hermeneutical sufficiency'.[89] Scripture itself, not the church, holds the keys to its own interpretation. Three interrelated principles underpin this assertion. Scripture is: perspicuous (*claritas scripturae*), sufficient and its own interpreter (*sacra scriptura sui ipsius interpres*). First, the Reformers argued that Scripture clearly communicates how God makes himself 'knowen to saluation'.[90] As such, Scripture is, second, sufficient to fulfil its purpose of showing human beings the way to eternal salvation. As the Thirty-Nine Articles state, 'Holye Scripture conteyneth all thynges necessarie to saluation'.[91] In turn, the clear and sufficient knowledge which Scripture provides about and for humans' salvation functions as an interpretive frame for the whole text: Scripture is its own interpreter. That is, the Reformers sought 'to interpret Scripture in terms of its own parameters', to 'return *ad fontes*', as McGrath describes the plan of action of the early Reformers Ulrich Zwingli and Martin Bucer.[92] Alluding also to the Reformation's contiguities with Renaissance humanism, Luther insists that 'all the fathers confess their own obscurity and only illumine Scripture with Scripture'.[93]

In Gadamer's assessment, the idea of *sacra scriptura sui ipsius interpres* gave rise to 'a new theological hermeneutics' that, importantly, seeded more 'a doctrine of the faith' than 'a doctrine concerning a technical skill'. As 'a doctrine of the faith', the emphasis of this theological hermeneutics is on the 'proclamation' of Scripture to the end that 'the Good News [. . .] reaches the simple person in such a way that he or she realizes that he or she is addressed and intended'.[94] By asserting Scripture's 'hermeneutical sufficiency', and denying Rome's prior hermeneutical control over it, the Reformers both democratised and personalised religious knowing.

These twin notions of democratisation and personalisation return us to Cranmer's and Protestantism's vision of 'all maner of persons' engaging directly with the Bible. *Hamlet*'s Gravedigger and Second Man offer a brief case study of what might ensue from such engagement. In the Folio *Hamlet*, the two characters banter over whether Adam 'was the first that ever bore arms' (V.i.33). The Second Man's 'Why, he [Adam] had none' stuns the Gravedigger: 'What, art a heathen? How dost thou understand the Scripture? The Scripture says Adam digged. Could he dig without arms?' (V.i.34–7).[95] The Gravedigger refers to his own knowledge of Scripture to support his deduction – 'The Scripture says' – while seeking to elicit the Second Man's take on the text: 'How dost thou understand the Scripture?' Simultaneously, the Gravedigger jestingly questions his companion's spiritual status – 'art a heathen?' – thus his hermeneutic fitness. This scene in which two plebian characters debate their opposing interpretations of Scripture captures an inevitable outworking, if not necessarily a primary intent, of the Reformers' doctrine of *sola scriptura* and accompanying push for vernacular Bibles.

One further influential Protestant doctrine framed this levelling and individualising of knowledge: the curiously named doctrine of the universal priesthood of all believers. How is it possible for all believers to be priests? Luther explains in *To the Christian Nobility of the German Nation* (1520), 'one of the most significant documents produced by the Protestant Reformation' according to James Atkinson.[96] The Reformer structures *To the Christian Nobility*'s first section around the trope of three walls to figure the 'stronghold' Rome had built around itself. His intention is to 'blast down these walls of straw and paper'. The same trenchant language serves as Luther's vehicle for each 'blast'. The first 'wall' he impugns is the 'pure invention that pope, bishop, priests and monks are called the spiritual estate while princes, lords, artisans, and farmers are called the temporal estate'. In actuality, 'all Christians are truly of the spiritual estate' as 'all have one baptism, one gospel, one faith, and are all Christians alike', Luther contends, citing 1 Peter 2: 9: 'You are a royal priesthood and a priestly realm.' A Christian is, as a matter of course, a 'priest': a servant of Christ. Those who hold the vocational offices of priests, bishops and even pope are 'neither different from [. . .] nor superior to [. . . .] a cobbler, a smith, [or] a peasant'.[97]

Luther directs his second 'blast' against the 'claim that only the pope may interpret Scripture'. To Luther, this exclusivism 'is an outrageous fancied fable' with zero scriptural support. Instead, as all Christians are priests, all Christians have the 'power to test and judge what is right or wrong in matters of faith'. People's hermeneutic agency extends even to the actions of popes. Christians, Luther claims, can and should measure the pope against their own 'believing understanding of the Scriptures', that is, their reading of Scripture in concord with its purpose of inducing belief and salvation. Once Rome's first two 'walls' of protection are destroyed, the third, Luther asserts, 'falls of itself'. This 'wall' is the ruling that only the pope can 'call or confirm a council'. Again, Luther anchors his argument in the absence of scriptural support for the ruling, and provocatively suggests that it must be dismantled if it is the pope who is 'an offense to Christendom'. In this instance – on that very day, Luther implies – 'the first man who is able should, as a true member of the whole body [of Christ], do what he can to bring about a truly free council' that stands in judgement over the pope.[98] Luther's insistence that all Christians are priests who should have access to Scripture and the right to interpret it is the grounds for such a council.

The concepts of *sola scriptura* and the universal priesthood of all believers provided the theological ammunition to subvert both the authority of Rome and the privileged status of the clerical order. Moreover, the two doctrines supplied the theological rationale for, first, translating the Bible into the vernacular and getting it into lay people's homes, and second, using the vernacular in preaching, liturgies and theological publications. As shown in my earlier sketch of Shakespeare's England, these activities became chief characteristics of Protestant religious culture, undertaken to clear the way for all (Christian) people – a universal collective of 'priests' – to know God directly through reading and interpreting Scripture.

There is, of course, a degree of idealism about this vision, this hermeneutical situation in which ordinary people seemingly easily discern the saving gospel which Luther discovered through his reading of Scripture. As Holder and historians before him point out, this objective represents 'a certain "exegetical optimism"'. Down the track, the Reformers themselves realised that interpreting and understanding Scripture is not as straightforward as *sola scriptura* and universal priesthood might imply.[99] Indeed, as I will discuss, their own emphasis on the depth of human beings' fallen condition strongly suggests that this interaction between reader and text will inevitably, as Gadamer states, involve 'difficulty'.[100] As will be seen, divisive interpretive conflicts among Protestant leaders over the Lord's Supper exposed this difficulty. Nevertheless, while the matter of how people know the truth was more complicated than Luther had anticipated in his early years, his reforming acts contributed significantly to a refiguring of the self as an interpreter of knowledge. Shakespeare was born at a time when the Reformers' theology was reshaping the space in which human existence is enacted, such that both space and existence became increasingly hermeneutical. Recalling Bruns, since Luther, we have been concerned to deeply consider 'the question of what it is to inhabit a given hermeneutical situation'.[101]

Competing Narratives

Act 4, scene 1 of *Much Ado About Nothing* offers a vivid illustration of this question. In the aftermath of Hero and Claudio's wrecked wedding, the Friar speaks up from the sidelines of the action to challenge Hero's father Leonato. The Friar pits his reading of Hero against the report of infidelity concocted by Don John and which Leonato, Don Pedro and Claudio had all accepted as incontestable truth. The latter two ground their accusation in what they (falsely) saw and heard, while Leonato declares that 'the story [. . .] is printed in her blood' – that is, Hero's blushes (IV.i.91, 123). But the Friar interprets Hero differently. His response calls to mind the *BCP*'s 'read, mark, learn and inwardly digest'. From his 'noting of the lady', the Friar has also 'marked / A thousand blushing apparitions'. However, he continues, each blush has been 'beat[en] away' by 'a thousand innocent shames / In angel whiteness' (IV.i.160–3). Moreover, the 'fire' he saw 'in her eye' was a purifying flame of truth. It 'burn[s] the errors that these princes hold / Against her maiden truth', just as fire consumes heretics and their works (IV.i.164–6).[102] Hero is true, the princes in error, and the Friar is willing to underwrite his hermeneutical claim. If he is proved wrong, they can call him a 'fool' and herein trust neither his 'reading' nor his 'observations', neither his 'age [. . .] reverence, calling, nor divinity' (IV.166–72).

To Don Pedro, Claudio and Leonato, their knowledge claim about Hero is not up for debate. They do not admit the possibility of alternative interpretations. Indeed, they do not appear to understand themselves as involved interpreters of reality, but rather portray themselves as objective receivers, thus conduits, of the truth. The Friar's response suggests that he sees himself differently: not that he cannot know the truth, but that he does so as its interpreter. He allows for the possibility that he might be misinterpreting Hero and locates this possibility within his own person and character. He may not only be wrong, but also untrustworthy. Further, the Friar seems to recognise that he seeks understanding alongside other interpreting selves. As they disagree, further avenues to uncovering the truth must be explored. The Friar advises that Leonato 'pause awhile' before jumping to conclusions (IV.i.200).

In this charged hermeneutical situation, Shakespeare captures a sense of the self's hermeneutical condition via his Friar, a perspective on human subjectivity which I link back to the hermeneutic revolution developing out of the Reformation and, to a lesser extent, Renaissance humanism. This scenario in *Much Ado* also suggests the riskiness of this theologically informed way of knowing. The Friar stakes his reputation and livelihood on his interpretation of Hero. His language may be hyperbolic, and theatregoers know that we are watching a comedy – we anticipate a happy resolution, not the Friar's downfall. But from the characters' viewpoint, risk attends the Friar's choice to speak into the uncertainty, as well as his subsequent 'counsel' that they attempt to root out the truth by faking Hero's death (IV.i.203). Neither the Friar nor his fellow characters can be certain that he is right. The audience does have this knowledge, yet we do not know if the Friar will be vindicated.

I adopt the notion of risky hermeneutics from Gadamer as he elaborates on modern hermeneutics as 'a Protestant art of interpreting Scripture clearly related in a polemical way to the dogmatic tradition of the Catholic church'. For Gadamer, this 'art' 'really risks itself' because Protestantism's way of knowing is not 'dogmatically predisposed, so that it reads out of the text what it has put into it'. Instead, 'it assumes that the word of Scripture addresses us and that only the person who allows himself to be addressed – whether he believes or doubts – understands'.[103] For Gadamer, Protestant hermeneutics and modern hermeneutics share an approach to understanding as an event both personal to and outside the control of the interpreter. Thomas Torrance makes this point when he summarises Calvin's *De Scandalis* as expanding upon Luther's notion that 'the very point where genuine interpretation can take place and profound understanding can be reached' is where one's 'natural reason is offended by' Scripture.[104]

Jens Zimmermann echoes Gadamer's implication that this risky, confronting even, way of knowing extends across religious and non-religious domains and from early modernity to the present day. For both precritical theologians and postmodern critics, knowing, Zimmermann argues, has a theological character: it 'proceeds by faith and follows the dynamics of belief with its convictions and personal involvement'. 'Personal involvement' here alludes to both the interpersonal knowledge of God that is the Reformers' goal for people's engagement with Scripture and individuals' entanglement in their knowing.[105] To return briefly to *Much Ado*, unlike the other male characters who stand over Hero as an object of knowledge, we could say that Friar Francis is conscious that he is implicated in his reading of her. The Friar assumes that there is 'a living relationship' between interpreter and 'text'.[106] Hero can address him, and he is willing to absorb the risks of this encounter in the hope of attaining understanding.

This narrative of the evolving entwining of subjectivity and hermeneutics positions the Reformers' theology as a cornerstone of how we in the modern West understand individuals' relation to truth. I draw on this narrative to elucidate our sense that Shakespeare's dramatisations of selfhood seem modern, arguing that this sense can be traced back to ideas that seem very distant from our times. But not everyone sees this historiography of hermeneutics and the West as either desirable or correct. Brad Gregory and James Simpson represent two influential lines of thought that each single out the Reformation as the source of what their proponents believe to be objectionable mainstays of modernity.

Gregory is the spokesperson for the 'undesirable' camp. In his magisterial *The Unintended Reformation* (2012), Gregory argues that the 'unintended' fallout from the Reformation half a millennium after its inception is a 'western hyperpluralism' which underlies Western society's ills. These ills are first, an ever-widening political and cultural polarisation; second, an escalating and indomitable individualistic consumerism; and third, the exclusion of 'the category of truth in the domains of human morality, values, and meaning'.[107] These are serious accusations, however inadvertent the Reformers' culpability may be. Can Gregory sensibly attribute responsibility to the Reformers for a state of affairs that seems so antithetical to their concerns? Yes, he insists, because the Reformers' spurning of Rome's authority in favour of *sola scriptura* provoked irresolvable disagreements about how to interpret and apply the Bible, hermeneutic conflicts that underline what Gregory terms 'the de facto diversity and individualism of Protestant truth claims'.[108]

As evidence, Gregory calls as his witness the crisis that would prove the Protestant Reformation's most damaging: the divisive internal debates over the meaning of the Lord's Supper (or Eucharist). Disagreements over how to read Christ's words of institution, especially 'This is my bodie' ('*hoc est corpus meum*') in Luke 22: 19–20, were instrumental not only in the movement of the Protestant Church away from Rome, but also in splitting Protestantism into its Lutheran and Reformed arms. The main adversaries were Luther and Zwingli, the leader of the Swiss Reformation. While both Reformers repudiated the Roman Catholic doctrine of transubstantiation, they also fought one another over the interpretation of 'This is my bodie'.

Luther argued for a miraculous union between the Eucharist's physical elements and the actual body of Christ. '*Hoc est corpus meum*', he asserts, means 'no crass eating' (which he equates with transubstantiation) 'but nonetheless a true partaking of the one Jesus Christ'. Zwingli ridiculed this idea. It is not possible to deny transubstantiation, he argues, while clinging on to a literal reading of '*hoc est corpus meum*', which he interprets as a trope fostering faith in the resurrected, ascended Christ.[109] '"Is"', according to Zwingli, means '"signifies"': '"is" cannot be taken literally, for the bread is not the body'.[110] The two Reformers could not be reconciled. At the 1529 Colloquy of Marburg, they agreed on fourteen out of fifteen articles of doctrine and five out of six points in the fifteenth article. But Luther's and Zwingli's minds would not meet on the interpretation of '*hoc est corpus meum*' – the last article's final point. In McGrath's analysis, 'two very different ways of interpreting Scripture underlay this disagreement', this hermeneutic impasse that in turn provoked doubt over the Reformers' claims about Scripture's perspicuity and the ease with which it can be interpreted.[111]

According to Gregory, modern-day interpreters of these events should not underestimate the 'ecclesial and social' implications of the Reformers' hostile doctrinal deadlock. In Gregory's reading of the situation, such theological divisions among Protestants resulted in social division (most immediately, between Lutheran and Reformed 'moral communities') and the self-undermining of 'the Reformation's foundational truth claim': *sola scriptura*. Because he reads *sola scriptura* as having this splintering effect, Gregory situates the doctrine as the fountainhead of 'Western hyperpluralism' and its above-mentioned consequences – all indications that 'Western modernity is failing'. Gregory sees the Reformation's continuing fallout in the displacement of 'shared answers to [. . .] Life Questions' ('serious questions *about* life, with important implications *for* life') with 'a hyperpluralism of divergent secular and religious truth claims' and the prizing of individualism.[112] This loss of commonality is for Gregory the heavy toll that Western culture is paying for the Reformation. If modern hermeneutics is an overflow of the Reformation, then, in Gregory's narrative, its origin is decidedly dubious.

In *Burning to Read* (2007), James Simpson advances a contrasting polemic which distances the Reformation from modern hermeneutics. In his 'history of evangelical reading', Simpson sets out to dismantle what he terms the 'Protestant case': the idea that the liberal tradition is indebted to Luther because his defiance of Rome birthed 'individual reading capacity, liberty and resistance to institutional disciplines'. Instead, Simpson asserts that 'evangelical reading' (Simpson prefers 'evangelical' to 'Protestant' or 'Reformed') produced neither liberty nor freedom, but rather religious fundamentalism and violence.[113] For Simpson, 'evangelical reading' signifies a paradoxical and damaging mode of being enforced by the principles of *sola scriptura* and *sola fides*. In this way, Simpson continues an influential perspective on the Reformation that goes back to critics such as John Stachniewski. In *The Persecutory Imagination* (1991), Stachniewski seeks to show how Calvin's and 'Calvinism's' soteriology 'fanned despair'. Stachniewski's language choices do not leave his readers guessing about his unfavourable view of the Reformers. Calvin is, for instance, 'the remorseless Calvin' whose theology is 'extremist'. In discussing Erich Fromm's 'highly suggestive' *The Fear of Freedom* (1942), Stachniewski groups 'the Protestantism of Luther and Calvin' with 'authoritarian ideologies in modern history'. To Simpson, Stachniewski's study is 'penetrating'.[114]

As he takes up his predecessor's critical perspective, Simpson depicts the idea of *sola fides* as stripping away for 'the terrified Christian [. . .] the obvious resources [sacraments and good works] for placating an angry God' available within Roman Catholic theology, hence 'confidence in any human resource whatsoever'. Christians' only recourse is 'faith in God's own initiative', faith mediated not by the church, but solely through the text of Scripture. For Simpson, faith and Scripture offer no solace as the 'evangelical emphasis on the literal sense leads directly to a despotic institutional account of textual authority'.[115] Reading Scripture for its 'literal sense' is Simpson's particular bone of contention. He defines 'literal sense' as the idea 'that the meaning of the words is wholly contained in the words themselves', and asserts that even evangelicals recognised that this narrow hermeneutic would not yield common understanding of the meaning of Scripture. Evangelicals, therefore, required a 'pre-textual event' to occur, an action against which Simpson rails: God's action of predestining some people for salvation.[116]

Predestination is colossal, and controversial, as is the broader doctrine of divine election of which predestination is a subset. Divine election is often the first idea associated with the Protestant Reformers, and regularly discussed in relation to Shakespeare's dramas. For most Reformers, divine election is, alongside justification by grace through faith alone, fundamental to their understanding of saving grace as solely intrinsic to and effected by God. Election confirms the absolute gratuity of salvation. Because it takes no account of human works, Simpson finds this soteriology incomprehensible. For Simpson, the notion of divine election, coupled with *sola scriptura*, license a Protestant form of institutional violence. Evangelicals, Simpson contends, replaced one institution – the visible Roman Catholic Church – with another: the 'invisible' 'True Church of the Elect'. Only members of the 'True Church' can rightly and authoritatively interpret Scripture. Yet such belonging is dependent on faith, and the catch is that faith can only be experienced when God's Spirit writes it as 'an anterior text' upon one's heart.[117]

Further, in Simpson's narrative, evangelicals' emphasis on the literal sense ironically 'displaces hermeneutic complexity to the entire life of the Christian': the world becomes 'a very complex and finally unreadable text that is incapable of answering the question: am I saved?' For Simpson, *sola scriptura* and *sola fides* cannot relieve the anxiety attending the sixteenth century's most pressing question. Instead, evangelicals' 'punishing textual culture' imposed a psychic violence 'which pushed its victims into rigid, exclusivist, persecutory, and self-punishing postures' still experienced today. We, Simpson contends, have inherited this 'imprisoning moment'.[118] If Simpson is right, we should not locate modern hermeneutics' heritage in the Reformation. Rather, the interpretive liberty essential to hermeneutics opposes the Reformers. Their ideas either subjugated individual readers to institutional despotism or created hermeneutic confusion. This latter critique suggests a perhaps surprising alliance between Simpson's and Gregory's viewpoints.

Do the charges stick? Did the Reformers and their theology give rise to the fracturing and pervasive figure of the autonomous Western individual or, alternatively, promote a cocktail of oppressive, schismatic fundamentalism and crippling hermeneutic uncertainty? Asking these questions reminds us of our own hermeneutic condition. We feel our affinity with

Much Ado's Friar when faced with three competing narratives about how the momentous events of the sixteenth century have tracked into our own: Gregory's, Simpson's and the genealogy underlying this book that links the Reformation to the modern Western assumption that understanding through interpretation is the mode of human being. Following Shakespeare's Friar, I suggest that 'marking' and 'noting' how the Reformers and their heirs understood the hermeneutical implications of their theological concerns will tell a different story to both Gregory's and Simpson's. This story (mostly) absolves the Reformers of Gregory's accusation of precipitating individualism and secularism and, contrary to Simpson, affirms the Reformers' central place in both the development of a hermeneutic consciousness and an emphasis on human knowing as vital and bounded that bridges Shakespeare's age to ours.

Calvin's famous opening to his *Institutes* headlines the Reformers' theological hermeneutics. 'Knowledge of God, and of our selues', the Reformer asserts, comprise 'the whole summe in all maner of all our wisedome'.[119] The problem of knowing is Calvin's keynote. If knowledge of God and self are the twin dimensions of wisdom, what does it mean, first of all, to have knowledge of God? As McNeill points out, for Calvin, knowledge is 'never "mere" or "simple" or purely objective knowledge'; instead, 'existential apprehension' best captures the Reformer's use of 'knowledge' – here, as he begins his *chef-d'œuvre*, and throughout the work. Knowledge of God, or better, knowing God, cuts to the very core of human being, involving 'mind and heart, affections and will, worship and devout work', as David Steinmetz puts it.[120] For Calvin, this experience of knowing God comes through knowing him as both Creator and Redeemer, the latter through Christ.[121] As McGrath shows, Calvin's humanist education is immediately evident as he begins the *Institutes* by agreeing with Cicero that the natural world reveals 'fragmentary and at times contradictory' knowledge of the existence and nature of a divine being or beings. But then Calvin parts ways with 'classical wisdom'. Scripture, he avers, unveils both more certain knowledge of God and 'knowledge of God of which nature knows nothing – the *cognitio Dei redemptoris*'.[122] For the Reformers, one ultimately knows God by being redeemed by him.

Knowledge of God is the pulse of Calvin's and his fellow Reformers' theology, knowledge that is personal and interpersonal, ontological and existential, salvific and transformative. Moreover, for Calvin, knowing God is inseparable from knowing oneself, an idea which echoes through Augustine's writings.[123] Calvin foregrounds this interconnectedness in the title and thesis of the first chapter of his *Institutes*: 'That the knowledge of God, and of ourselues, are things conioyned, and how they be linked the one with the other.' As he elaborates, Calvin lays stress on the mutual operation of 'these two knowledges': 'yet whether goeth before or engendreth the other, it is hard to discerne'.[124] To Zimmermann, Calvin's thesis marks out the Reformers' 'hermeneutical circle of self-knowledge': 'we cannot understand ourselves and the human situation without reference to the divine other'. Or, as Gadamer puts it as he explains 'that the concept of self-understanding has an originally theological stamp' (via the work of the eighteenth-century Counter-Enlightenment Protestant philosopher Johann Georg Hamann): 'we do not understand ourselves unless it be before God. But God is the Word.'[125]

Calvin begins Book Two of his *Institutes* by setting forth what he believes to be the essential features of self-knowledge attainable only before God. He starts with an allusion to the Delphic maxim, 'Know thyself': 'Not without cause hath the knowledge of himselfe beene in the old Prouerbe so much commended to man.' Calvin then states that this knowledge consists of his readers knowing two things about themselves. First, they are dependent upon God's 'gracious fauour toward' them, demonstrated both at creation and in the creator's continuing care for his creatures after the Fall. Second, Calvin urges his readers to recognise their current 'miserable estate' – the consequence of that ruinous primordial event.[126] In the rest of this chapter, I explore how, in Protestant hermeneutics, this two-pronged knowledge of self, centred on the Augustinian themes of divine grace and human fallenness, informs a perspective on human subjectivity and human beings' hermeneutical condition in which risk is inherent to understanding oneself and all things.

The Fall and the Interpreting Self

The Genesis 3 narrative of humanity's Fall and its aftermath, a motif that runs through the rest of Scripture, was well known to early modern English people. Through the liturgy and sermons, works of art and popular ballads, men, women and children heard and reheard, saw and saw again, what was considered the 'historically real' account of their, and all humanity's, undoing. Hannibal Hamlin suggests that the Fall narrative was so woven into the way that early modern English people instinctively thought about themselves and the world, and organised their way of life, that their culture 'couldn't be imagined without it'.[127] The Fall, according to the Reformers, made finite and fallible humanity's hermeneutic being and agency in the world. To them, the events of Genesis 3 resulted in the breakdown of the self-knowledge and interpersonal knowledge of God that together form the Reformers' and Augustine's 'hermeneutical circle of self-understanding'.[128] Crucially, in the Reformers' thinking, no fallen person can autonomously repair this entwined hermeneutic and spiritual predicament. Understanding this claim takes us to the question of the Fall's impact on human ontology and to the controversial, knotty doctrine of original sin.

As the first person to apply the appellation 'original sin' to human beings' moral, epistemological, existential and spiritual condition after the Fall, Augustine has shaped the ensuing centuries of debate about the idea which *The Winter's Tale*'s Polixenes alludes to as 'the doctrine of ill-doing' (I.ii.72). In *City of God*, Augustine contends that the first occasion of human 'ill-doing', Adam's fall, 'changed and vitiated' that first human's very nature. Of even greater significance, Adam's action also had repercussions for 'human nature' per se. Adam become 'subject to sin and death', and so too, inescapably, 'by birth', are 'his descendants' – all people.[129] Original sin has its source in Adam. Furthermore, it is universal, inherited – a condition of being born into a fallen world – and inherent to human being.[130] The Reformers embraced these four facets of Augustine's perspective. In England, the Church Father's theological anthropology gained such ascendancy that, in Harrison's assessment, it 'dominated the theological agenda and became a crucial point of reference in broader social and intellectual discussions'.[131]

Article nine of the Thirty-Nine Articles captures the four key elements of Augustine's thinking:

> Original sinne standeth not in the folowing of Adam, (as the Pelagians do vainely talke) but it is the fault and corruption of the nature of euery man, that naturally is engendred of the ofspring of Adam, whereby man is very farre gone from originall ryghteousnes, and is of hys owne nature enclined to evyll.[132]

Pelagius was Augustine's principal contemporary antagonist. Contra Augustine, Pelagius insisted that humanity is not bound to Adam. Pelagius, and Pelagians (or semi-Pelagians) who have adopted his thinking, define original sin as 'folowing' Adam, that is, as acts of the will.[133] Human ontology is not essentially vitiated by the Fall. Rather, universal free will means that humans have the capacity to turn (back) to God of our own volition.

In the mid-1520s, Erasmus and Luther were locked in an intense theological battle over this issue of human agency in salvation. In arguing the affirmative position in *De Libero Arbitrio* (1524), Erasmus contends that the 'other side [. . .] immeasurably exaggerate original sin'. By levelling out differences between individuals, that is, grouping together as Adam's sin-suffused descendants people 'with outstanding qualities, as though they were born to virtue [. . .] and others with minds so prone to crime that they seem almost borne onward by fate', Luther's doctrine, Erasmus claims, 'mak[es] God almost cruel'. Erasmus invokes the ancient figure of Pelagius to imply that some people can behave in ways that see them rewarded with eternal life. Specifically, individuals who have experienced God's gracious forgiveness of their sin also have their wills restored to the extent that they can freely choose actions that help qualify them for salvation.[134]

While Erasmus's allegiance to Pelagius is not clear (after all, Pelagianism was deemed heretical at the Council of Carthage in 418), he does appear to suggest some affinity between his own theology and that of the anti-Augustinian campaigner. In contrast, Luther shows his Augustinian colours, declaring, in his characteristically frank manner, that when it comes to salvation, original sin 'leaves free choice with no capacity to do anything but sin and be damned'. Luther, of course, is not arguing that, beyond the matter of salvation, people possess no freedom whatsoever. Anticipating that Erasmus will produce this critique, Luther refutes it: 'We know there are things free choice does by nature, such as eating, drinking, begetting, ruling, so that Diatribe cannot laugh us out of court.'[135]

Erasmus and Luther's debate brings to the surface what Henri Blocher terms the 'core difficulty' in the Augustinian doctrine. If 'a bent towards sinning' is universal, inherited and inherent, does this absolve individuals of responsibility and guilt for the wrong we enact – that is, for what seems, as Blocher puts it, 'a most personal exercise of freedom, namely, sin'? Blocher argues for the need to uphold what may appear to be a paradoxical dialectic central to the doctrine's 'design' (while also addressing the many missteps in this endeavour throughout Christian history). This dialectic 'tries to account for sin as a universal phenomenon and yet a matter of personal responsibility', that is, for sin as 'being "natural" in a sense and yet contrary to our true "nature"'.[136] The language of the Thirty-Nine Articles, for instance, strains to maintain this essential tension, juxtaposing the claim that original sin is part and parcel of being Adam's 'ofspring' with the assertion that sin is also personal to each individual. Original sin corrupts 'the nature of euery man'. Yet, each man 'of hys owne nature' is 'enclined to evyll', responsible to some extent for his propensity to 'folow' Adam.

This brief discussion highlights the doctrine's relevance to the age-old metaphysical puzzle of how to marry human perceptions and experiences of necessity and responsibility, determinism and freedom, especially when it comes to acts of wrongdoing and the problem of evil – an issue I take up in Chapter 2. For now, my focus is the hermeneutical implications of the Reformers' teaching that the Fall and original sin impacted human ontology. Luther unfolds these implications in his exposition of Genesis 1: 26. The verse begins: 'Furthermore God said, Let vs make man in our image according to our lickenes [likeness]'. Luther reads 'image' as the creator's endowment of the creature with 'an enlightened reason, a true knowledge of God, and a most sincere desire to love God and his neighbor'. For Luther, Adam's embodiment of these 'qualities' made him a true representation and reflection of God. The first human bore 'eternal life, everlasting freedom from fear, and everthing that is good' in his very being. Eve too, Luther asserts, shared Adam's 'mental gifts'; indeed, 'her very nature was pure and full of the knowledge of God'. The Fall devastated this life for both the first humans and their progeny. Not only did Adam and Eve's sin significantly distort their imaging of God, but it also ensured that all humanity after them 'cannot grasp it even with our intellect'.[137]

In consequence, no one can live as the first humans did: with 'a most perfect knowledge of God', a foundational interpersonal knowing that extended to every aspect of their existence. They were free of moral corruption, intellectual disorderliness, physical imperfections and existential dread. Every aspect of their experiences and being mapped onto both God's nature and reality. It need hardly be said that human existence as we know it could be encapsulated by reversing Luther's descriptions. Most importantly for Luther, humans' knowledge of God consists of 'feeble and almost completely obliterated remnants', and death's overshadowing means that 'we are never secure in God'.[138] Even Scripture – now the means to knowing God – while perspicuous in itself, is 'veiled' by its readers' fallen condition.[139] Similarly, to Calvin the 'minde is subiect to blindnes'. The fallen, blind mind cannot discern God's 'powers', hence God himself, in his works. Instead, 'monstrous trifles' replace knowledge of the 'one true God' even, Calvin claims, among 'those that otherwise are indued with singular sharpnesse of vnderstanding' – Plato included.[140]

Left to ourselves, human beings, the Reformers argued, cannot know God. And in Calvin's hermeneutical circle of self-knowledge, without knowing God people cannot know themselves. Specifically, 'since we in the person of the first man are fallen from our first estate', individuals' self-interpretations are awry, yielding only distorted knowledge of the two key parts of self-understanding: humanity's prelapsarian condition, 'the excellence of our nature, if it continued vncorrupted', and in contrast, our present 'miserable estate'. In the place of the latter, that is, understanding oneself as profoundly fallen, Calvin claims that 'the greatest part of men haue pernitiously erred' by seeing in themselves only their 'owne good things'. He expands on the consequences for those people with this high view of themselves – nearly everyone, in his opinion. Such a person does 'not profite in learning to know himselfe'.[141]

On the other hand, a person can become so dispirited by directing all his efforts to navel-gazing and judging himself 'by the rule of Gods iudgement' that he sees nothing but what is inside himself and 'leaueth to himselfe nothing toward the well ordering of his life'. Such people can discern neither humanity's 'first noblenes' in the past, nor the future when God will restore this unblemished nature, and with it immortality, to those who know him through faith. Without this insight into what God gave and what God will give people, one will not 'desire' this gift, attained through knowing God.[142] While not recognising the depths of one's own fallen condition thwarts self-knowledge, so too does ruminating too much on it. In this way, Calvin counsels against the despair and anxiety, the 'self-punishing postures', which Stachniewski and Simpson blame on his theology.[143]

Indeed, while noting that 'some people' found Calvin's theology of sin and salvation a cause for despair, Ryrie cautions against overstating the prevalence of this experience in early modern England. Ryrie adduces two historiographical complications to support his warning. First, 'the despairing Calvinist' is, Ryrie argues, 'an ahistorical caricature', a 'myth' conceived by Max Weber that, in Leif Dixon's words, 'has all too often been swallowed whole by scholars'.[144] Second, the sources available to us create an unbalanced picture. As Ryrie puts it, 'salvation-anxiety certainly produced a great deal of paper' as people minutely diarised their sins and ministers corresponded at length with the anxious, while also writing general treatises for the same audience. These are the voices now audible to us, while the thoughts and feelings of those who were 'untroubled, or positively comforted' by Calvin's theology and did not need pastoral correspondences are silent. Further, documenting one's own sin was, for early modern Protestants, a key reason for maintaining a spiritual diary. Here, Ryrie's analogy is useful: diary keeping 'does not mean you are obsessed with sin, just as keeping an account-book does not mean you are obsessed with money'.[145]

To the Reformers, the Fall and its binding of all people to sin and death precludes individuals putting themselves on the pathway to both knowledge of God and self. However, they are also adamant that such knowing is possible, and that it involves neither extolling oneself nor self-excoriation, but instead faith in God who has not only opened the pathway but will also lead people who entrust themselves to him to and along that road. As Calvin argues: 'Man's knowledge of God is God's own work.' Similarly, Zimmermann asserts that the 'theological tradition' to which Augustine and the Reformers belong affirms the possibility of self-knowledge, self-knowledge which rests on 'personal' divine revelation, a key aspect of God's activity of bestowing favour – grace – to his creation.[146] Or, in the words that Gadamer puts in his hypothetical theologian's mouth on the question of whether humans' 'effort to understand' comes from our own 'free decision' or from 'a neutral, completely objective concern':

> Oh no! Our understanding of the holy scriptures does not come from our own free choice. It takes an act of grace. And the Bible is not a totality of sentences offered willy-nilly as a sacrifice to human analysis. No, the gospel is directed to me in a personal way. It claims to contain neither an objective statement nor a totality of objective statements but a special address to me.[147]

The Reformers are central figures in a theological tradition that ascribes to divine grace the primary agency for desiring and attaining understanding. Grace illuminates God's 'special address', enabling the interpreting self to understand personally, albeit incompletely and provisionally.

Before exploring this interplay of grace and understanding, it is noteworthy that the Reformers did not shy away from applying their thinking about the hermeneutical implications of humanity's fallen condition to themselves, especially as people who claim to know God. One might assume that this self-understanding would prompt the Reformers to make bold claims about their hermeneutical agency. But they were more circumspect. In his *Lectures on Genesis*, Luther argues that while God's grace begins the work of repairing fallen humanity in his image, in this life this work is always unfinished: 'intellect and will indeed have remained, but both very much impaired'.[148] Calvin, in an epistle to his friend Simon Grynaeus (Gryney), applies this understanding of the continuing effects of original sin to both his own and corporate epistemological endeavours. While interpreters should not wilfully oppose the Word of God to itself through conflicting interpretations, nevertheless Calvin recognises that even careful interpreters 'haue not alwayes agreed amongst themselues'. Individuals' fallen constitutions vitiate their interpretive acts: 'God at no time hath voutchsafed his seruants with so singuler a blessing, that euery of them, shoulde bee indued with a full, perfect, and absolute knowledge.' Consequently, 'it is not to be looked for in this present life [. . .] that there were a perpetuall consent amongst vs'.[149]

The outworkings of this recognition that every individual's knowledge is necessarily limited and possibly fallible includes the Reformers' acknowledgment, at least in theory, of the presence of a plurality of potentially conflicting voices in the space of biblical interpretation and their practice of what Timothy George calls a '*churchly* hermeneutics'.[150] *Sola scriptura* does not make the church redundant. Luther, for instance, responds to Erasmus's charge of subjectivism by insisting that 'all spirits are to be tested in the presence of the Church at the bar of Scripture'.[151] As Kevin Vanhoozer observes, 'Luther never spoke of the priesthood of the *believer*, in the singular, and neither does the New Testament.' Similarly, *sola scriptura* does not mean '"*solo*" *scriptura*'. *Sola scriptura* upholds Scripture as 'the norm that norms other norms, in which case we can speak of a pattern of authority'. In contrast, *solo scriptura* makes Scripture 'the sole norm', thus potentially investing individuals with an interpretive authority that belies their belonging to the priesthood of believers (plural).[152]

Confessions and councils were among the 'normed norms' integral to the Reformers' corporate enactment of patterns of authority. Comparisons of Reformed confessions (including England's Thirty-Nine Articles) show both a unity of thought and allowance for 'a spectrum of views'. Church councils were the Reformers' preferred means of addressing serious doctrinal disputes. As Calvin states, the conclusions of councils are not always 'true and certaine'. But they do carry more weight than those of one person or a small group of individuals.[153] While its outcome was detrimental, the Colloquy of Marburg exemplifies the intent behind the Reformers' convocation of councils: Luther and Zwingli were brought together in the hope of finding a mediatory position. The Reformers' 'churchly hermeneutics' both complicates Gregory's choice of them as the chief antagonists in his narrative of how the West lost meaning, commonality and God, and resists the causal relationship that Simpson constructs between their seemingly alienating hermeneutics and violent schism. This is not to deny that factions developed and splits occurred within Protestantism. Certainly, after Marburg, Protestants 'found that they could not maintain a single identity'.[154]

There is no simple answer to the question of why the Protestant Church has experienced frequent schism. But the possibility of 'unhappy contests' over the meaning of pivotal phrases such as 'This is my body', the memory of which Calvin wishes 'we could bury [. . .] in perpetual oblivion', is, it seems, inherent to the DNA of the Reformers' theological hermeneutics.[155] To the Reformers, knowing is indeed risky for the fallen interpreting self. At the same time, they also insist that human existence does not play out within a futile hermeneutical situation. To return to Gadamer's theologian, knowing is possible through 'an act of grace', through God's 'special address' that is 'personal' to the self.[156]

Grace and the Interpreting Self

God's gracious revelation of himself, the Reformers assert, makes knowing him and oneself both possible and personal for human subjects. Language is the necessary medium of this divine self-revelation. As Calvin explains in different sections of the *Institutes*, God speaks to humanity in the illuminating Word of Scripture and through the incarnate Word – God the Son, 'the eternall Worde of God' who came into the world. For, while some knowledge of God can be discerned through viewing what he has done in creation, individuals' fallen condition ensures that 'we so ill profited therein'. Rather than leaving humanity in this helpless state, on their own unable to attain knowledge of him 'to saluation', God, Calvin writes, 'openeth his owne holy mouth' to reveal himself more directly and certainly.[157]

For the Reformers, God's nature is inextricably bound up with language. He is a communicator – of himself. Through both his textual and embodied address to humanity, God reveals not only his will, but also, more importantly, his character. As Tyndale puts it, 'God is not mans imaginacion but that only which he saith of hym selfe. [. . .] God is but his worde: as Christ saith John. viii. I am that I saye unto you / that is to saye / that which I preach am I.'[158] God's words map his nature. Unlike humans, whose words about ourselves are not necessarily trustworthy, God is his word. Moreover, as Tyndale notes, Christ the Word also applies the self-reflexivity of divine language to himself.

As he sets forth who he is so that he 'might be knowen to saluation', God's self-revelations manifest his grace. Calvin's notion of divine accommodation expands this point. Writing to refute 'Anthropomorphites', literalists in their reading of biblical anthropomorphisms, Calvin argues that even the 'slenderly witted' understand that God adapts his mode of communication to human limitations, 'speak[ing] as it were childishly, as nurses doe with their babes'. God is neither mortal nor finite. Rather, the 'maner' of God's speaking indicates his willingness to 'apply the vnderstanding of him to our slender capacitie'. To enable knowledge of himself, it was necessary that God 'descended a great way beneath his owne height'.[159] Here, Calvin clearly echoes Erasmus, who had written in his *Enchiridion militis christiani* (1503) that 'divine wisdom speaks to us in baby-talk and like a loving mother accommodates its words to our state of infancy'.[160] To Erasmus, divine accommodation exemplifies a central rhetorical axiom: 'if communication or persuasion is to take place, the higher must lower itself' (as lower persons cannot elevate themselves to the position of the higher).[161]

In Calvin's figuring of divine accommodation, Scripture and Christ are, to take up Vanhoozer's image, 'the "speech bridge" the infinite Creator traverses to communicate with finite creatures'.[162] Grace impels this divine journey. God built and crossed over the 'speech bridge' to secure human beings' redemption by re-establishing relationship with them. Paul Helm explicates how, in Calvin's thinking, divine grace drives divine linguistic accommodation. Since the 'ends that God seeks [. . .] are ultimately soteric in character [. . .] God's accommodation of himself in his language about himself [is] integral to his grace'. As implied by Calvin's image of God 'descending', as in a sense scaling himself down to the level of human comprehension, the divine's ultimate means of realising his goal of humanity's salvation is through 'the accommodation of God the Son in the Incarnation'.[163] God descended into the world in person to show himself and speak to bounded human beings.

As God's address to humanity is personal, it locates its recipients in a hermeneutical situation that is above all else relational. In this hermeneutical situation, understanding, according to the Reformers, develops for interpreting selves through their subjective encounters with the living voice of God. Such understanding is transformative, recasting individuals' identities and reorienting the way they see and interpret God, self and indeed all others in the world. This is how Luther situates himself in relation to the textual Word. As he elaborates on the idea of Scripture's hermeneutical sufficiency (*sacra scriptura sui ipsius interpres*), Luther writes:

> I do not wish to boast that I am more learned than all, but that Scripture alone should reign, nor do I pretend that it is to be interpreted by my spirit or that of other men. I wish to understand it by its spirit.[164]

Interpreting selves have a choice: either take possession of Scripture, bending its meaning to one's own desires, reason and will, or like Luther (or at least like Luther's account of his hermeneutics) seek to understand Scripture by opening oneself up to it such that the self's act of interpreting Scripture 'by its spirit' functions reflexively.

The latter approach is, for Luther, consistent with Scripture's nature. It is a 'pneumatic text', a living, answerable spirit, not a 'dead letter', that is, an object of inquiry and control for the rational mind. 'Pneumatic text' is Bruns's term, which he employs in describing Luther's conviction that interpreters' reading of Scripture must affect their very being if this engagement is to yield understanding. For Luther, in the hermeneutical situation comprising Scripture and reader,

> the reader is not so much the interpreter as the interpreted. [. . .] One's relation to the text is ontological rather than simply exegetical. [. . .] One's self-understanding or self-identity is reconstituted by the text. To understand the Scriptures is to see oneself in its light.[165]

People simultaneously attain (some) understanding of Scripture and themselves when they allow themselves to be redrawn by this encounter, to journey towards knowledge of self with, to recall Zimmermann, 'reference to the divine Other'. In Luther's words, 'Scripture is not understood, unless it is brought home, that is, experienced.'[166]

For Luther, this ontological, existential relationship between the divine Word and fallen human interpreters crystallises through the self's experience of Christ the embodied Word. This experience centres on Christ's historical crucifixion as the focal point of divine revelation. As he expands on his doctrine of justification by faith alone, Luther argues that, paradoxically, the cross both reveals and hides God. To Luther, the cross is a transcendent voice, a 'word' spoken from beyond the self to 'address' her.[167] Yet, when one looks at the spectacle of the cross, what is obviously discernible is not God, but instead a finite man – 'a man dying in apparent weakness and folly'.[168] This 'word of the cross', as Brian Gregor puts it, represents an 'astonishing mystery' to its addressees.[169] McGrath summarises Luther's point: 'God is particularly known through suffering.'[170]

In his 'Heidelberg Disputation' of 1518, Luther famously divides human responses to this surprising revelation: one can be a 'theologian of glory' or a 'theologian of the cross'. Expecting that the divine is manifest in 'strength, glory and majesty', the theologian of glory 'calls evil good and good evil'.[171] Such a person cannot perceive the cross as the ultimate site of divine revelation. The theologian of the cross, on the other hand, 'comprehends the visible and manifest things of God seen through suffering and the cross', especially that it is through this act of divine suffering that the self can be justified. This knowledge eludes human reason; it is grasped, instead, by 'faith alone'. Only through faith can interpreting selves first, recognise the exchange that occurred on the cross when 'Christ became sin on our behalf, in order that his righteousness might become our righteousness' and second, embrace the justifying 'power' of the cross as a mysterious gift of grace to them.[172]

Faith in the cross objectively changes the self's status before God who now views the justified person as righteous. This same gift also brings about the self's subjective, ontological transformation as one receives both 'the real and redeeming presence' of Christ the Word, that is, interpersonal knowledge of God, and a new understanding of oneself as 'ontologically reconstitute[ed]' by grace. Reflecting on Luther's distinction between theologians of glory and theologians of the cross, Gregor contrasts the 'ontology of self-justification' with the 'ontology of justification by faith'. The former binds individuals' identity to their 'own activity'; the latter's identity comes from outside the self – from God's recognition of them 'apart from any meritorious acts'.[173] Gadamer shows how this second configuration of the self links faith and self-understanding. 'From the theological point of view', the philosopher writes, self-understanding occurs as 'a gracious act of God that happens *to* the one who has faith'. As such, self-understanding, perhaps paradoxically, 'involves a moment of "loss of self"', of 'ecstatic self-forgetting'.[174] For, the primary agent of self-understanding is located not within, but outside the self: in the divine being.

As discussed, Simpson finds this theology highly objectionable. For Simpson, the idea that God gifts knowledge to some circumvents human volition to enact a covert, exclusionary form of institutional violence. Contra Simpson, the Reformers would argue that divine grace does not exclude, but includes; it does not supress human worth, but enables the indigent. To Simpson, Luther's soteriology 'makes a cruel and sadistic tyrant of God, and produces a Kafkaesque world of uncertainty for readers'.[175] To the Reformers, grace, for them the heartbeat of salvation, proves that the Creator is favourable towards his creation. Further, grace is pivotal to human beings' hermeneutic fitness and the possibility of understanding. Divine grace effects the interpreting self's ontological reversal by overturning an ontology of self-justification with an ontology of justification by faith. In so doing, grace does not '*perfect* natural interpretive acts', but instead '*restores* interpretive agents to right-mindedness and right-heartedness and *reorients* interpretation to its proper end' of knowing God and self.[176]

By transforming human being, divine grace ensures that knowing is possible. Yet, this inseparableness of knowing from ontology, from the self's finite, fallible being-in-the-world, also makes knowing risky. While divine grace, appropriated by faith, restores and reorients the justified interpreting self, human experience in this world frequently flies in the face of what individuals now know of God and themselves. Luther writes out of the context of his own struggles as he represents the Christian's temporal life as embodying an 'unending tension between faith and experience'.[177] Faith rests on divine self-revelation, particularly the unfathomable mystery of God dying on a repugnant cross so that fallen people can know him. Yet experience, including one's own experiences of suffering coupled with a continuing fear of God's judgement, will leave the believer 'always prone to doubt as to [. . .] whether God really is hidden' in the cross and thus knowable through faith, or is in fact 'simply absent altogether'. For Luther, the 'solution' is for the doubting self to return over and over to Scripture's 'correct definition' of Christ on the cross, to Paul's words in Galatians 1: 'who gave Himself for our sins'. By 'grasp[ing] the authentic Christ, and truly mak[ing] Him my own', Luther again perceives 'the true knowledge of God, of myself, of all creatures'.[178] Knowing is possible, but it comes as one walks the tightrope between faith and experience.

A similar tension exists in the Reformers' doctrine of predestination and its hermeneutical implications. As Luther and company cannot 'theoretically and doctrinally unravel' predestination, it is, in Marlow and Drewery's assessment, 'from one point of view a confession of ignorance and a very proper piece of Christian agnosticism'. Yet, predestination also represents 'a confession of faith and an affirmation of entirely legitimate Christian certainty', expressing 'the conviction that man's destiny is ultimately determined, not by his own fallible choices, and much less by luck or chance or arbitrary fate, but by the infallibly wise and good will of the gracious God revealed in Christ'.[179] In the incarnate, crucified Word, God showed that he is favourable to humanity. For fallen, fallible humans, anchoring their knowing and 'destiny' in the will of this God brings greater confidence that they will know him than entrusting this problem to their own doing.

As a confession of both ignorance and faith, the Reformers' ideas about predestination, indeed the breadth of their theology of grace, situates the interpreting self in a hermeneutical situation best navigated with interpretive humility. This idea of hermeneutic humility returns us to the essentially relational character of the hermeneutical situation brought into being by the Creator's personal address to his creation. In this interpretive space, the Reformers' theology of grace calls for a posture that Vanhoozer, re-sounding Luther, calls a 'hermeneutics of the cross'. Its antithesis? A 'hermeneutics of glory'. Within the paradigm of the hermeneutics of the cross, understanding occurs as interpreting selves willingly put themselves 'second' by submitting their 'interpretive theories to the test of the text'.[180]

Importantly, for the Reformers this recognition and honouring of the textual other necessarily applies beyond one's mode of reading the divine Word. It also maps the way interpreting selves respond to the words and being of all others. For those who know God, their new self-understanding, reflective of an ontology of justification by faith, orients them towards attentiveness to other selves. As Luther writes in *The Freedom of a Christian*, 'a Christian lives not in himself, but in Christ and in his neighbor. [. . .] He lives in Christ through faith, in his neighbor through love.' Neighbourly love, 'true love and the genuine rule of a Christian life' as Luther defines it, models itself on 'what Christ did for us', on his act of humble self-giving at the cross.[181] Sociality, more than that, a being-for-the-other, indeed for all others whom one encounters (as a neighbour is any other) is built into the architecture of the Reformers' understanding of what it is to know.

In this context, a hermeneutics of the cross positions individuals to listen to and act with humble love towards the transcendent, living voice of the other they are interpreting, rather than to stand over this 'text' – be it divine or human, written or enfleshed. This interpreting self is very unlike the individualistic, atomistic self whom Gregory links back to the Reformers, a self akin to the autonomous knowing subject forged out of the Enlightenment and its 'spirit of rationalism'.[182] Like Gregory, Sarah Beckwith also charges the Reformers with undermining human morality and community. To Beckwith, 'the Lutheran and Calvinistic understanding of justification' constructs a subjectivity that robs humans of agency as the self is no longer seen 'as an ethical subject capable of growth'. In this scenario, 'love could no longer be the central concept in Christian life'.[183] But the Reformers would recognise neither Beckwith's human subject nor its circumstances.

Calvin anticipates arguments like Beckwith's: 'That also is most false, that the minds of men are withdrawen from the affection of weldoing, when we take from them the opinion of meriting.' Instead of cooling the justified person's desire for 'weldoing' by denying that moral actions function meritoriously for salvation, Calvin argues that this person now has the capacity to understand and follow Scripture's ethical imperatives: 'Can we be pricked forward to charitie with anie more liuely argument then that of Iohn, that we should mutually loue one an other as God hath loued vs?'[184] For the Reformers, justification by faith lifts from people the impossible burden of hitching their salvation to what they do and who they are.

Once justified, a person is free – free to do good towards others. With their identity no longer bound up in their moral performance but instead with the divine grace and love given to them, justified selves, Eberhard Jüngel argues from the Reformers' theology, will '*manifest*' that grace and love 'in dealings with fellow human beings'.[185] Interpreting selves have been given the cross as a hermeneutic to shape their reading of and being towards others – a risky hermeneutic indeed.

By refiguring individuals' relation to how they attain crucial knowledge of God and themselves, the Reformers' ideas of *sola scriptura* and the priesthood of all believers contributed significantly to seeding a hermeneutic revolution. Seeking understanding as an interpreter became the self's mode of being. Moreover, according to the Reformers' thinking about the repercussions of humanity's fall and the nature of divine grace, interpreting selves are at once essentially relational and inescapably implicated in their efforts to understand. Knowing for the self is personal, yet not individualistic; humbling and risky, yet not humiliating nor futile; finite and fallible, yet possible. Gadamer's many conversations with Protestant hermeneutics suggest that while this rendering of human subjectivity is built on unfamiliar ideas, it is not entirely lost from Western culture today. If Shakespeare's interpreting selves continue to feel familiar to us in the modern world, the hermeneutical genealogy connecting his theologically full culture to ours may well account (to some extent) for this impression.

Notes

1. Hans-Georg Gadamer, 'Hermeneutics as Practical Philosophy', in *The Gadamer Reader: A Boquet of the Later Writings*, ed. and trans. Richard E. Palmer (Evanston, IL: Northwestern University Press, 2007), 241.
2. Jean Grondin, *Introduction to Philosophical Hermeneutics*, trans. Joel Weinsheimer (New Haven: Yale University Press, 1994), 39.

3. Charles Taylor, *Sources of the Self: The Making of the Modern Identity* (Cambridge, MA: Harvard University Press, 1989); Gadamer, 'Hermeneutics as Practical Philosophy', 241.
4. William Whitaker, *A Disputation on Holy Scripture, Against the Papists, Especially Bellarmine and Stapleton*, ed. and trans. William Fitzgerald (Cambridge: The University Press, 1849), 235; Thomas Cranmer, 'A Prologue or Preface,' in *The Byble in Englishe that is, the olde and new Testament, after the translacion appoynted to bee read in the Churches* (London: Edwarde Whitchurche, 1549), 4; Thomas Fulton and Kristen Poole, 'Introduction: Popular Hermeneutics in Shakespeare's London', in *The Bible on the Shakespearean Stage: Cultures of Interpretation in Reformation England*, ed. Thomas Fulton and Kristen Poole (Cambridge: Cambridge University Press, 2018), 1. Italics original; Judith Maltby, 'Foreword', in John E. Booty (ed.), *The Book of Common Prayer 1559: The Elizabethan Prayer Book* (Charlottesville: The University of Virginia Press, 1976, reissued 2005). Unless otherwise stated, I will use the 1559 *BCP* (rather than the 1549 or 1552 versions).
5. Booty, *The Book of Common Prayer 1559*, 79.
6. R. Ward Holder, 'Revelation and Scripture', in *T&T Clark Companion to Reformation Theology*, ed. David M. Whitford (London: Bloomsbury, 2012), 40, 477n31.
7. Gordon Campbell, *Bible: The Story of the King James Version, 1611–2011* (Oxford: Oxford University Press, 2010), 22.
8. Hereford and Worcester Record Office 802 BA 2764, p. 137, quoted in Caroline Litzenberger, *The English Reformation and the Laity: Gloucestershire, 1540–1580* (Cambridge: Cambridge University Press, 1997), 40.
9. Peter Marshall, *Beliefs and the Dead in Reformation England* (Oxford: Oxford University Press, 2002), 55; David Daniell, 'Shakespeare and the Protestant Mind', *Shakespeare Survey* 54 (2001): 7, 3–4.
10. Booty, *The Book of Common Prayer 1559*, 17.
11. Maltby, 'Foreword', viii, viii–ix.
12. Ibid. viii–ix; Booty, *The Book of Common Prayer 1559*; Alec Ryrie, *Being Protestant in Reformation Britain* (Oxford:

Oxford University Press, 2013), 318. Preces are prayers in which the minister and congregation say or sing alternate lines.

13. Ryrie, *Being Protestant*, 336, 317, 336.
14. Daniel Swift, *Shakespeare's Common Prayers: The Book of Common Prayer and the Elizabethan Age* (Oxford: Oxford University Press, 2012), 40.
15. Booty, *The Book of Common Prayer 1559*, 17.
16. Swift, *Shakespeare's Common Prayers*, 48, 45, 44.
17. Thomas Dabbs, 'Paul's Cross and the Dramatic Echoes of Early-Elizabethan Print', in *Paul's Cross and the Culture of Persuasion in England, 1520–1640*, ed. Torrance Kirby and P. G. Stanwood (Boston: Brill, 2014), 232.
18. Naseeb Shaheen, *Biblical References in Shakespeare's Plays* (Newark: University of Delaware Press, 1999), 38–9.
19. Michael Jensen, '"Simply" Reading the Geneva Bible: The Geneva Bible and Its Readers', *Literature & Theology* 9, no. 1 (1995): 31.
20. Lloyd E. Berry, 'Introduction to the Facsimile Edition', in *The Geneva Bible (1560 Edition)* (Peabody, MA: Hendrickson Publishers, 2007), 14, 22; Femke Molekamp, 'Using a Collection to Discover Reading Practices: The British Library Geneva Bibles and a History of their Early Modern Readers', *eBLJ* (2006): 3. <http://www.bl.uk/eblj/2006articles/pdf/article10.pdf>.
21. Vivienne Westbrook, 'Versions of Paul', in *A Companion to Paul in the Reformation*, ed. R. Ward Holder (Leiden: Brill, 2009), 434; Fulton and Poole, 'Introduction,' 2; Helen Wilcox, 'Measuring up to Nebuchadnezzar: Biblical Presences in Shakespeare's Tragicomedies', in *Early Modern Drama and the Bible: Contexts and Readings, 1570–1625*, ed. Adrian Streete (New York: Palgrave Macmillan, 2012), 55–6.
22. Holder, 'Revelation and Scripture', 51. The final 1559 Latin version of the *Institutes* was published in English in 1561.
23. Andrew Pettegree, 'The Spread of Calvin's Thought', in *The Cambridge Companion to John Calvin*, ed. Donald K. McKim (Cambridge: Cambridge University Press, 2004), 210; Anthony B. Dawson and Paul Yachnin, *The Culture of Playgoing in Shakespeare's England* (Cambridge: Cambridge University Press, 2001), 180.

24. Pettegree, 'Spread of Calvin's Thought', 210.
25. Peter Marshall, 'Choosing sides and talking religion in Shakespeare's England', in *Shakespeare and Early Modern Religion*, ed. David Loewenstein and Michael Witmore (Cambridge: Cambridge University Press, 2015), 55.
26. Naomi Tadmor, 'The Bible in English Culture: The Age of Shakespeare', in *The Oxford Handbook of the Age of Shakespeare*, ed. Malcolm Smuts (Oxford: Oxford University Press, 2016), 391–2.
27. Tessa Watt, *Cheap Print and Popular Piety, 1550–1640* (Cambridge: Cambridge University Press, 1991), 6–8; Heidi Brayman Hackel, 'The "Great Variety" of Readers', in *A Companion to Shakespeare*, ed. David Scott Kastan (Malden, MA: Blackwell Publishers, 1999), 139–42.
28. Lawrence Manley, 'Literature and London', in *The Cambridge History of Early Modern English Literature*, ed. David Loewenstein and Janel Mueller (Cambridge: Cambridge University Press, 2002), 401.
29. Marshall, 'Choosing sides', 55.
30. Peter Harrison, 'The Bible and the Emergence of Modern Science', *Science & Christian Belief* 18, no. 2 (2006): 116.
31. Diarmaid MacCulloch, *Reformation: Europe's House Divided 1490–1700* (London: Penguin Books, 2004), 77; Paul Oskar Kristeller, 'Humanism', in *The Cambridge History of Renaissance Philosophy*, ed. C. B. Schmitt et al. (Cambridge: Cambridge University Press, 1988), 113; Alister E. McGrath, *The Intellectual Origins of the European Reformation*, 2nd ed. (Malden, MA: Blackwell, 2004), 35.
32. MacCulloch, *Reformation*, 81.
33. McGrath, *Intellectual Origins*, 66, 38.
34. Alister E. McGrath, *Reformation Thought: An Introduction*, 4th ed. (Chichester: Wiley-Blackwell, 2012), 40.
35. MacCulloch, *Reformation*, 78, 81.
36. McGrath, *Intellectual Origins*, 128.
37. Ibid. 129, 125.
38. MacCulloch, *Reformation*, 84.
39. McGrath, *Reformation Thought*, 50; MacCulloch, *Reformation*, 99.

40. MacCulloch, *Reformation*, 84.
41. McGrath, *Intellectual Origins*, 58–9.
42. McGrath, *Reformation Thought*, 50.
43. MacCulloch, *Reformation*, 114.
44. McGrath, *Intellectual Origins*, 64; MacCulloch, *Reformation*, 111, 179.
45. MacCulloch, *Reformation*, 110, xxiii.
46. John T. McNeill, 'Introduction', in *Calvin: Institutes of the Christian Religion*, ed. John T. McNeill, vol. 1 (Philadelphia: Westminster Press, 1960), lvii; Bradley J. Gundlach, 'Augustine of Hippo', in *Evangelical Dictionary of Theology*, ed. Walter A. Elwell (Grand Rapids, MI: Baker Academic, 2001), 122–3.
47. McNeill, 'Introduction', lvii–lviii; Gundlach, 'Augustine of Hippo', 123.
48. McNeill, 'Introduction', lviii.
49. MacCulloch, *Reformation*, 77, 105–7.
50. McGrath, *Intellectual Origins*, 42–3.
51. L. E. Semler, 'A Proximate Prince: The Gooey Business of "Hamlet" Criticism', *Sydney Studies in English* 32 (2006): 107.
52. Grondin, *Introduction to Philosophical Hermeneutics*, 39; Kevin J. Vanhoozer, 'Discourse on Matter: Hermeneutics and the "Miracle" of Understanding,' in *Hermeneutics at the Crossroads*, ed. Kevin J. Vanhoozer, James K. A. Smith and Bruce Ellis Benson (Bloomington: Indiana University Press, 2006), 28–9.
53. McGrath, *Reformation Thought*, 117.
54. Richard Hooker, *The Ecclesiastical Polity and Other Works*, vol. 3 (London: Holdsworth and Ball, 1830), 379.
55. *Articles, whereupon it was agreed by the Archbishoppes and Bishoppes of both prouinces, and the whole cleargie, in the Conuocation holden at London in the yere of our Lorde God 1562* (Poules Churchyard, London: Richarde Iugge and Iohn Cawood, 1571), article 11.
56. Ralph S. Werrell, 'Reformation Conflict Between Stephen Gardiner and Robert Barnes, Lent 1540', in *Paul's Cross and the Culture of Persuasion in England, 1520–1640*, ed. Torrance Kirby and P. G. Stanwood (Boston: Brill, 2014), 136, 131.

57. Stephen Gardiner, *A declaration of suche true articles as George Ioye hath gone about to confute as false* (London: Iohannes Herforde, 1546), fol. ix.
58. Hastings Robinson (ed.), *Original Letters Relative to the English Reformation*, vol. 2 (Cambridge: The University Press, 1846 and 1847), 616–17.
59. Werrell, 'Reformation Conflict', 137.
60. Alister E. McGrath, *Iustitia Dei: A History of the Christian Doctrine of Justification*, 3rd ed. (Cambridge: Cambridge University Press, 2005), 42.
61. Martin Luther, 'Preface to the Complete Edition of Luther's Latin Writings', in *Career of the Reformer IV*, ed. and trans. Lewis W. Spitz (Philadelphia: Muhlenberg Press, 1960), 328, 336–7.
62. Ibid. 337.
63. Carl R. Trueman, *Luther on the Christian Life: Cross and Freedom* (Wheaton, IL: Crossway, 2015), 67. See McGrath, *Reformation Thought*, 120 and Markus Wriedt, 'Luther's Theology', in *The Cambridge Companion to Martin Luther*, ed. Donald K. McKim (Cambridge: Cambridge University Press, 2003) for two perspectives on the timing of Luther's conversion.
64. Martin Luther, 'The Freedom of a Christian', trans. W. A. Lambert, rev. Harold J. Grimm in *Career of the Reformer I*, ed. Harold J. Grimm (Philadelphia: Muhlenberg Press, 1957), 343, 363.
65. Alister E. McGrath, *Christianity's Dangerous Idea: The Protestant Revolution – A History from the Sixteenth Century to the Twenty-First* (HarperCollins e-books, 2007), 43–4.
66. *The Oxford Dictionary of the Christian Church*, 3rd ed. (2005), s.v. 'Exsurge Domine'.
67. McGrath, *Christianity's Dangerous Idea*, 251.
68. Peter Harrison, 'Philosophy and the Crisis of Religion', in *The Cambridge Companion to Renaissance Philosophy*, ed. James Hankins (Cambridge: Cambridge University Press, 2007), 241.
69. Kevin J. Vanhoozer, *Biblical Authority After Babel: Retrieving the Solas in the Spirit of Mere Protestant Christianity* (Grand Rapids, MI: Brazos Press, 2016), 145.

70. Gadamer, 'Hermeneutics as a Theoretical and Practical Task', in *The Gadamer Reader: A Boquet of the Later Writings*, ed. and trans. Richard E. Palmer (Evanston, IL: Northwestern University Press, 2007), 255.
71. McGrath, *Christianity's Dangerous Idea*, 53, 2.
72. Gadamer, 'Hermeneutics as a Theoretical and Practical Task', 255.
73. Trueman, *Luther on the Christian Life*, 34.
74. Erik Herrmann, 'Luther's Absorption of Medieval Biblical Interpretation and his Use of the Church Fathers', in *The Oxford Handbook of Martin Luther's Theology*, ed. Robert Kolb, Irene Dingel, and L'ubomír Batka (Oxford: Oxford University Press, 2014), 71, 72, 74.
75. Brian Cummings, *The Literary Culture of the Reformation: Grammar and Grace* (Oxford: Oxford University Press, 2002), 19; McGrath, *Intellectual Origins*, 144–5.
76. Vanhoozer, *Biblical Authority After Babel*, 112.
77. McGrath, *Reformation Thought*, 92–3.
78. David C. Steinmetz, 'The Council of Trent', in *The Cambridge Companion to Reformation Theology*, ed. David A. Bagchi and David C. Steinmetz (Cambridge: Cambridge University Press, 2004), 237–8.
79. McGrath, *Reformation Thought*, 93. Italics original.
80. Steinmetz, 'The Council of Trent', 237–8. Italics original.
81. Hans-Georg Gadamer, *Truth and Method*, trans. Joel Weinsheimer and Donald G. Marshall, 2nd, rev. ed. (London: Continuum, 2004), xxx; Holder, 'Revelation and Scripture', 52.
82. Martin Luther, 'Explanations of the Ninety-five Theses', in *Career of the Reformer I*, ed. Harold J. Grimm (Philadelphia: Muhlenberg Press, 1957), 209.
83. Jared Wicks, 'Roman Reactions to Luther: The First Year (1518)', *The Catholic Historical Review* 69, no. 4 (1983): 530.
84. *D. Martini Lutheri opera Latina varii argumenti* (Frankfurt and Erlangen, 1865), 1: 347, quoted in and trans. Wicks, 'Roman Reactions', 529. Italics original.
85. David P. Daniel, 'Luther on the Church', in *The Oxford Handbook of Martin Luther's Theology*, ed. Robert Kolb,

Irene Dingel, and L'ubomír Batka (Oxford: Oxford University Press, 2014), 338.

86. *The Canons and Decrees of the Sacred and Ecumenical Council of Trent, Celebrated under the Sovereign Pontiffs, Paul III, Julius III and Pius IV*, trans. James Waterworth (London: C. Dolman, 1848), 19.
87. Jean Calvin, *The Institution of Christian Religion*, trans. Thomas Norton (London: Arnold Hatfield, 1599), 1.7.1.
88. Whitaker, *A Disputation on Holy Scripture*, 352–3, 415.
89. Kevin J. Vanhoozer, *Is There a Meaning in This Text? The Bible, the Reader, and the Morality of Literary Knowledge* (Grand Rapids, MI: Zondervan, 1998), 305.
90. Calvin, *The Institution of Christian Religion*, 1.6.1.
91. *Articles, whereupon it was agreed*, article 5.
92. McGrath, *Intellectual Origins*, 157.
93. Martin Luther, 'Answer to the Hyperchristian, Hyperspiritual, and Hyperlearned Book by Goat Emser in Leipzig – Including Some Thoughts Regarding His Companion, the Fool Murner', trans. Eric W. Gritsch and Ruth C. Gritsch, in *Church and Ministry I*, ed. Eric W. Gritsch (Philadelphia: Fortress Press, 1970), 164.
94. Gadamer, 'Hermeneutics as Practical Philosophy', 233; Gadamer, 'Hermeneutics as a Theoretical and Practical Task', 258.
95. William Shakespeare, *Hamlet: The Texts of 1603 and 1623*, ed. Ann Thompson and Neil Taylor, Arden Shakespeare Third Series (London: Cengage Learning, 2006).
96. James Atkinson, 'Introduction: To The Christian Nobility of the German Nation Concerning the Reform of the Christian Estate', in *The Christian in Society I*, ed. James Atkinson (Philadelphia: Fortress Press, 1966), 117.
97. Martin Luther, 'To The Christian Nobility of the German Nation Concerning the Reform of the Christian Estate', trans. Charles M. Jacobs, rev. James Atkinson, in *The Christian in Society I*, ed. James Atkinson (Philadelphia: Fortress Press, 1966), 126–7, 130.
98. Ibid. 135, 136–7.
99. Holder, 'Revelation and Scripture', 44, 45.

100. Gadamer, 'Hermeneutics as a Theoretical and Practical Task', 255.
101. Gerald L. Bruns, *Hermeneutics Ancient and Modern* (New Haven, CT: Yale University Press, 1992), 158.
102. William Shakespeare, *Much Ado About Nothing*, ed. Claire McEachern, Arden Shakespeare Third Series (London: Bloomsbury, 2015), IV.i.162–3n.
103. Gadamer, *Truth and Method*, 328.
104. Thomas F. Torrance, *The Hermeneutics of John Calvin* (Edinburgh: Scottish Academic Press, 1988), 158.
105. Jens Zimmermann, *Recovering Theological Hermeneutics: An Incarnational-Trinitarian Theory of Interpretation* (Grand Rapids, MI: Baker Academic, 2004), 79, 78.
106. Gadamer, *Truth and Method*, 327.
107. Brad S. Gregory, *The Unintended Reformation: How a Religious Revolution Secularized Society* (Cambridge, MA: The Belknap Press of Harvard University Press, 2012), 22, 15–20.
108. Ibid. 89–93, 355.
109. Robert H. Fischer, 'Introduction to Volume 37', in *Word and Sacrament III*, ed. Robert H. Fischer (Philadelphia: Muhlenberg Press, 1961), xix, xviii.
110. Ulrich Zwingli, 'On The Lord's Supper', in *Zwingli and Bullinger*, ed. and trans. G. W. Bromiley (London: SCM Press, 1953), 224–5.
111. McGrath, *Reformation Thought*, 183, 182.
112. Gregory, *Unintended Reformation*, 89, 205, 94, 92, 365, 74, 377. Italics original.
113. James Simpson, *Burning to Read: English Fundamentalism and Its Reformation Opponents* (Cambridge, MA: The Belknap Press of Harvard University Press, 2007), 2–3, 7, 29.
114. John Stachniewski, *The Persecutory Imagination: English Puritanism and the Literature of Despair* (Oxford: Clarendon, 1991), 27, 23, 3; Simpson, *Burning to Read*, 291n58.
115. Simpson, *Burning to Read*, 81, 84, 107.
116. Ibid. 107, 124–5.
117. Ibid. 108, 35, 139.

118. Ibid. 140, 141, 282.
119. Calvin, *The Institution of Christian Religion*, 1.1.1.
120. John T. McNeill (ed.), *Calvin: Institutes of the Christian Religion*, trans. Ford Lewis Battles, 2 vols (Philadelphia: Westminster Press, 1960), 1.1.1n1; David C. Steinmetz, 'The Theology of John Calvin', in *The Cambridge Companion to Reformation Theology*, ed. David A. Bagchi and David C. Steinmetz (Cambridge: Cambridge University Press, 2004), 120.
121. Calvin, *The Institution of Christian Religion*, 1.2.1.
122. McGrath, *Intellectual Origins*, 56, 57.
123. McNeill (ed.), *Calvin: Institutes*, 1.1.1n3.
124. Calvin, *The Institution of Christian Religion*, 1.1.1.
125. Zimmermann, *Recovering Theological Hermeneutics*, 20; Hans-Georg Gadamer, *Philosophical Hermeneutics*, ed. and trans. David E. Linge (Berkeley: University of California Press, 1976), 55.
126. Calvin, *The Institution of Christian Religion*, 2.1.1.
127. Hannibal Hamlin, *The Bible in Shakespeare* (Oxford: Oxford University Press, 2013), 127–33, 177, 178.
128. Zimmermann, *Recovering Theological Hermeneutics*, 269.
129. Saint Augustine, *The City of God, Books VIII–XVI*, trans. Gerald G. Walsh and Grace Monahan (Washington, DC: Catholic University of America Press, 1952), XIII.3.
130. Henri Blocher, *Original Sin: Illuminating the Riddle* (Downers Grove, IL: InterVarsity Press, 1997), 18.
131. Peter Harrison, *The Fall of Man and the Foundations of Science* (Cambridge: Cambridge University Press, 2007), 3.
132. *Articles, whereupon it was agreed*, article 9.
133. Blocher, *Original Sin*, 123.
134. Desiderius Erasmus, 'De Libero Arbitrio', ed. E. Gordon Rupp and A. N. Marlow, trans. E. Gordon Rupp, in *Luther and Erasmus: Free Will and Salvation*, ed. E. Gordon Rupp and Philip S. Watson (Philadelphia: Westminster Press, 1969), 93, 94, 49.
135. Martin Luther, 'De Servo Arbitrio', ed. Philip S. Watson and B. Drewery, trans. Philip S. Watson, in *Luther and Erasmus:*

Free Will and Salvation, ed. E. Gordon Rupp and Philip S. Watson (Philadelphia: Westminster Press, 1969), 315, 286.
136. Blocher, *Original Sin*, 18, 12.
137. Martin Luther, *Lectures on Genesis: Chapters 1–5*, ed. Jaroslav Pelikan, trans. George V. Schick, (Saint Louis, MO: Concordia Publishing House, 1958), 63, 65, 66–7, 65.
138. Ibid. 66, 62, 67, 63.
139. Zimmermann, *Recovering Theological Hermeneutics*, 55.
140. Calvin, *The Institution of Christian Religion*, 2.1.9, 1.5.10.
141. Ibid. 2.1.1, 2.1.2.
142. Ibid. 2.1.3.
143. Simpson, *Burning to Read*, 282.
144. Ryrie, *Being Protestant*, 29; Leif Dixon, *Practical Predestinarians in England c. 1590–1640* (Farnham: Ashgate, 2014), 28.
145. Ryrie, *Being Protestant*, 29.
146. McNeill (ed.), *Calvin: Institutes*, 2.2.20; Zimmermann, *Recovering Theological Hermeneutics*, 270.
147. Gadamer, 'Hermeneutics as Practical Philosophy', 241.
148. Luther, *Lectures on Genesis: Chapters 1–5*, 64.
149. Jean Calvin, *A Commentarie vpon the Epistle of Saint Paul to the Romanes, written in Latine by M. Iohn Caluin*, trans. Christopher Rosdell (London: Thomas Dawson, 1583), image 8r.
150. Timothy George, 'Reading the Bible with the Reformers', *First Things* 211 (2011): 32. Italics original.
151. Nico Vorster, 'Sola Scriptura and Western Hyperpluralism: A Critical Response to Brad Gregory's Unintended Reformation', *Review of European Studies* 5, no. 1 (2013): 61; Luther, 'De Servo Arbitrio', 159.
152. Vanhoozer, *Biblical Authority After Babel*, 158, 120–1.
153. Richard A. Muller, 'John Calvin and Later Calvinism', in *The Cambridge Companion to Reformation Theology*, ed. David A. Bagchi and David C. Steinmetz (Cambridge: Cambridge University Press, 2004), 135; Vanhoozer, *Biblical Authority After Babel*, 132–6; Calvin, *The Institution of Christian Religion*, 4.9.13.
154. MacCulloch, *Reformation*, 172.

155. John Calvin, *Commentary on Corinthians – Volume 1*, trans. Rev. John Pringle (Grand Rapids, MI: Christian Classics Ethereal Library, 1848), 315.
156. Gadamer, 'Hermeneutics as Practical Philosophy', 241.
157. Calvin, *The Institution of Christian Religion*, 1.6.1, 3.1.2, 1.6.1.
158. William Tyndale, *The obedie[n]ce of a Christen man and how Christe[n] rulers ought to governe* (Antwerp: J. Hoochstraten, 1528), C3v.
159. Calvin, *The Institution of Christian Religion*, 1.6.1, 1.13.1; McNeill (ed.), *Calvin: Institutes*, 1.13.1n4.
160. Desiderius Erasmus, 'The Handbook of the Christian Soldier: *Enchiridion militis christiani*', trans. Charles Fantazzi, in *Spiritualia*, ed. John W. O'Malley , vol. 66 of The Collected Works of Erasmus (Toronto: University of Toronto Press, 1988), 35.
161. McGrath, *Intellectual Origins*, 54–5.
162. Kevin J. Vanhoozer, *Remythologizing Theology: Divine Action, Passion, and Authorship* (Cambridge: Cambridge University Press, 2010).
163. Paul Helm, *John Calvin's Ideas* (Oxford: Oxford University Press, 2004), 197.
164. Martin Luther, *D. Martin Luthers Werke: Kritische Gesamtausgabe*, vol. 7 (Weimar: Hermann Böhlau, 1892), 97–8, quoted in and trans. Bruns, *Hermeneutics Ancient and Modern*, 145–6.
165. Bruns, *Hermeneutics Ancient and Modern*, 147, 149, 146.
166. Zimmermann, *Recovering Theological Hermeneutics*, 20; *Dr Martin Luthers Tischreden (1531–46)*, vol. 3 (Weimar: Hermann Böhlaus, 1914), 170, quoted in and trans. Bruns, *Hermeneutics Ancient and Modern*, 147.
167. Brian Gregor, *A Philosophical Anthropology of the Cross: The Cruciform Self* (Bloomington: Indiana University Press, 2013), 44–5.
168. Alister E. McGrath, *Luther's Theology of the Cross* (Oxford: Blackwell, 1985), 167.
169. Gregor, *Philosophical Anthropology of the Cross*, 45; McGrath, *Luther's Theology of the Cross*, 173.
170. McGrath, *Luther's Theology of the Cross*, 150.

171. Ibid. 167; Martin Luther, 'Heidelberg Disputation', trans. Harold J. Grimm, in *Career of the Reformer I*, ed. Harold J. Grimm (Philadelphia: Muhlenberg Press, 1957), 40.
172. Luther, 'Heidelberg Disputation', 40; McGrath, *Luther's Theology of the Cross*, 160, 168, 173–5.
173. McGrath, *Luther's Theology of the Cross*, 175; Gregor, *Philosophical Anthropology of the Cross*, 46, 44, 42.
174. Gadamer, *Philosophical Hermeneutics*, 54, 51, 55. Italics original.
175. Simpson, *Burning to Read*, 253.
176. Vanhoozer, *Biblical Authority After Babel*, 65. Italics original.
177. McGrath, *Luther's Theology of the Cross*, 169.
178. Ibid. 172, 173; Martin Luther, *Lectures on Galatians 1535: Chapters 1–4*, ed. Jaroslav Pelikan and Walter A. Hansen, trans. Jaroslav Pelikan (Saint Louis, MO: Concordia Publishing House, 1963), 39.
179. A. N. Marlow and B. Drewery, 'Introduction', in *Luther and Erasmus: Free Will and Salvation*, ed. E. Gordon Rupp and Philip S. Watson (Philadelphia: Westminster Press, 1969), 23.
180. Vanhoozer, *Is There a Meaning?* 465.
181. Luther, 'The Freedom of a Christian', 371.
182. Gadamer, *Truth and Method*, 273.
183. Sarah Beckwith, *Shakespeare and the Grammar of Forgiveness* (Ithaca, NY: Cornell University Press, 2011), 47, 48.
184. Calvin, *The Institution of Christian Religion*, 3.16.2.
185. Eberhard Jüngel, *Theological Essays*, ed. and trans. John B. Webster, vol. 2 (Edinburgh: T&T Clark, 1995), 238. Italics original.

CHAPTER 2

HAMLET, THE FALL AND HERMENEUTICAL TRAGEDY

> The fault, dear Brutus, is not in our stars,
> But in ourselves
>
> *Julius Caesar*, I.ii.141–2

> Of man's first disobedience, and the fruit
> Of that forbidden tree, whose mortal taste
> Brought death into the world, and all our woe
>
> John Milton, *Paradise Lost*, i, 1–3[1]

> O God, Horatio, what a wounded name,
> Things standing thus unknown, shall I leave behind me!
> If thou didst ever hold me in thy heart
> Absent thee from felicity awhile
> And in this harsh world draw thy breath in pain
> To tell my story.
>
> Hamlet, *Hamlet*, V.ii.328–33

As Hamlet dies, hermeneutical concerns are on his mind, as they have been throughout the play. Hamlet fears that he will be misunderstood. Not even death offers him release from the unknowing that shadows *Hamlet*'s characters as they are carried forward, seemingly inescapably, to their tragic ends.

Theirs is, indeed, a 'harsh world'. Moreover, as suggested by Shakespeare's foregrounding of his characters' interpretive predicaments, it is a harsh world that brings out the hermeneutic nature of their being in it. Hans-Georg Gadamer's influential thesis about modern human subjectivity rings true, it seems, of *Hamlet*. For Gadamer, understanding is both intrinsic to human being and always interpretive. As such, individuals' mode of experiencing all things – other people, one's situatedness in history, one's own existence and the world – 'constitute[s] a truly hermeneutic universe'.[2]

Pairing *Hamlet* with this hermeneutic framing of subjectivity points to a preoccupation within the ever-expanding hermeneutical situation of the play's afterlife. Since the late eighteenth century, the task of unearthing the self signified by Shakespeare's characters, especially his protagonist, has occupied a sizeable portion of the vast field of *Hamlet* criticism. Hamlet has come to represent the liberal humanist self, or the socially delineated self, or the secular (or else the spiritual) self, and more. Other writers have summarised the mountain of now-familiar, conflicting arguments about selfhood (both early modern and modern) that invoke Shakespeare's hero.[3]

My focus is the concept of the self that emerges by bringing together Shakespeare's figuring of Hamlet as an interpreting self, *Hamlet* as a tragedy and the perennial puzzle of human freedom. Is Hamlet answerable for his unknowing and the accumulation of interpretive missteps that appear to cut a path to his tragic end? Or do his own 'too too sallied flesh', the 'unweeded garden' in which he abides and the genre of the English revenge tragedy – significant threads in the web of constraints to which he is subject – so attenuate Hamlet's agency that to attribute responsibility to him would be a misreading on our part (I.ii.129, 135)? To rephrase *Julius Caesar*'s Cassius, is the fault in the stars or in Hamlet? This is a loaded issue in our age. As Henri Blocher puts it, we moderns 'are caught between the tide of determinism and the cult of the autonomous self'.[4] Time and again, from the bear pit of social media to the battleground of public policymaking, uncompromising assertions of one or the other side of this dialectic polarise individuals and societies. Of greatest relevance to this chapter is the question of how one's perspective on human freedom informs one's interpretation of the interpreting self.

Key aspects of the Protestant hermeneutics of Shakespeare's day ring through *Hamlet*'s provocation of such deliberations. Specifically, the play abounds with allusions to the doctrines of the Fall, original sin, revelation and grace. As discussed in earlier chapters, the Reformers' teaching on these doctrines gave shape to a configuration of the self as interpretive that Gadamer (and others) identify as a forerunner of his philosophical account of human being. Ideas that may seem distant from our day contribute significantly to our sense that we find in Hamlet and his experiences plangent echoes of ourselves and our times.

The Fall and its consequences – corporeal death and original sin – loom large as Hamlet and his fellow characters seek to overcome their unknowing. What's more, the knowledge disclosed by the ghost seems a parody of divine revelation, while intimations of divine grace in the forms of forgiveness and providence offer momentary hope that Hamlet will receive the understanding he needs to arrest the plot's course towards tragedy, only to have the opposite effect of escalating his uncertainty. In the play-world, aspects of grace are present only as ironic shadows. *Hamlet* offers its audience a theologically inflected depiction of a 'harsh world': a world in which fallen human beings do not receive assistance from outside the Fall's jurisdiction, a world bereft of clear revelation and reversing grace. In such a world, the interpreting self experiences little relief from misconstrual and unknowing. Hamlet's story, we could say, embodies 'the tragedy of hermeneutical experience'.[5]

In figuring 'the tragedy of hermeneutical experience', Gerald Bruns extends Gadamer's thoughts about human experience. Gadamer turns to ancient Greek tragedy, specifically Aeschylus' *Agamemnon*, as a 'witness' to what is, for the modern philosopher, an essential dimension of all human experience. Tragedy shows us that 'experience is experience of human finitude'. Gadamer highlights Aeschylus' 'formula [. . .] of "learning through suffering" (*pathei mathos*)', as especially elucidatory of how the tragic expresses this inevitability. In Aeschylus, 'what a man has to learn through suffering is not this or that particular thing, but insight into the limitations of humanity, into the absoluteness of the barrier that separates man from the divine'. Suffering, 'real experience' (as Gadamer calls it), confronts humans with our inability to escape our mortal nature – 'our own historicity' – such that it is no longer possible to believe that 'everything can be reversed, that there is always time for everything and that everything somehow returns'. Rather, suffering makes one aware 'that all the expectation and planning of finite beings is finite and limited': we do not hold our futures in our hands; we do not belong among the gods. 'Experience teaches us to acknowledge the real', or, as Bruns puts it, to acknowledge 'reality as historicality or limit [. . . .] reality as other, not as the same: reality as that which is more Fate than Fact.'[6]

To Bruns, such acknowledgement is 'what happens in hermeneutical experience, where understanding is an achievement not of objective consciousness but of openness and answerability, where openness means exposure', that is, when interpreting selves are brought face to face with the cold reality of their boundedness. Indeed, Bruns finds that he 'wants to say' that such exposure characterises all hermeneutical experience. To him, hermeneutical experience 'always entails an "epistemological crisis"' and provides 'little comfort, unless it is simply that now we know how awful things can get'.[7] Sophocles' Oedipus exemplifies the iron-fisted hold of this tragic 'structure of meaning' (as Gadamer terms it) over the destiny of the interpreting self.[8] For, as Bruns reads him, 'Oedipus never misunderstands himself – he will always be the man who solved the riddle of the Sphinx – but this self-understanding cannot contain the other that his fate inscribes', the other being the immutable 'Fate' awaiting him 'beyond self-recognition', a reality he must accept.[9]

It is worth noting that, for Gadamer, in Greek tragedy, indeed all tragedy (here Gadamer mentions Shakespeare), the tragic hero is not alone in being both exposed to the tragedy of human (hermeneutical) experience and compelled to acknowledge its reality. Building on Aristotle's definition of tragedy that incorporates 'its *effect* [Wirkung] *on the spectator*', Gadamer argues that tragedy involves spectators in such a way that they too receive tragic hermeneutical insight into 'a metaphysical order of being that is true for all'. As a structure of meaning, tragedy exists in both art and 'life'.[10] A theatregoer, like the characters he watches, experiences 'an excess of tragic suffering' when he 'recognises himself and his own finiteness in the face of the power of fate'. In Oedipus, we see 'the ambiguities of fate hanging over every one of us', ambiguities that, by their very nature, entangle finite interpreting selves as we try to make sense of them.[11] For Gadamer, Greek tragedy explains a significant dimension of modern hermeneutical experience.

What about Shakespeare's tragedy and its protagonist who must know? Of course, as an English revenge tragedy, complete with the necessary ingredients of a ghost which provokes its hero into a bloody-minded pursuit of vengeance, that hero's (assumed) madness, a play-within-a-play, a graveyard scene and a gory collection of corpses, *Hamlet*'s dramatic lineage reaches back through Seneca to Aeschylus, Sophocles, and also Euripides. Are the ancients' notions of human finitude, irreversible actions and, above all, ineluctable fate the defining features of Shakespeare's dramatisation of the tragedy of hermeneutical experience? Some people contend in the affirmative and do so by pointing to the Christian, more specifically, early modern Protestant ideas about the fallen human condition and the operation of divine grace that are conspicuous throughout *Hamlet*. As I will discuss, to some critics, the Reformers' renderings of these doctrines situate human beings as casualties of an inscrutable divine determinism that subjugates human freedom.

In contrast, I argue that the Reformers' perspective on human (hermeneutical) experience intersects with, but does not neatly map onto, what Gadamer terms 'the classical sense of the power of destiny' and the 'disproportion between guilt and fate' it represents.[12] The Reformers' account of human subjectivity challenges and complicates interpretations of *Hamlet* which shackle the theological resonances in the play to a model of tragic fatalism that minimises human freedom and responsibility. Gadamer himself offers a clue to the difference as he briefly comments that 'Christian tragedy presents a special problem', an exception to the tragic genre. Gadamer gives two reasons to support this opinion. First, within a Christian cosmology, fate does not unduly outweigh guilt. Second, for Gadamer, the Christian message of 'divine salvation' disrupts the determining power which 'the values of happiness and haplessness that constitute tragic action' have over individuals' ends.[13] Indeed, while Gadamer holds up Greek tragedy as a mirror on the finitude that interpreting subjects cannot transcend, he also leans into Christian ideas of divine revelation and grace to analogise the possibility of understanding. As Jens Zimmermann notes, in setting forth this possibility, Gadamer both turns to 'the tradition of Augustine's theory of illumination' centred on Christ as the divine, incarnated revelatory Word and is 'drawn to the theological definition of self-understanding as dependent on grace'.[14]

Gadamer's rationale for why Christian tragedy introduces a 'special problem' suggests ways in which *Hamlet* rings some changes on the classical formulation of the tragic nature of human hermeneutical experience as the play engages with theological concerns of Shakespeare's time. On one hand, the many allusions to the Fall and its repercussions, which knit an anthropological pessimism into the texture of *Hamlet*'s mood, suggest that we cannot read Hamlet as able to be an autonomous actor in his hermeneutical situation. When it comes to human understanding, the hermeneutical insights Gadamer gains from Greek tragedy and the hermeneutical implications of the Reformers' doctrines of the Fall and sin cover much common ground. Roger Lundin notes that both classical and Christian perspectives on the human condition trace the tragic limits on understanding to human beings' inability to bridge the distance separating us from the divine. Kevin Vanhoozer insists on the interconnection: 'No description of the human hermeneutical condition is complete if it mentions only finitude and not fallenness besides.'[15] As a fallen interpreting subject in a harsh world, Hamlet is helpless to turn around his epistemological crisis. And he will suffer.

Yet, by attesting to 'the personality of God and the responsibility of sinners', the Christian doctrines also complicate readings of Hamlet and his unknowing as entirely fated by his environment and his necessarily finite understanding.[16] In the biblical narrative of the origins of the tragic human condition with which Shakespeare and his contemporaries were well acquainted, God, not fate, possesses supreme power within and over the cosmos. Above all else, this God is personal. Hence, the human-divine connection is in essence interpersonal – a dynamic emphasised in the Reformers' expositions of the Fall as, at heart, a fracturing of the divine-human relationship. As Jean Calvin puts it, the 'roote' of the Fall was the first humans' 'infidelitie' to God as they repudiated both 'the so great liberalitie of God wherewith [they were] enriched' and God's authority as expressed in his word.[17] By implication, humanity was created with at least some freedom – freedom to refuse God's generosity and authority, and thus the divine other himself. From the perspective of theological hermeneutics, human beings had a major hand in undoing the interpersonal hermeneutical circle of understanding (comprised of mutually dependent knowledge of God and self).[18] Humanity bears some responsibility for its downfall and subsequent unknowing. Fate does not disproportionately surpass guilt in either the Reformers' theology or, I argue, Shakespeare's play.

Rather, we could say that Shakespeare's tragic hero embodies 'the duality of experience': a twofold theological configuration of human subjectivity that absolutises neither determinism nor freedom.[19] Hamlet's necessary epistemological quest sets him on a tragic trajectory which is caught up in his role as the death-bound protagonist in a revenge tragedy. At the same time, as the plot heads towards this tragedy there are multiple moments when we sense that the fault may, indeed, be in him. To some extent, Hamlet can be called to account as an interpreter of himself, others and the world. Meanwhile, the hermeneutic agency that would turn things around for him must be, but is not, granted to him from beyond his temporal sphere. Much of *Hamlet*'s dramatic energy derives, it seems, from an anticipation of this reversal – of, it could be said, grace expressed in a dramatic register. Gestures to this turn, yet its ultimate exclusion, compound Shakespeare's assimilation of Protestant ideas about the Fall into his play-world and are pivotal to *Hamlet*'s variation on the theme of the tragedy of hermeneutical experience. I turn now to explore the allusions to the Fall and its aftershocks – clouded senses, death and original sin – underlying the theological resonance of *Hamlet*'s tragic interpreting subjects and their 'truly hermeneutic universe'.

'I know not'

Hamlet's action is increasingly caught up in the magnetic orbit of Genesis 3 and 4, in the mythology of the origins of human beings' unknowing and woe. Those early chapters of the Bible attribute this state of affairs to the first humans' privileging of the Serpent's version of reality over God's. Whereas God had empowered Adam and Eve to 'eat frely of eurie tre of the garden' except the one that would cause him to 'dye the death', the Serpent insinuates that God is holding out on them – mendaciously denying them freedom, not granting them it: 'Ye shal not dye at all [. . .] ye shalbe as gods knowing good and euil' (Gen. 2: 16–17, 3: 4–5). The subsequent conjunction in the Geneva translation explicitly connects these words and the couple's actions: 'So the woman [. . .] toke of the frute thereof, and did eat, and gaue also to her husband with her, and he did eat' (Gen. 2: 6).

To the Reformers, this act of taking and eating is laden with interpersonal and hermeneutical implications. William Perkins comments that Adam and Eve 'transgresse[d] the will of God'. To Calvin, they 'did not beleeue' God's word and instead 'assented to the sclaunders [slanders] of Satan, wherein he accused God of lying, enuie, and niggardly grudging'. Moreover, preferring the Serpent's reading of their situation over God's showed that they had but 'a colde and small feeling of the perill of death' and ensued in the corruption of their senses.[20] To the Reformers, the Fall was a site of confounded interpersonal, existential and empirical knowing.

As *Hamlet* opens, Shakespeare foregrounds the shortcomings of the senses by drawing his audience's attention to Barnardo's and Francisco's anxieties about not knowing: 'Who's there? / 'Nay answer me. Stand and unfold yourself' (I.i.1–2). Ironically, neither watchman can rely on his sight to satisfy his need to know. This uncertainty keys in to the Reformers' views about the Fall's impact on human senses.

Martin Luther, in *Table-Talk*, contrasts Adam's sight and hearing pre- and post-Fall:

> I believe that before the fall he could have seen objects a hundred miles off better than we can see them at half a mile, and so in proportion with all the other senses. No doubt, after the fall, he said: 'Ah, God! what has befallen me? I am both blind and deaf.' It was a horrible fall.[21]

This is pure speculation. Nowhere does the biblical narrative suggest that, at creation, Adam was endowed with superhuman senses. But Luther's imagining does shed light on his belief in the Fall's thoroughgoing undoing of humans' capacity to know. Calvin writes similarly, juxtaposing Adam before the Fall with his postlapsarian progeny. 'Uncorrupted' senses complemented the governance of Adam's mind by 'the light of true vnderstanding', as well as his moral uprightness. Together, Adam's 'minde, will, and all the senses, doe set before vs the diuine order'. But when he fell, Adam, with Eve, lost 'reason and iudgement: and seeing they were the bondeslaues of Sathan, he had their senses also captiue'. How does the first humans' enslavement affect their descendants? Calvin states that only 'obscure lineaments' of the divine image remain in the human race.[22] Luther agrees.

Here, as Peter Harrison shows, these leading Reformers followed Augustine's thinking. Humankind's experience of 'irremediable epistemological confusion' is, for Augustine, a significant repercussion of the Fall.[23] As the early modern Protestant world absorbed this view of human knowing, its knock-on effect was felt across all knowledge producing domains. The practices of English natural philosophy, built upon an underlying mistrust of the senses, offer a germane illustration. For instance, in *Novum Organum* (1620) and *The Great Instauration* (1620), Francis Bacon imputes significant responsibility for humans' defective knowledge of the created world to the innate obtuseness and unreliability of the senses. This guiding anthropological perspective prompted Bacon to encourage methods to redress the senses' shortcomings and the faulty knowledge they produce. For Bacon, experimentation especially fulfilled this role as this approach employed meticulous processes and emphasised their incremental yield of not certain but provisional knowledge.[24]

Of course, in *Hamlet*'s first scene, the hermeneutical focal point is supernatural, rather than natural. What is the nature of the elusive 'thing' that 'appeared', the 'dreaded sight twice seen of us' (I.i.20, 24)? The short answer, in Horatio's words, is 'I know not' (I.i.66). Despite their efforts, Marcellus, Barnardo and Horatio can discern neither the ghost's ontology nor its purpose from their experience of it (I.i.57, 66). Indeed, no intellectual activity, even on the part of a 'scholar' such as Horatio, can produce understanding (I.i.41). Understanding a supernatural being requires a special epistemological (and theological) category: revelation. Marcellus seems to recognise that their knowing depends upon the ghost revealing knowledge of itself. Three times, he urges Horatio to 'speak to it' (I.i.28, 41, 44).

In doing so, Marcellus follows the widely held belief that one must speak to a ghost to educe speech from it.[25] In Q1 and F, Q2's third 'Speak to it Horatio' (line 44) is 'Question it Horatio.'[26] These texts further emphasise that the role of interpreters in this hermeneutical situation when empirical observation is especially unproductive is, as Gadamer puts it, to 'bring out the undetermined possibilities of a thing' by questioning it.[27] This is what Horatio seeks to realise: 'What art thou that usurp'st this time of night [. . .]? / By heaven, I charge thee speak' (I.i.45–8). It refuses, of course. And before anyone hears the ghost speak, Shakespeare, through several direct allusions to the Fall and its outworkings, further entwines this theological accounting for the tragic human condition with *Hamlet*'s turbulent, hermeneutic world.

Evidently, Claudius's evocation of 'the first corpse' is one such allusion (I.ii.105). As has been often noted, 'first corpse' incorporates the longer Fall narrative – Genesis 4 in addition to Genesis 3 – into *Hamlet.* In Genesis 3, Adam and Eve fall, but do not immediately suffer the (sole) judgement foreshadowed as the consequence of their deed: death. Instead, they procreate (Gen. 4: 1–2). When death finally eventuates, the first person to 'dye the death' is neither Adam nor Eve, but their son: 'Káin rose vp against Hábel his brother, and slewe him' (Gen. 4: 8). Catherine Belsey proposes that, through frequent representation, Cain's fratricide was 'remarkably familiar in early modern culture'. More to the point, the event was often part of visual depictions of the Fall that made explicit for viewers 'a direct link between the Expulsion and the first murder'.[28]

Heather Hirschfeld concurs, but strengthens the connection. Citing Thomas Browne's *Pseudodoxia Epidemica* (1646), Hirschfeld argues that in early modern thought, Abel's death was more than just a consequence of Adam and Eve's sin, but '*required* in order for them to believe that they have incurred death'.[29] Abel's corpse was the necessary proof to Adam and Eve that they had fallen. Writing several generations before Browne, Calvin disagrees. To him, although Adam did not instantly die, 'the sorrowes and miseries' he experienced after the Fall are so categorically different from his prelapsarian existence that life and death rightly signify the contrast. As such, Calvin considers the question of why God appeared not to carry out his stated punishment of Adam 'vaine and superfluous'.[30] Nevertheless, the fact that Calvin addresses this interpretation of the Fall narrative suggests its influence.

Certainly, Cain's perpetration of the archetypal murder gave fresh force to the harsh reality of living in a fallen world. In *Hamlet*, the first allusion to this event is embedded into the fraught interactions of another unhappy family: 'How is it that the clouds still hang on you?' Claudius asks of Hamlet

(I.ii.66). Hamlet is disaffected, and Claudius is uncomfortable. The king is anxious to, but cannot, work the prince out. Gertrude follows with her own question: 'Why seems it so particular with thee?' (I.ii.76). These are the first of many questions asked to and about Hamlet. From the start, audiences see him as the focus of others' attempts to make sense of him, to control him. Before Hamlet is positioned as an 'observer', he is 'th'observed' (III.i.153).

Claudius's appropriation of 'the first corpse' as he shifts gears from scrutiniser to controller of Hamlet is, of course, heavy with irony. How long should a son mourn, or better, appear to mourn, his father? Less time than Hamlet has given to showing 'obsequious sorrow' for old Hamlet, the new king contends via a potted history of human mortality (I.ii.92). Such 'obstinate condolement' is

> a fault to heaven,
> A fault against the dead, a fault to nature,
> To reason most absurd, whose common theme
> Is death of fathers, and who still hath cried
> From the first corpse till he that died today
> 'This must be so.'
>
> (I.ii.93, 101–6)

Heaven, nature, the dead and reason, an intimidating roll call of witnesses, all testify to the necessity of sons losing their fathers: 'you must know your father lost a father, / That father lost lost his' (I.ii.89–90). Yet, by tracing this lineage of human mortality back to the first father's loss of his son – to the act that reverses his reasoning – Claudius complicates his own argument and unwittingly betrays himself.

The king attributes 'fault' to Hamlet. But the way he figures this fault shifts its locus from Hamlet's 'unmanly grief' to the Fall and its peculiar aftermath (I.ii.94). There is considerable aural and linguistic slippage between 'fault' and 'fall'. The etymological roots of 'fault' include the Vulgar

Latin *fallita* ('a shortcoming, falling') and the Latin *falsus* ('deceptive, feigned, spurious').[31] Elizabeth Watson observes that the play's 'compulsive repetition of *fault*' (in this speech, and most notably in Claudius's soliloquy in Act 3, scene 3), 'puns on *fall*, hint[ing] that Claudius has caused the fall of his brother from kingship and heaven, the falling off of Gertrude, and his own fall as a murdering Cain'.[32] In this scene, the proximity of 'fault' to 'first corpse' in the king's tortuous logic puts emphasis on the last fall in Watson's list. Claudius is Denmark's living royal brother. As he invokes Abel's corpse to constrain Hamlet, the king's presence calls to mind Cain and intimates the potential typological significance of both biblical brothers.

The ghost, of course, develops this implicit Claudius-Cain connection, and the king himself makes the analogy explicit in the prayer scene. Claudius's depiction as a type of Cain seems to fit him perfectly for the role of murderous villain in Shakespeare's revenge tragedy. Moreover, Cain's notorious prominence in the longer fall narrative suggests that, as the Fall permeates *Hamlet*'s unfolding of the tragedy of hermeneutical experience, culpability for the characters' inability to know the truth should be heaped on the king's shoulders. Certainly, this reading would absolve Hamlet of responsibility for his uncertainty that appears to bear directly on the play's tragic end. Yet, crucially, Shakespeare does not only implicate the Fall in aspects of Hamlet's hermeneutical situation external or less personal to him. Claudius's immorality circumscribes Hamlet's, and other characters', knowing. So too does the nature of the hermeneutic world in which they exist, marked out as fallen by the play's immediate focus on the unreliability of the human senses. But *Hamlet* also hints at the Fall's undermining of the prince's interpretive fitness from within himself. Several figurations of inward moral corruption suggest the idea of original sin. Original sin especially brings into view the interplay of Hamlet as an interpreting subject, *Hamlet* as a tragedy and the enduring question of whether humans can freely choose our actions.

'Some vicious mole of nature'

The Protestant Reformers rekindled Augustine's idea that all Adam's descendants inherit his fallen nature. In England, original sin supplied much of the grammar for anthropological discourses. As John Gillies argues in his article on *Hamlet* and original sin, the doctrine struck a chord with the age's prevailing distrust of human nature: 'That the timber of humanity is crooked – the heart desperately wicked – is never in need of demonstration.'[33] To recall the Thirty-Nine Articles, original sin 'is the fault and corruption of the nature of euery man, that naturally is engendred of the ofspring of Adam, whereby man is very farre gone from originall ryghteousnes, and is of hys owne nature enclined to evyll'.[34] As discussed in Chapter 1, Augustine's and the Reformers' doctrine holds in tension two seeming polarities: sin as a universal necessity and sin as the responsibility of individuals. Must all people sin? Yes, as all are Adam's descendants. Does necessity excuse everyone, or anyone? No. The Articles' authors assert that sin is not only individuals' inevitable lot, but also their 'fault'; thus 'euery person [. . .] deserueth Gods wrath and damnation' as one who enacts actual sin.[35] As Calvin puts it, all people are simultaneously 'corrupted in Adam' and 'guiltie through our own fault'.[36]

This rendering of the doctrine flies in the face of prevailing conceptions of it which yoke it to an absolutising determinism. Most modern critics who have analysed *Hamlet* in relation to original sin follow this line of thought. To Gillies, these '"leveling" readings', including Hirschfeld's, belong together in the 'anti-Hamlet school and the original-sin school' as they each variously excavate the doctrine's presence in the play to argue for the moral parity of the prince and his antagonists.[37]

Hirschfeld reads what she terms *Hamlet*'s 'intense theological underpinnings' in tandem with psychoanalytic theory to argue that Hamlet embodies 'the traumatizing impact of the doctrine of Original Sin'. Here, Hirschfeld assumes Augustine's largely discredited idea that original sin and its transmission are bound up with the act of procreation. To Hirschfeld, original sin is 'a foundational moment of transgressive sexuality and irretrievable loss'.[38] Hirschfeld aligns *Hamlet*'s structure with the two stages of Christian typology in which the later event of Christ's crucifixion undoes the devastating effects of the earlier Fall. However, the redemption anticipated by this 'typological axis of Fall and Crucifixion' remains unrealised as the psychic potency of original sin (as Hirschfeld understands it) compels frequent 'repetition' of the Fall's events. As such, the doctrine traps humans into 'the logic of trauma [that] overrides the logic of typology'. For Hirschfeld, *Hamlet*, with its repeated allusions to the Fall, 'reveal[s] typology's traumatic core'.[39]

Gillies differentiates himself from Hirschfeld, and the 'anti-Hamlet' and 'original-sin' schools, by arguing for Hamlet's distinctiveness. But Gillies's 'pro-Hamlet' interpretation only surfaces after he establishes that Shakespeare's appropriation and reshaping of the Reformers' doctrine does have a levelling effect through its 'aesthetic assimilation to character'. According to Gillies, the Reformers, especially Calvin, 'normaliz[ed] the agents of Genesis' for the pastoral and rhetorical purpose of helping their readers recognise their own fallen condition. Elsinore's inhabitants, Gillies asserts, are similarly 'ordinary'. Every character, including Hamlet, embodies 'normal crookedness'. But in *Hamlet*'s last scene, Hamlet, for Gillies, rises above his ordinariness. The prince's 'final deference to providence' is critical to Gillies's proposal. At this moment, Hamlet draws on the resources of the Reformation – especially faith – to transcend both his 'obsession with original sin' and his 'revenge dilemma'.[40]

While levelling readings that pair contemporary notions of original sin with Shakespeare's representation of Hamlet's subjectivity lean heavily towards determinism, Gillies's account of Hamlet's last-gasp liberation from original sin also somewhat elides the dialectical tension inherent in the Reformers' doctrine. This perspective rests on the prince's ability to accurately interpret the workings of divine providence – an assumption I question later in this chapter. In contrast to these anti-Hamlet and pro-Hamlet perspectives, I suggest that Shakespeare works the duality of necessity and responsibility within the doctrine of original sin into his construction of character and into *Hamlet*'s aesthetic, narrative and moral heart.

Act 1, scene 4 is key. As Hamlet, Horatio and Marcellus gird themselves for the ghost's reappearance, it seems that original sin is underwriting the prince's thoughts about the king's actions and the human condition. Q2's stage directions indicate that Claudius is, as promised, celebrating Hamlet's earlier expression of filial duty (I.iv.6 SD, I.ii.121–8). In Hamlet's disparaging sketch of him, the king comes across as anything but stately: Claudius 'keeps wassail' with 'swaggering upspring reels' and by 'drain[ing] his draughts of Rhenish down' (I.iv.9–10). The king may be following a time-worn 'custom', but to Hamlet its 'observance' by its head reduces the Danes to the nations' laughing stock and hollows out Denmark's 'achievements' (I.iv.16, 19–22).

Hamlet's association of the losses sustained by Denmark with the king's behaviour is suggestive of the idea of originating original sin. Why the seeming tautology: originating original? Blocher explains that the church has traditionally 'distinguished between *originated* original sin (the tendency to sinfulness with which all people are born) and the *originating* original sin (the transgression Adam perpetrated in the Garden and through which sin and death invaded our world)'.[41] A parallel can be drawn between the dynamics of the latter – originating original sin – and Hamlet's critique of the king. Romans 5 is the decisive biblical source for the concept of originating original sin. Showing 'what wee lost in Adam', as Calvin puts it, Paul situates Adam as the federal head of fallen humanity: 'Wherefore, as by one man sinne entred into the worlde, and death by sinne, and so death went ouer all men: for asmuche as all men haue sinned' (Rom. 5: 12).[42] The first person's sin and death guarantee that all will sin and die. There are hints of this pattern in Hamlet's linking of king and nation.

Hamlet more explicitly alludes to originated original sin as he continues in his somewhat sermonising vein by analogising from Denmark and its king to a more universal element of the human condition:

> So oft it chances in particular men
> That, for some vicious mole of nature in them,
> As in their birth wherein they are not guilty
> (Since nature cannot choose his origin),
> [. . .]
> Carrying, I say, the stamp of one defect
> (Being Nature's livery or Fortune's star),
> His virtues else, be they as pure as grace,
> As infinite as man may undergo,
> Shall in the general censure take corruption
> From that particular fault: the dram of eale
> Doth all the noble substance of a doubt
> To his own scandal –
>
> (I.iv.23–38)

Thompson and Taylor describe this as 'one of the most notoriously obscure passages in the entire canon', citing J. M. Nosworthy as one critic (among others) who contends that Shakespeare could not master these lines and intended to cut them.[43] The Folio excludes them altogether. Philip Edwards 'doubt[s] whether removing the speech decreases the effectiveness of the scene or diminishes our understanding of the play'.[44] While I agree with Edwards's point about dramatic 'effectiveness' (Hamlet's speech does introduce a certain tediousness to the scene), the matter of 'understanding' hinges upon one's perception of the importance of original sin to *Hamlet*'s meaning. For, although some of Shakespeare's syntactical and lexical choices seem inscrutable, the gist of the passage is not: an indwelling blight can sabotage the whole person.

For Gillies, this passage is one of several that exemplify how original sin 'saturates the motif of hidden corruption' in *Hamlet*. To Hirschfeld, Hamlet's speech encapsulates original sin's 'most essential premises: that human corruption is natural, reproducible – that is, inheritable'.[45] Hamlet certainly intimates that an inward bent towards evil is both covert in nature and transmitted from one generation to the next. 'Mole' signifies both a naturally occurring blemish or fault, and also, from around the time that Shakespeare was writing *Hamlet*, a figure who 'works underground' or 'in darkness or in secrecy'.[46] The prince associates 'the vicious mole of nature' with individuals' 'birth[s]'. This imagery resonates with the tropes the Reformers turned to in their expositions of original sin. Take, for example, John Foxe's sermon at Paul's Cross that includes this description of original sin: 'there lurketh also inwardly in the bottome of our nature a priuy *fomes* [spark], a breeder of sinne, an originall infection'.[47]

Moreover, when Hamlet asserts that 'the stamp of one defect', a 'particular fault', can corrupt an otherwise virtuous man, his language calls to mind the often-maligned idea of total depravity. Total depravity, an outworking of original sin in the Reformers' thinking, is not only notorious, but also often misunderstood. In Protestant theology, total depravity does not mean people are as sinful as they can possibly be: without conscience and unable to do good.[48] Rather, 'total' signifies that the Fall affected every part of human being and praxis: individuals' thoughts and affect, speech and actions. Alec Ryrie shows how elucidating total depravity was high on the church's agenda in Shakespeare's homeland.[49] Perhaps surprisingly, the issue of salvation drove this priority. For instance, the homily 'A Sermon of the Salvation of Mankind' lists a diversity of human experiences – 'Faith, Charity, Hope, Dread, Thoughts, Words, and Works' – and argues that original sin has corrupted them all. As such, people cannot justify themselves before God; they can, and can only, 'receive' justification from God 'freely, by his Mercy, without our deserts, through true and lively Faith'.[50] Grace is the correlate of total depravity (and original sin more broadly), a crucial pairing to which I will return.

More immediately, what makes Hamlet's speech interesting is its engagement with the tension inherent to conceptualisations of original sin, and the metaphysical dilemmas it precipitates. The weight of the prince's perspective lands, it seems, on the side of viewing the human condition and the actions to which this estate gives rise as determined, with the added implication that this circumstance may well be unjust. By paralleling 'some vicious mole of nature in them' with 'As in their birth wherein they are not guilty', Hamlet does not quite claim outright that humans should be free from blame for their inward corruption. The plain reading of these lines associates 'not guilty' with individuals' births – an odd, but true, observation. But the crescendo in lines 23–5 towards 'not guilty' and the natural pause that follows these words have the effect of extending this verdict to the previous line's image of the 'vicious mole of nature' as it lingers in theatregoers' minds.

Transposed into a more overtly theological key, the prince might well be questioning the justice of imputing guilt for human evil given that original sin is the lot of anyone with the misfortune of being born. If human beings are not free to choose what we are born with and as, are we responsible for inheriting a disposition towards evil? To what extent should we bear (at least some of) the guilt as agents of our actions, as the Reformers suggest we should? Two of Hamlet's lines, placed in parentheses in the Arden edition, appear to gesture to a response. The first parenthesis, '(Since nature cannot choose his origin)', with its obvious linguistic echoes of original sin, follows, and seems to make more emphatic, Hamlet's 'not guilty'. Lack of freedom negates guilt. In qualifying 'the stamp of one defect', the second parenthesis, '(Being Nature's livery or Fortune's star)', is also about origins. The prince alludes to the common Renaissance opposition of inborn character and external circumstances, and debates about which plays a greater role in shaping human existence and experience.[51] Is the source of people's proliferating 'defect' the characteristics they inherit at birth, or a higher power, be it chance or fate? Either way, Hamlet distances individuals from responsibility for their 'defect' by suggesting their lack of agency over its presence and corrupting influence.

The ghost's reappearance interrupts Hamlet's musings. With this juxtaposition, the prince's long speech, steeped in notions of original sin, frames this pivotal interpretive moment. As he follows Horatio's instruction to 'Look', Hamlet immediately voices his consciousness of the hermeneutic load that is now his to carry:

> Be thou a spirit of health or goblin damned,
> Bring with thee airs from heaven or blasts from hell,
> Be thy intents wicked or charitable,
> Thou com'st in such a questionable shape
> That I will speak to thee.
>
> (I.iv.39–44)

Like Horatio, Hamlet tries to elicit understanding from this 'questionable shape'. His three binaries suggest his perplexity about how he should read the supernatural being's ontology ('spirit of health or goblin damned'), origin ('heaven' or 'hell') and purpose ('wicked or charitable').

Early seventeenth-century theatregoers, however, probably did not share Hamlet's dilemma. To them, a ghost signalled genre: a revenge tragedy, patterned on Seneca's bloodthirsty plots, including a ghost who calls for the avenging of past wrongs, was playing out before them. This knowledge would have also sealed Hamlet's fate for the play's first audiences. Hamlet will relinquish his agency, ultimately his life, in the pursuit of vengeance. The sense of fatality portended by the ghost's presence reinforces, it seems, the general drift of Hamlet's theologically inflected sentiments in his 'mole of nature' speech. By introducing the ghost as Hamlet articulates concerns about the interplay of original sin, freedom and justice, Shakespeare brings together a well-known dramatic convention and his culture's dominant anthropology.

How do we read this juxtaposition? It may call attention to the injuriousness of the Reformers' theological anthropology. Hirschfeld's argument exemplifies such a reading. For Hirschfeld, *Hamlet*'s embodiment of the trauma engendered by the doctrine of original sin is reflective of 'the entire genre of the revenge tragedy'. Hirschfeld frequently employs a vocabulary that emphasises necessity and fate as she contends that, collectively, Elizabethan revenge tragedies express the solicitude caused by the religious belief that a child is born with 'a taint that is both motive and result of the sullied parental sexuality that begot them and to which they are destined'. In these dramas, revenge functions as a 'structurally and psychically necessary restaging of a traumatic religious scene (the Fall)' and the protagonist believes that by enacting revenge he can 'undo or set right the original traumatic violation'. But this hope is a mirage. Revenge 'must recoil on him' as it enfolds him back into, rather than releasing him and his world from, the original scene. With echoes of Gadamer's thoughts about ancient tragedy, the protagonist's pursuit of redemption 'become[s] a form of suffering'.[52]

When *Hamlet*'s ghost finally speaks, its words propel Hamlet along the path of the tragic avenging son (I.v.23–5). The ghost reveals and commands, and Hamlet falls into line: he will 'sweep to [his] revenge' (I.v.31). Hirschfeld's argument implicates what seem to be the harsh notes of determinism within Protestantism's doctrine of original sin in the tragic script given to Hamlet that binds him to revenge. Nevertheless, before hastening off like Hamlet – for us, along a fairly well-trodden road that situates the Reformers' theology within an absolutising paradigm comprising fatalism, determinism and oppressive religious conditioning – it should be noted that, as the plot progresses, other significant moments appear to break away from this mould. Instead, they suggest that the characters are at least somewhat answerable for their 'owne nature[s]' that are 'enclined to evyll', and for actions reflective of this disposition.[53]

As Claudius soliloquises, his struggle to repent, because of what such an action will cost him, is palpable. Nevertheless, the play strongly suggests that we should hold him responsible for not repenting. As the dead bodies accumulate in the final scene, Laertes emphatically points to the king as the one who is 'to blame' (V.ii.305). Notably, individual responsibility is also a feature of specific references to original sin, such as the well-recognised allusion in the nunnery scene. Original sin, Hamlet implies, is the reason why, as he says to Ophelia: 'You should not have believed me. For virtue cannot so inoculate our old stock but we shall relish of it. I loved you not' (III.i.116–18). Hamlet's metaphor comes from the horticultural practice of grafting a cutting from one plant onto the roots and stem of another – the 'old stock'. When it comes to humans' moral condition, inoculating (grafting) virtue into individuals' fallen nature will not negate the influence of the 'old stock': the 'relish' (taste) of original sin.[54]

These theological implications come into focus with Hamlet's next acidic injunction: 'Get thee to a nunnery! Why wouldst thou be a breeder of sinners? I am myself indifferent honest but yet I could accuse me of such things that it were better my mother had not borne me' (III.i.120–3). The taint of original sin, Hamlet assumes, is inherited. Marriage, sex and procreation multiply the 'old stock', and are thus implicated in original sin. Yet, as one whose birth inevitably confirms and condemns him as a sinner, Hamlet also knows that he is culpable for his own sins: for 'such things' as pride, revenge and ambition (III.i.123–6). Original sin is inborn, but Hamlet can still 'accuse' himself, admit his guilt. Here, his reasoning (unlike in his 'mole of nature' speech) points to the dialectic of necessity and individual responsibility that the Reformers tried to hold in tension within their conception of original sin.

Another possible allusion to original sin occurs in the previous scene. Hamlet asks Polonius to 'see the players well bestowed' (II.ii.460–1). In response to Polonius's 'My lord, I will use them according to their desert' (II.ii.465–6), the prince retorts: 'God's bodkin, man, much better! Use every man after his desert and who shall scape whipping?' (II.ii.467–8). Hamlet's assertion that punishment is the logical action if Polonius employs 'desert' as the guide for his treatment of 'every man' points again to a pessimistic perspective on human beings' natural state. What is noteworthy about this echo of original sin is that Hamlet's soliloquised self-interrogation of his inability to carry out the ghost's instruction follows soon after:

> Why, what an ass am I: this is most brave,
> That I, the son of a dear murdered,
> Prompted to my revenge by heaven and hell,
> Must like a whore unpack my heart with words
> And fall a-cursing like a very drab,
> A stallion! Fie upon't, foh! About, my brains!
>
> (II.ii.517–22)

This agonised Hamlet presents a sharp contrast to the character theatregoers observe earlier in the scene. After declaring his determination to take on the role of revenge tragedy hero (I.v.186–7), the prince's next on-stage appearance (from II.ii.164 SD) seems to indicate that he is on track. As he outwits the credulous Polonius and exposes the purpose behind Rosencrantz and Guildenstern's visit, Hamlet presents as driven and resolved. It appears that he has willingly submitted himself to enacting the ghost's revenge plot as its tragic hero. But Hamlet's soliloquy reveals otherwise. Uncertainty about this prescribed role stalls his performance of it, diluting the ardour that impelled him to give his word to the ghost. Now, like a whore who proffers enticing, yet empty, promises of love, the prince severs his words from action.

How does the glance at original sin before this soliloquy, which in turn recalls previous soundings of the doctrine, inflect how we interpret Hamlet's disclosure of his state of mind? In at least two ways, I suggest. First, evoking the belief that all interpreting subjects' cognitions, motivations, emotions and actions are necessarily vitiated because of their congenital 'sallied flesh' (to employ Hamlet's earlier expression) affirms the lack of conviction that appears to underlie Hamlet's inertia (I.ii.129). The prince should be wary – of himself. His initial reading of the ghost's narrative and command had prompted him to declare: 'It is an honest ghost – that let me tell you' (I.v.137). But in this soliloquy he back-pedals: 'The spirit that I have seen / May be a de'il' (II.ii.533–4).

How could 'honest ghost' evolve into 'may be a de'il'? Here, the notions of human hermeneutic finitude (modern philosophical hermeneutics) or fallenness (theological hermeneutics), together with Gadamer's figuring of interpreters' situatedness via the concept of horizons are instructive. For Gadamer, 'horizon' 'characterize[s] the way in which thought is tied to its finite determinacy, and the way one's range of vision is gradually expanded'.[55] Several moments in *Hamlet*'s first act hint at how Hamlet's hermeneutic finitude, indeed fallenness, may circumscribe his horizon as he seeks to make sense of the ghost's narrative and command. A. D. Cousins demonstrates how, in his first soliloquy, Hamlet, through metaphor, 'unwittingly creates at once a very personal and duplicitous map': 'So excellent a king, that was to this / Hyperion to a satyr' (I.ii.139–40). Old Hamlet was godlike, Claudius is a rapacious monster – in Hamlet's mind. As Cousins notes, Hamlet's representation of old and new kings occurs after contrary depictions of the two (I.i.61–2, 83; I.ii.1–39).[56] In the same scene, Hamlet, when speaking with Horatio, appears circumspect about the ghost's status: 'If it assume my noble father's person' (I.ii.242). In contrast, in soliloquy he is far less ambivalent: 'My father's spirit' (I.ii.253).

These brief windows on Hamlet's interpretive horizon suggest his susceptibility to the ghost's narrative in the charged hermeneutic situation in which grieving son encounters a possibly sinister 'pleasing shape' (II.ii.535). The prince's immediate reaction to the seeming knowledge that the ghost reveals is not surprising: 'O my prophetic soul! / My uncle!' (I.v.40–1) At this stage, the plot provides no solid evidence of Claudius's guilt. Rather, 'honest ghost' is a good fit with the prince's own horizon. But by Act 2, scene 2, 'honest ghost' seems too constricting. As the vast body of scholarship on this topic tells us, the ways that Shakespeare engages the religious pressure points in his own context contribute significantly to his protagonist's discomfort.

Theological narratives complicate the dictates of genre. For Eleanor Prosser, *Hamlet*'s ghost is definitively demonic. In post-Reformation England, revenge was prohibited and placed revengers in spiritual danger. Since Prosser published her influential *Hamlet and Revenge* (1967), her argument has been contested but, nevertheless, continues to be part of critical conversations.[57] And, of course, much discussion has taken place around the implications of the revenant's purgatorial quarters, especially because, as Peter Marshall observes, Shakespeare's ghost is the only English Renaissance stage ghost that associates its origins with what the Reformers repudiated as the 'Romyshe doctrine concerning purgatorie'.[58] Possibilities other than 'honest ghost' cloud Hamlet's horizon. In this hermeneutical situation, personalising his allusions to original sin by holding back on fulfilling his word to the ghost may actually save the prince from a misguided act, damnation even. After all, can Hamlet really trust himself and his hermeneutic aptitude?

Further, the juxtaposition of responsibility and compulsion that the doctrine of original sin embodies may add to Hamlet's equivocalness. Even as he is swept into the fast-flowing current of the ghost's narrative and imperative, the dynamics of which can be likened to the forces of determinism and necessity operating within Protestant notions of original sin, intimations of the opposing forces of individual agency and responsibility are ever-present. Uncertainty about the ghost's moral and spiritual condition centres *Hamlet* and its audience not on following the revenge tragedy's plot, but on scrutinising its designated hero because of the heavy hermeneutic responsibility he carries. Hamlet must rightly interpret his adviser; he must know if the ghost is 'a spirit of health or goblin damned' before he can give himself over to its plot (I.iv.40).

If we had not already felt the exigency of this hermeneutic task, it becomes impossible to ignore as Hamlet spells out the consequences of getting it wrong. 'Perhaps', Hamlet speculates, the ghost 'Abuses me to damn me!' (II.ii.535–8). While Hamlet may berate himself for his passivity, while he may denounce himself as a coward, it is not hard to empathise as he concludes the soliloquy by embarking on what seems an oblique course of action, hoping that it will grant him surer knowledge:

I'll have grounds
More relative than this. The play's the thing
Wherein I'll catch the conscience of the King.
(II.ii.506, 538–40)

Hamlet's long soliloquy exposes theatregoers to his internal torment, occasioned by the bind he is in. Hamlet is at once the fated hero of a revenge tragedy, and a fallen, yet accountable, interpreting subject in a Fall-constrained hermeneutic situation. His well-being, temporal and eternal, rests on the sense he makes of the words of an opaque supernatural being and the character of a king he is predisposed to resent.

Can Hamlet escape? The prince's seemingly inalienable bind is shot through with the implications of the Fall, death and original sin. But the Fall does have a theological counterpoint: grace. Hamlet evokes grace as a mode of intersubjectivity that reverses the status of helpless subjects when he opposes Polonius's modus operandi of acting towards the players 'according to their desert'. The prince charges his interlocuter to 'use them after your own honour and dignity – the less they deserve the more merit is in your bounty' (II.ii.468–70). There is, undoubtedly, some irony in Hamlet's allusion to Polonius's 'honour and dignity'. But the irony inherent to the specific situation doesn't take away from the general meaning. Let generosity, not whether others deserve it, function as the yardstick of how you act towards them, Hamlet prescribes.

Hamlet's mention of 'merit', that contested battlefield at the Reformation's frontline, points to the theological resonances in the interpersonal paradigm he sketches. For the prince, merit resides in the one who gives, an attribution that calls to mind Luther's pivotal doctrine of justification by grace through faith alone. Humanity's means of justification comes from beyond its fallen realm, effected solely by 'the merite of our Lord & Saviour Jesus Christ' that reckons people 'righteous before God', to recall the Thirty-Nine Articles on justification.[59] As the Reformers understood it, grace is the counterpoint to the Fall and its implications. However, the dynamics of fall and grace are not parallel. The difference hinges on the issue of agency. While all people are limited by their sinful nature, yet answerable for their sin, no one, according to the Reformers, can effectively release themselves from the hold of either Adam's originating original sin, or their own will to sin and its ultimate consequence: death. Humanity's fallen condition makes opaque the knowledge of God needed for this reversal. As Thomas Wilson describes it in his popular *The Arte of Rhetorique* (1553), 'after the fall of our first Father, sinne so crept in that our knowledge was much darkened'.[60]

For the Reformers, only divine grace, ultimately revealed, embodied and enacted in the person of Christ on the cross, can lift human beings out of this predicament. In his crucifixion, Christ absorbed human sin and gave his merit to effect ontological change, the 'ontology of justification by faith' (as Brian Gregor terms it), in those who have faith in this act of grace.[61] Grace makes knowing God, and oneself, possible. Indeed, the Reformers followed Augustine in arguing that such grace-dependent knowing extends beyond the knowledge needed for one's salvation. They insisted, Harrison, citing Augustine's *On Nature and Grace*, observes, that 'Adam's offspring' need divine grace 'not merely for their salvation (healing), but also for knowledge (illumination). [. . .] In its dependence on God, the mind was thus a *lumen luminatum* (illuminated light) not a *lumen illuminatas* (illuminating light).'[62] For Wilson, God's willingness 'to repaire mankinde through his free mercie' enables two essential features of a cohesive society: human eloquence and reason.[63] As noted, Gadamer also invokes Augustine's concept of divine illumination as he accounts for the possibility of understanding.

In the hermeneutic universe of Shakespeare's play-world, *Hamlet*'s characters' knowledge is 'much darkened'. Yet they seem powerless to steer their pressing hermeneutic endeavours towards greater certainty. All within their harsh world, but Hamlet especially, need light: reversal patterned after divine grace. Indeed, hints of this grace are present at moments when knowing the truth is crucial for Hamlet. But at these junctures, Shakespeare complicates the representation of grace in ways that compound the prince's epistemological and hermeneutic darkness, and drive the play towards hermeneutical tragedy. In the rest of the chapter, I focus on three key hermeneutical situations that feature problematic or ironic gestures to grace: Hamlet's readings of the ghost, Claudius's posture of prayer and the workings of divine providence.

'What art thou?'

'What art thou?' (I.i.45). The first words addressed to *Hamlet*'s ghost underline the hermeneutical difficulty it poses. Horatio's question is a query about ontology. Marshall argues that the centrality of this concern sets Shakespeare's play apart from most other contemporary stagings of ghosts that do 'not unduly agonize over their [ghosts'] precise ontological status'.[64] Prosser's study offers a possible explanation for *Hamlet*'s difference. She shows that of the fifty-one ghosts portrayed by Elizabethan and Jacobean dramatists, the provenances of forty-seven are not located within a Christian construction of the cosmos. A further three, while conceptualised within a Christian framework, are only parenthetically Christian and, moreover, do not charge visitees to do anything (such as enact revenge) that contradicts Christian teaching. *Hamlet*'s revenant alone both situates itself within a Christian context and incites Hamlet to unchristian action.[65] This circumstance frames, indeed requires, inquiries into the ghost's very being, especially as the self-proclaimed spirit of the prince's father implies possible analogies between itself and its story, and the storyteller and story central to Christianity.

As his ghost meets his protagonist, Shakespeare brings into play the well-known conventions of English revenge tragedy, and then refigures his spectral character and the genre. As he does so, the echoes of a religious narrative likely more familiar to Shakespeare's first audience than that of the revenge tragedy offer insight into *Hamlet*'s unusual interest in its ghost's ontology. This narrative tells the story of divine grace. Like the revenge tragedy, the religious story unfolds through performance. Christ first enacted its script at the Jewish Passover meal before his crucifixion – his Last Supper. His role included breaking the unleavened Passover bread, giving it to his disciples and instructing them to 'do this in remembrance of me' (Luke 22: 19). Like *Hamlet*'s dramatic scene, this religious scene represents a crucial, and complex, hermeneutical situation for its interpreters. Hamlet, and *Hamlet*'s audience, must make sense of the ambiguous ghost and the knowledge it reveals. Christ's words are likewise revelatory and also contain within them the potential for misunderstanding by his addressees – his disciples and his church.

Shakespeare, I propose, hints at this biblical event via *Hamlet*'s ghost's self-presentation, its story about the past and the script it commands the prince to enact. The revenant's parting injunction especially suggests the influence of the biblical scene: 'Adieu, adieu, adieu, remember me' (I.v.91). By evoking the Eucharist, Shakespeare also infuses into the encounter of prince and ghost the emotional freight accumulated throughout the sixteenth century as the sacrament became a site of interpretive uncertainty and conflict. In Chapter 1, I outlined how a failure to come to a common understanding of Christ's words instituting the Lord's Supper fractured the unity of the early Reformers and the Protestant Church. An ontological question lay at the heart of the hermeneutic dispute. What did Jesus mean when he broke bread and stated: '*hoc est corpus meum quod pro vobis datur*':

'This is my bodie, which is giuen for you' (Luke 22: 19; see also, Matt. 26: 26, Mark 14: 22, 1 Cor. 11: 24)?

To recap, Martin Luther and Ulrich Zwingli were the main combatants in the Protestant in-fighting. Luther read *hoc est corpus meum* as representing the miraculous, coexisting presence of the sacramental bread and Christ's body, and the sacramental wine and Christ's blood; Zwingli interpreted the bread and wine as pure metaphor. A permanent divide within Protestantism (the emergence of distinct Lutheran and Reformed churches) ensued from the two Reformers' inability to reconcile their hermeneutical differences. Among the next generation of Protestants, agreement was eventually negotiated among non-Lutheran theologians. In 1549, Zwingli's successor Heinrich Bullinger joined with Calvin to produce what Diarmaid MacCulloch describes as a 'remarkable piece of theological statesmanship': the *Consensus Tigurinus*.[66] In opposition to both Luther's literalism and Zwingli's reductionism, Calvin argued that Christ is not physically but is spiritually present in the sacrament. Calvin reads *hoc est corpus meum* as a 'speech by figure of transnomination [metonym] which is commonly vsed in the Scripture, when mysteries are entreated of'. Metonymic 'signes' in Scripture, including the Eucharistic bread and wine, 'beare a sure and not deceitfull signification, and haue the truth adioyned with them'. Although the bread and wine are 'corporall and visible' and Christ is 'spirituall and heauenly', Christ's name can, nevertheless, 'rightly accorde with' them.[67] Calvin's 'symbolic instrumentalism', as Brian Gerrish terms it, went further than Bullinger was prepared to go with his 'symbolic parallelism'.[68] But 'after prolonged and often acid-toned correspondence during the 1540s', Bullinger and Calvin united, realising that what they could assent to about the Lord's Supper outweighed their differences.[69]

The *Consensus* states that the main 'end' of the Eucharist is that God 'may [. . .] testify, represent, and seal his grace to us'. Humanity's corporeality and inclination towards doubt and despair are accommodated as the material immediacy of the Eucharistic elements 'bring the death of Christ and all his benefits to our remembrance, that faith may be the better exercised'.[70] Remembrance rings through the high point of the *BCP*'s communion liturgy. As the congregation kneels, the minister delivers the bread (and then the cup) to each person, concomitantly interpreting his and their actions. I will quote the passage related to the bread:

> The body of our Lord Jesus Christ which was given for thee, preserve thy body and soul into everlasting life: and take and eat this, in remembrance that Christ died for thee, and feed on him in thy heart by faith, with thanksgiving.[71]

Calvin's influence, his assertion of the sacrament as metonym, is evident. (Indeed, the Church of England closely aligned itself with Calvin's position.) Communicants feed on Christ himself; but while the eating is physical, the feeding is spiritual. Remembrance, then, requires more than one's mind: body and soul are drawn into this drama of divine grace. So too is history, in particular the turbulent recent history precipitated by the disputed question of ontology. The first half of the statement could imply Christ's physical presence in the elements, even as his atoning death to which the bread (and wine) are tied is firmly anchored in the past. In a somewhat jarring juxtaposition, the second half unambiguously locates Christ solely in that historic hour of his death, accessible only through symbolism and memory.

Most people in Shakespeare's England participated in a re-enactment of this charged hermeneutic situation at least every Easter; some communicated more often.[72] In church, they also heard Christ's contested words – 'This is my bodie' – and the entire account of the Last Supper conveyed by four biblical authors on the holy days leading up to Easter:

Matthew 26 on the Sunday before Easter, Mark 14 on Monday, Luke 22 on Wednesday and 1 Corinthians 11 on Good Friday Eve. According to Ryrie, despite people's infrequent celebration of the Eucharist, the sacrament itself 'could hardly have been more prominent' in their minds because of their knowledge and, for some, personal experiences, of the ruptures and violence caused by the disputes over Christ's words.[73] My suggestion is that Shakespeare's contemporaries' experiences of the restaging of this pivotal scene in the unveiling of divine grace, this impelling, yet unsettling and perplexing, accretion of history, situated them as especially alert viewers of another charged hermeneutic situation. This is the moment when *Hamlet*'s ghost speaks to the prince. 'Mark me', the revenant's initial illocution, immediately locates Hamlet as the solitary interpreter of what this supernatural figure 'shall unfold' (I.v.2, 6). The prince must 'lend [his] serious hearing' to this revelatory discourse, whose climax and crux are remembrance (I.v.5).

The spectre's final words before exiting the stage take hold of the prince. 'Adieu, adieu, adieu, remember me', the ghost charges, having 'unfolded' his story of past murder and adultery (I.v.91). As with his earlier response to the ghost's demand for revenge, Hamlet does not hesitate to enfold himself proleptically into the revenant's script. 'Remember thee?' (I.v.98). The prince will empty his memory of all else: 'thy commandment all alone shall live / Within the book and volume of my brain' (I.v.102–3). In making this promise, he dedicates more than his mind to the ghost. As he concludes his soliloquy by taking up the revenant's words as his own – 'Now to my word. / It is "Adieu, adieu, remember me"' – Hamlet also implicitly obligates himself to revenge: to giving his body and soul to fulfilling these words (I.v.110–11). For in keeping with the conventions of revenge tragedy, for the son, avenging his father's death is, as Michael Neill phrases it, 'merely remembrance continued by other means'.[74] Yet, as time progresses, while the ghost and his words increasingly consume his mind, Hamlet separates remembrance and revenge. In the closet scene, the ghost reunites the two: 'Do not forget! This visitation / Is but to whet thy almost blunted purpose' (III.iv.106–7). Remembrance entails revenge; memory requires action.

Earlier, I linked Hamlet's 'forgetting' to the mood of uncertainty occasioned by the Fall's ascendancy in Shakespeare's depiction of Elsinore's hermeneutic world and its subjects' hermeneutic condition. Here, what the ghost indicates about its own nature when it first speaks to Hamlet seems to inject even more uncertainty into Hamlet's hermeneutical situation. 'Remember me', with its Eucharistic overtones, takes on the ambiguity and anxiety associated with the religious hermeneutical situation, especially as it draws attention to the problem of ontology. In fixing itself at the centre of Hamlet's consciousness and establishing itself and its story as the grounds for the mode of remembering to which it commits the prince and his future, the revenant calls to mind the supernatural figure at the heart of the Christian sacrament. But it does this in a way that suggests parody and thus invites doubt.

For what the ghost reveals about itself and its story suggest the antithesis of Christ and his story: the Fall saturates the former, grace the latter. Of course, the fingerprints of the Fall are smeared all over deadly revenge. Conversely, as Calvin puts it, although 'the maner of partaking of' Christ in the Eucharist is disputed, every person 'vnlesse he be altogither without religion' agrees that 'Christ is the bread of life, wherewith the faithfull are nourished into eternall salvation.'[75] Luther, Zwingli and their followers all agreed that eating and drinking gestures in some way to God's grace for fallen humanity. While both Christ and the ghost command memorialisation, the forms these acts should take are poles apart.

The dramatic scene contains further inverted echoes of the biblical scene. As *Hamlet*'s ghost commences its narrative, it binds its telling to the particularities of time. 'My hour is almost come', the revenant informs Hamlet (I.v.2). As the actor gives voice to these words, some early modern theatregoers' minds may have turned to the pronouncement of another hour. In Luke's gospel, the narrator frames his account of Christ's institution of the Eucharist with an emphasis on its timeliness: 'And when the houre was come, he [Christ] sate downe, and the twelue Apostles with him. Then he said vnto them, I haue earnestly desired to eat this Passeouer with you before I suffre' (Luke 22: 14–15). Christ's final Passover is ready. In this 'houre', he prefigures a new expression of divine grace and humanity's future experience of this grace, which he will achieve in his own suffering body. In so doing, he makes claims about himself as both being and materialising grace and truth.

Suffering will also be the experience of *Hamlet*'s ghost in its forthcoming 'hour'. But while Christ will shed his blood for others – for humanity's sins – the spirit of Hamlet's father is 'Doomed for a certain term to walk the night / And for the day confined to fast in fires' (I.v.10–11). Old Hamlet may not be responsible for his premature arrival in his spiritual 'prison-house'. Nevertheless, his soul must endure a time of punishment for his own 'foul crimes' (I.v.14, 12). As dawn approaches, so too does the 'hour' of that soul's return to purgatory. If the fierce contemporary contests over the very existence of purgatory already problematise the ghost's self-representation as the revealer of truth, so too do its vivid depictions of the former king's sins that must now be expiated.

The ghost's insistent allusions to these sins and to purgatory continue *Hamlet*'s signalling of the Fall's overshadowing of critical interpretive moments in its plot. So also does the ghost's association of Claudius with the Edenic deceiver – Satan himself: 'The serpent that did sting thy father's life / Now wears his crown' (I.v.38–9). While alone with the revenant, Hamlet responds to its truth claims with unquestioning belief and a resolute determination to remember. Soon after, however, theatregoers hear him worry that Satan is actually operating through another instrument. Perhaps it is the spectre that is 'a de'il' masked in a 'pleasing shape': the explanation for ghost sightings frequently offered by Protestant preachers and writers (II.ii.534–5). What if the ghost is not old Hamlet's spirit? Perhaps, and here the prince reflects another Elizabethan commonplace, his own constitution – his 'weakness' and 'melancholy' – exposes him to the devil's schemes (II.ii.536).[76]

The ghost's indeterminate nature serves as a spotlight on Hamlet's status as an interpreting subject. Making sense of the supernatural being is, for the prince, the crucial precursor to performing the next scene in its script. The glare of the spotlight illuminates Hamlet's unenviable circumstance. By foregrounding the problem of its own ontology, the ghost's allusions to the Lord's Supper also accentuate its opacity. For, in intimating parallels between itself and Christ, the ghost situates itself as Christ's contrary. Grace, Christ and his Supper's keynote, advances understanding, while the dominance of the Fall in the ghost's story and self-representation suggests that Hamlet should expect hermeneutic uncertainty. Moreover, he should be distrustful. As a parody of Christ, this seeming revealer of truth could quite possibly, as Hamlet goes on to speculate, embody something other than truth and reality. The traces of the Eucharist in the revenant's discourse tantalise. They hold out before the prince the possibility of understanding, of truth, only to obfuscate both. This predicament, in a further twist on the Eucharist, isolates Hamlet.

When the ghost first singles out Hamlet from the astounded trio, Horatio observes that it desires 'some impartment' to the prince 'alone' (I.iv.58–60). 'Alone' adumbrates the deleterious impact of Hamlet's decision to leave his companions and 'follow it' (I.iv.63, 68, 79). Horatio and Marcellus do catch up with him, but he is nevertheless very much alone, isolated by the unprovable knowledge and singular instruction he has received. Not only does Hamlet refuse to tell his companions his 'news', he and the ghost also bind them to a type of sacrament: swearing an 'oath' of secrecy (I.v.118, 143–79). The overflow of their promise – Hamlet's aloneness – signifies the inverse of the intended outcome for Christians who share together in the Lord's Supper: communality. The Eucharist is a fundamentally intersubjective act. One eats and drinks, one remembers, with others. Indeed, as Arnold Hunt notes, popular understandings of the sacrament in early modern England viewed it as the locus of reconciliation and community.[77]

With the telling exception of the players, Hamlet henceforth experiences little affinity with others. As Hamlet soliloquises about his delay and the possibility that the ghost 'may be a de'il', he expresses confidence in the truth-revealing function of play-acting (II.ii. 534, 539). Upon Claudius's abrupt curtailing of *The Mousetrap*, the prince declares his epistemological tactic a success. Hamlet trumpets his certainty: 'O good Horatio, I'll take the Ghost's word for a thousand pound' (III.ii.278–9). In sharp contrast, Horatio's guarded response (it turns out that Hamlet has told him his news) exhibits only tepid belief (III.ii.278–83). Harold Fisch makes the point that Hamlet's staging of his own play shows that, unlike the protagonists in a Greek drama or a Senecan revenge play, he has some agency, 'a share in determining the shape of the plot'. Hamlet's ability to influence *Hamlet*'s plot gestures to 'a dialectic of coercion and free will' as a feature of the play's narrative structure.[78] But Hamlet's own plot goes awry. Rather than exposing Claudius's guilt to others, it seems that the prince's play further intensifies others' gaze upon him – and deepens their perplexity. Rosencrantz's 'Good my lord, what is your cause of distemper?' encapsulates the solicitude of all (III.ii.328–9). The celebratory recorders Hamlet calls for become a metaphor for his disaffection and estrangement: 'you would sound me from my lowest note to my compass. [. . .] Yet you cannot make it speak' (III.ii.358–60).

When Hamlet does speak, only the audience hear him:

> 'Tis now the very witching time of night
> When churchyards yawn and hell itself breaks out
> Contagion to this world.
>
> (III.ii.378–80)

Hamlet situates himself and the charge he is yet to fulfil under the malevolent dominion of the force he had feared as the spectre's origin. In another parody of the Eucharistic drama, he attests to his readiness to

> drink hot blood
> And do such business as the bitter day
> Would quake to look on.
>
> (III.ii.380–2)

On one hand, we could say that the vacillating revenge tragedy hero has evolved. Having uncovered the truth (to himself), he now has the resolve to actuate damnable revenge. That is Hamlet's singular perspective. *Hamlet*'s audience may be less sure. Should we share Horatio's ambivalence? Is Hamlet's hermeneutical approach – play-acting – a trustworthy medium of revelation? Hamlet's misreading of Claudius's enactment of prayer offers answers that are both deeply ironic and conflicting.

'Pray can I not'

Early modern English people may have been especially aware of the theatrical dimension of prayer. The *BCP*'s Morning and Evening Prayer services functioned as twice-daily prayer scripts to use 'either privately or openly', by oneself, or with others in church or at home.[79] Ramie Targoff suggests that 'to pray in the English church meant always to perform'.[80] Of course, prayer is not only performance. To Calvin, prayer is 'a certaine communicating' (or 'communion', as Ford Lewis Battles translates it) 'of men with God, whereby they entring into the sanctuarie of heauen, do in his owne presence call to him touching his promises'.[81] Prayer is relational. It evinces and expresses one's personal knowledge of God, taking the self out of this world while remaining in it. Prayer is thus both a corporeal and spiritual act, and in this confluence of secular and sacred, material and otherworldly, lies the possibility that what may look like prayer may not be prayer at all. This potential paradox underlies the dramatic tension in *Hamlet*'s 'prayer' scene. Hamlet is right: right to 'take the Ghost's word'; right also to believe that play-acting can strike 'to the soul' and cause 'guilty creatures' to 'speak' (III.ii.278, II.ii.524–8). Unfortunately, however, when the king speaks and 'proclaim[s] [his] malefactions', he does so in soliloquy (II.ii.527).

A soliloquy could be a religious speech act: 'talke alone with god in contemplation', as the sixteenth-century bishop Thomas Cooper states.[82] Described this way, it is easy to imagine how soliloquising could morph into praying. But as he reveals his guilt, Claudius makes it clear that, while God is indeed on his mind as he talks alone, he is unable to talk to God:

> O, my offence is rank: it smells to heaven;
> It hath the primal eldest curse upon't –
> A brother's murder. Pray can I not.
>
> (III.iii.36–8)

Claudius cannot take himself into God's presence. But he knows that God is aware of him, and that divine judgement awaits. God has inhaled the stench of the 'offence' which proves Claudius's affinity to Cain.

But the king also knows that his judge is merciful:

> What if this cursed hand
> Were thicker than itself with brother's blood?
> Is there not rain enough in the sweet heavens
> To wash it white as snow? Whereto serves mercy
> But to confront the visage of offence?
> And what's in prayer but this twofold force
> – To be forestalled ere we come to fall
> Or pardoned, being down? Then I'll look up:
> My fault is past.
>
> (III.iii.43–51)

As 'fall' and its linguistic cousin 'fault' ring the Fall through Claudius's soliloquy, mercy, accessed through prayer, is its counterpoint. In a postlapsarian world, prayer has a 'twofold force': it can 'forestall' an individual from retreading the original path of sin and fall; and, for those already on this path, it is the door to pardon. Claudius, of course, needs the latter. But he can invoke the divine promise of mercy, mercy that will 'wash [. . .] white as snow' his 'cursed hand' / [. . .] thicker than itself with brother's blood'.

This stunning imagery picks up on God's words to the wayward nation of Israel in Isaiah 1: 15–18:

> Thogh ye make manie prayers, I wil not heare: for your hands are ful of blood. Wash you, make you cleane [. . . .] Come now, & let vs reason together, saith the Lord. Thogh your sinnes were as crimsin, they shalbe made white as snowe.

God will not listen to Israel's prayers while they refuse to repent of their sin, until they 'wash'. When they do, presenting themselves before God to 'reason' with him, the promise in these verses is that he will make their sins 'white as snowe', taking away the sting of guilt and condemnation. The same pattern of repentance and receipt of forgiveness shapes the beginning of Morning Prayer. Having been reminded that they sin, the congregation (or individual praying alone) say a general confession: 'Almighty and most merciful Father, we have erred and strayed from thy ways.' This confession includes a plea for divine grace – 'But thou, O Lord, have mercy upon us miserable offenders' – followed by a pronouncement of absolution: 'Almighty God, the Father of our Lord Jesus Christ [. . .] he pardoneth and absolveth all them which truly repent, and unfeignedly believe his holy gospel.'[83] Shakespeare absorbs this Protestant pattern of divine-human relations into Claudius's words: confession, request for God's forgiveness and mercy, and God's response of certain grace is available even to Elsinore's murderous king.

But there is one obstacle: he must repent. Repentance is part and parcel of the prayer that asks for the divine mercy which will 'confront the visage of offence' by erasing one's guilt. In Genesis 4, God asks Cain, 'Where is Hábel thy brother?' (Gen. 4: 9). This divine speech act, according to Calvin, represents a 'prouocation to repentance', an opportunity to turn back to God.[84] But Cain refuses repentance and God: 'Am I my brothers keper?' (Gen. 4: 9). Etymologically considered, 'the name of repentance in Hebrew is deriued of conuerting or returning, in Greeke of changing of the minde or purpose'.[85] As the *BCP*'s authors put it, returning to God to receive his forgiveness requires a person's 'whole mind and true heart'.[86] Repentance ties a person's actions to their words. For Claudius, to return, to change his mind, necessitates relinquishing 'those effects for which [he] did the murder' (III.iii.54). 'May one be pardoned and retain th'offence?' the king asks, knowing full well the answer (III.iii.56). In his circumstance, not repenting equates to both not praying and not receiving forgiveness:

> But O, what form of prayer
> Can serve my turn: 'Forgive me my foul murder'?
> That cannot be
>
> (III.iii.51–3)

Moreover, Claudius knows that he cannot hold on to the spoils of his sin and fool God into granting him grace. In heaven, 'there is no shuffling', no trickery as there is 'in the corrupted currents of this world (III.iii.61, 57).[87] 'A right prayer requireth repentance' Calvin pronounces as he comments on God's refusal to hear Israel in Isaiah 1: 15.[88]

The king adumbrates that no right prayer will issue from his mouth: 'Yet what can it, when one cannot repent?' (III.iii.66). Claudius says 'cannot'. But as Shakespeare conveys a sense of his character's agency by emphasising his internal conflict, 'cannot' seems almost a smokescreen for 'will not'. Like Cain before him, at this crossroads the king appears to have a choice:

> O wretched state, O bosom black as death,
> O limed soul that struggling to be free
> Art more engaged.
>
> (III.iii.66–9)

By opening himself up to the possibility of divine mercy and forgiveness, Claudius reinforces the extent to which the sin from which he cannot, will not, return has 'limed' (trapped) his 'soul'. He already feels the grip of the spiritual death that, without grace, is his to a certainty.

The king's unwillingness to repent renders his next words somewhat surprising. With them, he does cast his voice into the supernatural sphere – 'Help, angels, make assay' – before he directs his 'stubborn knees' to 'bow' (III.iii.69–70). Why does Claudius assume a posture that signifies penitent prayer? He cannot be deliberately dissembling. There is no human audience before which to perform, and he has already acknowledged that God sees through insincere prayer. Joseph Sterrett interprets Claudius's kneeling as meaningless because of the '"unheardness"' of his 'confession soliloquy'. To Sterrett, the form of the king's 'confession' signals why he 'cannot find a prayer': his outward act of speaking alone signifies that his external self is cut off from others and his own soul, the two possible anchor points of meaningful prayer. By grounding his reading in a view of the human subject as divided, Sterrett, broadly speaking, represents the mainstream postmodern critical position on Renaissance subjectivity. Claudius's inability to pray, Sterrett argues, is *Hamlet*'s 'centrepiece' as it encapsulates the play's futile preoccupation with uncovering its characters' inward states.[89] But this perspective cannot account for Claudius's assumption that his prayer would not be 'unheard'. God will hear him and grant him mercy, if only he could, would, repent. Nor does Sterrett explain why, if the king 'visualises his sin to be so great as to prevent the act of kneeling or, if not, to prevent the act from having any meaning', he does kneel.[90]

In challenging the notion of the divided Renaissance subject, Targoff suggests that a concomitant and contrary belief in the 'direct correspondence' between the external and internal self also existed in early modern England. Targoff links this alternate account of subjectivity to the emphasis on the public domain of the church as the locus for expressions of faith. This accent on public worship prompted English Protestant churchmen to 'construct a theological justification' that affirms, first, the possibility that external religious devotion could authentically express internal spiritual health, and second, that authenticity may be read from the body. In consequence, 'the worshiper's physical posture, the tone of her words, and the nature of her expression, came to determine her devotional state'. Kneeling in prayer, for instance, evidenced the sincerity of one's prayers, and thus genuine faith. Moreover, in a reversal of Calvin's and the *BCP*'s logic, Targoff suggests the counter-influence of a 'behaviorist philosophy': 'Renaissance Protestants frequently imagined performative behavior to have a causal as well as reflective relation to the internal self.'[91] Conforming one's body into the mould of prayer could transform one's spiritual condition.

As Targoff observes, Claudius, it seems, subscribes to this belief.[92] If he can tame his 'stubborn knees', his heart, calcified against turning to receive mercy, may follow and become 'soft as sinews of the new-born babe' (III.iii.70–1). He could return himself to a state of being unconcerned with the trappings of this life. 'All may be well' (III.iii.72). Does Claudius's pose signify a turn to grace via his yielding body and heart, a reversal of his subjectivity that just might mark a turning away from tragedy in the play's plot? Or is his external action unrepresentative of his internal desires, like Isaiah's unrepentant addressees whose many prayers God rejects? Whether Claudius sincerely wants internal spiritual transformation to ensue as he folds his body into a gesture of contrition, its immediate effect is to create a complex hermeneutical situation.

For theatregoers, Hamlet's entrance and long speech delay the possibility of knowing if Claudius experiences a change in his heart. Instead, shifting the focus to Hamlet's dilemma accentuates both the potential for paradox inherent in the act of praying and the hermeneutic perplexity it can engender. Hamlet, as we know, arrives a moment too late to receive definitive confirmation of Claudius's guilt. But proof is not the prince's primary concern. After *The Mousetrap*, Hamlet is sure enough. In this next hermeneutical situation, a different problem occupies his thoughts. Should he strike while the king appears to be praying? Hamlet's interpretation of what he sees proves determinative:

> Now might I do it. But now 'a is a-praying.
> And now I'll do't [*Draws sword.*] – and so 'a goes to heaven,
> And so am I revenged! That would be scanned:
> A villain kills my father, and for that
> I, his sole son, do this same villain send
> To heaven.
>
> (III.iii.73–8)

Playgoers may be uncertain about whether Claudius is truly repenting. But Hamlet is convinced that he is, and as the prince understands the economy of divine grace, dying while praying guarantees one's passage to heaven. While issue has been taken with both Hamlet's spitefulness and his theology, these are not the questions that imbue this scene with dramatic potency, and irony.[93] Rather, the tension centres on Hamlet's hermeneutic fallibility. In a heartbeat, he determines that Claudius's posture indicates authentic repentance. Nevertheless, Hamlet draws his sword, a sight that causes spectators to wonder if he will kill Claudius, even as he expounds his belief that doing so does not fulfil the letter of the ghost's command: 'Why, this is base and silly, not revenge' (III.iii.79). Will Hamlet 'do it'? Eventually, we hear his definitive 'No' and see him sheath his sword (III.iii.87 and SD). Hamlet will wait until Claudius is 'about some act / That has no relish of salvation in't' (III.iii.91–2).

Hamlet has, of course, got it very wrong. But he has no way of knowing this. Having mistimed his entry into the scene, he also miscues his exit out of it. Theatregoers hears what the prince does not: 'My words fly up, my thoughts remain below. / Words without thoughts never to heaven go' (III.iii.97–8). Contrary to Sterrett's proposal that Claudius here articulates 'the inevitable unknowability of one's spiritual condition', the king appears to possess clear insight into his soul's standing before God.[94] He knows that his thoughts betray his allegiance to his 'offence' and the earthly gain he has reaped from it. Whatever he said, he was not repenting. His words did not take him into the 'sanctuarie of heauen' to take hold of God's promise of grace.[95] Claudius knows that his posture of prayer did not comprise even a 'relish' of salvation.

Having disagreed with Sterrett, I do concur with his opinion, shared by John Cox, that Shakespeare accords this underanalysed scene a pivotal role in his play.[96] *Hamlet* has reached a critical juncture with this juxtaposition of Claudius's and

Hamlet's psychic and spiritual struggles, this cumulation and intersection of the theological, hermeneutical and existential cruxes underlying much of the play's imaginative and emotional dynamism. Earlier, I asked if play-acting, Hamlet's chosen hermeneutical method, is a reliable way of knowing. Yes, and no, this prayer scene shows us. But the no ironically undercuts the yes. Claudius's revelation of his guilt proves that Hamlet was right about the correspondence of his own theatre to reality. Yet the prince is wrong about the king's performance: he fails to recognise the alternate case in which play-acting does not map onto truth. The king perchance and the prince definitely believe that bowed knees signify proximity to God's mercy and forgiveness. But Claudius's posture confirms the opposite. This inverse correlation of the appearance of prayer and grace entangles Hamlet in a hermeneutical situation that again brings out both his condition as a fallen interpreting subject and, in a further irony, his own urgent need for the grace he thinks Claudius is receiving: the grace which makes knowing possible.[97]

Hamlet's need and the absence of such 'illuminating light' in his hermeneutic universe becomes more and more pronounced.[98] His accidental murder of Polonius and the chain of unnecessary deaths which follow reify the tragedy of hermeneutic experience by bringing further disorder, further outworkings of the Fall, into their world. 'One woe doth tread upon another's heel' (IV.vii.161). It could be argued that by wrongly interpreting Claudius's performance of prayer and its relationship to divine grace, Hamlet did forestall his enactment of revenge and thus his own possible damnation. But it seems better to understand the prince's misreading as speeding his and the play's ineluctable movement towards their mutually tragic ends. Not killing Claudius leaves open the possibility that Hamlet will mistake Polonius for Claudius and allows Claudius to plot Hamlet's demise. In *Hamlet*'s last scene, the coincidence of Claudius's plot and what appears to be Hamlet's misreading of grace, specifically divine providence, becomes the catalyst for the play's tragic dénouement.

'Special providence'

Most people in early modern England subscribed to the idea of divine providence. As Alexandra Walsham explains, the single word 'providence' stood for a 'bundle of assumptions about the intrusion of the supernatural in the secular sphere'. Providence knits together two critical beliefs about God: he is all-knowing and all-powerful. God had ordered the universe from his vantage point of eternity, and is always superintending and busily involved in his creation.[99] Providence supplied the lens of transcendent action through which one should view all temporal events and concerns, irrespective of their magnitude or outcome. George Abbot, for instance, in his sermons on Jonah (published in 1600) attributes to divine providence occurrences as diverse as: winds that advance and winds that frustrate a person's business; the growth of Christianity; the effective preaching of Luther who was 'no great man'; Queen Elizabeth's preservation, as well as her perseverance in 'reform[ing] Religion'; and the eradication of plague from an unnamed English city.[100] In Shakespeare's England, providentialism was 'the single teleological thread which wove together past, present, and future'.[101]

When Hamlet returns to his native soil, he twice credits divine intervention for his recent escape from Claudius's murderous scheming, before invoking providentialism as the framing narrative for his present and future (V.ii.10, 48). Horatio urges Hamlet to follow his misgivings about Claudius's proposed fencing match. But in his famous reply, Hamlet decides otherwise:

> Not a whit. We defy augury. There is special providence in the fall of a sparrow. If it be, 'tis not to come. If it be not to come, it will be now. If it be not now, yet it will come. The readiness is all, since no man of aught he leaves knows what is't to leave betimes. Let be.
>
> (V.ii.197–203)

As has been frequently observed, Shakespeare has in mind Matthew 10: 29–31, verses frequently employed to explicate providentialism:

> Are not two sparrowes solde for a farthing, and one of them shal not fall on the ground without your Father?
> Yea, and all the heeres of your heade are nombred.
> Feare ye not therefore, ye are of more value then manie sparrows.

The prince's frequent allusions to providence as Shakespeare's play spirals towards tragedy, especially this explicit reference to a key biblical text, have, unlike the prayer scene, excited much critical attention. Has Hamlet, broadly speaking, 'converted' to a Christian world view? Jesse Lander suggests that the prince's words 'offer what is in effect a confession of faith'. Or is his perspective more fatalistic, his words expressing, as Alan Sinfield argues, a 'Stoic world weariness [. . .] despite the distinctively Protestant phraseology'?[102] Weighing these divergent interpretations requires some teasing apart of the doctrine of providence.

It is worth noting that belief in providence bridged the chasm of sixteenth-century confessional differences. Protestants and Catholics alike turned reflexively to providentialism to help them account for the seeming unpredictability of their lives and the adversities they faced. Nevertheless, the doctrine especially engaged the energies of Protestants: Protestant teachers discussed it in 'exhaustive detail and with wearisome frequency'. Walsham attributes this preoccupation to two centrepieces of the Reformers' theology: original sin and justification by grace through faith alone. Providence is a natural corollary of Protestantism's emphasis on human beings' reliance on God's mercy in the critical matter of salvation, of how one knows God.[103] Introducing salvation raises the connection between providence and the controversial doctrine of election, inclusive of notions of predestination and assurance. In England, providence, according to Walsham, was often folded into the doctrine of election: 'Predestination thus defined the interpenetration of [God's] sovereignty into the self.' Preachers exhorted their audiences to read all their experiences, 'calamities as well as mercies', as affirmations of their election.[104] As discussed in Chapter 1, such ruminations could induce 'self-loathing, melancholy, and debilitating despair'.[105] As also discussed, despair was less characteristic of the state of mind of early modern Protestants than is often asserted in modern commentary, including influential interpretations of the allusions to providence in *Hamlet*.

Sinfield's reading is paradigmatic of these interpretations. Neither Shakespeare nor we, Sinfield contends, can find comfort in the providentialist discourse Hamlet invokes. For, Shakespeare's imagined world is too like his own. To Sinfield, 'the violent and punitive providence of Calvin and even of [Lancelot] Andrewes' functions as an agent of oppression in both worlds. But Shakespeare does more than reflect this orthodoxy. He also, Sinfield contends, registers his disquiet with it. Hamlet ascribes his circumstances to the workings of the divine hand, but Shakespeare refuses to allow him to express the responsiveness and joy that, in Calvin's theology, such recognition should animate. Instead, Hamlet embodies 'Senecan resignation'. This modulation of Christian providence into fatalism, culminating in Hamlet's stoic 'Let be' is, for Sinfield, the source of *Hamlet*'s tragedy.[106] Aaron Landau concludes similarly, arguing that in Elsinore Shakespeare reproduces a sense of the intellectual 'benightedness' that the Reformation brought to his world. Hamlet's 'oscillation between incompatible discursive modes' (religious and otherwise) manifests this confusion. He eventually takes on a posture that, in Landau's assessment, is Stoic rather than Protestant and the 'tragedy of errors' at *Hamlet*'s close testifies to Shakespeare's denial of 'special providence' and a Protestant world view.[107]

I will return to this nexus of *Hamlet*, providence, fatalism and tragedy. For now, the key idea to unfold is that, while providence and predestination were (and can be) considered conterminously, early modern Protestants understood God's providential actions under the umbrella of a conception of divine grace that covers more than the matter of salvation: grace as 'the gift of God's beneficent presence and activity'.[108] As Brian Cummings points out, 'early modern thinking about providence is much broader and more widespread, and yet also more complex and more ambiguous, than we have got used to thinking'.[109] This expansiveness and nuance can be seen in Calvin, whose name is most often connected to providentialism, and who – incidentally, but not unimportantly – separated his teaching on providence and predestination in his *Institutes*. Whereas the latter is discussed in Book Three, Calvin locates the bulk of his explication of divine providence in Book One: 'The Knowledge of God the Creator'. It is in relation to this ultimate epistemological and existential concern – how one can know God – that Calvin addresses the doctrine. Vanhoozer notes that in Christian tradition divine providence 'exposits God's relation to the world in terms of care and control'. To care and control Vanhoozer adds 'divine *communicative* action': God's self-revelation.[110]

Care, control and self-revelation all feature in Calvin's writings about providence. To draw on David Steinmetz's summary, for Calvin, God's active involvement in his creation is self-revelatory ('the *opera Dei*'), even if human beings' fallen condition prevents them from recognising that the divine hand is upholding the world. Providence has limited the Fall's impact, ensuring that it 'served to mute rather than extinguish' God's self-revealing care and control. Access to this knowledge comes by way of the other source of divine self-revelation: Scripture ('the *oracular Dei*'). Scripture elucidates the understanding of God that one can read from observing his world.[111] Calvin sets forth what this knowledge is. Like Hamlet, he references Matthew 10: God acts within creation as its 'perpetuall gouernour and preseruer [. . .] by susteyning, cherishing and caring for, with singular prouidence euerie one of those things that he hath created euen to the least sparrow'.[112]

'Singular prouidence' emphasises the distinction that can be drawn between God's universal oversight of his creation – general providence – and his particular care for and control over individual creatures, extending even to the sparrow. Sinfield observes that in this section of the *Institutes*, Thomas Norton's translation interchanges 'singular prouidence' with words that must ring in the ears of anyone familiar with *Hamlet*: 'speciall prouidence'.[113] This language of 'special providence' was not exclusively, nor originally, Calvin's. Lander, via Charlotte Methuen, points out that Aquinas and Luther had previously distinguished between general and special providence; moreover, in Elizabethan England 'special providence' was a topic of interest to Catholic, as well as Protestant, writers.[114] Nevertheless, evident resonances exist between Calvin's treatise and Shakespeare's drama, including the linguistic proximity of special providence and the humble sparrow. In commenting on Christ's appeal to the sparrow, Calvin expands on Christ's a fortiori argument to emphasise the intimate nature of God's oversight of human lives: 'with so much neere care doth God prouide for vs'. For Calvin, knowledge of the proximity and particularity of God's 'singular prouidence' brings assurance as one experiences good and evil at others' hands, a solace which especially shelters the 'Christian hart'.[115]

Several critics read Hamlet's fusing of divine providence into his own story as indicating that he has in some, not necessarily uncomplicated, way had a transformative experience of this solace. Evidently, these approaches contrast sharply with the interpretations of Sinfield and those after him that present an overwhelmed, fatalist prince. Central to the transformation argument is the idea that, at some point, Hamlet modifies his self-understanding. This change may have taken place on board the ship that should have transported him to his death, or perhaps in the graveyard. The most relevant analyses engage Shakespeare's historico-religious context as they variously link what Mark Matheson terms Hamlet's 'subjective transformation' to his interpretation of his own circumstances in the light of divine providence.[116] For instance, both Lander and Fisch attribute Hamlet's words about providence to Protestantism's stress on *sola scriptura*, and its cultivation of what Lander terms 'biblical culture' and Fisch 'Reformation Biblicism'.[117] Lander and Fisch each contend that, in *Hamlet*'s final act, Christ's teaching about providence guides the prince towards a newfound humility that enables responsive action. Providence helps Hamlet overcome what Lander sees as his overblown hero complex. For Fisch, the 'dialogic' relationship Hamlet enters into with providence convinces him to stop staging his own play as a means of extracting the truth, and to 'humbly cooperate with the metaphysical order': a 'larger play'.[118] Hamlet takes on a readiness to 'act in response to events' and especially, both critics emphasise, to die.[119]

Hamlet's readiness takes on a political edge for Gillies who associates the change in Shakespeare's protagonist with the interplay of Protestant discourses of providence and conscience present in Act 5. Given that the king 'hath killed my King and whored my mother' (and more), 'Is't not perfect conscience', Hamlet reasons to Horatio, 'To quit him with this arm?' (V.ii.64, 67–8, F). According to Matheson, Hamlet's justification for regicide reflects the high view of the conscience held by some Reformers, including Calvin and Perkins. While subservient to God, individual conscience can vindicate dissension against a tyrannous state.[120] But for Gillies, Hamlet's words mask a courtly revenge ethic in the guise of a '*faux* Protestant piety'.

Gillies argues that two occasions of chastening self-recognition steer the prince away from unchristian revenge towards true faith. First, immediately after he invokes 'perfect conscience' as an apology for regicide, Hamlet alludes to original sin: 'this canker of our nature' (F V.ii.690). As he foregrounds the universality of humanity's fallen condition, Hamlet realises that he, too, is implicated in his accusation against his uncle. He is given further pause for thought when he glimpses in the supercilious Osric the same 'courtly emulation', inclusive of a revenge ethic, he himself had typified and from which he turns to take recourse in 'special providence'. Instead of pressing conscience into the service of revenge, Hamlet now embodies 'a simple "readiness" to await whatever providence may send one's way', an action that may ultimately achieve justice through 'lawful violence' and affirm the prince's political and spiritual rightness.[121]

Each of these 'pro-Hamlet' narratives assume that Shakespeare's hero more or less reads the doctrine of divine providence according to its grain, and that he brings this understanding to bear upon his circumstance. Hamlet experiences the solace of mapping God's self-revelation, care and control onto his past, present and future, and responds accordingly: he is ready – ready to wait or fight, ready to act and die. The final sentence of Lander's nuanced discussion captures this reading of Hamlet's hermeneutics: 'despite the worry over "wild and whirling words" [I.v.132], Matthew 10: 29 is presented as a simple text, a reliable confirmation of a providential order that remains fundamentally mysterious'.[122] But what if original sin, the 'canker of our nature' which Gillies adduces against Hamlet's appeal to conscience, also confounds the prince's interpretation of the biblical text so that, while the text may be reliable, his reading of it is not? What if his words remain 'wild and whirling', if the deep impression made by the Fall upon Hamlet's hermeneutical situation and his own hermeneutical condition muddies the transparency of his reading and application of divine providence and grace?

When Hamlet invokes the biblical text on providence, he does so to check Horatio's offer to defer the fencing match:

> Hamlet — Thou wouldst not think how ill all's here about my heart – but it is no matter.
> [. . .]
> Horatio — If your mind dislike anything, obey it. I will forestall their repair hither and say you are not fit.
> Hamlet — Not a whit. We defy augury.
>
> (V.ii.190–7)

Hamlet's intuition seems right. Everyone present in that hermeneutical situation – Horatio and theatregoers – knows that Claudius wants Hamlet dead. He should feel disquiet.

Falling back on divine providence to silence one's premonitions might appear pious, but Calvin would have likely responded differently. In his thinking on secondary causality, Calvin argues that divine providence often operates through earthly means. This includes human beings' ability to plan to avoid predictable future dangers:

> He that hath limited our life within appointed bounds, hath therewithal left with vs the care thereof [. . .] If God hath committed to vs our owne life to defende, our dutie is to defend it. If he offer vs helps, our duety is to vse them. If he shew vs dangers before, our duetie is not to runne rashlie into them.[123]

This section of the *Institutes* emphasises the role God gives to human agents within the domain of his providential workings. Calvin singles out 'madde men': 'prophane men' who 'in manner confound heauen and earth together'. To these 'madde men', heavenly oversight of the world negates the need for human action within it. It is pointless to occupy ourselves in the business of avoiding death, they reason, as God has already fixed the day of our deaths and is safeguarding our lives until that day.[124]

John McNeill identifies the 'prophane men' as belonging to the Libertine sect against whom Calvin wrote the pamphlet *Contre la secte phantastique et furieuse des Libertins* (1545).[125] Calvin sits his contemporary antagonists' distortions of divine providence alongside the pagan fatalism of Plautus' Pistoclerus in *Bacchides* and those like him who 'by desperation throwe themselues into destruction' in anticipation of being 'carried away by destinies'. For Calvin, divine providence does not amount to fatalism. A few pages earlier, he had reacted against his critics who 'would bring [. . .] in hatred' his account of providence by equating it with what 'the Stoikes teach of *Fatum* or Destenie'.[126] As Torrance Kirby observes, by collapsing secondary processes into a perspective on fate and destiny as relentlessly determinative, a Stoic view of divine providence effaced 'secondary causality, and with it any truth to human individuality'.[127]

Calvin's concern to distance Christian providentialism from this 'dogma of fate' was shared by English Protestant clergy. (Walsham names Ralph Walker, Robert Hill and Edward Cradocke.) To these clergymen, English people too regularly mistook '"stoicall destinie"' for divine providence.[128] Calvin realises that his own readers could do likewise and replicate his opponents' erroneous thinking. He thus intersperses addresses to the 'madde men' with a more vaguely directed 'thou': 'Thou gatherest that danger is not to be taken heede of [. . .] but the Lord doth therefore enioyne thee to take heede of it.' Like the Libertines, Calvin's ordinary readers could also wrongly interpret providential determinism as something akin to fatalism. How would this misreading play out? Unlike the 'circumspect man' who can protect himself from danger, the 'foole' – the 'thou' who ignores signs of danger – 'perisheth by vnaduised rashnes', even as both 'folly and wisedome are instruments of Gods disposition'.[129]

We are back to balancing on a knife-edge between divine determinism and human responsibility. Whatever the complexities and paradoxes in Calvin's thinking, it is hard not to glimpse Hamlet in the Reformer's 'foole' who misreads the workings of divine providence. Indeed, Calvin's 'vnaduised rashenesse' recollects Hamlet's first allusion to providence as he tells Horatio of his escape from Claudius's machinations. Having established that he could not sleep, 'rashly' begins a new sentence that diverts the prince from his narrative along a side track of unfinished thoughts – stepping stones that lead from 'Rashly – / And praised be rashness for it –' to 'There's a divinity that shapes our ends / Rough-hew them how we will' (V.ii.7–11). These lines underscore the complexity of a hermeneutical situation in which providence is part of the mix. In the present, Hamlet brings together his past 'rashness' (commissioning Rosencrantz's and Guildenstern's deaths) and his future 'ends', human and divine agency, and implies that meaning can be found in this pairing.

One cannot know if Shakespeare had Calvin explicitly in mind, but the echoes are suggestive. What can be made of Hamlet's linking of rashness and providence, especially as, for Hamlet (contra Calvin), the former seems to serve the latter by preventing his perishing? Is Shakespeare ironising Calvin? Is Shakespeare co-opting Calvin to spotlight Hamlet's foolish thinking about providence? Perhaps the most that can be said is that the possibilities for interpretive ambiguity and multiple (mis)readings abound in this pile-up of past, present and future, of divine actors who 'shape' human ends and human actors who behave rashly and 'rough-hew' these same ends.

Calvin says as much. He asserts the likelihood that people 'encomber themselues with entangled doubts' by wrongly applying the doctrine of providence. Calvin continues by contrasting the tumultuous nature of temporal existence – 'all things are confounded and troubled togither' – with what is happening simultaneously in heaven. There 'remaineth [. . .] the same quietnesse and calmenesse that was before', as God enacts his governance of all things. For Calvin, the disparity between earth and heaven means that his readers should 'keepe modestie' ('cherish moderation') when it comes to judging God's actions.[130] It is 'vnorderly' that many people reserve such 'modestie' for their judgements of fellow mortals, preferring to 'suspend our iudgment [of others] than to incur the blame of rashnes' (there's that word again), while at the same time 'boldly call[ing] the workes of God to account [. . .] and giu[ing] vnaduised sentence of things vnknowyen'.[131]

Whether or not Shakespeare was thinking about (and critiquing) Calvin's and Protestantism's views on providence, the mood of his play-world could well be described in the Reformer's terms. To Elsinore's inhabitants, 'all things are confounded and troubled togither'. Amid this maelstrom of unknowing in the real world, Calvin argues that it is 'a Christian hart', the person impacted by divine grace, who finds assurance in the knowledge that 'the singular providence of God [. . .] will suffer nothing to happen, but that which shall turne to his good and saluation'.[132] Unlike the commentators who argue for Hamlet's subjective transformation, I do not think that his allusion to 'special providence' reflects a change in the condition of his heart. Of course, our text is drama, not spiritual biography, so to focus the argument on the question of whether Shakespeare's hero has 'converted' is somewhat off the mark.

Rather, as suggested throughout this chapter, it seems that the play-world's mood does not shift via the agency of something approximating the divine grace that regenerates human hearts: 'grace' in a dramatic register, which we find in the comedies and romances. In *Hamlet*, there is no equivalent of *Much Ado's* Friar whose sagacity adverts tragedy;

there is no miraculous revelation that brings about restoration as there is in *The Winter's Tale*. Even as hints of grace filter into *Hamlet*'s last scene through the gestures to divine providence, Hamlet's misreading of divine action confirms the Fall's dominance in his world. To reprise an earlier metaphor, the prince is not given the light he needs to interpret his own disquiet and Horatio's offer as potentially part of the 'things vnknowyen' that make up God's 'beneficent presence and activity' in that hermeneutic moment. Hamlet does not have the grace that will help him make sense of grace.

Considered in this way, while Hamlet may remind us of Calvin's 'foole', we should, perhaps, temper our censure of him. Preferring 'moderation' over rash judgements about the workings of God's providence is difficult enough (if Calvin is to be believed). But understanding providence is even more perplexing when one's hermeneutical situation, moreover, one's ability to enact one's being as an interpreting subject, is hemmed in by the Fall. Hamlet, I feel, again invites our empathy as he invokes providence and 'runne[s] rashlie', to use Calvin's phrase, into the staged fencing match: an event that we know will not go well for him. Yet, at the same time, it seems that we cannot completely absolve the prince of responsibility for misreading providence as fate, and for the tragedy that ensues.

The play does not allow us to do this, to collapse providence into fatalism. 'Let be' may come across as a deep sigh of stoic resignation, but Hamlet's very next words give the impression of agency. At length, he elaborates upon his request for Laertes' 'pardon' as he attributes the 'wrong' he has done to his 'sore distraction' and 'madness' (V.ii.204–21). Hamlet may be disingenuous. Theatregoers know that he had decided to play-act madness. Or he may be sincere. Either way, the prince speaks as though he, through his words, will affect the personal and political dynamics of the scene orchestrated for him to star in, and die in. Whether he is exposing this situation as a pretence or using words to work against the grain of his world's scepticism, Hamlet does not present himself as the passive victim of an overpowering deity.

In this chapter, I have shown how the rich vein of Protestant hermeneutics that Shakespeare taps into is productive of this potential for, indeed predicament of, duality in our responses to his hero. The insistent peals of the Fall and original sin in *Hamlet* inform an understanding of Hamlet as an interpreting self whose knowing is vitiated, yet is to some extent morally answerable for his interpretive (mis) judgements and their consequences. A theological perspective illuminates the conundrum deeply embedded in Hamlet's characterisation: the irresolvable tension wrought by the opposing forces of necessity and responsibility, determinism and agency. Moreover, the logic of Protestant hermeneutics points us to Hamlet's need for interpretive assistance: the semblance of intersubjective grace offered from outside his world which seems within reach, but is ultimately withheld. Shakespeare's particular remix of influential theological discourses of his day provides a complex lens through which to bring into focus Hamlet's story: the story the dying prince wants Horatio to tell.

Of course, there is also another lens, another force at work in Shakespeare's drama. The directing hand of genre, of revenge tragedy, seems to pull against this view in favour of fatalism. Without doubt, *Hamlet*'s plot elements closely resemble the English revenge tragedy's key conventions. Yet in this play, plot is not pre-eminent: it does not engulf nor nominalise the Christian ideas about human subjectivity and the nature of the cosmos which Shakespeare encountered everywhere in his culture, and which rise to the surface throughout his play. As these ideas come into contact with the revenge tragedy plot, they add layers of meaning to it. They bend its trajectory away from fatalism to tell a story of the tragedy of hermeneutical experience in a key that chimes within a theologically full culture.

At *Hamlet*'s end, Horatio (somewhat vaguely) adumbrates Hamlet's story. The tragic 'sight' before Fortinbras's eyes evidences evil human motives and actions, unintended misinterpretations and unknown reasons (V.ii.346, 351, 385, 365–69). These diverse factors cannot be disentangled. Hamlet's story situates him as neither a pawn controlled by cosmic or social determinism, nor as the poster child of human autonomy and freedom. Perhaps it is this open-endedness in his subjectivity, the lack of absolutising, that both perplexes us and keeps drawing us back to him as interpreting subjects endeavouring to make sense of our own stories, and the human story.

Hamlet and *Hamlet* push back against our modern world's absolutising tendencies. Binding oneself to either the pole of determinism or the pole of autonomy might simplify one's necessary hermeneutic relationship to ourselves, others and the world, especially in our readings of others. But interpretive foreclosure comes at a cost, not least of which is the growing misunderstanding and mistrust across private and public spheres of interaction that, I suggest, are contributing to our present-day realisation of hermeneutical tragedy. 'Who's there?' The theological hermeneutics of Shakespeare's day that prompts us to wrestle with the complexities of his protagonist's hermeneutic condition could also assist us to consider this question afresh, perhaps with a little less self-assuredness and a little more fellow feeling, as we shift our gaze from the stage back to our own 'truly hermeneutic' world.

Notes

1. John Milton, *Milton: Paradise Lost*, ed. Alastair Fowler, 2nd ed. (London: Routledge, 2007), I.1–3.
2. Hans-Georg Gadamer, *Truth and Method*, trans. Joel Weinsheimer and Donald G. Marshall, 2nd, rev. ed. (London: Continuum, 2004), xxvii, xxiii.

3. For summaries, see Margreta de Grazia, 'When did Hamlet become modern?', *Textual Practice* 17, no. 3 (2003): 489–96; L. E. Semler, 'A Proximate Prince: The Gooey Business of "Hamlet" Criticism', *Sydney Studies in English* 32 (2006): 107–11, 15; Graham Holderness, '"The Single and Peculiar Life": Hamlet's Heart and the Early Modern Subject', *Shakespeare Survey* 622 (2009): 298–301. Studies representative of different perspectives on Hamlet's subjectivity published after these summaries include: Brian Cummings, *Mortal Thoughts: Religion, Secularity and Identity in Shakespeare and Early Modern Culture* (Oxford: Oxford University Press, 2013), 207–35; Peter Holbrook, *Shakespeare's Individualism* (Cambridge: Cambridge University Press, 2010), 43–99; Rhodri Lewis, *Hamlet and the Vision of Darkness* (Princeton: Princeton University Press, 2017); and some of the chapters in Tzachi Zamir (ed.), *Shakespeare's Hamlet: Philosophical Perspectives* (New York: Oxford University Press, 2018).
4. Henri Blocher, *Original Sin: Illuminating the Riddle* (Downers Grove, IL: InterVarsity Press, 1997), 94.
5. Gerald L. Bruns, *Hermeneutics Ancient and Modern* (New Haven, CT: Yale University Press, 1992), 179.
6. Gadamer, *Truth and Method*, 350–1; Bruns, *Hermeneutics Ancient and Modern*, 186.
7. Bruns, *Hermeneutics Ancient and Modern*, 186, 187, 184, 189.
8. Gadamer, *Truth and Method*, 125.
9. Bruns, *Hermeneutics Ancient and Modern*, 185.
10. Gadamer, *Truth and Method*, 125, 128, 125. Italics original.
11. Hans-Georg Gadamer, *The Relevance of the Beautiful and Other Essays*, ed. Robert Bernasconi, trans. Nicholas Walker (Cambridge: Cambridge University Press, 1986), 128, 71.
12. Gadamer, *Truth and Method*, 127.
13. Ibid. 127.
14. Jens Zimmermann, *Recovering Theological Hermeneutics: An Incarnational-Trinitarian Theory of Interpretation* (Grand Rapids, MI: Baker Academic, 2004), 259–60.
15. Roger Lundin, 'Meeting at the Crossroads: Fiction, History, and Christian Understanding', in *Hermeneutics at the Crossroads*,

ed. Kevin J. Vanhoozer, James K. A. Smith and Bruce Ellis Benson (Bloomington: Indiana University Press, 2006), 143; Kevin J. Vanhoozer, 'Discourse on Matter: Hermeneutics and the "Miracle" of Understanding,' in *Hermeneutics at the Crossroads*, ed. Vanhoozer et al., 28–9.

16. Lundin, 'Meeting at the Crossroads', 143.
17. Jean Calvin, *The Institution of Christian Religion*, trans. Thomas Norton (London: Arnold Hatfield, 1599), 2.1.4.
18. Zimmermann, *Recovering Theological Hermeneutics*, 30.
19. Blocher, *Original Sin*, 95.
20. William Perkins, *An Exposition of the Symbole or Creed of the Apostles* (Cambridge: Iohn Legatt, 1595), 92; Calvin, *The Institution of Christian Religion*, 2.1.4; Jean Calvin, *A Commentarie of Iohn Caluine, vpon the first booke of Moses called Genesis*, trans. Thomas Tymme (London: Thomas Dawson, 1578), 90, 91.
21. Martin Luther, *The Table Talk of Martin Luther*, ed. and trans. William Hazlitt (London: H. G. Bohn, 1857), 57.
22. Calvin, *A Commentarie of Iohn Caluine*, 44, 45, 94, 44.
23. Peter Harrison, *The Fall of Man and the Foundations of Science* (Cambridge: Cambridge University Press, 2007), 32.
24. Ibid. 174, 175, 6–7.
25. *Hamlet (Second Quarto Text)*, ed. Ann Thompson and Neil Taylor, I.i.41n.
26. Ibid. I.i.44n; William Shakespeare, *Hamlet: The Texts of 1603 and 1623*, ed. Ann Thompson and Neil Taylor, Arden Shakespeare Third Series, (London: Cengage Learning, 2006), 1.35 and I.i.44.
27. Gadamer, *Truth and Method*, 375.
28. Catherine Belsey, *Shakespeare and the Loss of Eden: The Construction of Family Values in Early Modern Culture* (Basingstoke: Macmillan, 1999), 130, 131.
29. Heather Hirschfeld, 'Hamlet's "First Corse": Repetition, Trauma, and the Displacement of Redemptive Typology', *Shakespeare Quarterly* 54, no. 4 (2003): 425. Italics original.
30. Calvin, *A Commentarie of Iohn Caluine*, 71.
31. *Online Etymology Dictionary*, s.v. 'fault (n.)'.

32. Elizabeth S. Watson, 'Old King, New King, Eclipsed Sons, and Abandoned Altars in *Hamlet*', *The Sixteenth Century Journal* 35, no. 2 (2004): 483. Italics original.
33. John Gillies, 'The Question of Original Sin in *Hamlet*', *Shakespeare Quarterly* 64, no. 4 (2013): 400.
34. *Articles, whereupon it was agreed by the Archbishoppes and Bishoppes of both prouinces, and the whole cleargie, in the Conuocation holden at London in the yere of our Lorde God 1562* (London: Richarde Iugge and Iohn Cawood, 1571), article 9.
35. Ibid. article 9.
36. Calvin, *A Commentarie of Iohn Caluine*, 96.
37. Gillies, 'The Question of Original Sin', 424, 396–8.
38. Hirschfeld, 'Hamlet's "First Corse"', 427, 426, 430. On Augustine's viewpoint, see Blocher, *Original Sin*, 27–8, 111–12.
39. Hirschfeld, 'Hamlet's "First Corse"', 446, 447, 448.
40. Gillies, 'The Question of Original Sin', 422, 409, 411–12, 415, 412, 424, 418.
41. Blocher, *Original Sin*, 37. Italics original.
42. Jean Calvin, *A Commentarie vpon the Epistle of Saint Paul to the Romanes, written in Latine by M. Iohn Caluin*, trans. Christopher Rosdell (London: Thomas Dawson, 1583), 65.
43. *Hamlet (Second Quarto Text)*, ed. Thompson and Taylor, I.iv.23–38n. See J. M. Nosworthy, '*Hamlet* and the player who could not keep counsel', *Shakespeare Survey* 3 (1950), 74–82. See also Philip Edwards, 'Apendix 1: Textual Analysis', in *Hamlet, Prince of Denmark*, ed. Philip Edwards (Cambridge: Cambridge University Press, 2019), 259.
44. Edwards, 'Apendix 1', 259.
45. Gillies, 'The Question of Original Sin', 403; Hirschfeld, 'Hamlet's "First Corse"', 438.
46. *OED Online*, s.vv. 'mole, n.1', 'mole, n.3 (and adj.1)'.
47. John Foxe, *A Sermon of Christ Crucified, Preached at Paules Crosse* (London: Iohn Daye, 1570), fo. 7v.
48. Charles Caldwell Ryrie, 'Depravity, Total', in *Evangelical Dictionary of Theology*, ed. Walter A. Elwell (Grand Rapids, MI: Baker Academic, 2001), 337.

49. Alec Ryrie, *Being Protestant in Reformation Britain* (Oxford: Oxford University Press, 2013), 50.
50. *Certain Sermons or Homilies Appointed to Be Read in Churches in the Time of Queen Elizabeth* (London: George Wells, Abel Swall and George Pawlett, 1687), 28–9.
51. *Hamlet (Second Quarto Text)*, ed. Thompson and Taylor, I.iv.32n.
52. Hirschfeld, 'Hamlet's "First Corse"', 435, 436.
53. *Articles, Whereupon It Was Agreed*, article 9.
54. *Hamlet (Second Quarto Text)*, ed. Thompson and Taylor, III.i.116–18n; *OED Online*, s.vv. 'innoculate, v.', 'relish, v.1'.
55. Gadamer, *Truth and Method*, 301.
56. A. D. Cousins, 'Shakespeare's Hamlet 1.2.153', *The Explicator* 62, no. 1 (2003): 5–7.
57. Eleanor Prosser, *Hamlet and Revenge* (Stanford: Stanford University Press, 1967); see John Gillies, 'Calvinism as Tragedy in the English Revenge Play', *Shakespeare* 11, no. 4 (2015): 366.
58. Peter Marshall, *Beliefs and the Dead in Reformation England* (Oxford: Oxford University Press, 2002), 258; *Articles, Whereupon It Was Agreed*, article 14.
59. *Articles, Whereupon It Was Agreed*, article 11.
60. Thomas Wilson, *The Arte of Rhetorique* (London: Ihon Kingston, 1560), preface.
61. Brian Gregor, *A Philosophical Anthropology of the Cross: The Cruciform Self* (Bloomington: Indiana University Press, 2013), 44, 42.
62. Harrison, *The Fall of Man*, 41.
63. Wilson, *The Arte of Rhetorique*, preface.
64. Marshall, *Beliefs and the Dead*, 257–8.
65. Prosser, *Hamlet and Revenge*, 255–60.
66. Diarmaid MacCulloch, *Reformation: Europe's House Divided 1490–1700* (London: Penguin Books, 2004), 251.
67. Calvin, *The Institution of Christian Religion*, 4.17.21; John T. McNeill (ed.), *Calvin: Institutes of the Christian Religion*, trans. Ford Lewis Battles, 2 vols (Philadelphia: Westminster Press, 1960), 4.17.21.

68. Brian Gerrish, 'Luther and the Reformed Eucharist: What Luther Said, or Might have Said, about Calvin', *Seminary Ridge Review* 10, no. 2 (2008): 15.
69. MacCulloch, *Reformation*, 251.
70. John Calvin, *Tracts Containing Treatises on the Sacraments, Catechism of the Church of Geneva, Forms of Prayer, and Confessions of Faith*, trans. Henry Beveridge, 3 vols, vol. 2 (Edinburgh: The Calvin Translation Society, 1849), 214.
71. John E. Booty (ed.), *The Book of Common Prayer 1559: The Elizabethan Prayer Book* (Charlottesville: The University of Virginia Press, 1976, reissued 2005), 264.
72. Arnold Hunt, 'The Lord's Supper in Early Modern England', *Past & Present*, no. 161 (1998): 41.
73. Ryrie, *Being Protestant*, 336.
74. Michael Neill, 'English Revenge Tragedy', in *A Companion to Tragedy*, ed. Rebecca W. Bushnell (Malden, MA: Blackwell, 2005), 345.
75. Calvin, *The Institution of Christian Religion*, 4.17.5.
76. Marshall, *Beliefs and the Dead*, 249, 250.
77. Hunt, 'The Lord's Supper', 47, 62.
78. Harold Fisch, *The Biblical Presence in Shakespeare, Milton, and Blake: A Comparative Study* (Oxford: Oxford University Press, 1999), 91.
79. Booty, *The Book of Common Prayer 1559*, 17.
80. Ramie Targoff, 'The Performance of Prayer: Sincerity and Theatricality in Early Modern England', *Representations* 60 (1997): 57.
81. Calvin, *The Institution of Christian Religion*, 3.20.2; McNeill (ed.), *Calvin: Institutes*, 3.20.2.
82. Thomas Cooper, *Thesavrvs Lingvae Romanae & Britannicae* (Londini: Henry Denham, 1578), s.v. 'soliloquum'.
83. Booty, *The Book of Common Prayer 1559*, 50–1.
84. Calvin, *A Commentarie of Iohn Caluine*, 139.
85. Calvin, *The Institution of Christian Religion*, 3.3.5.
86. Booty, *The Book of Common Prayer 1559*, 319.
87. *Hamlet (Second Quarto Text)*, ed. Thompson and Taylor, III. iii.61n.

88. Calvin, *The Institution of Christian Religion*, 3.20.7.
89. Joseph Sterrett, 'Confessing Claudius: sovereignty, fraternity and isolation at the heart of *Hamlet*', *Textual Practice* 23, no. 5 (2009): 755, 739, 752, 756.
90. Ibid. 755.
91. Targoff, 'Performance of Prayer', 50, 55, 57, 58, 60.
92. Ibid. 62.
93. On Hamlet's spitefulness, see *Hamlet (Second Quarto Text)*, ed. Thompson and Taylor, III.iii.73–95n. On Hamlet's theology, see Watson, 'Old King, New King', 481.
94. Sterrett, 'Confessing Claudius', 756.
95. Calvin, *The Institution of Christian Religion*, 3.20.2.
96. Sterrett, 'Confessing Claudius', 739; John D. Cox, 'Shakespeare's Religious and Moral Thinking: Skepticism or Suspicion?', *Religion & Literature* 36, no. 1 (2004): 59–60.
97. Harrison, *The Fall of Man*, 41.
98. Ibid. 41.
99. Alexandra Walsham, *Providence in Early Modern England* (Oxford: Oxford University Press, 2001), 3, 8–10.
100. George Abbot, *An Exposition Vpon the Prophet Ionah* (London: Richard Field, 1600), 46, 109–10, 301.
101. Walsham, *Providence in Early Modern England*, 9.
102. Jesse M. Lander, 'Maimed Rites and Whirling Words in Hamlet', in *The Bible on the Shakespearean Stage: Cultures of Interpretation in Reformation England*, ed. Thomas Fulton and Kristen Poole (Cambridge: Cambridge University Press, 2018), 198; Alan Sinfield, 'Hamlet's Special Providence', *Shakespeare Survey* 33 (1980): 95.
103. Walsham, *Providence in Early Modern England*, 2–3, 225, 9.
104. Ibid. 15.
105. Ibid. 15, 17.
106. Sinfield, 'Hamlet's Special Providence', 97, 94–5, 97.
107. Aaron Landau, '"Let Me Not Burst in Ignorance": Skepticism and Anxiety in Hamlet', *English Studies* 82, no. 3 (2001): 220, 221, 29.
108. Kevin J. Vanhoozer, *Biblical Authority After Babel: Retrieving the Solas in the Spirit of Mere Protestant Christianity* (Grand Rapids, MI: Brazos Press, 2016), 53.

109. Cummings, *Mortal Thoughts*, 231.
110. Kevin J. Vanhoozer, *Remythologizing Theology: Divine Action, Passion, and Authorship* (Cambridge: Cambridge University Press, 2010), 367. Italics original.
111. David C. Steinmetz, 'The Theology of John Calvin', in *The Cambridge Companion to Reformation Theology*, ed. David A. Bagchi and David C. Steinmetz (Cambridge: Cambridge University Press, 2004), 120–1. Italics original.
112. Calvin, *The Institution of Christian Religion*, 1.16.1.
113. Sinfield, 'Hamlet's Special Providence', 92. See Calvin, *The Institution of Christian Religion*, 1.16.1, 2, 4, 7; 1.17.6.
114. Lander, 'Maimed Rites', 200.
115. Calvin, *The Institution of Christian Religion*, 1.17.6.
116. Mark Matheson, '*Hamlet* and "A Matter Tender and Dangerous"', *Shakespeare Quarterly* 46, no. 4 (1995): 393.
117. Lander, 'Maimed Rites', 191; Fisch, *Biblical Presence*, 84.
118. Lander, 'Maimed Rites', 202; Fisch, *Biblical Presence*, 109–11.
119. Lander, 'Maimed Rites', 199, 202; Fisch, *Biblical Presence*, 113. Also see Huston Diehl, 'Religion and Shakespearean Tragedy', in *The Cambridge Companion to Shakespearean Tragedy*, ed. Claire McEachern (Cambridge: Cambridge University Press, 2003), 92–3; and Raymond B. Waddington, 'Lutheran Hamlet', *English Language Notes* 27, no. 2 (1989): 38–9. Julia Reinhard Lupton argues similarly from the perspective of postmodern political theology: Hamlet's trust in providence transforms his 'passive tendencies into a form of *dynamis*'. Julia Reinhard Lupton, *Thinking with Shakespeare: Essays on Politics and Life* (Chicago: The University of Chicago Press, 2011), 238–9.
120. Matheson, '*Hamlet* and "A Matter Tender and Dangerous"', 392–3, 395–6.
121. Gillies, 'The Question of Original Sin', 423, 403, 420, 423, 422, 423–4. Italics original.
122. Lander, 'Maimed Rites', 203.
123. Calvin, *The Institution of Christian Religion*, 1.17.4.
124. Ibid. 1.17.4, 3, 4.
125. McNeill (ed.), *Calvin: Institutes*, 1.17.3n10.
126. Calvin, *The Institution of Christian Religion*, 1.17.3; 1.16.8.

127. W. J. Torrance Kirby, 'Stoic and Epicurean? Calvin's Dialectical Account of Providence in the *Institute*', *International Journal of Systematic Theology* 5, no. 3 (2003): 314.
128. Walsham, *Providence in Early Modern England*, 22.
129. Calvin, *The Institution of Christian Religion*, 1.17.4.
130. Ibid. 1.17.1; McNeill (ed.), *Calvin: Institutes*, 1.17.1.
131. Calvin, *The Institution of Christian Religion*, 1.17.1.
132. Ibid. 1.17.6.

CHAPTER 3

NOT KNOWING THYSELF IN *TROILUS AND CRESSIDA*

A poet exhibiting people who are irascible and indolent should show them as they are, and yet portray them as good men – in the way that Homer made Achilles both a good man and a paradigm of stubbornness.

Aristotle, *Poetics*, XV[1]

The sacred writ pronounceth them to be miserable in this world, that esteeme themselves. Dust and ashes (saith he) what is there in thee, thou shouldest so much glory of?

Michel de Montaigne, 'An Apologie of Raymond Sebond', *Essayes*[2]

Not without cause hath the knowledge of himself beene in the old Prouerbe so much commended to man.

Jean Calvin, *The Institution of Christian Religion*, 2.1.1

Self-knowledge and morality are inseparable in, and central to, *Troilus and Cressida* – Shakespeare's caustic, ironic, genre-bending take on both the Trojan legend and the famous, ill-fated love affair of his titular characters. Via its less than savoury characters (to follow the play's frequent metaphorical allusions to taste), *Troilus* offers viewers and readers a sceptical, at times contemptuous, perspective on humans as 'self-interpreting animals', as Charles Taylor describes us.[3] The play exudes moral suspicion as its characters' self-regarding misreadings of themselves contort their being towards both the other characters and the exigent moral questions within the hermeneutical situations they inhabit. Shakespeare certainly does not follow Aristotle's injunction that poets should represent classical heroes as 'good men', even as they expose their faults. Shakespeare's Achilles, Homer's hero, comes across as anything but 'good' and the same can be said for nearly all the mythological figures now relocated onto the late Elizabethan stage. *Troilus*'s audience could well take up Montaigne's words to ask of Homer's warriors and Chaucer's sympathetic protagonists: 'what is there in thee, thou shouldest so much glory of?'

Ironically, there is nothing to glory of in *Troilus*'s legendary characters. Shakespeare, it seems, draws upon the theologically informed, dominant and pessimistic anthropology of his day to engender doubt about these characters, and what they might represent about the interpreting self. He had done so in *Hamlet*. *Hamlet*, one could say, takes its audience to the edge of elegy as early modern Protestant accounts of the Fall's impact on human subjectivity inform Shakespeare's figuring of hermeneutical tragedy. *Troilus* has a decidedly different effect. A pervasive cynicism keeps *Troilus*'s audience at arm's length emotionally, even as the play often seems to cue us to side with its (sometimes comic) ridiculing of its famous heroes and their world. Indeed, *Troilus*'s uncertain, hybrid genre – we could call it a genre mash-up in our modern parlance – underscores the tone Shakespeare adopts to press home doubt from his play's Prologue to its final line. *Troilus*, commentators suggest, is perhaps 'ironic tragedy', or it may be 'satiric comedy', or 'skeptical satire', or 'tragic satire'.[4] While the label we might attach to *Troilus* is debatable, each iteration cited reminds us that neither the play's

Greek nor its Trojan civilisations escape the scrutiny of its disbelieving gaze.

'Fallen' could well encapsulate the society full of self-regarding interpreting subjects that Shakespeare stages. Of course, *Troilus*'s pre-Christian setting precludes the explicit thematising of the Fall which we find in *Hamlet*. There is no mention of Adam nor Cain, no 'first corpse' nor 'primal eldest curse' in *Troilus*. Yet, the play's sustained animus towards the affections, attitudes and ambitions upheld as virtues in classical literature (pride, honour, fame and so forth), in tandem with its satirical probing of its characters' shallow self-knowledge transport its Homeric and Chaucerian characters and settings into the world of late Elizabethan England. There, men and women were exhorted to reframe pride and cognate classical virtues through the lens of an Augustinian anthropology which emphasises humans' fallen condition and the necessity of knowing oneself as a fallen knowing and moral subject.

Troilus's Greek and Trojan warriors alike are proud, preoccupied with worth and honour, both individual and corporate, and the play does not allow its audience to view the characters' 'esteeme' of themselves with even a mite of approval. The Catholic Montaigne's reading of 'the sacred writ' as stressing the impropriety of such a self-perception allies him with the perspective of the Protestants of his age. As 'dust and ashes' are all people's end, glorying in oneself only confirms fallen human beings' 'miserable' estate in this world. Montaigne alludes, of course, to God's judgement of Adam after the Fall in Genesis 3: 19. Montaigne's and Protestantism's mutual strong opposition to humans' deep-seated 'blinde loue of themselues' (as Jean Calvin phrases it) reflect Augustine's influential configuration of sin.[5]

As Calvin explains, for Augustine, 'pride was the beginning of al euils'.[6] Taylor argues that Augustine's theology was a cultural 'hypergood [that arose] by superseding earlier views'. 'Hypergoods' are 'goods which not only are incomparably more important than others but provide the standpoint point from which these must be weighed, judged, decided about'. The specific 'superseded' hypergood Taylor has in mind is the 'Homeric-inspired honour ethic' that bestowed 'fame and glory' on those men who were its embodiment: 'the warrior, or citizen, or citizen-soldier'. Augustine's contrary world view (and Plato's before him, according to Taylor) overturned the high standing of this ethic and the values it inscribed into society. Pride, fame and glory, once virtues, became 'temptations'.[7]

Renaissance humanists' enthusiasm for the ancient world ensured that pride and honour were hot topics in early modern England.[8] It should be noted that opinions about pride and honour were not solely negative, nor entirely unilateral. Jennifer Clement observes that the Aristotelian ideal of magnanimity – 'proper pride', pride moderated by humility – carried some weight in early modern England's 'honor culture'.[9] 'The demands of honor' as a motive for action, Alexander Welsh notes, 'were openly debated'.[10] Nevertheless, Augustine's perspective was preponderant. The English populace were, on the whole, educated to think of pride as the antagonist of humility (thus, as will be seen, of self-knowledge), and to agree with Augustine that the pursuit of glory is 'an enemy of Christian faith'.[11] As theologians and preachers taught and promulgated that faith, they traced emotions, attitudes and behaviours that elevate the self over others, especially God, to the Fall and its ongoing corruption of human nature and morality.

In *A Learned Sermon of the Nature of Pride* (1612), Richard Hooker, like Augustine, locates pride at the core of humanity's descent into sin and continued ensnarement by it. Pride 'setteth the whole world out of course'. Throughout his sermon, Hooker's central metaphor for pride and its effects is the image he reads in Habakkuk 2: 4: 'His minde swelleth and is not right in him.' For Hooker, this pathology is entwined with self-knowledge – and so is its healing. In Hooker's diagnosis of fallen human beings, 'there is in the heart of every proud man, first an errour of vnderstanding'. The proud person does not know himself: 'he thinketh his owne excellencie, and by reason thereof, his worthinesse of estimation, regard, and honour, to be greater then in truth it is'. This misreading produces inflated affections towards oneself, which in turn shape the proud self's 'outward acts'. Just as misunderstanding oneself fans the flames of pride, Hooker is keen to stress that self-understanding is essential to its 'cure'. Understanding oneself aright will 'abate the error which causeth the minde to swell'.[12] To attain such understanding, one must cultivate humility. Hooker represents the mainstream view at the time as he ties self-understanding to humility, and humility to acknowledgement of one's spiritual and moral impoverishment: one's fallenness.[13]

To Calvin, such humility is the engine of moral action. The Reformer agrees with the exhortation encapsulated in the 'old Prouerbe': 'Know thyself'. Without self-knowledge, humans are 'altogither blinded' as we make necessary decisions about how to act. But he disagrees with 'some' philosophers for whom the 'ende' of knowing oneself is a person's awareness of 'his owne dignitie and excellence'. Instead, Calvin argues, self-understanding comes from, first, recognising God's 'gracious fauour' towards humankind and second, remembering humanity's collective 'miserable estate after the fall of Adam'. Such knowledge deflates pride and fosters the humility necessary 'if we will attaine the true marke both of right knowledge and well doing'. Elsewhere in his *Institutes*, Calvin discusses the relation of understanding as a human faculty and well doing: human action. Arguing that understanding and will are the two fundamental faculties within the human soul, Calvin follows Aristotle's belief that understanding directs the will (or 'appetite' as Aristotle calls it). Further, Calvin states that he will not 'confute' the ancient philosophers who maintain 'that there are three beginnings of doing: that is to say, Sense, Vnderstanding, and Appetite', although Calvin collapses sense into understanding.[14]

Where Calvin finds himself 'constrained somewhat' to depart from Aristotle is over the question of whether 'man may rightly gouerne himself' by way of his understanding. Here, Calvin points out that because the 'Philosophers' were ignorant of the doctrine of the Fall they 'confound[ed]' human capacity before this decisive moment in history with humans' debilitated understanding after it.[15] Putting all this together, for the Reformers, understanding, especially self-understanding, shapes what the self does, while sin, especially pride, impedes the self-understanding needed for the self to know truly and act rightly as a knowing, moral agent. A propensity towards both hermeneutic blindness – misjudging what is before one's eyes – and moral wretchedness is a significant storyline in the Reformers' account of the human drama.

Troilus's action and the society on show fragment under the pressure of the destructive mix of its characters' mutual hermeneutic blindness, especially their want of self-insight, and their questionable morality and actions. The play lays bare the desires at the core of its male-centric world by showing its characters engaging in morally suspect acts of valuing. Pride, as well as the 'universal wolf' of lust – a self-consuming 'appetite' for praise, fame, vengeance and sensual satisfaction – drive much of the valuing which takes place in Shakespeare's drama (I.iii.120–1). And there is much of it. *Troilus* frequently depicts its characters putting a construction upon the actions and 'worth' (another word which echoes throughout the play) of other people, or themselves. In addition to valuing, the characters weigh, prize, read and taste. Indeed, if *Hamlet* emphasises the senses, *Troilus* does this even more, via its allusions to taste and especially to sight. In *Troilus*, eyes and sight figure the relation of self-understanding and morality.

In the second scene, Alexander describes Ajax as 'purblind Argus, all eyes / and no sight' (I.ii.29–30). Like the mythological Argus, the play seems to be 'all eyes'. There are constant allusions to eyes – to their physical functions and, more often, to the expansive figurative meanings which they mediate as tropes not only for knowledge and knowing, but also for knowers. Puns on eye/I underscore the necessary coincidence of subjectivity and knowing, especially knowing oneself as a moral subject. The 'eye itself' cannot 'behold itself', Achilles states in the discussion Ulysses orchestrates with him on 'speculation' about one's own 'virtues' (III.iii.106–7, 110, 101). 'Speculation' is another sight-related word. It suggests knowledge: 'intelligent or comprehending vision' as the *OED* defines it.[16] Theatregoers hear both 'eye' and its homonym 'I' as the two characters agree that 'speculation' about the 'I' can only be found in the eye of another: in 'eye to eye opposed' (III.iii.108). (Here, Shakespeare revisits a notion he first introduces in *Julius Caesar*.)[17] Yet, in a move emblematic of Shakespeare's Homeric characters, Achilles 'reduces' (as Frank Kermode notes) this self-understanding from knowing one's virtues – one's inherent, especially moral, qualities – when they 'shin[e] upon', 'heat' and are reflected back by others, to something altogether more superficial (III.iii.100–3).[18] For Achilles, self-understanding extends no deeper than knowledge of one's own 'beauty', one's 'form' (III.iii.104, 109).

Some of Shakespeare's already-famous characters also assert apparent self-knowledge via gestures (ironic for the play's audience) to the 'fixed' identities (Linda Charnes's formulation) which literary history had already cemented for them.[19] Most notably, the play's main lovers delay heading to the bedroom in favour of elaborating at length on these identities. 'I am as true as truth's simplicity', Troilus declares, while Cressida apprehends a future day when, 'if I be false', the memory of her betrayal of Troy's prince, already realised in literary history, but not in this iteration of their unhappy romance, will outlive the city itself (III.ii.165, 179–86). As will be seen, Troilus may be true, but his self-awareness is perhaps even more shallow than Achilles' figuring of self-understanding, while Cressida's falseness maps the limits of her self-knowledge and precipitates its erosion. As *Troilus* progresses, it becomes increasingly evident that, despite many acts of interpretation and much talk about knowing, speculation is in short supply in Shakespeare's play-world. Specifically, *Troilus*'s characters display very little insight into themselves as moral agents. They are, instead, hermeneutically blind.

'That fool knows not himself'

Troilus's exposé of self-understanding gone awry contributes significantly, I suggest, to the modern feel of what David Hillman calls 'Shakespeare's most self-consciously philosophical play'.[20] Indeed, *Troilus* has (for various reasons) been described as anticipating the concerns and mood of modernity.[21] Shakespeare's representations of hermeneutic blindness call to mind the configuration of the interpreting self as a 'moral being' in the hermeneutics of Hans-Georg Gadamer and other modern philosophers in the post-Heideggerian tradition.[22] These philosophers' development of the ideas of earlier authors (especially Aristotle and Christian thinkers) make vivid for us both Shakespeare's engagement with the Protestant hermeneutics of his day and the present-day resonances of his sordid characters and unsettling play-world.

As I stress throughout this book (often by adducing Gadamer himself), juxtaposing early modern theological hermeneutics with modern-day philosophical hermeneutics brings together two overlapping (rather than remote) ways of apprehending human being. For Gadamer, (self-)understanding for the interpreting self comes about not objectively nor independently, but out of one's status as a 'moral being' situated intersubjectively – among other interpreting selves.[23] Moral knowledge is integral to self-understanding, that is, to moral self-understanding, which necessarily ensues in action. The influence of Protestantism in Gadamer's thinking is evident in the affinities between Calvin's trio of self-knowledge, right knowledge and well doing, and Gadamer's hermeneutic cluster of self-understanding, moral knowledge and action.

What is it that interpreting selves ideally come to understand about themselves, about being human? For Gadamer, self-understanding is inevitably moral knowledge. He expands on this point as he argues for the 'hermeneutic relevance' of Aristotle's ethics (or practical philosophy). What Aristotle terms 'self-knowledge' is, according to Gadamer, the 'kind of knowledge that [man] has of himself in his moral being', knowledge which most of *Troilus*'s characters seem to sorely lack.[24] Application is integral to this knowledge, as seen in Aristotle's notion of 'phronesis'. Phronesis is 'practical knowledge' or 'practical wisdom' that comes from knowing oneself as a moral being.[25] Phronesis is something the knower of self does in a given situation in response to 'what he sees'. A 'moral decision', Gadamer asserts, is 'doing the right thing in a particular situation – i.e., seeing what is right within the situation and grasping it'. Reminiscent of both Calvin's description of fallen humanity and *Troilus*'s characters, to Gadamer, the opposite of enacting a moral decision is 'not error or deception but blindness'. Error or deception suggest 'theoretical' or 'technical' knowledge, having the ability, for instance, to make something other than oneself: 'pure knowledge detached from any particular kind of being'. Blindness, in contrast, emphasises being: the condition of knowers rather than what is known. The interpreting self inflicted with blindness, the self wanting morally constituted self-understanding, does not have the knowledge which 'governs [one's] *action*': phronesis.[26]

Further, Gadamer lays stress on the interpersonal dimension of this action. The interpreting self acts in relation to other interpreting selves. If phronesis is 'the virtue of thoughtful reflection' which issues in the self's ethical action in a given situation, then, as Gerald Bruns shows, for Gadamer, these situations always involve other people. Phronesis 'means responsiveness to others'.[27] Like Aristotle, Gadamer pairs phronesis with 'synesis', which incorporates empathy and affect into this 'responsiveness'. Synesis is 'being habitually understanding toward others'. It describes one's posture in situations when someone else, rather than oneself, must make a moral decision. In such circumstances, interpreting selves who embody synesis involve themselves in the other's dilemma, seeing and feeling 'as if he too were affected'.[28] In thinking about phronesis and synesis together, Taylor's aphoristic observation (as he differentiates the study of the self from other objects of scientific enquiry) is apt. The individual self-interpreter cannot be investigated in isolation, Taylor asserts, as 'a self only exists among other selves'.[29] Phronesis and synesis require a company of interpreting selves enacting what Gadamer calls 'a kind of communality in virtue'.[30]

Gadamer identifies the sixteenth century as the era when Aristotle's ethics became relevant to hermeneutics, a circumstance he attributes to both humanism and the Reformation.[31] Gadamer focuses on the Protestant church service, especially the increasing proportion of the service allotted to the sermon, as exemplary of the fusion of self-knowledge and application. To Gadamer, the privileging of the sermon was a consequence of the Reformers' keynote doctrine of justification by grace through faith alone. That is, because the doctrine radically altered (by refuting) people's belief that their meritorious acts would contribute to their salvation, the organising force behind the Protestant service was the need to show 'through the interpretation of scripture in the sermon' that while faith does not justify the self, it does produce 'good works'. Through this Protestant practice, 'application', phronesis and synesis in Aristotelian terms, came to 'occup[y] [the] true core of understanding itself'.[32]

What does a society look like when there is little 'application', when its citizens are largely indifferent to their moral being? In scene upon scene, across the deflated love and war narratives, *Troilus* lifts the veil on such a world. As the characters increasingly manifest their mutual hermeneutic blindness and accompanying want of phronesis and synesis, the Trojan and Greek sides of the parapet more and more resemble mirror images of atomising societies, societies marked, one could say, not by a communality in virtue, but by a kind of communality in vice. Or, to draw on a more explicitly theological paradigm, a communality in fallenness.

I have noted how, in *Troilus*, the undercurrent of distrust towards human pride and the pursuit of honour and glory (individual and collective) reflects early modern Protestants' association of these feelings and ambitions with humanity's fallen condition. Added to this, a specific line in Act 3 suggests the Fall and original sin. 'One touch of nature makes the whole world kin', Ulysses states to explain the Greek commanders' en masse snub of Achilles which he (Ulysses) had just choreographed (III.iii.176, 140). To an early modern Protestant ear, Ulysses might be paraphrasing the Thirty-Nine Articles: 'Original sinne [. . .] is the fault and corruption of the nature of euery man'.[33] Ulysses implies that Achilles' peers have turned their collective 'present eye' from Achilles to 'the lubber Ajax' as the commanders share a hermeneutic fallibility: a proclivity to be taken in by the latest novelties because of their faulty sight (III.iii.180–5, 140). Ulysses speaks disingenuously of course, to provoke Achilles' pride. But the general principle and suspicion he evokes, underlined by the theological ring in his language, could well apply to the 'whole world' of *Troilus*. Ulysses' words are not the only occasion when the play alludes to religious imagery to emphasise its characters' suspect moral and hermeneutic conditions. Later in this chapter, I will look more closely at Shakespeare's use of two images that have links to Scripture: 'the botche' and the 'deafe adder'.

Like Ulysses with Achilles, *Troilus*'s characters do, at certain moments, say things – about themselves or others, or about moral and ethical issues – which appear judicious, suggestive of phronesis. Yet, as with Ulysses' words to Achilles, these articulations are inevitably undermined by self-contradiction, self-interest or mistrust. They do not produce right action. Indeed, throughout the play, almost everything the characters say alienates them from one another, and the audience. Taylor observes that 'we judge [people] morally on the basis of what they see or do not see'. For instance, what a person expresses may both reveal and compound his 'failure' to 'see the point of some moral advice proffered' or 'to see what he is doing to others'.[34] Shakespeare, it seems, invites his audience to judge his characters morally as their words expose their circumscribed insight and have the effect of atomising and unravelling individuals, relationships and society. In Gadamerian terms, very little 'real dialogue' takes place during the play.[35]

To conceptualise 'real dialogue', Gadamer draws on Protestantism's dialogic model of self-understanding, comprising grace, transcendence and faith. With echoes of Calvin's hermeneutical circle of self-knowledge (which I discuss in Chapter 1), the philosopher notes that, theologically, knowledge of oneself requires the actions of two interlocutors: first, God the transcendent Word who, through speaking in the biblical text, 'promises us a better understanding of ourselves'. The other dialogue partners are those who respond with faith in God's words. These people realise that the text of Scripture is not inert. Rather, it both speaks 'directly' to individuals and invites them to speak to it: Scripture 'gives ever new answers to the person who questions it and poses ever new questions to him who answers it'. Self-understanding follows as 'we overcome the abysmal ignorance about ourselves in which we live' through this dialogic engagement with the Word.[36] This is a picture of interpreting selves who, as the Reformers depict them, have experienced the theological passage from human fallenness to hope via faith in the divine other's transcendent acts of grace – an existential journey which resurfaces throughout this book.

Gadamer's account of the transformative effect of Scripture on its readers calls to mind Luther on *sola scriptura*. For Luther, interpreting oneself, or allowing oneself to be interpreted, from the transcendent standpoint of Christ's redemptive grace communicated in God's Word overhauls one's 'self-understanding or self-identity'.[37] Notably, Calvin connects this reconstructed self to ideas at the heart of this chapter on *Troilus* in his contention that, as Raymond Kemp Anderson phrases it, 'external grace is the source of inalienable status'. Grace offers its recipients sure knowledge of their 'full permanent worth'. Such knowledge frees the self from the shackles of 'self-centered egotism'.[38] As Gadamer transposes this theological model into the domain of human discourse, he describes interpersonal dialogue as entering into another's 'thought world' and thus 'adapt[ing] ourselves to each other'. This initial openness to the other – to, we could say, having faith in the words of another person beyond, transcending, oneself – continues until 'real dialogue begins'.[39] To Gadamer, the interpreting self who participates in 'real dialogue' experiences, not 'a loss of self-possession, but rather [. . .] an *enrichment* of our self'. A theological and dialogic dynamic of faith and transcendence underlies Gadamer's exposition of self-understanding. In effect, as Jens Zimmermann summarises, Gadamer's 'real dialogue' is 'an experience of transcendence'.[40]

Troilus's interpreting selves have a lot to say. But their verbal exchanges rarely, if ever, approach 'real dialogue'. The society depicted on Shakespeare's stage is largely empty of the interplay of faith and transcendence, that is, the building blocks of the 'real dialogue' which furthers self-understanding. No character represents a transcendent voice who elicits others' – other characters' and the audience's – sustained trust. Or, to flip the perspective, the characters do not appear open to entering into one another's thought worlds. They do not trust one another (and we do not trust them). As the narrative progresses, nothing changes. Or perhaps better, *Troilus*'s plot advances its characters and their world inevitably, irretrievably towards self-destruction, towards the logical end of coexistence without the 'real dialogue' which can redress the hermeneutic blindness that is its characters' and their society's default condition.

While this absence overshadows the entire drama, we perhaps feel it most acutely when the play positions us to morally judge Hector and Cressida. As will be seen, on different occasions, *Troilus*'s action seems to move in a direction that might engender a type of faith in Cressida and Hector, only to leave the two characters enmeshed in their society's ubiquitous hermeneutic blindness and moral wretchedness. The play's war and love narratives coalesce in bringing to light a society that is, to invoke one of *Troilus*'s memorable epithets, 'putrefied' to its very 'core' (V.ix.1). While the two plots overlap and become increasingly entangled, in the following sections of the chapter I will focus initially on the war plot and then the love plot, considering first the characters who most evidently exhibit the play-world's 'putrefied' condition in each narrative strand before showing how the play hints at the possibility that Hector and Cressida may stand apart from their world, only to twice pull the rug out from under this possibility.

'One touch of nature makes the whole world kin'

First, the war plot. As a prelude to reading Shakespeare's play alongside early modern configurations of the interplay of human fallenness, self-knowledge, and pride and other classical virtues, I must briefly consider a prior hermeneutical question. *Troilus*'s setting distinguishes it from the other problem plays. What, then, is the relation between the familiar pre-Christian setting, storylines and characters that are the palpable stuff of Shakespeare's play-world, and the understanding of the interpreting self, no doubt inflected by Christian ideas, in his real world? If early modern Protestant ideas about human fallenness, faith and transcendent grace, and the hermeneutic implications of these ideas, do influence Shakespeare's dramaturgy (as I argue), and if, as Maurice Hunt claims, he and several 'others', have found a 'multitude of Christian allusions' in the play, how do we make sense of Shakespeare's anachronism without depicting the playwright as demonstrating 'a naive lack of proper historicism' (as Hannibal Hamlin phrases it)?[41] Did Shakespeare, like some Renaissance readers of Homer, regard the ancient poet as 'an honorary Christian'?[42]

These questions take us to the issue of how Shakespeare and his fellow English men and women read ancient texts. Their reading was, of course, mediated by the translators and compilers of editions of the numerous classical works brought to the fore by Renaissance humanism. As with any editorial acts, contemporary political, civic and social concerns found their way into early modern versions of the classics. Robert Miola summarises the attitude of humanists towards antiquity as a 'didactic, Christianizing appropriation'.[43] George Chapman's 1598 *Seauen bookes of the Iliades of Homere, prince of poets*, described by Tania Demetriou and Tanya Pollard as 'one [of] the most sustained and vivid engagements with Homer in the European Renaissance', offers a germane example.[44] Miola views Chapman's translation as a 'great Protestant reworking' and a 'moralistic translation' of the *Iliad*. For Miola, Chapman's *Iliad* takes on its Protestant, moralistic character through its refiguring of certain Homeric 'virtues' – Achilles' pride, for instance – as 'deadly sins'.[45] More broadly, Jessica Wolfe argues that Chapman seeks to present an 'ironic interpretation of Homer', that is, an interpretation that unearths the ironies in Homer. In adopting this hermeneutic, Chapman ascribes 'a godly status' to the ancient poet, and co-opts him in Chapman's perception of his own role as 'a poetic voice grounded in the "just reproof" of human vice and ignorance': a voice of 'moral correction'.[46]

Of the many vernacular retellings of the Troy narrative which likely informed Shakespeare's *Troilus* (Heather James describes the play as almost a 'palimpsest' of this legend) Chapman's *Seauen bookes* was evidently significant.[47] Aside from the 'structural and verbal echoes', the parallels between the Thersites of the play and the translation, and several analogous plot elements, Shakespeare also takes up the same 'Christian hermeneutic' that Chapman employs to reframe heroic values such as pride.[48] Marcus Nordlund points out that the eighteen appearances of 'pride' in *Troilus* account for 'a whopping 14 per cent' of Shakespeare's use of the word across his corpus.[49] Almost all eighteen occurrences condemn pride. *Troilus* also bears the imprint of Chapman's ironic interpretation of Homer. But Shakespeare's attention to Chapman's hermeneutic through his own use of irony also distances his play from Chapman's humanist ambitions. As Wolfe observes, *Troilus* enacts for theatregoers 'a more pessimistic and spiritually bankrupt version of Chapman's ironic Homer', a rendition which shows the evasiveness of self-knowledge for the self consumed by 'epic values' such as pride, and the desire for glory and honour.[50] James paints a picture of a Shakespeare who 'often chose the least favourable versions of [Homer's] legendary figures' upon which to base his characterisations in *Troilus*.[51] I would add that he also adds a further defaming twist or two to exacerbate his characters' foibles.

Shakespeare uses irony to let his audience in on his joke about these culturally ingrained, overdetermined characters, especially through their nods to their own, or others', literary histories and reputations. While these speech acts have a ring of familiarity, they are, on the whole, superficial and wooden, and convey moral dubiety. We have moved a long way from a historically naive Shakespeare to a dramatist who seems acutely conscious of the dissimilarities between his world and the ancient world, differences which he plays up while ironising. Of course, Shakespeare's approach was not unique. As Hamlin points out, the playwright's '"creative" anachronism' follows a well-trodden sixteenth-century path. Hamlin names Lucas Cranach the Elder and Lucas Cranach the Younger, Pieter Brueghel and Sir Thomas Wyatt as examples of Renaissance artists and humanists who, rather than naively collapsing past into present, embody 'historical awareness' in their works.[52] Moreover, *Troilus* – Shakespeare's own version of creative anachronism – aligns with many other 'irreverent treatments of Homer' circulating in England at the time.[53] Shakespeare's interpretive practice situates him within the intellectual and imaginative eddies of his day. He 'read the classics very much as a man of his age'. Contextualising him in this way does not entail pressing him and his work too firmly into any one mould, including that of humanism. But it does mean that the humanists' 'Christianizing' agenda did leave its mark upon the Shakespearean corpus.[54]

Troilus's frequent correlations of pride and a desire for glory and honour with both its characters' deficient (self-) understanding and imagery of infection, swelling and disease are evocative of contemporary theological discourses that implicated pride in humankind's fall. From its first epithet, *Troilus* dismantles its characters' obsessions with their own esteem. The Prologue describes the Greek princes as 'orgulous' (2). Inflated language immediately gives *Troilus*'s audience a sense of its characters' unseemly self-perceptions.

One image especially captures the Greek commanders' corporate turgidity. Punning on 'general', Thersites hypothesises: just say Agamemnon has boils, would the entire Greek camp be contaminated by its 'botchy core' if 'those boils did run', as then the 'general' would be running? (II.i.1–6)

Thersites' insult is all the more biting if we take into consideration the religious allusions it evokes. For some in Shakespeare's intended audience, 'botchy' may have called to mind Deuteronomy 28 or Revelation 16, or syphilis. In the biblical passages, 'the botche' (bodily swellings like ulcers, tumours, sores and boils) is threatened as a possible punishment for people who turn against God. Moreover, some early modern theological writings associate 'the botche' in these passages with syphilis – 'the Neapolitan bone-ache' which Thersites bitterly invokes as 'vengeance on the whole camp' (II.iii.16–18).[55] Syphilis emerged in epidemic proportions among the invading soldiers of Charles VIII of France's army in Naples in 1495 and spread across Europe throughout the sixteenth century. The Swiss Reformer Heinrich Bullinger imports this context into his reading of the 'botch' in Revelation 16, associating it with the 'pockes' that originated 'in the warre of Naples [. . .] in the campe of whores'.[56] Richard Leake was one English preacher who linked the botche in Deuteronomy 28 to a contemporary plague, which he attributes to present-day personal and corporate 'disobedience' in his present-day, and all humanity's inheritance as 'Adams branches and posteritie'.[57]

In *Troilus*'s Greek camp, the taint of their society's 'botchy core' affects all, sparing neither Agamemnon the general nor anyone in general. Achilles and Ajax especially exemplify what it looks like to be infected with pride. The other commanders attribute Achilles' refusal to 'untent his person' to pride, and that pride to his erroneous self-interpretation (II.iii.165). (*Troilus* does not mention the dispute between Achilles and Agamemnon, which in the *Iliad* precipitates

Achilles' withdrawal from the battle.) 'We think him over-proud', Agamemnon urges Patroclus to tell Achilles, 'And under-honest, in self-assumption greater / Than in the note of judgement' (II.iii.121–3). Here, 'judgement' connotes truth and wisdom – what is real – although, of course, the play's prior rendering of the other characters making these judgements as 'botchy' (including Agamemnon the speaker) detracts from their standing as interpreters.[58] Nevertheless, while *Troilus* positions its audience to doubt its characters, it still allows for the possibility that they can sometimes be speaking the truth, and it guides us to know when these times may be. In response to Ajax's 'What is he more than another?', Agamemnon reinforces the subjective nature of Achilles' 'self-assumption': 'No more than what he thinks he is' (II.iii.140–1).

Soon after, Ulysses amplifies Agamemnon's argument:

> Imagined worth
> Holds in his blood such swoll'n and hot discourse
> That 'twixt his mental and his active parts
> Kingdomed Achilles in commotion rages
> And batters down himself. What should I say?
> He is so plaguy proud that the death-tokens of it
> Cry 'No recovery.'
>
> (II.iii.169–75)

To Ulysses, Achilles' sense of his own great 'worth' is merely 'imagined'. As this misreading of himself overtakes his entire being, it also takes him to the brink of self-destruction. Shakespeare draws upon early modern faculty psychology to figure pride's ruinous impact on the self. The intensity of Achilles' feelings of pride – his 'active parts' – so inflate and inflame his blood that they go into battle with his 'mental' parts: his reason. There is no victor in this civil war.[59]

Like the plague, Achilles' pride is both pernicious and contagious. 'Many are infect', Nestor affirms in the earlier

Greek war council scene (I.iii.187). Nestor singles out Ajax, whose contrariness shows that he is 'in full as proud a place / As broad Achilles' (I.iii.189–90). Ulysses employs metaphors from horticulture and childbirth to echo Nestor's observation about the impact of Achilles' pride, contending that if the 'seeded pride' that has 'blown up' to 'maturity' in 'rank Achilles' is not 'cropped' it will 'breed a nursery of like evil, / To overbulk us all' (I.iii.316–20). A communality in vice, one might say, will be the defining mark of their society as Achilles' corruptive pride breeds and infects.

The hold which Achilles' self-regard has over him ensures that he is also plagued by the seeming withdrawal of his peers' esteem of him. After the Greek princes' manufactured snub of him, Achilles' pride is immediately piqued: 'What mean these fellows? Know they not Achilles?' (III.iii.70). Of course, the irony is that, in contrast to his illustrious literary reputation, Shakespeare's Achilles gives little cause for pride. Homer's Achilles is compelling – flaws and all. His 'banefull wrath' (in Chapman's opening line) is the story's mainspring, even if Chapman also injects a Christian disapprobation of human wrath into his translation. By Chapman's sixth line, readers know Achilles as 'Thetis Godlike Sonn'.[60] But when *Troilus* first – and belatedly – names Achilles, it also belittles him: 'Achilles? A drayman, a porter, a very camel' (I.ii.240). Pandarus conjures a doltish drudge, and Achilles' own side accords him little more prestige. Ulysses' language drips with sarcasm when he introduces 'the great Achilles' into the conversation in the Greek council (I.iii.142). As Shakespeare renders him, Homer's hero is idle, shallow and out of shape.

Ulysses' plot to deflate Achilles climaxes in the role Ulysses allocates himself: ''Tis like he'll question me' (III.iii.42). Does their ensuing lengthy exchange develop, in Gadamerian terms, into 'real dialogue' which helps Achilles see his pride? Not really. Ulysses had theorised that the lords' display of pride through their snubbing of Achilles would have a curative effect by illuminating Achilles' pride to himself:

> I have derision medicinable
> To use between your strangeness and his pride
> Which his own will shall have desire to drink.
> It may do good. Pride hath no other glass
> To show itself but pride.
>
> (III.iii.44–8)

However, there appears to be a fundamental flaw in Ulysses' method if healing Achilles' pride is truly his intention. 'If' is a crucial qualification. *Troilus*, of course, constantly reminds its audience to distrust its characters' motives, and Ulysses is no exception.

He and Achilles concur with one another that 'speculation' – knowledge of oneself – comes about 'by reflection': by seeing oneself in others' eyes, although (as discussed) Ulysses' focus is knowledge of one's virtues, whereas for Achilles self-knowledge is literally skin-deep (III.iii.110, 100). What is more problematic is that the two also agree that pride is the end of such knowledge. Having asserted that one does not know 'his parts', his virtues, until he translates them into deeds and receives praise for them from others – until he sees them 'formed in th'applause' – cunning Ulysses uses this idea to taunt Achilles as he capitalises on Achilles' pride (III.iii.101, 118, 120). 'Th'unknown Ajax's' 'parts', Ulysses suggests, have now superseded Achilles' as the reason for applause (III.iii.124–6). Even more pointedly, Ulysses explicitly appeals to Achilles' pride as a thing of value as he sets forth a seeming abstraction: 'How one man eats into another's pride, / While pride is fasting in his wantonness!' (III.iii.137–8). This is, of course, not mere theory, but artful manipulation in the guise of warning. Ajax is growing fat on the glory belonging to you Achilles, Ulysses cautions as, paradoxically, the recklessness and arrogance ('wantonness') ensuing from your pride induces complacency: your belief that you do not need to feed it.[61] To supposedly cure Achilles of his pride, Ulysses brings into play a conception of self-knowledge contingent upon bolstering one's pride and reaping glory.

Certainly, Achilles' response shows that Ulysses' ruse has provoked him: 'I see my reputation is at stake. / My fame is shrewdly gored' (III.iii.229–30). But recognising that his glory is on the wane is about all that Achilles sees after their dialogue. He does not perceive his own pride. There is a hint that Achilles senses that there is more he should know about himself. Yet that knowledge eludes him. The scene nearly ends with a poignant moment as Achilles expresses his inability to understand what is taking place within himself: 'My mind is troubled, like a fountain stirred, / And I myself see not the bottom of it' (III.iii.309–10). But, in keeping with *Troilus*'s overruling sardonic tone, Thersites immediately undercuts the possibility of Achilles' words engendering pathos: 'Would the fountain of your mind were clear again, that I might water an ass in it! I had rather be a tick in a sheep than such a valiant ignorant' (III.iii.311–13). Thersites has the final say in the scene. His mockery of the toxicity of Achilles' unknowing – not even an ass should drink from Achilles' mind in its current murky condition – focuses *Troilus*'s audience (again) on the play's critique of the inverse relation of pride and (self-)understanding.

Shakespeare embeds a farcical rendition of this theme into the scene as Thersites reports that Ajax is 'so prophetically proud of an heroical cudgelling' (by Hector) 'that he raves in saying nothing' (III.iii.250–1). Ajax 'knows not' Thersites, mistaking him for Agamemnon (III.iii.261–3). His utterances become so nonsensical that 'he's grown a very land-fish, languageless, a monster' (III.iii.264–5). Ajax's pride makes him grotesque, undoing his personhood. Thersites mimics him in 'the pageant of Ajax' by uttering monosyllables and clichés (III.iii.271–300). Earlier, in Ajax's presence, Thersites had described him as a 'fool' who 'knows not himself' (II.i.64). Minus some of the lampooning, unravelling of the self is also the outcome for Achilles when, as John Gillies remarks, he (like everyone else in the play-world) makes that self 'fatally beholden to a given peer group or social world' and ends up unable to see himself.[62] Achilles, too, 'knows not himself', and his benighted hermeneutic condition impacts his actions.

Here, the idea of phronesis offers a yardstick to judge what Achilles does after his pride is stung. For the Reformers, and also Gadamer, self-knowledge is moral knowledge, and key to well doing, that is, action that responds rightly to what a person sees: phronesis. After Achilles sees his damaged reputation, and little else, his actions, culminating in Hector's disturbing death scene, indicate his want of moral consciousness. Shakespeare's audience knows that Achilles will be the cause of Hector's death. But rather than taking place through single combat between the two characters (albeit with the intervention of the gods), the playwright has his character assign the act to his Myrmidons. The only thing Achilles does is speak. As with his earlier speech acts, but even more so, Achilles' words in this scene call for moral judgement.

By stripping away the epic context and diminishing his hero, Shakespeare refigures Achilles' victory so that it is redolent of the thuggery and hubris of a gang of bullies. Having found Hector unarmed, Achilles orders the surprise attack and then sends out his soldiers to trumpet the triumph as though his own hands had accomplished it: 'On, Myrmidons, and cry you all amain, / "Achilles hath the mighty Hector slain"' (V.ix.13–14). Most critics agree that Achilles' characterisation in this moment is, as Joseph Navitsky puts it, 'the exemplary instance of the play's subversion of epic heroism'.[63] *Troilus* depicts Achilles' defeat of Hector as an unethical act: at once cowardly and brutal, and not at all valorous. But Achilles misreads the nature of his unheroic deed as the rapacity of reputation drives him to claim credit for its enactment.[64] Circumscribed insight and moral failings follow as Achilles' esteem of himself darkens his (self-)understanding.

In this way, Achilles is representative of, rather than exceptional within, his world. In *Troilus*, the hermeneutic blindness of nearly all its interpreting selves is implicated in the unravelling of individuals and the body politic alike. Thersites may have his own side in mind when he insinuates that the general – all – are infected by their society's botchy core, but the play extends his metaphor across the battle-line. In Shakespeare's rendering of Trojan society, characters' valuing of worth, reflective of their pride and prizing of honour and glory, also precipitates suspicion about their insight and moral being. Again, biblical imagery, especially of human fallenness, adds weight to unfavourable moral judgements of these characters and their world. Here, I turn to the Trojan council scene. In it, we find further suggestions of humanity's fallen condition as the princes debate whether Helen is 'worth keeping' (II.ii.81). The exposure of their value system gives *Troilus*'s audience cause for doubting them all – including, ultimately, Hector.

'What's aught but as 'tis valued?'

Should Troy keep Helen? The Trojan princes' dispute over this question pivots on their evaluations of worth. Using vocabulary that reinforces the 'marketplace frame' evoked by 'worth', they disagree about how to 'weigh' and 'value' Helen's worth to them (II.ii.26, 52).[65] What scale should they use? Hector invokes a levelling measure to argue that, as every 'soul' is as 'dear' as Helen's, sacrificing thousands of souls to 'guard a thing not ours' means that Helen 'is not worth what she doth cost' (II.ii.18–19, 22, 51). To Troilus, Hector's 'reason' misses the point entirely because he employs the wrong measure. While Hector's primary motivation appears to be the preservation of life, Troilus asserts that corporate honour – 'the worth and honour of a king' – cannot be compared with 'common' lives (II.ii.24, 26–8).

For Troilus, value is relativistic: 'What's aught but as 'tis valued?' (II.ii.52). As a person's value is mediated by others, they can assign value to Helen according to how much honour they derive from her. Martial success feeds their reputation, and so Helen is of prodigious value to them. She is

> a pearl
> Whose price hath launched above a thousand ships
> And turned crowned kings to merchants.
>
> (II.ii.81–3)

Here, Shakespeare of course alludes to Christopher Marlowe's *Doctor Faustus*: 'Was this [Helen of Troy] the face that launched a thousand ships?' ('A' text, V.i.90). As Dawson notes, Shakespeare replaces Marlowe's 'face' with 'price'.[66] This change further emphasises Troilus' situating of the princes as subjective valuers of Helen's worth. So too does his recollection of their choric response of '"Inestimable!"' when Paris had returned home with his 'noble prize' ('prize' being a variant of 'price') (II.ii.88, 86).[67]

Yet, even as Troilus exerts the authority he believes he has as an interpreter of another's value, he simultaneously, ironically, casts doubt over his own hermeneutic fitness. In addition to Marlowe's *Faustus*, the words of Christ in Matthew 13: 45–6 also lie behind Troilus' comparison of Helen with a pearl. In the biblical verses, Jesus analogises 'the kingdome of heauen' with the 'perle of great price' which a 'marchat' (merchant) 'founde [. . .] and solde all that he had' to buy. In Matthew 5: 3, Christ had described the inhabitants of the kingdom of heaven as those who are 'poore in spirit', meaning the humble who, as the Geneva Bible's gloss explains, 'feele them selues voide of all righteousnes that they may onely seeke it in Christ'. By implication, humility is needed to see the true value of the pearl one finds, that is, the kingdom of heaven, and to act rightly in response to what one sees. As he unknowingly calls attention to this positive association of humility and hermeneutics, Troilus brings into question his own interpretation of Helen, motivated as it is by the antithesis of humility: his desire for personal and corporate honour.

While Troilus may implicitly undermine his own ability to determine another's worth, Hector takes exception to his premise. 'What's aught but as 'tis valued?' In opposition to Troilus' absolute statement about relativism, Hector argues that 'value dwells not in particular will' (II.ii.53). One person's worth is not solely decided by another. Rather, value is more complicated: it is both intrinsic to a thing, a person – ''tis precious of itself' – and inflected by the desires of those with a stake in that which is being valued – 'the prizer[s]' (II.ii.55–6). Kermode styles the brothers' theoretical debate as 'a conflict between Truth and Opinion', and sides with Hector as the one who speaks 'the truth'. Other critics concur. Hector's words represent 'a moment of lucidity' for Hunt, and 'a potentially rich and complex fusion' of 'intrinsic and conferred value' for Bevington. To Dawson, 'Hector has the better argument'.[68] As these examples indicate, critical discussions of *Troilus* have dwelt upon the holes Hector pokes in Troilus' circular reasoning, that is, the assertion that Helen is worth keeping because they say she is worth keeping.

Moreover, Hector's critique of Troilus (and Paris, who also argues that Helen's value lies in keeping her to preserve their honour) extends beyond their flawed thinking. He also contends that their impoverished moral consciousnesses skew their judgement. Having just claimed that Troilus and Paris would not be out of place among the young men 'whom Aristotle thought / unfit to hear moral philosophy', Hector continues his reprimand by connecting hermeneutic rationality and morality (II.ii.166–7). He interweaves humoral theory and the Old Testament to show his brothers what they appear unaware of about themselves: the 'reasons [they] allege' betray their unsound physical and spiritual conditions (II.ii.168). Troilus and Paris suffer from a humoral disturbance. Their 'distempered blood' means that 'hot passion', especially anger, so overrules their reason that they cannot determine ''Twixt right and wrong' (II.ii.169–71).[69] Hector's argument resonates in Gadamer's words as the philosopher expands on blindness as a hermeneutic and moral condition: 'A person who is overwhelmed by his passions suddenly no longer sees what is right to do in a given situation. He has lost his self-mastery and hence his own rightness – i.e. the right orientation within himself.'[70] Having become disorientated within themselves, Troilus and Paris are consumed with 'pleasure and revenge', and pleasure and revenge, Hector asserts, 'have ears more deaf than adders to the voice / Of any true decision' (II.ii.171–3).

This image comes from Psalm 58: 3–5, in which the future King David portrays the enemies who seek his destruction:

> The wicked are strangers from the wombe: *euen* from the belly haue they erred, & speake lies. Their poison is euen like the poison of a serpent: like the deafe adder that stoppeth his eare. Which heareth not the voyce of the inchanter, thogh he be moste expert in charming.

Shakespeare was taken with David's deaf adder. He also makes use of the image in 2 *Henry VI* (III.ii.76–7) and Sonnet 112.[71] In Morning Prayer, early modern English people would have encountered Psalm 58 and the deaf adder on the eleventh day of each month. The narrative and theology of the Fall saturate the verses Shakespeare draws on. The disaffectedness of the 'wicked' commences in the womb, an image evocative of the doctrine of original sin. The serpent and adder together suggest two aspects of the Fall. George Wither, archdeacon of Colchester, includes both creatures in his *An A.B.C. for Layemen* (1585). Wither's entry for 'serpent' is pure allegory:

'The sight of a serpent shoulde bring to minde the subtilty & malice of the diuell, whereby he deceiued and seduced oure first father Adam.'[72] I cannot say if encountering serpents was a regular experience for Wither's readers. But if they did come face to face with one, Wither wanted them to turn their thoughts to humanity's Fall in Genesis 3.

Wither also has something to say about adders, and Psalm 58 is clearly his source. For Wither, the adder figures fallen humanity: it 'expresseth the nature of obstinate wicked men'. Adders and wicked men alike are deaf to persuasion by either 'the charmer', or by 'wholesome doctrine and good counsell that proceedeth out of the Word', that is, by voices external to themselves.[73] Hector suggests that being governed by pleasure and revenge means that Troilus and Paris are even less likely to listen to transcendent voices – 'the voice / Of any true decision' – than the Psalmist's adder and its human parallel. As he continues to prosecute his case against his brothers, Hector appeals to external voices – to the 'moral laws / Of nature and of nations', specifically the laws binding wives and husbands to one another (II.ii.184–5). As Bevington notes, in early modern political and ethical thinking, the moral laws of nature are 'divine or "natural" law'; the moral laws of nations are 'man-made law' and are derived from divine law.[74] The cosmos decrees that returning Helen to Menelaus – wife to husband – is the right thing to do in their situation. Acting contrarily, Hector argues, threatens to rend the moral fabric of society, making 'wrong' 'much more heavy' (II.ii.187–8).

The evidence Hector adduces is persuasive. Classical ethics, humoral medicine, theology and law together discredit Troilus and Paris as evaluators of worth. Their faulty arguments combine their compromised morality with their self-centred, self-referential perspectives on value and honour. 'Hector's opinion / Is this in way of truth', he seemingly concludes; and the play appears to agree (II.ii.188–9). Hector's stance shows up, Calvin might say, the blindness of mind and the perverseness of heart that make his brothers' value systems suspect. Because they bear these characteristics and have this effect, Hector's words (of course) serve to ultimately condemn him as, mid-sentence, he abruptly, famously, U-turns:

> yet, ne'ertheless,
> My spritely brethren, I propend to you
> In resolution to keep Helen still;
> For 'tis a cause that hath no mean dependence
> Upon our joint and several dignities.
>
> (II.ii.189–93)

In the context of the lengthy debate, Hector's about-face is decidedly unexpected. Yet having been privy to Aeneas' earlier visit to the Greek camp, *Troilus*'s audience already knows what Hector confirms in this scene: 'I have a roisting challenge sent amongst / The dull and factious nobles of the Greeks' (II.ii.208–9). Hector never intended to return Helen. His prior action of challenging the Greeks to search out a warrior willing to meet him in one-to-one combat had already muddied his seeming occupation of the moral high ground throughout most of this scene.

When Hector leads off the debate in the Trojan council by contending that they should let Helen go and thereby end the protracted, costly war, this background knowledge generates confusion for viewers, and in so doing situates them as doubters. *Troilus* signals that we should be as wary of Hector as any other character. But, unlike most of his compatriots, and his adversaries, Hector lures us in to have faith in his words, to believe that he is opening up a 'real dialogue' with his brothers and the audience. His speech acts seem to embody hermeneutic insight. They are 'in way of truth', suggestive of seeing that prompts right moral conduct and gestures to transcendence. But by the scene's close, although the words themselves have become no less insightful as diagnoses of his society's captivation by fame, suspicion has been heaped upon their speaker. Hector shows that his earlier criticism of Troilus, that Troilus' 'will' (judgement and action) 'dotes' as it 'is inclineable / To what infectiously itself affects', applies equally to him (II.ii.58–60). Troilus' overriding desires ('affects') for honour govern his will, and so do Hector's.

Indeed, as Hector draws breath after juxtaposing 'truth' with 'yet', Troilus immediately, enthusiastically, affirms that Hector is one of them (II.ii.189). 'Why, there you touched the life of our design!' (II.ii.194). Troilus would not have pressed his case if, he asserts, it was their 'heaving spleens' which drove their continued 'defence' of Helen. But she is 'a theme of honour and renown'. The irony is unmissable: the 'valiant and magnanimous deeds' Helen inspires will bring both 'fame in time to come canonize us' and 'a promised glory' (II.ii.194–206). Hector, according to Miola, was Shakespeare's 'favourite Homeric hero'.[75] This paratextual titbit which might well emphasise that in *Troilus* no character, no interpreting self, rises above the play-world's design.

While Troilus might couch this value system in the seemingly heroic, idealistic language of worth, honour and valour, its actual fallout is moral and hermeneutic morass. Troilus himself may have unwittingly given the game away as he implies that their 'heaving spleens' are their real motivators by denying this possibility. Hector's unreserved embrace of their design and of his brothers disabuses the play's audience of any faith they may have been directing towards him in the belief that he is the play's moral, transcendent voice (II.ii.113, 207). Rather, Hector implicates himself in his society's hermeneutic blindness, a mode of being which plays out in *Troilus*'s final, fragmenting act as Hector's want of self-knowledge unmasks his own and the play-world's putrefied core. Before returning to the scene of Hector's demise, I will turn my attention from war to love, more precisely, to love in war. No character in the war plot offers hope amid its pessimism. The same is true of the love plot.

'The life of our design!'

In *Troilus*, love, like war, is mired in the hermeneutic blindness and moral decay characteristic of the life of the play-world's 'design'. But the love narrative complicates the hermeneutic act of judging its famous protagonists as it brings to the fore the question of whether we can read them as embodiments of (self-)interpreting persons – as selves whose interpretations, words and actions carry moral weight. Do they, to invoke Taylor, represent 'full human agent[s] [. . .] in the ordinary meaning', that is, moral beings?[76] This complication is brought to our attention as the love plot disrupts its own unfolding by placing emphasis on Troilus and Cressida's well-known story of sexual attraction, love and betrayal as already written, enacted and decided.

Shakespeare layers into his retelling of his characters' story a heightened self-consciousness of the literary history which has already determined their futures and how they will be known: their 'notorious "identities"', as Charnes calls them. 'Heightened' is key here. Undoubtedly, *Troilus* as a whole is (necessarily) intertextual. Or, as Hillman puts it, 'the characters are all massively *pre*-scripted'.[77] But it is in the love narrative, whose history is shorter and its prior reworkings less diffuse than the events associated with the war legend, that Shakespeare puts on each character's lips the singular trait which both identifies and confines them.

It is not just that Shakespeare's Troilus must be and is true, and Shakespeare's Cressida must be and is false – that they ineluctably walk a path predetermined since Benoît de Sainte-Maure first told their story in the twelfth century and Chaucer made it popular in England from the fourteenth. More than the inevitability of plot, Shakespeare conveys a strong sense of literary determinism as he writes it into the theme of self-understanding. The playwright seemingly binds his characters' self-knowledge in perpetuity by having them voice as future-oriented tropes what everyone already knows about them. When they come together in the '"trope-plighting" scene', as James calls it, Troilus boasts that in 'the world to come', 'cit[ing] / "As true as Troilus"' will definitively affirm any lover's faithfulness; Cressida acknowledges that her name may become a byword for the opposite: '"As false as Cressid"' (III.ii.168, 176–7, 191).[78]

What is the effect of giving Troilus and Cressida this ironic knowingness about their future identities? It certainly foregrounds the possibility of their ossified, one-dimensional self-understanding in the present, and that, paradoxically, as they speak, any sense of them as persons or selves could be disappearing into what Charnes aptly describes as 'the void of rhetorical citationality'.[79] Shakespeare offers his audience the pleasure of nodding knowingly and appreciating the way he has his characters seemingly snap close the trap of literary history that has already determined their destinies. Yet, at the same time, why, as Charnes asks, do even critics who have much to say about *Troilus*'s anti-essentialism respond to the play's characters as something more than ironised constructs by (unintentionally) evoking their presence?[80] How do we explain 'the powerful sense of personhood that accompanies the characters' rhetorical constructedness', as Dawson puts it?[81]

I suggest that even as Shakespeare's lovers' ironic, self-referential articulations pull against their personhood by fixing their identities and destinies in past texts that govern their futures, their simultaneous gestures to their self-understanding in the present situate them as moral beings (whether or not they acknowledge this status). On one hand, as Troilus gives voice to his knowledge of himself as 'true', he reveals that his self-understanding is in fact one-dimensional and also self-idealising: it does not exceed the confines of his tropic identity, nor extend to moral knowledge and action. On the other hand, what we hear Cressida say as she struggles (and fails) to be other than 'false' signals that, unlike Troilus, she may possess self-awareness and moral consciousness. Via the characters' contrasting interplays with their 'notorious identities', the play elicits from its audience moral judgements which treat both Troilus and Cressida as representations of personhood.

So far, my presentations of this argument could imply that the individual is the source of his or her status as a self. But as I will show, by contextualising its lovers' speech acts concerning their own identities within (parodic) moral frameworks, *Troilus* characterises personhood as coming into being in relation to others. Personhood does not equate to individualism. Indeed, it is when the lovers are atomised, and their self-understanding circumscribed through egotism (Troilus) or isolation (Cressida), that their speech and actions contradict their moral being and provoke (differing degrees of) moral judgement.

Here, the emphases in both early modern Protestant theology and modern philosophical hermeneutics on the inherent interpersonality of both the self and self-understanding bring to light *Troilus*'s suspicious stance towards its lovers. While, in Helen Cooper's words, Chaucer's *Troilus and Criseyde* reads 'as if it were one of the great love stories of the world', Shakespeare applies the attenuating blades of satire and doubt to the narrative he inherited as he holds up to view attraction and appetite unaccompanied by phronesis, synesis or real dialogue.[82] Like Gadamer, Taylor also links the self and self-understanding to intersubjectivity and dialogue. 'The interchange of speakers' is for Taylor central to self-definition, to one's response to the question of 'Who I am'. This necessarily relational structure of self-understanding is one of what he calls the 'transcendental conditions' of selfhood.[83] Along with

Gadamer, Taylor explicitly enfolds transcendence into one's understanding of oneself: self-understanding comes into consciousness through structures greater than the individual.

This greater than, as Taylor conceives it, consists not only of other people, but also of metaphysical spaces. 'I define who I am by defining where I speak from' as I locate myself in relation to others in the intimate, interpersonal and social geographies in which I participate, 'and also crucially in the space of moral and spiritual orientation within which my most important defining relations are lived out'.[84] *Troilus*'s lovers define themselves (as one another's antitheses) within the bounds of the intimate relationship determined for them by literary history, and Shakespeare frames their living out of their relation – what they say and do to one another – with the sense that these words are spoken and these actions are taking place within a 'space of moral and spiritual orientation'.

One culturally prominent space whose coordinates seem to map *Troilus*' tryst scene is the English wedding ceremony. In Shakespeare's England, marriage was a key site of moral and spiritual orientation. A 'holy wedlock', established as a couple pledge their mutual faithfulness, exchange rings and join hands, highlights a specific instance of the dialogic, intersubjective constitution of the self and self-understanding.[85] When Pandarus executes the role of go-between determined by his name, his unfolding interaction with *Troilus*'s lovers incorporates what appear to be parodic imitations of the marriage liturgy in *The Book of Common Prayer*'s 'Form of Solemnization of Matrimony'. Emily Ross describes the scene as Pandarus' 'inverted wedding service'.[86] When Troilus and Cressida finally come together, the go-between's voice, like that of the officiating minister, is interspersed throughout the scene. But while the liturgy gives the minister words that facilitate intimate dialogue which enacts the willing union of two individuals, Pandarus' 'meddling and intervention', as Hillman puts it, 'horribly mangle[s]' any possibility of an intimate conversation between the play's lovers.[87] A somewhat more direct parodic parallel between pander and pastor is suggested by what Pandarus says. As Troilus and Cressida kiss, Pandarus quotes a legal formula associated with indentures (duplicate documents of a deed between two parties): 'Here's "In witness whereof the parties interchangeably"', before urging the couple towards sexual consummation (III.ii.57–8).[88]

In addition to alluding to indentures, the phrase also contains echoes of the actions of witnessing and interchange written into another legal statement: the moment in the *BCP* marriage ceremony when the minister declares the union to be legally binding:

> Forasmuch as Name and Name have consented together in holy wedlock, and have witnessed the same before God and this company, and thereto have given and pledged their troth either to other, and have declared the same by giving and receiving of a ring, and by joining of hands: I pronounce that they be man and wife together.[89]

Pandarus implies that he has ratified a mock contract between Troilus and Cressida. When it seems that their union may prematurely conclude without consummation, Pandarus wears the masks of both celebrant and witness as he interposes himself in his role as a pander: 'Seal it, seal it; I'll be the witness. Here I hold your hand, here my cousin's. [. . .] Say "Amen".' (III.ii.192–9). The actor's enactment of these words also approximates an element of the *BCP* ceremony of matrimony. While saying, 'Those whom God hath joined together, let no man put asunder', the priest 'joins their right hands together'.[90] Shakespeare's first audiences knew that, according to the church and the law, a couple's joining of hands before a witness was a significant event, formalising an 'inviolable and irrevocable' union.[91]

In *Troilus*, hints of the authentic marriage ceremony function like an undertow as its simulacrum plays out on the surface in a parodic space of moral and spiritual orientation. Here, I should note that in reading the real-world religious and legal script as some sort of counterpoint to the exchange between the play's lovers, my interest is in neither speculating about whether or not Troilus and Cressida are married, nor co-opting Shakespeare for any viewpoint about the Protestant theology of marriage.[92] Instead, my focus is on how the contrast directs theatregoers' moral judgement and mistrust of the characters, first of all Troilus. If we cast our minds back to the Trojan council, in that scene the topic of marriage places Troilus and his fellow princes under scrutiny. By keeping Helen and thereby contravening the 'moral laws' safeguarding the sanctity of marriage, they expose the 'design' by which they live – a design animated by the hubris and morally suspect appetite driving that world's inner circle of men (II.ii.184). In *Troilus*'s male-centric society, men characterised by hermeneutic blindness designate the worth of women.

Shakespeare first introduces this masculinist hermeneutic stance in the context of his play's love narrative. In the opening scene, Troilus immediately becomes the object of the play's satire and suspicion. Having devoted many lines to stylising himself as a tormented Petrarchan lover – 'I tell thee I am mad / In Cressid's love' (I.i.47–8) – Troilus turns to commerce to refigure himself as a merchant venturer. Cressida's 'bed' is 'India', a telling conflation of lust and procurement (I.i.96). To the early modern English mind, India signals a far-removed 'great riche countrey'.[93] Troilus imagines Cressida on that bed: 'there she lies, a pearl' (as discussed, a trope he recycles to describe Helen) (I.i.96). Whereas Cressida is passive, ready to be acquired, Troilus sees himself as 'the merchant' (I.i.99).

In her parallel soliloquy, Cressida shows that she is attuned to male desire, to how men perceive women, and the vulnerable position of women in love affairs in a society where male subjectivity takes precedence: 'Things won are done [. . .] Men prize the thing ungain'd more than it is' (I.ii.279–80). Foreshadowing later uses of 'prize' to allude to men assessing women's value, Cressida here suggests that men unrealistically 'prize' yet-to-be-won women (see II.ii.86, 91; IV.iv.132–3). As noted, prize is etymologically close to another of the drama's recurring words: price.[94] A woman's price is higher before she is won. Revealing her love for her 'prizer' only leaves Cressida open to his devaluing of her. Although she loves Troilus, Cressida determines that 'Nothing of that shall from mine eyes appear' (I.ii.285–6). Of course, literary tradition is against her. We do not witness Cressida changing her mind and agreeing to the rendezvous. But we are promptly reminded of her vulnerability, even before it takes place.

Theatregoers cannot miss Troilus' euphoria as he fantasises about the sexual pleasure he expects to imminently enjoy:

> I am giddy; expectation whirls me round.
> [. . . .]
> What will it be,
> When that the wat'ry palates taste indeed
> Love's thrice-repured nectar?
>
> (III.ii.15–20)

Troilus could be an eager groom anticipating his bride's arrival. But he is not. Marriage is not on his lips and, perhaps more surprisingly, neither is the name of Cressida. When Troilus mentions love, he associates it with an image more suggestive of lust: the stimulation and satiation of his 'wat'ry palate'. Dawson points out that Troilus' elision of marriage in Shakespeare's version of the romance indicates an overstepping of cultural norms in a way that Chaucer's Troilus' relationship with Criseyde does not. While Chaucer's poem is the exemplary English work of courtly love, embodying conventions that include the necessarily transgressive nature of the love relationship, Shakespeare wrote within a society that, in Vanessa Harding's words, 'was deeply invested in the institution of marriage, promoting it as a universal aim'.[95] Marriage was ingrained in the moral framework of Shakespeare's England.

The Protestant Reformation was the main impetus behind this elevated view of marriage. While the Reformers denied the sacramental status of marriage, they, perhaps paradoxically, insisted on its 'sacred nature'.[96] The *BCP*'s liturgy begins by educating the congregation about the holiness of marriage: they gather 'in the sight of God' to join the couple in 'holy matrimony'. Marriage is 'an honourable estate' as it was instituted by God before the Fall, while, in a postlapsarian world it redresses the Fall's effects, being 'ordained for a remedy against sin, and to avoid fornication'. The *BCP* also describes marriage as a signifier of the divine-human relationship. Marriage symbolises 'the mystical union [. . .] betwixt Christ and his church': a 'spiritual marriage and unity'.[97] Susan Karant-Nunn shows how the bolstering up of marriage liturgies by the Reformers reflected the gravity they attached to the institution. They moved the ceremony from the church's doorstep to a place in front of the altar and it became more involved, including not just the couple's consent, but 'elaborate religious instruction'.[98]

Further, Protestant marriage liturgies added oaths 'before God' which couples were required to take to legitimate their union.[99] In early modern England, oaths were charged with moral valency. 'A Sermon Against Swearing and Perjury' (in the first *Book of Homilies*) equates the oaths taken by a marrying couple to 'profess[ing]' Christ and 'receiving the Sacrament of Baptism'. Both momentous speech acts invoke 'the Name of God' as a witness to 'holy promises'. In the case of marriage, these promises 'knitteth Man and Wife in perpetual love, that they desire not to be separated for any displeasure or adversity that shall after happen'.[100] Oaths (or vows) differentiate right from wrong for oath-takers thenceforth. As such, they imply that those who take them are capable of moral judgements and actions. Oaths and vows signify that humans are moral beings existing in a moral world. As Anthony Thiselton summarises, promising brings to the fore 'the commitments and responsibilities of agents of promise within an intersubjective, public, extra-linguistic world of ethical undertaking and address'.[101] In the Protestant matrimonial oaths, the assumption that agents of these promises are moral beings encompasses not only their ability to keep the oath itself by staying married, but extends also to their hermeneutic stance, and their conduct, within the marriage relationship.

The marriage ceremony, one might say, formalises 'real dialogue' as it anticipates ongoing 'real dialogue', as well as the enactment of phronesis and synesis. The *BCP* has couples each twice promising affection, solace and fidelity to the other: 'I N. take thee N. to my wedded wife/husband, to have and to hold from this day forward, for better, for worse', and so on.[102] These vows structure an exchange that resembles aspects of 'real dialogue'. They require each person to have faith in the other's promises. Moreover, the words individuals say as they make these promises locate the self within something greater than the self, that is, the experience of 'mutual society, help, and comfort' intended for marriage which, in turn, signifies, the divine-human 'mystical union'.[103]

In this way, the matrimonial vows are anticipatory: 'from this day forward'. And it is after the wedding, in the ongoing relationship adumbrated by these vows that, one could say, the couple's dialogic engagement moves off script and becomes a dynamic and open-ended interchange: a fuller sense of 'real dialogue' experienced as an '*enrichment*' of the self.[104] In addition, the reciprocity of the vows and their bringing together of particular circumstances ('in sickness, and in health', 'for better, for worse, for richer, for poorer') and promised actions ('forsaking all other, keep thee only to her/him', 'to have and to hold', 'to love and to cherish') call Gadamer's phronesis to mind.[105] As the couple 'plight' their 'troth' to one another, the self is constituted interpersonally and dialogically as each person commits to taking up a moral lens through which they will see themselves, their spouse and the world, and to a seeing that produces actions marked by 'responsiveness' to the other (to recall Bruns on Gadamer's interpretation of phronesis).[106]

In *Troilus*'s trope- or troth-plighting scene, Shakespeare evokes just enough of the language and form of the well-known ritual to alert theatregoers to the distance between the responsive selflessness evinced in the liturgy (whether or not this played out in actual marriages is another matter) and what the play's characters say to one another. The dissimilarity especially directs unfavourable moral judgement towards Troilus. I have observed how his undisguised anticipation parodies that of a groom, eliding Cressida as he imagines his own imminent sexual satiation. In contrast, Cressida's veiled entrance suggests that, while her own passion may have overcome her better judgement, her change of mind comes at a cost (III.ii.15, 37SD). Cutting somewhat across the grain of the play's satirical tone and its characters' abstract, overweening articulations, Shakespeare gives Cressida language that seems to express vulnerability.

As she speaks, her lover's anxiety to brush aside her feelings is a lesson in unresponsiveness. When Cressida states that her fears cause her to see 'more dregs than water' in the 'fountain' of their love, Troilus replies, 'Fears make devils of cherubims; they never see truly' (III.ii.64–7). When she also turns to the proverbial to suggest that fearing 'the worst' may prevent enacting 'the worse' (that which is less than 'the worst'), he – perhaps out of naivety and idealism, but no doubt also driven by sexual urgency – dismisses her fear: 'O, let my lady apprehend no fear. In all Cupid's pageant there is presented no monster' (III.ii.68–71).[107]

Troilus links male lovers and monsters to deny the association. But the connection sticks, and vow-making is the action which draws the two together. For Troilus, 'the monstruosity of love' is that men are backed into the corner of having to make outlandish vows to win over their mistresses: 'we vow to weep seas, live in fire, eat rocks, tame tigers'. Men are not monsters, love is monstrous to men, trapping them in a double bind: 'that the will is infinite and the execution confined; that the desire is boundless and the act a slave to limit' (III.ii.74–80). Cressida does not allow Troilus to shift the blame. Picking up on the idealism as well as the sexual connotations in his assertion, she suggests that using words to make unrealisable, thus self-annulling, vows is inhuman: 'They say all lovers swear more performance than they are able [. . .] They that have the voice of lions and the act of hares, are they not monsters?' (III.ii.81–6).

Cressida's quick wit does not offset her concern. Is a man who makes ostentatious, empty vows a person to be feared? By implication, should his mistress be wary, and walk away (as Cressida almost does later in the scene)? In his reply, Troilus denies Cressida's correlation of self-misrepresenting lovers with monsters ('Are there such? Such are not we'), before returning to the familiar themes which most of *Troilus*'s characters think make their world go round: subjective valuing and worth. Troilus confidently implies that when women 'taste' (or test) men, they will inevitably 'praise' them. (Praise derives from the same etymological roots as 'prize' and 'price'.) Women will 'allow' (which also means 'praise') men as the men 'prove' themselves (III.ii.87–90).[108] Then, ironically, as though Cressida's anxiety about lovers who over-promise has not registered, Troilus makes a vow: 'Troilus shall be such to Cressid as what envy can say worst shall be a mock for his truth, and what truth can speak truest not truer than Troilus' (III.ii.92–4).

Promissory rhetoric has a persuasive potency, and Cressida obviously feels (temporarily) assuaged. She responds by repeating verbatim (as a momentary act of faith perhaps) the earlier offer which she had all but retracted: 'Will you walk in, my lord?' (III.ii.95, 59). Yet, as an onlooker, it is difficult not to be suspicious of Troilus' tongue-twisting promise, which, according to John Kerrigan is precisely a potential effect of staged oaths and vows. In dramatic contexts, oaths and vows engage audiences as interpreters of vow-makers' motivations.[109] Especially given theatregoers' accumulating knowledge of Troilus' hermeneutic stance as a manifestation of his hermeneutic blindness and self-focus, his words come across as circling around, without settling into, the terrain of substantial promissory vows. Promissory vows commit their speakers to moral action towards the promisee. Troilus' vow, in contrast, seems too convenient, and at the same time, too idealistic, indeed too self-idealising. He mentions Cressida, but his overriding concern appears to be establishing himself as the apotheosis of truth.

This self-elevation – glorying in himself – through abstraction becomes the keynote of Troilus' final oath in the scene as he situates himself as the source and very epitome of truth:

> True swains in love shall in the world to come
> Approve their truth by Troilus. When their rhymes,
> Full of protest, of oath and big compare,
> Wants similes, truth tired with iteration
> [. . .]
> Yet, after all comparisons of truth,
> As truth's authentic author to be cited,
> 'As true as Troilus' shall crown up the verse,
> And sanctify the numbers.
>
> (III.ii.168–79)

Cressida has disappeared from Troilus' view, as has any sense that he is making a self-involving, concrete promise to her. His focus is on himself, on, we could say, defining himself – but that is not quite right. Self-idealisation, not self-definition, seems to better capture the nature of Troilus' speech act.

The overlaps and intersections between both Gadamer's and Taylor's conceptions of the dialogic constitution of the self and self-understanding, and the *BCP*'s marriage vows which the scene calls to mind, bring into view the ironies in Troilus' appropriation of the form of a vow as the medium for idealising himself. As he seemingly pledges a vow to Cressida, the individualistic, rather than interpersonal, cast of his words indicates the spurious nature, not only of his commitment to her (commitment being the purpose of vowing), but also of his self-understanding. For if a proper definition of one's own identity involves seeing oneself in relation to the other people in the metaphysical spaces of one's existence, the only others in Troilus' purview are abstract, future, poetry-writing wooers. These shadowy others will, Troilus forecasts, shore up his immortality. What they will not do is contribute to the prince's understanding of his personhood through 'real dialogue' with him. Indeed, no other person can do this, for Troilus has already closed the matter. He has fixed his identity as a figure of speech that, ironically, has already become the hackneyed, superficial cliché he insists he will never be.

By all means, Troilus (as discussed) must be a faithful lover. In Chaucer's narrative, this decided feature of the plot is consistent with Troilus' character. Chaucer's Troilus' much-emphasised 'trouthe' is a virtue, an inner quality – a significant aspect of his 'whole moral character'.[110] When Pandarus – more genial and well-intentioned than Shakespeare's cynical, lascivious go-between – tells Criseyde that Troilus abounds in 'aile vertue', including 'aile trouthe', she is impressed, agreeing that 'grete power and moral vertue' are a rare, yet honourable, mix of qualities in a king's son (ii.159–68).[111] In contrast, Shakespeare's Troilus is the only character in the play who explicitly, positively associates himself with truth. When he does, one senses that moral virtue is far from his mind. Instead, as he appropriates for himself the role of truth's originator, as he links future voicings of the maxim he constructs about himself with the divine action of sanctifying, Troilus' words again bring to the surface the appetite for glory and honour which motivated his argument in the Trojan council and punctuates his earlier vow in this tryst scene. Troilus the lover mirrors Troilus the warrior (or rather, the other way around).

We need wait no longer than the morning after to see how this warriors' honour ethic, and the manner of hermeneutic blindness it spawns, plays out in the actions of Troilus the lover. As he attempts to equivocate his way around confirming his lover's fear of her plummeting value – 'O foolish Cressid, I might have still held off, / And then you would have tarried!' (IV.ii.17–18) – Troilus seems to receive Aeneas' arrival announcing the exchange of Cressida for Antenor as almost a relief:

Aeneas		We must give up to Diomedes' hand
		The Lady Cressida.
Troilus					Is it so concluded?
(IV.ii.67–8)

After many lengthy, ardent declarations of passion and loyalty, Troilus accepts the turn of events in a miserly half-line. The impression that his response to the situation, to Cressida, is off-kilter, that it lacks phronesis, builds throughout the parting scenes. Troilus says and does nothing to quieten audiences' growing mistrust of his moral understanding as his focus turns immediately to himself – 'How my achievements mock me!' – and he presses upon Cressida his insistence that she 'be true' (IV.ii.71; IV.iv.56–81). The conclusion she comes to is unsurprising: 'O heavens, you love me not!' (IV.iv.81). Even Troilus' fleeting, belated defence of Cressida seems more show, more about his reputation than genuine concern for her, occurring when love meets war and Troilus finds himself in a verbal battle with the steely Diomedes over who gets to 'prize' Cressida (IV.iv.108–36). If a vow to be true in the context of love is a promise of so much more than a wafer-thin fidelity (as the marriage ceremony insists), Troilus has pretty much hollowed out any moral substance from his vows, or better, his vow-like words, by the time he hands the unwilling Cressida over to Diomedes.

'Words, words, mere words'

By now, it appears that Cressida is more than entitled to receive from audiences and critics the sympathetic understanding which Troilus fails to extend to her, especially when the play's other male characters join him in a chorus of unresponsiveness and disregard. Pandarus, for instance, on hearing of their separation, expresses distress for Troilus, not Cressida ('The young prince will go mad'); Diomedes brags that, once he has taken Cressida from Troy, 'I'll answer to my lust' (IV.ii.78; IV.iv.131). Then there is Ulysses' scorching depiction of Cressida as sexually brazen, his words surfeited with irony as his detailed inventory of her body (to supposedly emphasise the totality of her lasciviousness) betrays his own lust:

> There's language in her eye, her cheek, her lip,
> Nay, her foot speaks; her wanton spirits look out
> At every joint and motive of her body.
>
> (IV.v.56–8)

Without doubt, Cressida's fortunes are framed and constrained by her world's ascendant value system and the patriarchy it trumpets. She is hemmed in, isolated. Yet, Shakespeare does not allow us to take the easy route of interpreting her in these terms only. Here, I disagree somewhat with readings of Cressida (including in performance) which locate her wholly within a paradigm of victimhood and oppression. Grace Tiffany summarises such accounts of Cressida as victim as 'defenses [. . .] that posit her fundamental powerlessness to do anything but inscribe herself into a masculine ethic which so (de)values her'.[112] Painting Cressida in this way erodes the personhood we sense that Shakespeare gives her. Indeed, Cressida is the play's most complicated, ambiguous character. She is more difficult to pin down than the male characters, in part because she comes across as more than a victim of her warrior culture and its privileging of the male eye which, as Shakespeare portrays them, tars her male counterparts with the same, almost-caricaturing, brush. As Cressida engages dialogically in promise making, her consciousness of her moral being contributes significantly to her ambiguity and complexity. Otherwise put, she seems to possess an awareness of phronesis: there is a right thing to do in the particular situations in which she finds herself, even as, at the same time, it feels that her hands are tied.

We receive a strong impression of Cressida's insight into herself as a moral being in the moments before she reciprocates Troilus' ostensible vow. Having expressed a desire to 'shun' herself, which also (to Troilus' and Pandarus' horror) means walking away from the rendezvous, Cressida explains why:

> I have a kind of self resides with you,
> But an unkind self that itself will leave
> To be another's fool. Where is my wit?
> I would be gone. I speak I know not what.
>
> (III.ii.141–6)

Juxtaposed with the obvious irony underlying Cressida's self-prognosis, we see a character who, if we accept the truthfulness of her words, appears to possess a significant degree of knowledge of what it means to be a person. Cressida views herself and her future actions through the twin lens of intersubjectivity and (im)moral action. Her disquiet is born of the knowledge that the latter will undermine the former. She knows that she will not just 'leave' Troilus, but that such an action is 'unkind'.

This self-scrutiny, almost absent among the male characters, hints at the stern command given to the marrying couple at the beginning of the *BCP* marriage ceremony. The minister invokes 'the dreadful day of judgment' as he addresses the couple: 'if either of you do know any impediment why ye may not be lawfully joined together in matrimony, that ye confess it'.[113] When Troilus (most likely to hurry her on) commends Cressida for her wisdom, she describes her prior revelation of her internal conflict as 'a large confession' which she 'perchance' concocted 'to angle for your thoughts' (III.ii.147–50). Is Cressida dissembling to cover up her loss of 'wit' or even, as she tentatively suggests, in her 'confession' itself? The play offers no clear answer, but only a feeling that, just as disclosure of a potential 'impediment' must defer the exchange of vows in the wedding ceremony, it might be best for everyone if the pause button was hit right now so that Cressida's uncertainty can be addressed.

Of course, Cressida must press on and vow. Mirroring her lover's inflated language, Cressida draws from the same supply of hyperbole:

> If I be false, or swerve a hair from truth,
> When time is old and hath forgot itself,
> When they've said 'As false
> As air, as water, wind, or sandy earth,
> [. . . .]
> Yea, let them say, to stick the heart of falsehood,
> 'As false as Cressid'.
>
> (III.ii.179–91)

Leaving aside the rhetorical flourish, Cressida, in keeping with what appears to be moral consciousness, does (unlike Troilus) pledge concrete, self-involving moral action, albeit expressed in the conditional mood: 'If I be false'. Her vow is also negatively phrased. Both literary necessity and what

Kerrigan terms 'the rhetoric of their troth-plight' compel Cressida to match Troilus' 'true' with her 'false', locking her, it appears, into 'a default position of dishonesty'.[114] Once more, 'victim' feels like the right shorthand for Cressida and her circumstance. But again, *Troilus* pulls us up just short of using this language of victimhood.

To some extent, this is because Cressida keeps reminding us that she is a moral being by iterating her promise. Immediately after Pandarus tells her 'thou must be gone', she declares to the 'immortal gods' that she 'will not go', and then calls on the same gods to 'Make Cressid's name the very crown of falsehood / If ever she leave Troilus!' (IV.ii.91–102). Tellingly, as Troilus pressures her to affirm her loyalty, Cressida inverts her negative, conditional vow. She articulates a positive, commissive speech act: 'I'll be true' (IV.iv.68). It is hard to explain away the sense that genuine emotion underlies Cressida's words, that, one could say, she seems to be committing herself to engaging in 'real dialogue'. This effect amplifies the impression, already implied by the inherent moral implications of giving one's undertaking to another, that she sees herself as having some moral agency. Indeed, without some agency, Cressida's undoing inside the Greek camp would lose much of its dramatic potency and interpretive complexity. As Cressida inches towards consenting to Diomedes answering to his lust, as she (inevitably) fails to do the impossible – keep her conflicting vows to both Troilus and Diomedes – and as her own insight becomes opaque, Shakespeare makes his audience aware of the limits of our own hermeneutic condition by situating us to judge her morally.

There are many metatheatrical moments in *Troilus*. Cressida's final physical appearance in the play represents the most sustained occasion in which it draws playgoers' attention to our participation in the event unfolding before us. As Ulysses manoeuvres Troilus into place to overlook Cressida's interaction with Diomedes, Shakespeare locates his audience in a similarly uncomfortable position of watching and making sense of Cressida's words and actions. It is not that the playwright wants, or allows, his audience to adopt Troilus' perspective. Thersites is also present as another overlooker – separate from Ulysses and Troilus, and always ready to inject frequent doses of sleazy vitriol:

> Troilus [*to Ulysses, aside*]
> Cressid comes forth to him.
> Diomedes [*to Cressida*] How now, my charge?
> Cressida
> Now, my sweet guardian. Hark, a word with you.
> [*She whispers to him.*]
> Troilus [*aside*] Yea, so familiar?
> Ulysses [*to Troilus, aside*] She will sing any man at first sight.
> Thersites [*aside*] And any man may sing her, if he can
> take her clef. She's noted.
>
> (V.ii.7–13)

By multiplying and making diffuse the eyes looking at Cressida from within her world, the scene complicates the hermeneutic experience for those of us trying to read her from a greater distance. As Ulysses rubs salt into his companion's wounds, he wants Troilus to see the woman possessed by her 'wanton spirits' he had already damned Cressida to be. But the Cressida we meet in this scene is not so cut and dried; judging her is difficult.

There is a painful familiarity to Cressida's vacillation as she tries to, yet cannot, tell Diomedes to leave, as she gives him Troilus' love-token (a sleeve) and snatches it back. In this scene, Cressida is no less caught up in her society's masculinist ethic, shot through as it is with pride and lust, than she was in the assignation scene. One senses some solicitude, a self-protecting exigency, behind 'sweet guardian', even if her whispering and the provocative overtones in 'sweet' also call to mind Ulysses' branding of her as a 'daughter of the game' (IV.v.64). But the moral complication which further clouds interpretations of Cressida here is that she has both sworn an oath to Diomedes (V.ii.28) and made promises to Troilus.

In making concrete promises, Cressida, quite possibly in contrast to the male characters, has located herself as a moral being within (recalling Taylor) a 'space of moral and spiritual orientation'.[115] It may not seem fair that Diomedes demands – twice – that Cressida keep her oath (V.ii.17, 24). Nevertheless, she is the one who not only agrees to do so – 'In faith I will, la' – but also adds further emphasis to her commitment: 'Never trust me else' (V.ii.61). Troilus may be at his hyperbolic and idealistic best as he seeks to reconcile himself to Cressida's action. But Shakespeare's intended audience would probably have agreed with him about the weightiness of vows, especially the marriage vows to which the lovers' vows had parodically gestured:

> If souls guide vows, if vows be sanctimonies,
> If sanctimony be the gods' delight,
> If there be rule in unity itself,
> This is not she.
> [. . .]
> This is, and is not, Cressid.
>
> (V.ii.146–53)

The problem is that this is Cressid. She is one entity who has both succumbed to Diomedes and shown that she knows her obligation to Troilus. Cressida derides herself – 'O false wench!' – as she remembers that 'He [Troilus] loved me', his sleeve functioning metonymically as concrete proof of her vow: 'O pretty, pretty pledge!' (V.ii.73, 83). However suspicious we may be of the male characters, Cressida's internal conflict suggests that she agrees with their insistence that vows have moral and spiritual import. Cressida is the character who we most likely identify as having a moral consciousness, and thus the one whose downfall comes closest to tragedy. But the entanglement of the two, of her understanding of herself as a moral being with her inability to align her actions with this knowledge, focuses the audience's judgement in a way that withholds from her the status of a tragic character (like, say, Cordelia or Desdemona). Cressida herself anticipates unfavourable moral judgement: 'Ay, come. – O Jove! – Do, come. – I shall be plagued.' 'Plagued' alludes to both divine judgement and many sixteenth-century literary treatments of her as ultimately diseased and impoverished (especially in, and influenced by, Robert Henryson's *The Testament of Cresseid*) (V.ii.111).[116]

Cressida's last words embody the devastating effects of not being able to enact moral knowledge:

> Good night. I prithee [Diomedes], come. –
> Troilus, farewell! One eye yet looks on thee
> But with my heart the other eye doth see.
> Ah, poor our sex! This fault in us I find:
> The error of our eye directs our mind.
> What error leads must err. O, then conclude:
> Minds swayed by eyes are full of turpitude.
>
> (V.ii.112–18).

For Troilus, splitting Cressida in two denies reality. But Cressida has already made the same self-atomising move. In a final act of self-interpretation, she reduces her moral impasse, and her self-understanding, to a common hermeneutic and moral fault, indeed depravity, which she attributes to all women. The female interpreting self is untrustworthy, not just because her seeing is morally conflicted, but because it is morally compromised – 'full of turpitude'. There may be no other way out, but it is as though Cressida has taken recourse to the (blinded) male hermeneutic stance towards herself that she had feared – an interpretive posture which elides all self-understanding. Her insight is circumscribed, and while blaming her entirely for this is more than what the play does, it also does not release her from all responsibility.

Shakespeare leaves us with this unresolved tension, which somewhat differentiates his play from its literary ancestors. Troilus is Chaucer's hero, yet the poem's narrator interposes himself as the mediator of readers' responses to Criseyde by moderating Troilus' condemnation of her and alerting them to her remorse:[117]

> And if I myghte excuse hire any wise,
> ffor she so sory was for hire vntrouthe,
> I-wis, I wolde excuse hire ȝet for routhe.
>
> (v.1097–9)

In contrast, in Shakespeare's play, almost as confirmation of Cressida's atomisation, no one speaks up for her, or gives her a voice which affirms her integrity (her wholeness, if not her probity) as a moral being. Not even Pandarus is privy to the contents of the letter he delivers from Cressida to Troilus, as the prince dismisses her communication as 'Words, words, mere words, no matter from the heart' before ripping it up (V.iii.108). There is a hint that Cressida may be expressing regret in her letter. Shakespeare ensures that we will never know.

Our knowledge of Cressida becomes as opaque as what we sense her knowledge of herself has become. Any possibility of clarity, of 'real dialogue' both between the characters and between character and audience, is in shreds. But before we forget the extent to which Troilus and the 'design' that blinkers him are implicated, it is significant that he does the shredding. Of all *Troilus*'s characters, Shakespeare gives Cressida the greatest depth and complexity. She loves and is unfaithful; she exhibits the moral consciousness of a full human agent and undermines her moral knowledge. Her portrayal invites sympathy, but also doubt and judgement. She is not her play-world's transcendent heroine. We cannot place our faith in her. Cressida's fragmentation, and that of her love, is emblematic of the atomisation of her society which soon follows.

'Most putrefied core'

The play's scrutiny of its characters' hermeneutic blindness and its ruinous impact on self and society reaches its clamorous climax in Hector's death. Hector's refusal to listen to transcendental knowledge revealed to others signals his imminent demise. Andromache's pleading communication of her dreams 'of bloody turbulence' and Cassandra's affirmative – 'O, 'tis true' – cannot dissuade Hector from fighting Achilles (V.iii.10–11, 13). Andromache's and Cassandra's words are all-too-fleeting instances of transcendent voices breaking into the play-world's otherwise closed sphere of existence. But earlier scenes had already shown that this world's value system accords very little worth to these female characters. Alexander reports that Hector, angry at having been struck down by Ajax on the battlefield, had returned home and 'chid Andromache', a disregard which he repeats in this later scene (I.ii.4–35). Troilus dismisses Cassandra's frantic interruption of the Trojan council, writing her off as 'mad'. And while Hector contrastingly describes her premonition of Troy's destruction as 'high strains / Of divination', his insincerity in that moment soon becomes apparent (II.ii.122, 113–14). Hector's characterisation of Troilus and Paris in the council as having 'ears more deaf than adders' to transcendent voices rebounds on him as Andromache questions: 'When was my lord so much ungently tempered / To stop his ears against admonishment?' (II.ii.172; V.iii.1–2).

Hector's course was set when he took Achilles' hand and agreed to their 'match', and he lays claim to the superiority of his judgement (over Andromache's and Cassandra's) by calling on the gods as the ultimate recipients of his speech act: 'Begone, I say. The gods have heard me swear' (IV.v.268–70; V.iii.15). Even as he refuses to listen to external voices, Hector asserts that he has been heard, and approved. Nevertheless, given the earlier discussion of the spiritual and moral seriousness attached to oaths and vows, Hector might have a point.

One should keep one's vows. But Cassandra sees right through him: 'The gods are deaf to hot and peevish vows' (V.iii.16). Hector spoke his vows inside an echo chamber. Moreover, Cassandra's criticism again ironically recalls Hector's own (disingenuous, yet truthful) reproof of Troilus whose 'madly hot' blood and 'hot passion' prevent him from heeding Cassandra's earlier warning, and (along with Paris) from discerning right from wrong (II.ii.115–18, 169–71). Strong desires and irrational emotions can also corrupt vows, a truth which the audience had already witnessed in Troilus' suspect troth-plight with Cressida.

Cassandra shows that her brothers' devaluing of her is far from the mark as she seals her case with what Samuel Johnson considers to be 'all the coolness and judgment of a skilful casuist': 'It is the purpose that makes strong the vow, / But vows to every purpose must not hold' (V.iii.79, 23–4).[118] Vows are not absolutes, free of motive; they should not be instrumentalised to license a person's will. Kerrigan observes that Cassandra represents an 'orthodox' viewpoint, expressed in texts such as the 'Sermon Against Swearing and Perjury' and early modern casuistical literature. A condition oath-takers must fulfil, states the homilist, is that they 'must do it with judgment, not rashly and unadvisedly, but soberly, considering what an Oath is'.[119] One can hear the idea of phronesis in this injunction, and in Cassandra's logic: following through with his 'hot and peevish' promise is not the right thing for Hector to do in his situation.

But Hector is governed by something other than phronesis: 'Life every man holds dear, but the dear man / Holds honour far more precious-dear than life' (V.iii.27–8). To Hector, giving honour pre-eminence elevates him above 'every man'. Sound familiar? Hector's genuflection to an honour ethic, accompanied by his hubris, confirm the other occupants of his echo chamber: unsurprisingly, his fellow warriors, be they Trojan or Greek. It is his prior dialogue with these other prizers of honour and of self which matters to Hector and how he sees himself, not his current conversation with his wife and sister. As he declares to Priam, 'I do stand engaged to many Greeks, / Even in the faith of valour' (V.iii.68–9). Within the confines of Hector's value system, Cassandra's argument that, because he himself had invalidated his pledge he does not have to keep it, is perhaps incomprehensible and certainly preposterous. Hector sways Priam. But Cassandra stands firm as she devastatingly diagnoses Hector's hermeneutic blindness: 'Thou dost thyself and all our Troy deceive' (V.iii.90).

Hector's dual deception of self and society stands out amid the chaotic action of the play's concluding scenes. He spares Achilles, confirming Troilus' earlier objection: 'Brother, you have a vice of mercy in you, / Which better fits a lion than a man' (V.iii.37–8). Hector's 'vice' may appear noble. (Bevington and Dawson both note the fabled belief that lions show their dignity as the 'king of beasts' by sparing their lesser prey.)[120] Yet, in the context of war, Troilus' caution seems judicious. Achilles may well put his finger on Hector's real motive when, in response to Hector's offer to 'Pause, if thou wilt', he spits out his reply: 'I do disdain thy courtesy, proud Trojan' (V.vi.15–16). Mercy may just be a veil for presumption.

Undoubtedly, something other than mercy drives Hector as he pivots from releasing Achilles to 'hunt[ing]' the anonymous Greek bedecked in '[*sumptuous*] *armour*' (V.vi.32, 26SD). Again, audiences cannot miss the pointed irony as Shakespeare allows Hector only four brief lines to celebrate his success before Achilles returns with his Myrmidons:

> Most putrefied core, so fair without,
> Thy goodly armour thus hath cost thy life.
> Now is my day's work done. I'll take good breath.
> Rest, sword; thou hast thy fill of blood and death.
> [*He starts to disarm*]
>
> (V.ix.1–4)

Claire Kenward observes that Shakespeare follows medieval tradition in linking Hector's death to greed. Similarly, Kenneth Muir points out that John Lydgate's fifteenth-century *Troy Book* 'moraliz[es]' on covetousness immediately before narrating Achilles' killing of Hector.[121] Covetousness, of course, breaks the Tenth Commandment: 'Thou shalt not couet thy neighbours house [. . .] neither any thing that is thy neighbours' (Exodus 20: 17).

Associating Hector's death with greed and covetousness is a Christian refiguring of what was customary in Homer: taking the armour of a conquered foe as the spoils of war.[122] In his exposition of covetousness ('lust' in Thomas Norton's translation), Calvin contends that self-interest and self-importance stop people from seeing both themselves and the lust which covertly, insidiously, deceives and then destroys them. When one is 'blinded and drunke with loue of himself' and riddled with 'the 'disease of pride', 'the euils of lust are hidden in so deepe and crooked priuie corners, that they easily deceiue the sight of man'; lust 'destroieth miserable man so secretly, that he feeleth not the deadly dart thereof'.[123] This dark image of the unseeing and vainglorious self finds resemblance in Shakespeare's characters, especially, in these final scenes, in Hector, whose covetousness has far-reaching consequences beyond himself.

If Hector's desire for the 'goodly armour' is the final piece of evidence that proves Cassandra right about his calamitous self-deception, it also ensures his deception of Troy. Soon after, Achilles gloats over this prospect as he spells out Hector's and his city's mutual atomisation: 'Now, Troy, sink down! / Here lies thy heart, thy sinews, and thy bone' (V.ix.11–12). Hector is now Troy's 'putrefied core'. Or rather, especially given the double meaning of 'putrefied', he was always that, his physical demise signifying his own and his world's thoroughgoing moral corruption. Even now, *Troilus* does not offer theatregoers relief from its pessimism by allowing Hector's death to become tragic. Hector's final words, his call upon Achilles to adhere to his dubious battlefield ethic – 'I am unarmed. Forgo this vantage, Greek' – show his inability to recognise his own contribution to his downfall (V.ix.9). Unlike the heroes of the tragedies, Hector dies, as John Cox observes, without any perception of 'his dismal lack of self-knowledge'.[124] He is not given a spark of redemptive moral awareness.

For a moment, Troilus' prognostications of the aftermath of Hector's death lean towards tragedy:

> There is a word will Priam turn to stone,
> Make wells and Niobes of the maids and wives,
> [. . .]
> Hector is dead. There is no more to say.
> (V.xi.17–23)

Troilus' words are poignant and, of course, prove true. But Shakespeare has him deliver them in a register reflective of the style of later sixteenth-century writing 'that aspired to be "heroic"'. As Colin Burrow notes, the use of such 'an elevated register [. . .] was potentially appropriate for tragedy but dangerously close to the proximate vice of tumidity'.[125] When Shakespeare gives Troilus nine more lines to say, nine lines of overblown bravado, tumidity overrides potential tragedy. And with any possibility of tragedy drowned out by Hector's unknowing and Troilus' bombast, it is appropriate that Pandarus speaks *Troilus*'s epilogue, beginning with a parodic lament: 'A goodly medicine for my aching bones! O world, world, world!' (V.xi.35–6). Pandarus is putrefying in front of the audience he insults and indicts as 'Good traders in the flesh [. . .] Brethren and sisters of the hold-door trade' before he voices the play's last promise – to them: he will bequeath theatregoers his 'diseases' (V.xi.45, 51, 56).

Throughout *Troilus*, Shakespeare has beckoned his audience to come near and indulge in a little scoffing, to judge the celebrated characters he satirises as he puts on view the anthropological pessimism of early modern Protestant England. But these final lines, bitter and disquietingly funny, draw theatregoers uncomfortably close to Shakespeare's dramatisation of a kind of communality in vice or fallenness: to his pride-filled, atomised, market-driven societies in which the captivation of the eye by the desires of the I hollows out values and vows and leaves little room for either self-understanding or responsive seeing of others; to a world where the absence of transcendence manifests in a mistrust between persons that ultimately undoes the self. Little wonder that it feels as though *Troilus* has found a home in our day.

Notes

1. Aristotle, *Poetics*, ed. Anthony Kenny (Oxford: Oxford University Press, 2013), XV.
2. Michel Eyquem de Montaigne, *Montaigne's Essays*, trans. John Florio, vol. 2 (London: Dent, 1965), 199.
3. Charles Taylor, *Human Agency and Language: Philosophical Papers 1* (Cambridge: Cambridge University Press, 1985), 45.
4. Susan Snyder, 'The Genres of Shakespeare's Plays', in *The Cambridge Companion to Shakespeare*, ed. Margreta De Grazia and Stanley Wells (Cambridge: Cambridge University Press, 2001), 94; David Hillman, 'The Worst Case of Knowing the Other? Stanley Cavell and Troilus and Cressida', *Philosophy and Literature* 32, no. 1 (2008): 74; Camille Slights, 'The Parallel Structure of *Troilus and Cressida*', *Shakespeare Quarterly* 25, no. 1 (1974): 50.
5. Jean Calvin, *The Institution of Christian Religion*, trans. Thomas Norton (London: Arnold Hatfield, 1599), 2.1.2.
6. Jean Calvin, *A Commentarie of Iohn Caluine, vpon the first booke of Moses called Genesis*, trans. Thomas Tymme (London: Thomas Dawson, 1578), 92.
7. Charles Taylor, *Sources of the Self: The Making of the Modern Identity* (Cambridge, MA: Harvard University Press, 1989), 65, 64, 65, 20, 65.

8. Alexander Welsh, *What Is Honor? A Question of Moral Imperatives* (New Haven, CT: Yale University Press, 2008), 53–4.
9. Jennifer Clement, *Reading Humility in Early Modern England* (Farnham: Ashgate, 2015), 6.
10. Welsh, *What Is Honor?*, 54.
11. Clement, *Reading Humility*, 30; Saint Augustine, *The City of God, Books I-VII*, trans. Gerald G. Walsh, Demetrius B. Zema, and Étienne Gilson (Washington, DC: Catholic University of America Press, 1950), 5.14.
12. Richard Hooker, *A Learned Sermon of the Natvre of Pride* (Oxford: Ioseph Barnes, 1612), 8, 11, 14.
13. Clement, *Reading Humility*, 7.
14. Calvin, *The Institution of Christian Religion*, 2.1.1; 1.15.7, 6, 7.
15. Ibid. 1.15.6, 7.
16. *OED Online*, s.v. 'speculation, n.'.
17. See *Julius Caesar*, I.i.53–64.
18. Frank Kermode, '"Opinion" in *Troilus and Cressida*', *Critical Quarterly* 54, no. 1 (2012): 97.
19. Linda Charnes, '"So Unsecret to Ourselves": Notorious Identity and the Material Subject in Shakespeare's Troilus and Cressida', *Shakespeare Quarterly* 40, no. 4 (1989): 417.
20. Hillman, 'The Worst Case of Knowing the Other?', 74.
21. See, for instance, David Bevington, 'Introduction', in *Troilus and Cressida*, ed. David Bevington, Arden Shakespeare Third Series (London: Bloomsbury, 1998), 19; Hugh Grady, *Shakespeare's Universal Wolf: Studies in Early Modern Reification* (Oxford: Oxford University Press, 1996), 57–94; Douglas Cole, 'Myth and Anti-Myth: The Case of Troilus and Cressida', *Shakespeare Quarterly* 31, no. 1 (1980): 83.
22. Hans-Georg Gadamer, *Truth and Method*, trans. Joel Weinsheimer and Donald G. Marshall, 2nd, rev. ed. (London: Continuum, 2004), 314.
23. Ibid. 314.
24. Ibid. 311, 314.
25. Ibid. 19, 314; Jens Zimmermann, 'Ignoramus: Gadamer's "Religious Turn"', *Symposium* 6, no. 2 (2002): 212.

26. Gadamer, *Truth and Method*, 312, 314, 319, 314, 312. Italics original.
27. Ibid. 319; Gerald L. Bruns, *Hermeneutics Ancient and Modern* (New Haven, CT: Yale University Press, 1992), 261.
28. Hans-Georg Gadamer, 'Hermeneutics as a Theoretical and Practical Task', in *The Gadamer Reader: A Boquet of the Later Writings*, ed. and trans. Richard E. Palmer (Evanston, IL: Northwestern University Press, 2007), 261; Gadamer, *Truth and Method*, 319, 320.
29. Taylor, *Sources of the Self*, 35.
30. Gadamer, 'Hermeneutics as a Theoretical and Practical Task', 261.
31. Ibid. 254.
32. Ibid. 258.
33. *Articles, whereupon it was agreed by the Archbishoppes and Bishoppes of both prouinces, and the whole cleargie, in the Conuocation holden at London in the yere of our Lorde God 1562* (London: Richarde Iugge and Iohn Cawood, 1571), article 9.
34. Taylor, *Human Agency*, 37, 39, 38.
35. Hans-Georg Gadamer, *Philosophical Hermeneutics*, ed. and trans. David E. Linge (Berkeley: University of California Press, 1976), 57.
36. Ibid. 57, 58, 57, 55.
37. Bruns, *Hermeneutics Ancient and Modern*, 146.
38. Raymond Kemp Anderson, 'Corporate Selfhood and "Meditatio Vitae Futurae": How Necessary Is Eschatology for Christian Ethics?', *Journal of the Society of Christian Ethics* 23, no. 1 (2003): 35.
39. Gadamer, *Philosophical Hermeneutics*, 57; Jens Zimmermann, *Recovering Theological Hermeneutics: An Incarnational-Trinitarian Theory of Interpretation* (Grand Rapids, MI: Baker Academic, 2004), 97.
40. Gadamer, *Philosophical Hermeneutics*, 57; Zimmermann, *Recovering Theological Hermeneutics*, 260. Italics original.
41. Maurice Hunt, 'Shakespeare's *Troilus and Cressida* and Christian Epistemology', *Christianity and Literature* 42, no. 2 (1993): 243. David Kaula similarly argues that in *Troilus*

Shakespeare follows the practice of other Renaissance writers by interpreting a classical story 'from a Christian viewpoint'. David Kaula, '"Mad Idolatry" in Shakespeare's *Troilus and Cressida*', *Texas Studies in Literature and Language* 15 (1973): 37–8; Hannibal Hamlin, *The Bible in Shakespeare* (Oxford: Oxford University Press, 2013), 179.

42. Jessica Wolfe, *Homer and the Question of Strife from Erasmus to Hobbes* (Toronto: University of Toronto Press, 2015), 12.
43. Robert S. Miola, 'Reading the Classics', in *A Companion to Shakespeare*, ed. David Scott Kastan (Malden, MA: Blackwell Publishers, 1999), 182.
44. Tania Demetriou and Tanya Pollard, 'Homer and Greek Tragedy in early modern England's theatres: an introduction', *Classical Receptions Journal* 9, no. 1 (2016): 21.
45. Robert S. Miola, 'Lesse Greeke? Homer in Jonson and Shakespeare', *Ben Jonson Journal* 23, no. 1 (2016): 123, 114.
46. Wolfe, *Homer and the Question of Strife*, 243, 10–11.
47. Heather James, 'Shakespeare's Classical Plays', in *The New Cambridge Companion to Shakespeare*, ed. Margreta De Grazia and Stanley Wells (Cambridge: Cambridge University Press, 2010), 156; See Demetriou and Pollard, 'Homer and Greek Tragedy', 21n115, who state that, despite persisting scepticism, 'whether Shakespeare read Chapman's Homer was answered conclusively in the affirmative by [R. K.] Presson (1953)'. For more on Shakespeare's sources see David Bevington, '"Instructed by the Antiquary Times": Shakespeare's Sources', in *Troilus and Cressida*, ed. David Bevington, Arden Shakespeare Third Series (London: Bloomsbury, 1998); Anthony B. Dawson, 'Appendix: Sources of the Play', in *Troilus and Cressida*, ed. Anthony B. Dawson, The New Cambridge Shakespeare (Cambridge: Cambridge University Press, 2017), 267–75; Kenneth Muir, *The Sources of Shakespeare's Plays* (Abingdon: Routledge, 1977; repr., 2005), 141–57.
48. Demetriou and Pollard, 'Homer and Greek Tragedy', 21n115; Dawson, 'Sources of the Play', 377–9; Miola, 'Lesse Greeke?', 114.
49. Marcus Nordlund, 'Pride and Self-Love in Shakespeare and Montaigne', in *The Shakespearean International Yearbook 6:*

Special Section, Shakespeare and Montaigne Revisited, ed. Graham Bradshaw, Tom Bishop and Peter Holbrook (Aldershot: Ashgate, 2006), 83.

50. Wolfe, *Homer and the Question of Strife*, 300, 302.
51. James, 'Shakespeare's Classical Plays', 156.
52. Hamlin, *The Bible in Shakespeare*, 181. Hamlin draws on Thomas M. Greene's work to make this distinction.
53. Wolfe, *Homer and the Question of Strife*, 300–1.
54. Miola, 'Reading the Classics', 184, 182.
55. The Great Bible and the Bishops' Bible use 'botch' in Revelation 16; the Geneva Bible uses 'sore'. See Kaula, '"Mad Idolatry"', 31.
56. Heinrich Bullinger, *A Hvndred Sermons vpō the Apocalips of Iesu Christ*, trans. John Daus (London: Iohn Day, 1561), 482. Also see Kaula, '"Mad Idolatry"', 31.
57. Richard Leake, *Foure Sermons Preached and Publikely Taught by Richard Leake* (London: Felix Kingston, 1599), 59–65.
58. *Troilus and Cressida*, ed. Bevington, II.iii.122–3n; William Shakespeare, *Troilus and Cressida*, 2nd ed., ed. Anthony B. Dawson (Cambridge: Cambridge University Press, 2017), II.iii.113n.
59. Anthony Dawson and David Bevington both point out that the notion of the person or the body as a kingdom was a commonplace in early modern England. *Troilus and Cressida*, ed. Bevington, II.iii.172LN; *Troilus and Cressida*, ed. Dawson, II.iii.159n.
60. Homer, *Seauen Bookes of the Iliades of Homere, Prince of Poets*, trans. George Chapman (London: Iohn Windet, 1598), 1.
61. *Troilus and Cressida*, ed. Bevington, III.iii.137–8n; *Troilus and Cressida*, ed. Dawson, III.iii.136–7n; *OED Online*, s.v. 'wantoness, n.'.
62. John Gillies, 'The Question of Original Sin in *Hamlet*', *Shakespeare Quarterly* 64, no. 4 (2013): 402.
63. Joseph Navitsky, 'Scurrilous Jests and Retaliatory Abuse in Shakespeare's *Troilus and Cressida*', *English Literary Renaissance* 42, no. 1 (2012): 29.
64. Hector's death resembles the account of Troilus' death in William Caxton's *Recuyell of the Historyes of Troy* (1474)

and John Lydgate's *The Troy Book* (1513). See Bevington, '"Instructed by the Antiquary Times"', 390; Dawson, 'Sources of the Play', 272.

65. Dawson, 'Introduction', 38.
66. *Troilus and Cressida*, ed. Dawson, II.ii.81–2n.
67. *OED Online*, s.v. 'prize, n.1 and adj.'.
68. Kermode, '"Opinion" in *Troilus*', 100, 102; Hunt, 'Shakespeare's Troilus and Cressida', 252; Bevington, 'Introduction', 68; Dawson, 'Introduction', 38.
69. *Troilus and Cressida*, ed. Bevington, II.ii.169n.
70. Gadamer, *Truth and Method*, 319.
71. Naseeb Shaheen, 'Biblical Echoes in *Troilus and Cressida*', *Notes and Queries* 43, no. 2 (1996): 161.
72. George Wither, *An A.B.C. for Layemen* (London: Robert Waldegraue, 1585), 124.
73. Ibid. 2, 3.
74. *Troilus and Cressida*, ed. Bevington, II.ii.184–5n.
75. Miola, 'Lesse Greeke?', 119.
76. Taylor, *Human Agency*, 3.
77. Charnes, '"So Unsecret to Ourselves"', 415; Hillman, 'The Worst Case of Knowing the Other?', 78. Italics original.
78. Heather James, *Shakespeare's Troy* (Cambridge: Cambridge University Press, 1997), 106.
79. Charnes, '"So Unsecret to Ourselves"', 434.
80. Ibid. 427–9. Hillman is an exception. See 'The Worst Case of Knowing the Other?', 84–5.
81. Dawson, 'Introduction', 35.
82. Helen Cooper, *Shakespeare and the Medieval World* (London: Bloomsbury Publishing, 2012), 223.
83. Taylor, *Sources of the Self*, 35, 39.
84. Ibid. 35.
85. John E. Booty (ed.), *The Book of Common Prayer 1559: The Elizabethan Prayer Book* (Charlottesville: The University of Virginia Press, 1976, reissued 2005), 293.
86. Emily Ross, '"Words, Vows, Gifts, Tears and Love's Full Sacrifice": An Assessment of the Status of Troilus and Cressida's Relationship According to Customary Elizabethan Marriage Procedure', *Shakespeare* 4, no. 4 (2008): 421.

87. Hillman, 'The Worst Case of Knowing the Other?', 82.
88. *Troilus and Cressida*, ed. Bevington, III.ii.56–7n; Ross, '"Words, Vows, Gifts"', 434n16; *OED Online*, s.v. 'indenture, n.'.
89. *Troilus and Cressida*, ed. Bevington, III.ii.56–7n; Booty, *The Book of Common Prayer 1559*, 293.
90. Booty, *The Book of Common Prayer 1559*, 293.
91. *Troilus and Cressida*, ed. Bevington, III.ii.192–3LN.
92. Ross addresses the former issue in '"Words, Vows, Gifts'".
93. Thomas Cooper, *Thesavrvs Lingvae Romanae & Britannicae* (Londini: Henry Denham, 1578), s.v. 'India'.
94. Dawson points out that the Quarto text uses 'price' here. *Troilus and Cressida*, ed. Dawson, I.ii.249n.
95. Dawson, 'Sources of the Play', 269; K. A. Brown, 'Courtly love', in *The Princeton Encyclopedia of Poetry and Poetics: Fourth Edition*, ed. Roland Greene et al. (Princeton: Princeton University Press, 2012), 312; Vanessa Harding, 'Families and Households in Early Modern London, c. 1550–1640,' in *The Oxford Handbook of the Age of Shakespeare*, ed. Malcolm Smuts (Oxford: Oxford University Press, 2016), 604.
96. Susan C. Karant-Nunn, 'Reformation society, women and the family', in *Reformation World*, ed. Andrew Pettegree (London: Routledge, 2000), 449.
97. Booty, *The Book of Common Prayer 1559*, 291, 290, 296.
98. Karant-Nunn, 'Reformation society', 449.
99. Ibid. 449.
100. *Certain Sermons or Homilies Appointed to Be Read in Churches in the Time of Queen Elizabeth* (London: George Wells, Abel Swall and George Pawlett, 1687), 72.
101. Anthony C. Thiselton, 'Further Implications and the Paradigmatic Status of Promise as Communicative Action', in *The Promise of Hermeneutics*, ed. Roger Lundin, Anthony C. Thiselton, and Clarence Walhout (Grand Rapids, MI: Wm. B. Eerdmans, 1999), 234.
102. Booty, *The Book of Common Prayer 1559*, 291–2.
103. Ibid. 291.
104. Gadamer, *Philosophical Hermeneutics*, 57. Italics original.

105. Booty, *The Book of Common Prayer 1559*, 290–1. The one asymmetrical promise in these vows is the wife's additional pledge of obedience to her husband.
106. Ibid. 292; Bruns, *Hermeneutics Ancient and Modern*, 261.
107. *Troilus and Cressida*, ed. Bevington, 69–70n.
108. C. C. Barfoot, 'Troilus and Cressida: "Praise Us as We Are Tasted"', *Shakespeare Quarterly* 39, no. 1 (1988): 53.
109. John Kerrigan, 'Shakespeare, Oaths and Vows', in *Proceedings of the British Academy Volume 167, 2009 Lectures*, ed. Ron Johnston (Oxford: Oxford University Press, 2011), 65.
110. Barry Windeatt, *Troilus and Criseyde* (Oxford: Clarendon Press, 1992), 247.
111. All references to *Troilus and Criseyde* are to: Geoffrey Chaucer, *Troilus and Criseyde*, ed. Barry A. Windeatt (London: Routledge, 1991).
112. Grace Tiffany summarises prominent 'defenses' from the 1970s and 80s, and critiques them as denials of Cressida's self-authoring agency. Tiffany, 'Not Saying No: Female Self-Erasure in *Troilus and Cressida*', *Texas Studies in Literature and Language* 35, no. 1 (1993): 45–8, 52. For a more recent reading of Cressida as victim see Laurie E. Maguire, 'Performing Anger: The Anatomy of Abuse(s) in "Troilus and Cressida"', *Renaissance Drama* 31 (2002). Jami Rogers surveys significant late twentieth-century productions which followed Juliet Stevenson's pioneering performance of Cressida as a victim in Howard Davies's 1985 Royal Shakespeare Company production (and contrasts these with 'post-feminist' twenty-first-century performances). Jami Rogers, 'Cressida in Twenty-First Century Performance', *Shakespeare* 10, no. 1 (2014).
113. Booty, *The Book of Common Prayer 1559*, 291.
114. Kerrigan, 'Shakespeare, Oaths and Vows', 82.
115. Taylor, *Sources of the Self*, 35.
116. *Troilus and Cressida*, ed. Bevington, V.ii.111n; Shakespeare, *Troilus and Cressida*, ed. Dawson, V.ii.104n. Henryson's *Testament* was first published as an addition to Chaucer's *Troilus* in William Thynne's 1532 edition and was included

with all subsequent sixteenth-century editions of Chaucer. Holly A. Crocker, *The Matter of Virtue: Women's Ethical Action from Chaucer to Shakespeare* (Philadelphia: University of Pennsylvania Press, 2019), 79–80.

117. Nikki Stiller, *The Figure of Cressida in British and American Literature: Transformation of a Literary Type* (Lewiston, NY: The Edwin Mellen Press, 1990), 37.
118. *Plays*, ed. Samuel Johnson, 8 vols (1765), quoted in *Troilus and Cressida*, ed. Bevington,V.iii.24n.
119. *Certain Sermons or Homilies*, 71.
120. *Troilus and Cressida*, ed. Bevington, V.iii.38n; *Troilus and Cressida*, ed. Dawson, V.iii.38n.
121. Claire Kenward, '"Of Arms and the Man": Thersites in Early Modern English Drama', in *Epic Performances from the Middle Ages into the Twenty-First Century*, ed. Fiona Macintosh et al. (Oxford: Oxford University Press, 2018), 432; Muir, *The Sources of Shakespeare's Plays*, 146.
122. *Troilus and Cressida*, ed. Bevington, V.vi.28n; *Troilus and Cressida*, ed. Dawson, V.vi.26SDn.
123. Calvin, *The Institution of Christian Religion*, 2.7.6.
124. John D. Cox, 'Shakespeare's Religious and Moral Thinking: Skepticism or Suspicion?', *Religion & Literature* 36, no. 1 (2004): 51.
125. Colin Burrow, 'Shakespeare and Epic', in *Epic Performances from the Middle Ages into the Twenty-First Century*, ed. Fiona Macintosh et al. (Oxford: Oxford University Press, 2018), 38.

CHAPTER 4

SEEING MERCY, STAGING MERCY IN *MEASURE FOR MEASURE*

The world's a Theater, the earth a Stage,
Which God, and nature doth with Actors Fill.

Thomas Heywood, *An Apology for Actors*[1]

Be ye merciful. Judge not, and ye shall not be judged. Condemn not, and ye shall not be condemned. Forgive, and ye shall be forgiven. Give, and it shall be given unto you; good measure, and pressed down, and shaken together, and running over, shall men give into your bosoms. For with the same measure that ye mete withal, shall other men mete to you again. And he put forward a similitude unto them. Can the blind lead the blind? [. . .] Why seest thou a mote in thy brother's eye, and considerest not the beam that is in thine own eye? [. . .] First thou hypocrite, cast out the beam out of thine own eye, and then shalt thou see perfectly to pull out the mote that is in thy brother's eye.

Luke 6: 36–42

Fourth Sunday after Trinity gospel reading,
The Book of Common Prayer 1559[2]

This self-overcoming of justice: one knows the beautiful name it has given itself – *mercy*; it goes without saying that mercy remains the privilege of the most powerful man, or better, his – beyond the law.

Friedrich Nietzsche, *On the Genealogy of Morals*[3]

For centuries, *Measure for Measure* has provoked spirited responses around the tensions which Nietzsche strikingly, provocatively captures. As Nietzsche sees it, when justice overcomes, when it surpasses itself as mercy, it becomes something sublime. Yet, there is a catch. Mercy sounds beautiful, but it is also the prerogative of those in authority.[4] It is the 'powerful' who have the capacity and the utility for benevolence, for action 'beyond the law'. Does the granting of mercy ultimately elide, or does it satisfy, the claims of justice? Can it simultaneously do both? Moreover, if mercy is given by the 'powerful', does this act divest its recipients of their own agency? *Measure* immerses its audience in these dilemmas as it sets forth the seemingly enigmatic, and complex, interconnections of justice, law, human agency and action, and the ideas behind the word which Shakespeare uses more times in this play than any other: mercy.[5]

Measure opens with its world's 'most powerful man' – Vienna's Duke – handing over his authority to his deputy, instructing him that 'Mortality and mercy in Vienna / Live in thy tongue and heart', and to 'enforce or qualify the laws / As to your soul seems good' (I.i.44–5, 65–6). Given this thematic interest, it is not surprising that *Measure* is Shakespeare's 'most biblical', 'most theological' drama.[6] Shakespeare gives his main characters religious identities and *Measure for Measure* is the only play title which he took directly from Scripture – Luke 6: 38: 'For with the same measure that ye mete withal, shall other men mete to you again.' The playwright did not have to reach too deeply into his memory to recover his scriptural source. Throughout their lifetimes, early modern people heard it read in church at least annually on the fourth Sunday after Trinity: one day in the English summer. Luke 6: 36–42 is that day's gospel reading. Like *Measure*, the biblical passage hinges on interplays between mercy, justice and law, between those who give and impose, and those who receive and accept. On the face of it, the reciprocity implied in Shakespeare's specific source (Luke 6: 38) signals retributive justice: measure for measure, the 'eye for eye, tooth for tooth' of Exodus 21: 24. Yet the verse's biblical and liturgical contexts insist that its readers and hearers think about mercy.

The Lucan excerpt, part of Christ's so-called Sermon on the Plain (Luke 6: 17–49), begins with mercy. 'Be ye merciful' is the foundational injunction, framing the actions which follow: 'judge not', 'condemn not', 'forgive', 'give' a 'good measure'; and, most memorably, Christ's 'similitude' (parable), which offers a specific instance of hermeneutic blindness: hypocrisy. Before correcting another person's vision, hypocrites must first 'remedy' – to employ one of *Measure*'s motifs – their own sight so that they can 'see perfectly' (or 'clearly').[7] Seeing is the pivotal trope in this reading. Early modern parishioners who were taking note (and it seems that Shakespeare was one of them), likely felt the weightiness of the seven pithy verses in which Christ exhorts his listeners to be clear-sighted interpreters of God, other people and themselves. In the logic of this passage, people's reading of divine mercy informs their view of themselves and motivates their day-to-day interactions. The implications of seeing and understanding divine mercy are personal and concrete.

That much is apparent. But what is the character, the scope, of the divine mercy which Christ tells his listeners to imitate? In Shakespeare's post-Reformation, Protestant England this was a pressing question, taking people from the church pews to a site of fierce theological contention. *Measure*'s Lucio alludes to this doctrinal battleground: 'Grace is grace, despite of all controversy' (I.ii.21). Hermeneutic disputes about the workings of divine grace and mercy (and their theological cognates forgiveness and pardon) figured largely in the seismic division of the Catholic Church and reconfigurations of people's understanding of human being. Hans-Georg Gadamer identifies the pivotal ideas that brought about these changes. For him, the Reformers' 'return to Scripture' (*sola scriptura*) and democratisation of Bible reading (the priesthood of all believers) 'turned up [. . .] the very message of the holy scriptures'. Scripture's leitmotif is that 'not obedience to the law and the performing of meritorious works but faith alone [. . .] promises justification', that is, salvation.[8]

Justification is of course the close neighbour of justice. Is the Reformers' insistence that people are justified only through placing their faith in divine grace the self-overcoming of justice with mercy? Certainly, this view of salvation was disquieting, standing 'in the way of the natural prior self-understanding that human beings had of themselves' (as Gadamer phrases it).[9] By 'natural prior self-understanding', Gadamer alludes to Roman Catholicism's doctrine of justification that appears to accommodate justice, derived as it is from the belief that God accounts sinful people righteous through the aggregate of his merciful forgiveness of them and individuals' moral merit and religious works. Elsewhere, Gadamer connects 'the genuine task of hermeneutics' to what he calls the 'fundamental strangeness and alien quality' of Protestantism's undoing of this thinking about salvation. A Protestant theology of grace, Gadamer states, 'represents a challenge that shatters all our natural expectations, for it does not correspond to our guiding ideas of reward and punishment or merit and blame'.[10] In the sixteenth century, this counter-intuitive message precipitated much controversy.

Not a lot has changed. Whether expressed in religious or secular keys, the idea of mercy, especially mercy entirely uncoupled from merit and works, continues to represent a challenge and, at times, provoke much indignation. Mercy without merit, an 'ontology of justification by faith' over an 'ontology of self-justification' (as Brian Gregor puts it), can be an affront to the modern Western sense of justice and understanding of the self as, above all else, a free agent.[11] Charles Taylor contends that a defining mark of the modern self is 'the independence of the subject, his determining of his own purposes without interference from external authority'. The modern self is a 'disengaged subject' who, as Ruth Abbey elaborates in her commentary on Taylor, 'rather than imagining itself as connected to some wider cosmic-cum-moral order [. . .] believes that it can properly understand and define itself in the absence of any attachment to this ambient reality'.[12] To critics such as Peter Holbrook, Shakespeare's works anticipate our own, post-Romantic, 'modern values' which cluster around this image of the independent, disengaged, self-determining subject, values such as 'freedom, individuality, self-realisation, authenticity'.[13] Claims that individuals do not have a hand in their own salvation swim against the fast-flowing current of this powerful discourse that brings together Shakespeare and modern identity.

Objection to the Reformers' seeming negation of this view of the self in their answer to that most urgent of questions in Shakespeare's day (how does a human being attain eternal salvation?) registers in some critical responses to *Measure*. To Sarah Beckwith, for instance, the Reformers' doctrine of justification deprived human beings of their personhood as 'it was axiomatic to reformed grace that as God-given, and to be God-given, it must be free of all human words and deeds'. Shakespeare, Beckwith argues, 'utterly abjures [this] eradication of the human' and exposes it in *Measure*.[14] Similarly, Devin Byker maps *Measure*'s central themes of mercy and justice onto the 'antagonistic relationship' of pre-Reformation and Reformation soteriology, opposing Catholic Isabella's enactment of 'intercessory speech' to the 'substitutionary logic' of the 'precise' – Puritan – Angelo.[15] Byker reads Shakespeare's play as siding with the former. Praying for the dead, priestly absolution and other forms of intercessory speech widely practised in late medieval England affirmed selfhood and agency, and also community, as these speech acts facilitated one person's contribution to another's salvation.[16] In contrast, 'by reducing intercession to a unique action appropriate to Christ alone', the Reformers' 'substitutionary logic' took away the opportunity for humans to speak and act meritoriously on others' behalf, leaving people alone to speak for themselves, and worse, unable to do so.[17]

Positioning Shakespeare as the Reformers' disputant rests on reading *Measure*'s two main figures of authority – the Duke (disguised for much of the play as a friar) and his deputy Angelo – as unambiguous theatrical analogues of the Protestant God or a Protestant theo-political ruler (a 'Christian prince' akin to England's James I), or more broadly, as exemplary of Protestantism.[18] Precise Angelo's *modus operandi* is, for Byker, emblematic of Protestantism's reductionistic, isolating 'substitutionary' soteriology. The Duke, as Beckwith interprets him, similarly demonstrates the ill effects of Protestantism. He represents the merger of church and state into a single, oppressive figure. Much like Protestant teaching, the Duke co-opts the 'internal forum' of the confessional for the service of the state and thus evacuates confession of inwardness and efficacy. In its place, he has 'theatricalized confession and evolved a form of theater to replace it', theatre which 'bypass[es] the volition of those involved'. The Duke becomes a figure of tyranny, exemplifying the dangers of a theo-political state and its '"remedies" for sin in the post-Reformation setting', that is, the Reformers' effacing theology of grace.[19] Neither the Duke nor the Reformers' theology fare well as Beckwith brings them together.

To focus on Shakespeare's character, Beckwith's reading certainly reflects the tide of critical opinion which has turned against him in recent decades. The Duke has, as Robert Watson puts it, been 'demoted' by most modern-day scholars and theatre practitioners. Formerly viewed as 'a wise, resourceful leader', he is now more often than not seen as embodying something much darker.[20] As Beckwith's argument indicates, much of the suspicion focuses on the Duke's puppeteer-like theatricality. *Measure* opens with him distributing executive roles to Angelo and Escalus, and declaring that he will 'privily away' (I.i.67). 'I love the people', the Duke insists, 'But do not like to stage me to their eyes' (I.i.67–8). Yet, in a categorical contradiction of this assertion, publicly staging himself is exactly what the Duke does across the play's duration, as he doubles in the roles of absent sovereign and present (surveilling) spiritual counsellor. His ambiguous subjectivity, together with the questionable theatre he scripts, stage manages and enacts, are for many critics *Measure*'s chief crux.

The awkward comic reversal the Duke engineers in the play's final act has especially galvanised much critical displeasure. The resonance of this metatheatrical climax with a scene of judgement sets up the expectation of Vienna's ruler-judge both disburdening himself of his role-playing and dramaturgy, and bringing about a just resolution. The Duke does neither. Instead, he stages Isabella's and Mariana's shaming before he arranges marriages (including his own) and distributes pardons (mercy) with a seemingly heavy-handed, imperious command of his own, and Shakespeare's, stage.

Of course, not everyone considers this dénouement and the figure holding centre stage problematic and vexatious. Debora Kuller Shuger describes the Duke's forgiveness of Claudio, Angelo, Barnardine and Lucio as 'his extravagant abjuration of the penal [. . . that] enacts, in an uncomfortably literal fashion, the ideal of Christian justice'. Shuger groups the Duke's 'exercise of penitential justice' with what she sees as his pastoral concern for his subjects' salvation. This pairing styles the Duke as a 'sacral ruler' (God-like monarch) – the figure pivotal to a 'Christian social order', this being the 'ideal [. . .] of Christian polity' that 'Anglican orthodoxy' (which Shuger distinguishes from English puritanism) shared with James I.[21] Shuger's reading manifests belief: belief in the Duke, and belief in the (Protestant-Anglican) theo-political model of mercy she sees him enacting.[22]

Shuger's study has been prominent, but the weight of responses to *Measure* differ diametrically from hers. Along with Beckwith and Byker, more critics have doubted, indeed often expressed deep scepticism about both the Duke and (as they understand it) a Reformed figuring of mercy and grace which they associate with him, and his deputy.[23] Jeremy Tambling's working analogy is less specific – 'If the Duke is to be thought of as like God' (rather than like the God of Protestantism) – but Tambling's conclusion aligns with this disbelieving strain of criticism: *Measure*'s Duke-cum-God figure 'shows that theocracy depends on the assertion of the will, which includes the power of forgiveness.'[24]

In contrast to these polarised perspectives, *Measure*, it seems to me, elicits from its audience a mix of doubt and belief. Too often, the actions the Duke scripts for himself and others, including his own performance of mercy, cause us to question his self-perception, motives and his seeming overpowering of others' wills. The way the Duke inhabits his hermeneutical situation (to recall Gerald Bruns) is troubling.[25] But our suspicion need not extend to the Reformers' logic of grace as it features in *Measure*. Rather, in *Measure*, allusions to the Protestant account of how divine mercy meets human need brings to light the hermeneutic blindness, problematic nature and limitations of its play-acting Duke, and in so doing suggest his disconcerting likeness to his hypocritical deputy. Specifically, within their respective hermeneutical situations, neither judge clearly sees himself and, in consequence, neither enacts genuine mercy when confronted by the seemingly competing claims of mercy and justice.

'Heaven doth with us as we with torches do'

In this chapter, I draw on a popular Renaissance trope – *theatrum mundi* – to show the many-sided intersections between the Reformers' theology and *Measure*'s interrogation of the Duke and his fellow characters, especially Angelo. *Theatrum mundi*: the world as theatre, and reciprocally, the theatre as world. This topos chimes with *Measure*'s self-conscious metatheatricality. It was regularly used in the philosophy of the Stoics and Neoplatonists (including Seneca and Marcus Aurelius) and the theology of the Church Fathers (from John Chrysostom and Augustine to Bernard of Clairvaux), before becoming a 'general commonplace' again in the sixteenth century. Of course, the notion that the theatre stages a world which is itself theatricalised turns many people's thoughts at once to *As You Like It*'s Jacques's much recited 'All the world's a stage, / And all the men and women merely players' (II.vii.139–40). But prior to its introduction into the theatre by Shakespeare and others, the *theatrum mundi* trope had already gained currency via early modern theological works.[26]

Jean Calvin's employment of the metaphor is especially frequent, and panoramic. Robert White identifies 160 examples in his survey of approximately one-fifth of Calvin's voluminous oeuvre. In the *theatrum mundi*, as Calvin conceptualises it, God and humans are both sometimes protagonists and sometimes audience. As chief actor (and scriptwriter), God reveals and enacts his nature via his creation, his church and Christ.[27] In his commentary on Isaiah, Calvin figures creation as 'this faire theater of the world, where Gods glory shines round about and beneath vs' and the church as 'the most excellent theater of [God's] glorie'. It is in the New Testament that Calvin locates the pinnacle of divine revelation: 'the vncomparable goodnesse of God appeared vnto all the whole worlde vpon the crosse of Christe, as vppon a most gorgeous Theatre.'[28] Within the divine theatre, humans are, first of all, interpreting spectators, 'placed in this world, as vpon a spacious Theatre to behold the acts of our God [. . .] [and to] diligently and attentiuely [. . .] obserue and consider' God's self-revelation in creation, the church and, ultimately, Christ on the cross.[29]

Further, Calvin exchanges the roles of God and humanity. Humans are also actors. Our script is the will of God: enacting virtue.[30] Of all the virtues, to the divine playwright there is none 'more pleasing [. . .] then liberalitie', that is, mercy. Here, humans need divine intervention: God's mercy to be merciful. As Calvin puts it, 'mercifull men may as well be taken in the passiue signification, namely, for such to whom the Lord shewes mercie'.[31] Mercy must be first passively received before it is actively given. This emphasis on humankind's indigence does indeed confront the 'natural prior self-understanding' expressed in the view of the self which the Reformers disputed.[32] As interpreters and actors in the *theatrum mundi*, human beings are 'exposed' – visible, ultimately, before the divine protagonist who is not only creator and saviour, but also righteous ruler and judge.[33] Humans find themselves in need, Calvin suggests – in need of mercy from this judge.

Is *Measure*'s Duke an earthly counterpart of the divine judge and dispenser of mercy? The Duke certainly appears to think of himself as a sacral ruler or God figure, a self-understanding which is perhaps borne out by the religious attire with which he clothes himself. But *Measure* does not smooth the way for its audience to readily agree with the Duke. Instead, it directs us to question his interpretation of himself as it situates him as requiring mercy, rather than as a univocal embodiment of transcendent grace. Much more than an analogue of the divine playwright, *Measure*'s Duke is an exposed human actor. His overbearing, clumsy handling of his subjects shows that, like them, he too is 'frail'. In *Measure*, frailty images characters' moral shortcomings. Ironically, the play introduces this idea through Angelo. His 'we are all frail' cannot be more than a reflex, given that Angelo says these words as he denies leniency to Claudio for transgressing sexually while brazenly attempting to coerce Claudio's sister Isabella into sleeping with him (II.iv.132). By giving in to the very desire which he had boastingly declared that he could resist ("'Tis one thing to be tempted, Escalus, / Another thing to fall'), Angelo is, without doubt, the morally and spiritually bankrupt 'hypocrite' Isabella declares him to be (II.i.17–18; Vi.i.41).

Later, the Duke (as Friar) re-sounds Angelo's religiously charged vocabulary as he reflects on his deputy's duplicity: 'frailty hath examples for [Angelo's] falling' (III.i.181). But as *Measure*'s action unfolds, the role-playing Duke unwittingly betrays his own frailty, his fallenness. Like Angelo, the Duke manifests both religious pride (as will be seen) and hypocrisy. On the latter, I take my cue for my reading of Duke and deputy as hypocrites from the etymological roots of 'hypocrisy' and its theatrical resonances. Hypocrisy conveys notions of stage acting, feigning and pretence. As the Puritan preacher and author Robert Bolton explains, the Greek word for hypocrite (*hypokritēs*) 'signifieth a stage-plaier'.[34]

Hypocrisy was much discussed in Protestant England, in the main in relation to 'false religion'.[35] Alec Ryrie describes hypocrisy, the 'white Devil', as a 'perennial Protestant fear', a preoccupation which, as Lucia Nigri argues, goes a long way to explaining why the character of the hypocrite featured so regularly on the early modern English stage. This anxiety about hypocrisy went hand in hand with a new, and growing, concern with the 'ideal of sincerity', which John Jeffries Martin traces to the Reformers' theology.[36] As Jane Taylor notes, by the seventeenth century, 'hypocrisy' and 'insincerity' were almost interchangeable terms, as evidenced in texts such as Thomas Cooper's *The Estates of the Hypocrite and Syncere Christian* (1613), which connects hypocrisy and sincerity by contrasting them.[37] Interestingly, hypocrisy (insincerity), along with pride, are the only human 'vices' Calvin explicitly uncovers upon the stage of the *theatrum mundi*, the stage that should feature human beings' acts of mercy.[38]

In *Measure*, hypocrisy and religious pride cloud both Angelo's and the Duke's seeing of themselves and others, and direct the two rulers down problematic paths that either elide mercy (Angelo) or instrumentalise it (Duke). Unchecked hypocrisy and pride within the self distort these characters' postures in relation to mercy – a way of being, I suggest, which arouses the suspicion each attracts. Here, there are echoes of the Reformers' thinking. For them, hypocrisy and pride at once declare one's own self-determining independence and deny one's own need for mercy. Such an assertion of self-sufficiency is a 'self-contradiction': it undermines a person's humanity, defined, according to Luther and others, in the doctrine of justification by grace through faith alone.[39]

Eberhard Jüngel explains how the Reformers came to the seemingly paradoxical conclusion that relinquishing one's agency in the matter of salvation is key to realising one's humanity. Premised on an understanding of humans as 'ordered toward recognition', the Reformers contended that it is God's 'justifying activity' and the faith (absent of works) it elicits that gives humans 'irrevocable recognition'. Through this divine recognition, humans 'come to themselves outside of themselves [. . .] in relation to others and in relation to God'. Human being is interpersonal. By displacing God's already accomplished justification with the 'I' who is questing for self-recognition, individuals estrange themselves from others and God, and thus their own humanity.[40] One becomes, as Luther (and Augustine before him) put it, '*incurvatus in se*': 'turned in upon' oneself.[41]

Measure's Duke and Deputy come into focus as Jüngel expands on how, for the Reformers, striving for self-determining justification (before God) turns one in upon oneself and strikes at interpersonal connections. Not anchoring one's need for recognition in God's recognition opens the door to the possibility of 'the abuse of the wealth of relations in order ruthlessly to realise oneself in all relations' – the antithesis of mercy. Misuse of 'social positions of power' may be the vehicle for such mistreatment of others. But so too, Jüngel stresses, could 'moral rigorism': 'a kind of dictatorship of ruthless, moralistic egocentricism'.[42] Fuelled by a pride not dented by his own hypocrisy, Angelo's unyielding moralism is expressed in his merciless application of the law that evolves into his self-proclaimed descent into tyranny (II.iv.170). While Angelo refuses to be merciful (in the language of *Measure*'s biblical source), the sense that the Duke appropriates mercy for his own self-realisation, that is, insincerely, makes for a troubling end to his script.

Some characters have greater insight into mercy: Escalus, the Provost, Mariana and Isabella who, as I will show, particularly articulates and (eventually) embodies the Reformers' logic of grace. Isabella's actions in *Measure*'s final act are especially reminiscent of the climactic scene of divine grace: Christ's crucifixion. No doubt there is some irony to this association of a character who is desperately keen to be a Roman Catholic nun with one of the Reformers' flagship doctrines. But the same could be said of readings of the Duke-as-Friar's actions as emblematic of Protestantism. It is perhaps fitting that in a play deeply interested in disjunctions between outward appearance and inner reality, Isabella's theological professions do not neatly map the habit which the actor playing her usually wears. The 'rich confusion', as Kenneth Graham puts it, which ensues as Shakespeare obviously, yet superficially and unreliably, signals his principal characters' religious identities and sets his play in a Catholic locale, may be, Brian Gibbons and David Scott Kastan both suggest, a tactic the playwright employs. The eclectic configuration of place and characters in *Measure* dissociates Shakespeare's play from accusations of treading too near prominent theo-political issues and identities of early seventeenth-century Protestant London (a society which *Measure*'s Vienna just happens to resemble).[43]

Certainly, as Isabella puts forward Protestant-sounding reasons for why Angelo should be merciful to Claudio, she appears to assume that she and the deputy share a mutual understanding of the operation of divine mercy. Isabella is the character closest to the play's moral centre. This does not make her straightforward. Like the Duke, she has divided critics, animating much displeasure and much praise.[44] Isabella is not easily likeable, in some ways problematic and, as she affirms, also frail (II.iv.125–31). She is the character who most clearly expounds divine mercy. Yet this very same mercy, because of its personally challenging nature, brings out Isabella's particular embodiment of frailty, especially in *Measure*'s early acts. Mercy, the very action she must seek from Angelo, is at variance with Isabella's own disposition. She appears much more at home viewing and judging herself and others from within a hermeneutic of moral rigorism and retributive justice. Should mercy set aside the demands of law and justice? In different circumstances, Isabella and Angelo, one senses, might find themselves agreeing on their responses to this question.

'Like man new made'

In many ways, Isabella more closely resembles the judge to whom she appeals for mercy than the brother on whose behalf she speaks. When Lucio disdainfully describes Vienna's new ruler as one who 'doth rebate and blunt his natural edge' with 'study and fast', Isabella does not seem to share Lucio's disgust (I.iv.57–61). Indeed, Lucio's presentation of Angelo's abnormally dispassionate demeanour compares with the 'strict restraint' which Isabella seeks in the religious world of the cloister (I.iv.4). While showing Isabella's dissimilarity to the base Lucio may not trouble her (or anyone), *Measure* also explicitly contrasts her with the provost – a character who remains humane throughout the play. The provost makes himself vulnerable to the deputy's power play ('Do you your office, or give up your place') when he questions the necessity of Claudio dying for 'this vice' which 'all sects, all ages smack of' (II.ii.13, 5). Moments later, Isabella introduces her petition with that same word: 'vice'. Whereas to the provost Claudio's sexual transgression shows his humanity, Isabella distances herself from the common masses: 'There is a vice that most I do abhor, / And most desire should meet the blow of justice' (II.ii.30–1). This is moral rigorism hand in glove with retributive justice. Isabella's language is harsh; Angelo would likely applaud her tone and sentiment. At first blush, Isabella does not make for a promising heroine of a drama whose title upholds a mode of seeing and judging informed by mercy.

This is not to say that *Measure* pits law and justice against licence and pardoning, as though mercy is Vienna's silver bullet. In the previous scene, Escalus, another figure of moderation, had not only agreed with Angelo that Pompey the 'bawd' and company should be whipped, but had also reluctantly admitted that, while Claudio's death sentence 'grieves' him, Angelo's severity 'is but needful' to curb their city's immorality (II.i.187, 121–2, 240–3). Escalus acknowledges that 'pardon is still the nurse of second woe', a model of law and order which Angelo repeats when he denies Isabella's petition (II.i.245, II.ii.102–7). Justice is not mercy's antithesis. But where justice is impartial, mercy operates in a different, more personal, register. Escalus 'would save' Claudio in part because he 'had a most noble father'. The judge knows the offender's family (II.ii.6).

As she begins her suit, Isabella uses a narrow vocabulary, language which is very comfortable for Angelo to hear, and refute: please see Claudio's 'fault', not him, as the law's violator (II.ii.36–7). This is the domain of abstract, impersonal justice. Attributing responsibility to the fault alone strips the 'actor' of his agency as a human being, as though what was done and what will be done are transactions between law and act, involving no persons (II.ii.38). Isabella had already voiced her reluctance about saying even this. She is 'at war 'twixt will [plead] and will not [plead]' (II.ii.32–4). Not surprisingly, she easily cedes defeat to the 'just but severe law', a response which resounds in Angelo's 'Maiden, no remedy' (II.ii.43, 49). It is Lucio who compels Isabella to start again. He urges her to cease being 'too cold', and to instead 'entreat' and 'kneel', to 'hang upon his gown' and show that she does actually care more about her brother's life than her need for an object as trivial as 'a pin' (II.ii.44–7).

At this point, the keynote of Isabella's plea shifts from law and justice to mercy – from the impersonal to the personal. To repurpose Nietzsche, Isabella needed in a sense to overcome herself – that is, her default way of judging even her own brother – to enable her desire for justice to overcome itself as mercy. She calls on Angelo to do likewise. Isabella asks the deputy to see himself as the law's active interpreter, rather than its disinterested conduit, and to simultaneously view Claudio with humanity. 'Yes', there is a remedy, your honour: you. 'I do think that you might pardon him, / And neither heaven nor man grieve at the mercy' if you allow 'remorse' (sorrow or compassion, rather than personal guilt) to move your 'heart' (II.ii.49–50, 55).[45] Here, Angelo (and *Measure*'s audience) should recall his commissioning when the Duke had also connected Angelo's heart and his rule (I.i.44–5). But Angelo shows no signs of remembering.

Isabella's argument provides a suitable moment to highlight two ways in which Shakespeare's characterisation of the law in *Measure* reflects his own context. First, Isabella's contention that pardoning Claudio would not trouble heaven gestures to the close association of theological and legal discourses in England's Protestant polity. As David Loades explains, 'it was universally asserted that a valid statute must be consistent with the law of God'.[46] This belief flowed from the top down. James I figured a ruler as God's earthly 'Lieutenant'. The King should 'Obserue the statutes of your heauenly King / And from his Law, make all your Lawes to spring'.[47] The shaping influence of the Bible's moral law on English law can be seen in the involvement of the courts in matters of sexual 'sin'. From about 1580, law-breaking 'fornication', mirrored in Angelo's description of Juliet as 'the fornicatress', included 'ante-nuptial sexual activity', that is, the long-standing and accepted tradition of pre-church wedding espousals (II.ii.24). It is important to note that, as Diarmaid MacCulloch points out, most of the English populace did not meet 'the new discipline' with dissension. Rather, this 'severe law' (in Isabella's words), 'went hand in hand with increasingly widespread strictness in sexual morality'.[48] Even *Measure*'s Claudio attributes his own sexual 'offence' to 'too much liberty' (I.ii.103, 107).

England's laws were strict. And yet their severity was balanced by the frequent practice of mitigating punishment. As B. J. Sokol and Mary Sokol point out, this leniency was a product of an ethos of 'sympathy'. Such fellow feeling was grounded in a belief in the inherent sinfulness of all people – the notion of original sin that has been a recurring motif throughout this book, and which Isabella alludes to as she tries to sway Angelo.[49] Another idea present in Protestant discourse, and implied in Isabella's situating of Angelo as the law's interpreter, underpins the very possibility of extending mercy to lawbreakers. The law, according to the Reformers, is a living text which must be interpreted to be rightly applied. As Calvin writes, 'in all the commaundements it is so manifest, that there are figurative speeches, meaning more in expressing part that he may worthily be laughed at that will restraine the meaning of the lawe to the narrownesse of the words'.[50]

Because it is laughable to restrict the law's meaning to its letter, 'it is euident', Calvin argues, 'that sober exposition doest passe beyond the wordes'. For him, the two key principles in God's moral law are that it directs first, the worship of God 'with pure faith and godlinesse', and second, the 'embrace of men with vnfained loue' – 'the rule of charitie'. Love (charity) was also, in Calvin's reading of the Old Testament, the foundation of ancient Israel's judicial laws.[51] For Calvin, the rule of charity should be the linchpin of all laws in the post-biblical world. This proposition affords much capaciousness. Judicial laws must differ between nations and across time as 'enrollèd penalties' (as Claudio puts it) are interpreted, reworked and applied within the context of their use (I.ii.145).[52] The hermeneutical nature of this process provides the grounds for the clemency and equity evident in early modern English legal pronouncements, an understanding of the law echoing through the Duke's instruction to 'enforce or qualify the laws', Isabella's 'you might pardon him', and both the provost's and Escalus' earlier calls for Angelo to moderate Claudio's sentence.[53]

Angelo, of course, thinks differently, insisting on the law's moral strictness and immutability rather than its hermeneutic nature (II.ii.56, 72). Further, Angelo refuses to admit the personal dynamic at play in his judgement: 'It is the law, not I, condemn your brother' (II.ii.82). He denies that he 'can' pardon Claudio, that the rule of charity 'can' apply in this situation if he allows 'remorse' into his 'heart' (II.ii.52, 53, 55). As Isabella attempts to change Angelo's heart and thus his mind, she invokes both 'heaven' and 'man' as judges of his judgement. In the temporal sphere, as Angelo moves among men, he would adorn himself with that which best befits a man occupying his office by pardoning Claudio. More than 'the king's crown', 'the deputed sword', 'the marshal's truncheon' or 'the judge's robe', mercy is the highest attribute of those in authority (II.ii.61–2). But the deputy shows no interest in hearing how he should do his job. Realising this, Isabella escalates her case by assigning him an entirely different role. He is no longer the judge, but the one under judgement – God's judgement.

Viewed from heaven's perspective, human judges are indistinguishable from all other people. Angelo had pronounced Claudio 'a forfeit of the law'. Isabella could be reading from the Reformers as she refracts Angelo's words through a theological prism: 'Why all the souls that were, were forfeit once' (II.ii.73, 75). Vienna's law condemns Claudio. The effect of God's 'spirituall lawe', Calvin asserts, is the forfeit of all souls.[54] Here, the problem is not the law, but human lawbreakers. For if any person could perfectly keep God's moral law, they would indeed be 'accounted righteous before the heauenly throne of iudgement'; they would be rewarded with 'eternall saluation'.[55] However, humanity's fallen condition makes it 'impossible to keepe the lawe'. As such, 'of it selfe [the law] can doe nothing but accuse, condemne and destroy'.[56] Taking his readers on a lightning-fast journey to the 'farthest time in memorie', Calvin insists that not one of the 'holy men' of history has 'attained to the full perfection of loue' codified in the law, nor 'not beene troubled with concupiscence (sin)'. Calvin challenges his readers to deny his reading of the human condition: 'Who can say nay?'[57]

As the vehicle of divine justice, God's moral law convicts all. This appears a grim take on both the God who rules the *theatrum mundi*, and the predicament of frail human actors whom he has seemingly ambushed by giving them a law that inevitably condemns them and thus causes despair. Calvin acknowledges this possible grievance: 'Wilt thou say then, Doth the Lord so mocke us? For how finally doth it differ from mocking, to shew foorth a hope of felicitie [. . .] when in meane season the entrie vnto it is foreclosed and impossible to be come to?'

In his response, Calvin recognises that despair is quite possibly a person's experience if all one sees is the law.[58] However, he argues, human misery is not the end of the law.

Rather, because it causes people to realise their indigence, the law turns the human gaze away from itself to grace:

> And whereas the iniquitie and condemnation of vs all is sealed by the testimonie of the law, it is not done for this purpose [. . .] God hath concluded all vnder vnbeliefe [. . .] that they being naked and emptie, may flee to his mercie [. . .] [and] take hold of it alone insteede of righteousnesse and merites.[59]

Mercy does not so much overcome justice as fulfil its demands. For Calvin, it is when Christ on the cross took up the centre stage of world history ('as vppon a most gorgeous Theatre') that God simultaneously enacted justice and mercy. In Christ's substitutionary death, 'the damnation of all men was shewed, sinne was abolished [and] saluation was giuen vnto men': divine justice was satisfied and divine mercy proclaimed.[60]

As she takes Angelo into terrain which should be familiar to him, Isabella's line of argument resembles Calvin's logic. Although divine justice necessitates that all souls are forfeit, 'he that might the vantage best have took / Found out the remedy' (II.ii.75–7). Isabella hypothesises about Angelo's destiny if God was only just and not also merciful:

> How would you be
> If he, which is the top of judgement, should
> But judge you as you are?
>
> (II.ii.77–9)

Isabella implies, of course, that Angelo would fare badly if his judge were not forgiving. Puritan Angelo would have found it difficult to dispute Isabella's theology as a general principle. However, given the growing indications that Angelo believes himself to be exceptionally righteous, one can imagine him flinching when Isabella lumps him together with the rest of humanity as needful of heaven's merciful judgement. Further, he may especially take issue with her omission of any suggestion that his own moral strictness has gained him at least some credit with the divine judge.

Both sides of this equation – human sin does not nullify God's mercy; human merit does not contribute to God's mercy – re-sound the Reformers' account of how God saves humans. Jüngel's synthesis of the implications of this theology is elucidatory. The meaning of 'justification of sinners' 'forbids identifying the self either with the *best act* one has committed or with the *worst act*'.[61] It is this disengagement of people's actions from their salvation, their agency from their identity and destiny, that Beckwith and early modern Roman Catholic theologians before her object to. The Reformers' theology of justification, Beckwith argues, makes 'any hermeneutics of human agency impossible'. Or, in the words of the Council of Trent's 'Decree on Justification' (1547), any person is 'anathema' who says that 'nothing else [besides faith alone] is required to co-operate in order to the obtaining the grace of Justification, and that it is not in any way necessary, that [the impious] be prepared and disposed by the movement of his own will'.[62]

In contrast, for the Reformers, it is emphasising what a person does which threatens personhood. To them, because personhood comes by way of 'God's recognition' of oneself, people must be seen, and see themselves, as 'more than simply an agent'. The self is 'constituted through the very exclusion of human self-realisation'.[63] Does this theology shape an account of human subjectivity that excludes human action, and by implication disregards the self's moral and social being and responsibility? Not according to the Reformers, for whom 'justification can have consequences in human action, but it can never have causes in it'. These are Beckwith's words, yet with her next sentence she elides the nuance in her first clause: 'This is an astonishing, impossible obliteration of the world of human action, and of the human conditions of feeling, acting, and doing.'[64] The Reformers thought otherwise. Luther captures their consensus: 'We do not become righteous by doing righteous deeds but, having been made righteous, we do righteous deeds.'[65]

Isabella concludes her initial argument for Claudio's life with a plea for action reflective of this transformation. 'Think on' God's merciful treatment of you Angelo, 'And mercy then will breathe within your lips / Like man new made' (II.ii.79–81). Isabella's construction – someone else does the re-making – brings to mind Calvin's insistence on using the passive tense to describe the event of salvation.[66] Isabella wants Angelo to do righteous deeds, specifically, to enact in the divine *theatrum mundi* the virtue which (according to Calvin) God most desires human actors in receipt of his mercy to perform. This movement from passively accepting divine mercy to actively being merciful to others follows the logic of *The Book of Common Prayer* (*BCP*) that allocates Shakespeare's biblical source – Luke 6 – to the fourth Sunday after Trinity. In the annual rhythm and flow of the liturgy, the Trinity Sundays, which focus on how justified believers should live, do not stand alone. Instead, the springtime season of Easter, the church's celebration of God's acts that secured humans' justification, precedes the Trinity Sundays. To be merciful 'as your Father also is merciful', one must first experience mercy as a person who has been 'new made' through Christ's crucifixion and resurrection.

Cultivating humble, sober self-awareness in the light of what Easter signifies about human beings' mutual wretchedness and need for mercy is, according to Calvin, key to understanding Luke's passage. Calvin reads 'judge not' as Christ not 'preciselye restrain[ing] from iudgeing'; instead, he wants to cure people from the almost universal 'disease' that causes 'euery man [to be] a seuere censor against others'. Christ's words call for 'iudgement according to the rule of charitie' that, crucially, must be preceded by the judge's 'iudgement at himselfe'.[67] Judging oneself first holds in check one's judgement of others. Charity and self-awareness frame Christ's articulation of the idea of 'measure for measure' that, in Luke's gospel, elaborates on an already-stated posture of generosity: 'give, and it shall be given unto you'. In Calvin's interpretation, Christ puts the onus on the first actor in an interpersonal hermeneutical situation to 'sheweth himselfe louing, gentle, and right towardes his brethren'. For the most part, this person 'shall feele the same gentlenesse of others towardes himselfe'.[68]

Not everyone reads 'measure for measure' this way. Tambling, for one, argues that the saying denotes law – specifically, fulfilment of the Old Testament law, inclusive of revenge – and the *lex talionis*. In the gospels, Christ, according to Tambling, upholds this notion of 'eye for eye, tooth for tooth': tit for tat; balancing the scales; reactive, retributive justice.[69] Contrary to Tambling, Calvin reads Christ's words as taking his listeners a long way from the *lex talionis* and into the domain of charity and self-understanding. Isabella urges Angelo to adjust his own vision with this perspective on 'measure for measure'. By clearly seeing his own indigence and God's largesse toward him, Angelo will judge 'like man new made'. When he refuses, Isabella, with increasing boldness, links Angelo's unwillingness to the two specific vices which Calvin features in the unfolding drama within the divine *theatrum mundi*: pride and hypocrisy.

'False seeming'

In his commentary on Isaiah, Calvin derides Sennacherib, King of Assyria and Israel's enemy, for his pride. To Calvin, Sennacherib is a 'tyrant', whose 'belch[ing]' out of blasphemies, oblivious to God's imminent destruction of him, 'manifests and brings his vntamed pride forth vpon the stage'.[70] Isabella's tone takes on a similarly contemptuous quality as she lays the blame for Angelo's resistance to tempering 'justice' with 'pity' on the deputy's 'tyrannous' use of his 'giant's strength' (II.ii.102, 103, 111). Like proud Sennacherib, Angelo has overlooked the distance between himself and God. 'Jove' possesses the power to 'thunder', to issue a 'sharp and sulphurous bolt'; in contrast, 'man, proud man' is merely 'dressed in a little brief authority' (II.ii.115, 114, 119, 121–2).

By figuring human authority as an integument, Isabella emphasises that it is extrinsic to human nature, and ephemeral. Granting humans the omnipotence of Jove is not the solution. Unlike 'merciful heaven', who reserves condemnatory judgement for the 'unwedgeable and gnarlèd oak', while sparing the 'soft myrtle', if humans could 'thunder' as Jove does, 'every pelting officer / Would use his heaven for thunder, nothing but thunder!' (II.ii.119–20, 117–18). This is a ratcheting up of Calvin's assertion that all people (even those who have experienced divine mercy) lean towards harshness in their judgement of others. Sovereign power in human hands would be frightening, marked by unceasing oppression of others rather than mercy, Isabella charges.

Indeed, Isabella identifies a double danger in investing humans with some authority. Not only is 'proud man' inclined towards tyranny, but he is also a prime candidate for hypocrisy. In the form of two 'sayings', Isabella articulates a maxim which is no less true in our own day than it was in Shakespeare's: people in authority appear immune from the rules condemning the same behaviour in those of lesser status (II.ii.137, 131–2, 134–5). It is this social inequity, accompanied by a sense of privilege and protection, which makes positions of power fertile grounds for hypocrisy. 'Authority', Isabella contends,

> though it err like others,
> Hath yet a kind of medicine in itself
> That skins the vice o'th'top
>
> (II.ii.138–40)

Power can lead individuals to think that they can fool others into believing that they are spiritually and morally healthy, and into enacting what Robert Bolton called 'grosse hypocrisie'. Gross hypocrisy is blatant, knowing dissimulation 'by which a man professeth that which is not in his heart at all, and so deceiues others, but not his owne heart' (rather than 'formal hypocrisie', which includes self-deception). Utilising the *theatrum mundi* metaphor, Bolton depicts the 'grosse hypocrite vpon the stage of this world' as 'a very painted sepulchre and whited wall, glorious indeed in outward fashions and solennities'.[71]

As Angelo propositions and threatens Isabella, gross hypocrisy, grounded in assumptions of privilege and protection, is exactly what he flagrantly declares he will perform, in a move which echoes with chilling familiarity in present-day revelations of the interactions between powerful men and vulnerable women (and is also reminiscent of Cressida's predicament in *Troilus*). The deputy invokes his reputation ('my unsoiled name'), his religious persona ('th'austereness of my life'), the influence of his word ('my vouch against you'), and his position in society ('my place o'th'state') to flout Isabella's intention to 'proclaim' him for his 'seeming' (II.iv.156–7, 151–2). As Isabella had predicted, Angelo does abuse his authority. Yet, a warning is embedded in her choice of metaphor, a choice which chimes with Bolton's imagery. 'Medicine' implies illness. To Bolton, the hypocrite is a walking, well-attired, tomb. Merely covering over one's vice (applying authority's 'medicine') is, Isabella argues, no cure at all.

Instead, the path away from pride-fuelled hypocrisy and the self-destruction it foreshadows begins with a thorough self-examination which sees beneath the 'skin' and leads one towards mercy:

Go to your bosom,
Knock there, and ask your heart what it doth know
That's like my brother's fault. If it confess

> A natural guiltiness, such as is his,
> Let it not sound a thought upon your tongue
> Against my brother's life.
>
> (II.ii.140–5)

Isabella draws together ideas previously put to Angelo. She (and Escalus) had suggested that Angelo and Claudio are more alike than the deputy could imagine, or want to admit (II.ii.66, II.i.10–16). Both men could 'confess / A natural guiltiness'. 'Natural guiltiness' is reminiscent of the idea of original sin – universal human frailty. Continuing the play's focus on Angelo's heart, Isabella suggests that if he looked into its inner recesses he would find knowledge of his own fallen nature. She appeals to him to pair this self-knowledge with merciful action towards Claudio. The two men's manner of life may distinguish them, but their hearts unite them.

This time, Isabella's words appear to strike home. 'She speaks, and 'tis such sense / That my sense breeds with it' (II. ii.146–7). Isabella's 'sense' – the wisdom of her words – has given Angelo a glimpse into his heart, indeed into his possession of a heart as he experiences the arousal of his 'sense': libidinous desire. Isabella's twofold 'turn back' may be more germane than she intends (II.ii.148, 150). She, of course, wants Angelo to turn back to continue the conversation until he overturns his judgement of Claudio. But Isabella also, perhaps unwittingly, puts her finger on Angelo's suddenly urgent personal crisis as he finds himself dangerously close to a spiritual precipice. Earlier, Angelo had proudly asserted his immunity to temptation; now, he acknowledges (in an aside) that 'I am that way going to temptation' (II.i.17–18, II.ii.163). Across two soliloquies, *Measure*'s audience witness Angelo's inner turmoil as he comes face to face with the truth about himself, yet refuses to turn back.

His first soliloquy charts the abrupt reversal of his self-understanding as he is confronted with his own desire to yield to temptation. Musa Gurnis highlights the rapid-fire questions (eleven in twenty-six lines), thirty-two caesuras and fourteen extrametrical lines which convey the disturbance of body, feeling and mind quickening within the deputy:[72]

> What's this, what's this? Is this her fault or mine?
> The tempter or the tempted who sins most, ha?
> Not she, nor doth she tempt; but it is I
> That lying by the violet in the sun
> Do as the carrion does, not as the flower,
> Corrupt with virtuous season.
>
> (II.ii.167–72)

Here, Angelo shows lucidity and humility (which he will soon negate) as he acknowledges that his sin originates with him, not Isabella. The image he draws upon to figure his condition suggests that he is (at last) applying to himself the doctrine which he should know: original sin. Gurnis cites two Elizabethan writers, William Burton and Gervase Babington, who both point to the polarising action of the sun on flowers and carrions as analogies for God (the sun) and fallen human nature (the carrion). While God stands behind human actions, he does not, both men argue, cause these actions to become evil. Rather, the innate evil in human nature is brought out by God's inducement of the action, just as the sun's rays, while stimulating the sweetness of flowers, simultaneously intensify the stench of carcasses.[73] Relatedly, 'carrion' suggests the frequent biblical and theological use of 'flesh' to denote unregenerate human nature. Calvin, for instance, uses 'flesh' as the emblem for all human beings' entire postlapsarian state. 'Corrupted' flesh is in need of 'regeneration'.[74]

By comparing himself with the carrion, Angelo acknowledges his 'fleshliness'. Moreover, he accepts that he cannot separate this knowledge of who he is from what he does, especially what he does as a judge of others, as he pairs ontology and action: 'Oh fie, fie, fie, / What dost thou or what art thou, Angelo?' (II.ii.176–7). That same day, Angelo, believing himself to have scrupulously observed the law, had argued that its application is independent of human interest (II.i.18–31). Now that he is en route to committing the very wrongdoing which will end Claudio's life, Angelo realises that law enforcement is not so cut and dried:

> O let her brother live!
> Thieves for their robbery have authority
> When judges steal themselves.
>
> (II.ii.179–81)

Angelo does not transcend the fallen condition of those whom he judges. This newly discovered self-knowledge also refigures his understanding of his relation to the law. He admits that the law may be hermeneutical. In his office, he does possess agency to 'enforce or qualify the laws' and, as the Duke had suggested, his 'soul' is implicated in these actions (I.i.65–6). Claudio's life rests as much in Angelo's own keeping – in the workings of the law enforcer's inner life – as the law's. In recognition of their mutual fleshliness, the deputy knows that he could look upon Claudio with fellow feeling, turn back, moderate his application of the law and let Claudio live.

But there are strong hints that Angelo will not do this. He concludes this soliloquy by juxtaposing his horrified recognition of his susceptibility to temptation with an interpretation of the process redolent with religious pride. When coupled with authority, pride, Isabella had warned Angelo, is the seedbed of hypocrisy and tyranny. Here, he affirms her insinuation that she was not just speaking theoretically as he almost sanctifies his own version of lust: 'O cunning enemy, that to catch a saint / With saints dost bait thy hook!' (II.ii.184–5). Biblically, the appellation 'saints' (*hagios*, a most holy thing) applies to all Christians corporately. One joins the company of the saints, according to Luther, by the grace of God. Saints are 'holy', but their holiness has been 'freely receaue[d]', not 'as they them selues haue gotten by their owne industrie, good workes and merites'.[75] Saints have, one could say, a passive, rather than an active, holiness. Angelo, however, appears to have active holiness in mind when he singularises 'saint'. It becomes a self-designation, a self-justification. The 'enemy's' need to resort to tempting him with a fellow saint only emphasises his own saintliness. Even as Angelo demonstrates some comprehension of his and Claudio's mutual frailty, his vainglory persists, underscored by his insistence that, although 'virtuous' Isabella 'subdues me quite', his 'temper', his composure, had never been 'stir[red]' by 'the strumpet' (II.ii.187–90).[76]

The next day, the warning signs multiply. Like *Hamlet*'s Claudius, Angelo cannot pray:

> When I would pray and think, I think and pray
> To several subjects: heaven hath my empty words,
> Whilst my invention, hearing not my tongue,
> Anchors on Isabel. Heaven in my mouth,
> As if I did but only chew his name,
> And in my heart the strong and swelling evil
> Of my conception.
>
> (II.iv.1–7)

One can imagine Angelo having a restless night. This time, he is the one who brings up the subject of his heart. Isabella had urged him to look inward and see what his heart reveals about himself. Now he knows, and that knowledge is foreboding. Angelo realises that, because of the state of his heart, his attempts to pray are nothing more than mastication. And for an early modern Protestant, an inability to pray would have been troubling, indicating that he is in a spiritually perilous position.[77]

Yet his predicament need not have been fateful. All Protestants, Ryrie notes, knew that there was one prayer anyone 'could and must' pray and that, importantly, God would answer: 'a prayer of heartful repentance'.[78] As discussed in Chapter 2, repentance is a spiritual turning back: a 'changing of the minde or purpose' such that one experiences 'a true turning of our life vnto God'.[79] Angelo does not repent. Instead, he moves himself further away from God. In this soliloquy, the deputy casts off his previously cherished 'gravity' and reduces himself to his base appetites:

> Blood, thou art blood:
> Let's write 'Good Angel' on the devil's horn
> 'Tis not the devil's crest.
>
> (II.iv.9, 15–17)

More than acknowledging his 'natural guiltiness', which is what Isabella had asked him to do, Angelo now centres his identity on evil. The title 'Good Angel' will not reform his 'devil's horn' (his true identity) and Angelo has hardened himself with unconcern about this 'false seeming' (II.iv.15).[80]

On Isabella's return, Angelo shows how his blood will dictate his actions as he places her in a double bind. She could 'redeem' Claudio. How? By 'giv[ing] up [her] body' to Angelo (II.iv.53–4). Redemption is, of course, a theologically resonant metaphor. Christ's willing sacrifice of his body redeems fallen humans from eternal death. The redemptive act Angelo seeks to coerce from Isabella is a monstrous parody of the exchange at the heart of this divine undertaking. It is 'foul redemption', as Isabella exclaims, the antithesis of 'lawful mercy' (II.iv.113–14). When his 'pernicious purpose' sinks in, Isabella's immediate impulse expresses, I think, what we all want: justice through the exposure of Angelo's 'seeming, seeming' (II.iv.151). She drops her deferential form of address: 'I will proclaim thee, Angelo [. . .] I'll tell the world aloud / What man thou art' (II.iv.152, 154–5). She will unmask him. But she cannot. Angelo's flawless reputation and powerful station, as well as his testimony (lies) against her, he threatens, will 'stifle' her words (II.iv.155–60). He will exploit his 'false seeming' to silence Isabella even as he 'prove[s] a tyrant' to Claudio (II.iv.15, 170).

Ironically, it is the deputy's change of mind about the law's hermeneutic nature which facilitates his enactment of gross hypocrisy via this conception of himself as a tyrant. In his previous conversation with Isabella, Angelo had situated himself as entirely uninvolved in his administration of the law. Now, he collapses the proper boundaries between himself and the law: 'I, now the voice of the recorded law, / Pronounce a sentence on your brother's life' (II.iv.61–2). Escalus soon confirms Angelo's intimation that he views himself as synonymous with the law: 'my brother justice have I found so severe that he hath forced me to tell him he is indeed Justice' (III.ii.215–7).

Asserting one's own status as justice itself shows that, if he already was not, Angelo has now become thoroughly turned in upon himself. Previously, he had placed himself under the law's authority (II.i.29–31). Here, consumed by his lust, Angelo subjects both the law and others to his devilish will. He crushes the law and others' personhood as he restates to Isabella the bitter choice he puts before her:

> I give my sensual race the rein
> [. . .]
> redeem thy brother
> By yielding up thy body to my will.
>
> (II.iv.161–5)

If Isabella refuses, Angelo will ensure that Claudio dies a cruel death (II.iv.166–8). Making one's will law, 'bidding the law make curtsey to their will, / Hooking both right and wrong to th'appetite' (as Isabella phrases it), is self-realisation manifest as ruthless self-interest (II.iv.176–7).

Angelo does 'stifle' Isabella and she foresees only one – tragic – end: Claudio's death (II.iv.159, 178–9). *Measure*'s audience, however, know differently. For us, the continued presence within the *theatrum mundi* of the disguised Duke adumbrates the possibility that Isabella's and Claudio's fortunes will be reversed. The juxtaposition of Isabella's words of resignation and exit with the Duke's reappearance and his first words to Claudio amplifies this possibility: 'So then you hope of pardon from Lord Angelo?' (III.i.1). Hope momentarily takes the place of despair as *Measure*'s spotlight shifts from Angelo to the Duke. However, another juxtaposition, the parallels between his deputy's hypocrisy and the Duke's own donning of an external (religious) persona to conceal his true nature, complicate and subvert expectations that *Measure*'s plot will now track straightforwardly towards a comic conclusion. Instead of transcending and resolving his city's problems, the Duke is soon entangled in them in ways that bring out his ambiguous subjectivity, indeed his frailty, as he takes over the plot in Vienna's *theatrum mundi*.

'Craft against vice'

When the Duke first announces his intention to make use of the theatrical nature of his world, it seems that the primary role he scripts for himself is that of spectator. He will 'behold [Angelo's] sway' from within the costume that allows him to 'bear [himself] / like a true friar' and predicts that his deputy will reveal himself as a 'seemer' (I.iii.44–5, 48–9, 55). This arrangement of roles in his theatre may well offer us a clue to the Duke's self-understanding. Across the multifarious usages of the *theatrum mundi* topos from antiquity to the seventeenth century, spectators were often figured as superior to actors (a hierarchy we have evidently reversed in the modern world). Reflecting on this commonplace idea via a quotation attributed to Pythagoras, Enno Ruge notes that actors were considered '"slavish men" who foolishly and compulsively pursue worldly aims'. In contrast, spectators were '"the best people"'. They have the wisdom to stand apart from the 'world of appearances' and evaluate that which is before their eyes, specifically, 'the vanity, hypocrisy and falseness of people'.[81]

The Duke's figuring of himself as a spectator also associates him with other disguised ruler protagonists of early Jacobean dramas. Through covertly observing the failings of his subjects and substitutes, the disguised ruler comes to recognise that he alone can rule and reform his domain. His sovereignty thus affirmed, he then precedes to reveal his real identity.[82] *Measure*'s Duke sets himself up in his *theatrum mundi* as wise, moral spectating ruler (who will likely uncover Angelo's vanity, hypocrisy and falseness). He beholds, Angelo acts. However, the theological configuration of the trope, a constant background presence throughout Shakespeare's play, works against the Duke's arrangement of his theatre. Not only do human actors inadequately execute the divine playwright's script (which thematises mercy), but also, as Ruge observes of Calvin's employment of the *theatrum mundi* metaphor, humans prove equally unfit as spectators.[83] Postlapsarian blindness frustrates human beings' ability to truly interpret God's actions in his theatre as revelatory of his 'glorie'. As such, 'scarsely the hundreth man [one person in a hundred] is a true beholder' of divine glory.[84] Calvin doubts the hermeneutic ability of human 'beholders' – the very role *Measure*'s Duke takes upon himself.

Moreover, to Calvin, a person is at once audience and actor in God's *theatrum mundi*. Vienna's sovereign initially figures himself as omniscient, but he is soon drawn into the play-world's action both in the assumed role of Friar and in those moments when he – sometimes unwittingly, sometimes knowingly – steps outside this part to enact another character: the Duke who speaks and acts in Friar's integument. *Measure* directs its audience to evaluate the Duke as both spectator and actor, especially his interpretations of himself as he performs different parts. As we carry out this hermeneutic role, we have an analogue from within the play: Lucio. Lucio (without an equivalent in Shakespeare's key sources), is the self-appointed interpreter of the Friar-Duke and of another character whom the Duke creates: 'the absent Duke', an appellation only used by the Duke himself (III.i.195, III.ii.106, IV.ii.115).[85]

As Lucio forms his judgement of the Friar-Duke via ironic contests with this character over the truth about the absent Duke, theatregoers become increasingly aware of the Duke's belief in his own exceptionalism. Like Angelo, this self-understanding centres on his sexual abstinence. In a society in which 'lechery' is 'too general a vice', chastity becomes a distinguishing mark of a righteous life (III.ii.86, 88). When Lucio postulates that the Duke 'had some feeling of the sport, he knew the service', the Friar-Duke's response is categorical: 'The absent Duke', he insists, was not 'much detected for women, he was not inclined that way' (III.ii.104–7). Lucio's knowledge claims about his sovereign are incendiary. His words could well have him convicted of slander in the Court of Star Chamber.[86] All the same, the Duke seems too concerned to deny his interest in women. His refutation of Lucio repeats his earlier self-description as he charges Friar Thomas to 'Believe not that the dribbling dart of love / Can pierce a complete bosom' (I.iii.2–3).

The similarities between the Duke and the character he sets himself over to behold are unmissable. Both Duke and deputy idealise temperance and, more to the point, see themselves as representatives of this ideal. To Friar Thomas, the Duke portrays Angelo as barely human. Angelo 'scarce confesses / that his blood flows, or that his appetite / Is more to bread than stone' (I.iii.53–4). Ironically, the Duke cannot hear in his censure of Angelo the echoes of his very recent declaration of his own invulnerability to human passion. He 'hath a purpose', the Duke tells Friar Thomas, 'more grave and wrinkled', more virtuous, 'than the aims and ends / Of burning youth' (I.iii.4–6). The obvious religious associations of the Duke's self-description suggests that his choice to garb himself in religious clothing is more than just a convenience. Rather, his disguise expresses his perception of himself. As Beckwith notes, across several Jacobean disguised-ruler plays, *Measure*'s Duke is the only authority figure who chooses to take on a friar's persona.[87]

Like Angelo, religious pride disposes the Duke to self-righteousness. Moreover, as each claims to be invulnerable to sexual temptation, the two rulers also share a want of self-knowledge. Each disavows the possibility, but both characters find themselves desiring intimacy with a woman, indeed the same woman. For all Lucio's braggadocio, by *Measure*'s end the play proves him right when he says that the Friar is deceived about the Duke (III.ii.108). That is, the Duke is deceived about himself. Further (as with his deputy), the rift that opens between the glimpses which audiences receive of the Duke's inner self and the religious persona which he puts on engenders a growing sense that the Duke is turned in upon himself, bent on self-realisation.

His concern for his reputation is a significant case in point. When the Duke stages his departure in *Measure*'s opening scene, he depicts himself as humble and prudent. While he loves his subjects, he does not 'relish well / Their loud applause and aves vehement' (I.i.67, 69). Yet as the play progresses, the Duke comes across as anything but the self-effacing persona he constructs before Angelo and Escalus. Again, it is Lucio who appears able to get under the Friar-Duke's skin, indeed the Duke's religious disguise, as he characterises the absent Duke as 'a very superficial, ignorant, unweighing fellow' (III.ii.121). Ruffled, the Friar-Duke takes the bait, coming across as too eager to correct Lucio: 'Either this is envy in you, folly, or mistaking. The very stream of his life and the business he hath helmed must, upon a warranted need, give him a better proclamation.' The absent Duke's qualities and accomplishments, the Friar-Duke claims, would be apparent even to the 'envious' (III.ii.122–6). Perhaps the Duke can be excused for reacting to Lucio's provocations. However, later in the same scene the Duke engineers an opportunity to turn his conversation with Escalus to the absent Duke's reputation: 'I pray you, sir, of what disposition was the Duke?' 'What pleasure was he given to?' (III.ii.197–8, 201). Indications of vanity, hypocrisy and falseness evoke doubt about the role-playing Duke.

This suspicion grows when the Duke assumes the additional functions of playwright and stage manager in Vienna's *theatrum mundi*. The Duke's exertion of his controlling hand within his theatricalised world becomes more apparent when he scripts and directs the notorious bed-trick as his 'remedy' for Isabella's predicament (III.i.192). This foregrounding of the Duke as self-designated auctor occasions comparisons between Shakespeare's character and the divine scriptwriter. In theological uses of the *theatrum mundi* trope, God and humans exchange the parts of actors and spectators. But God alone is figured as (concurrently) transcendent playwright and stage manager. Sir Walter Raleigh takes up the metaphor: 'God hath written out for us, and appointed us all the parts we are to play.'[88] Calvin (in Ford Lewis Battles's summary), emphasies that, as scenes of 'creation, alienation, return, and forgiveness' unfold in Scripture and history, the main theme of 'the divine playwright's' narrative is his own unceasing concern to make himself known to his human audience and actors. Culminating in Christ's salvific crucifixion, all the divine acts within his 'universal theater [. . .] decode the message of a just and merciful God to his errant offspring'.[89]

The Friar-Duke presents his proposed bed-trick in language reminiscent of justice and mercy. That he does so only serves to emphasise the problematic nature of his plot development and raise questions about his motivation. The moral status of the bed-trick is, of course, contentious (III.i.192). Verna Foster outlines alternative interpretations of the act: Is it an 'immoral solution' or a 'necessary evil out of which good will come'? Among critics, the bed-trick has, Marliss Desens observes, elicited more disquiet than any other 'convention of the English Renaissance stage'.[90] Shakespeare further complicates our reading of his use of this device in *Measure* by offering a close-up of its orchestrator. The bed-trick invites the play's audience to search out the Duke's motives and thus question his likeness to the divine playwright.

Significantly, it is while enacting the part of Friar that the Duke presents Isabella and Marianna with his script, and the roles he has conceived for them. Isabella believes that it is Friar Lodowick who asks her to 'fasten [her] ear on [his] advisings' (III.i.191). He represents a figure of trust, which he perhaps plays up when he attributes his 'advisings' 'to the love I have in doing good' (III.i.191). Before she hears the details, it is already hard for Isabella to refuse. Marianna's decision to participate rests on her experience of the Friar-Duke as 'a man of comfort', a 'good friar' (IV.i.8, 50). 'She'll take the enterprise upon her, father', Isabella reports, repeating the word the Friar-Duke had used with her: 'If you advise it' (IV.i.63–4). The lineation and language here underscore the Friar-Duke's eagerness as he finishes Isabella's half-line: 'It is not my consent, / But my entreaty too' (IV.i.64–5).

Whereas Isabella and Marianna are swayed by the 'advisings' of the man they believe to be a good friar, *Measure*'s audience understand this character differently. Just before the Friar-Duke approaches Isabella with his scheme, we had seen him compromise, take advantage of perhaps, the religious office he signals. First, he asks the Provost to conceal him so that he can overhear Claudio and Isabella's conversation. Then, he seemingly violates the seal of confession and actually lies by telling Claudio that he is Angelo's confessor and that the deputy never intended to force sexual relations on Isabella (III.i.52, 159–67).

Claudio does not register alarm about the Friar-Duke's eavesdropping, nor his breach of the sacred trust of the confessional. Claudio has bigger worries, compounded by the Friar-Duke's blunt 'tomorrow you must die' which, the audience knows, is also disingenuous, hence almost cruel (III.i.166). Unlike Claudio, those of us who have a spectator's perspective do have cause to query the script of the Duke as Friar and the heavy hand he employs to execute it. Equivocal may be the best way of summing up the set of reasons he gives for the role he writes for Isabella: 'you may most uprighteously do a poor wronged lady a merited benefit, redeem your brother from the angry law, do no stain to your own gracious person, and much please the absent Duke' (III.i.192–5). Even as the bed-trick works dramatically for Shakespeare, his framing of its occurrence in his plot prompts disbelief towards his Duke. For one, we know that the Duke's second and third reasons are spurious: Claudio's life and Isabella's honour would be swiftly secured if the Duke stopped play-acting.

The Friar-Duke's first reason unconsciously (from his perspective) brings to the surface the taint of expediency affixed to his strategy. Marianna's wronging by Angelo calls for sympathy, but is the planned deceit of Angelo any less morally problematic? After all, while breaking off a betrothal because of a sunken dowry is a mercenary act and an 'unjust unkindness', Angelo did not contravene the law (III.i.227). He could legally break his 'contract' – the *sponsalia per verba de future*: a promise to marry in the future (III.i.206).[91] The idea of duping Angelo into having sex with Marianna bears too uncomfortable a resemblance to the deputy's blatantly immoral coercion of Isabella. Again, *Measure* hints at the two rulers' similarities. Or perhaps there is more than a hint. Both men make use of religious language to put the burden of responsibility on Isabella to 'redeem' Claudio through actions that compromise her morally and leave her vulnerable. Yet, both men could easily effect this 'redemption' by disclosing their own play-acting.

Out of character, and in soliloquy, the Duke draws a definite line between the two characters' actions: 'craft against vice I must apply' (III.ii.239). But in *Measure* that line becomes increasingly blurred. Indeed, the Friar-Duke's own circuitous language may betray that he feels some unease about his 'craft': 'I do make myself believe' (III.i.192). Evidently, the Friar-Duke does quiet his own concerns. Isabella, too, believes, which may just be a token of her own frailty. She expresses 'content' as the Friar-Duke concludes his presentation of his plan with a piece of consequentialist reasoning: 'the doubleness of the benefit defends the deceit from reproof' (III.i.240–1, 243). What is the double benefit, the justifiable ends, which the Friar-Duke lands on? First, his already-stated aims of extricating Isabella, Claudio and Marianna from their respective difficulties. To these he adds another hoped-for outcome, a new motivation: 'and the corrupt deputy [will be] scaled' (III.i.238–9).

The sense of 'scaled' here is of weighing, comparing.[92] Against what will Angelo's 'corrupt' behaviour be weighed and compared? Perhaps the Friar-Duke has in mind Vienna's law, or Angelo's own rigorous application of it. Or perhaps the 'deceit' inherent in the bed-trick itself will balance out the deputy's prior hypocritical duplicity. Certainly, Angelo's punitive experience of justice appears to be at the forefront of the Friar-Duke's mind as the crowning marker of the bed-trick's success. This is measure for measure, stripped of its biblical and liturgical context. The Friar-Duke has a point: from what we have seen, 'well-seeming Angelo' warrants a return measure for his behaviour; he deserves to be scaled (III.i.212). At the same time, by making exact, retributive justice the high point of his script, the Friar-Duke situates it several removes from the drama of mercy playing out in the divine *theatrum mundi*. This contrast shows the Duke's unlikeness to the divine playwright. When the Friar-Duke first introduces the bed-trick to Isabella, he states that it will 'much please the absent Duke' – the fourth reason for its enactment (III.i.195). Without dismissing his intention to benefit Marianna, is the Duke also pleased at the prospect of seeing Angelo get his comeuppance? The latter seems to be uppermost on the Duke's mind as he concludes his soliloquy:

> So disguise shall by th'disguised
> Pay with falsehood false exacting
> And perform an old contracting.
>
> (III.ii.241–4)

Of course, events after the bed-trick thwart the Friar-Duke's plotting of what, speaking as the Duke in an aside, he self-assuredly predicts will be a straightforward transaction: Claudio's pardon for Angelo's 'sin' (IV.94–5). Instead, the deputy's wrongdoing has the effect of reinforcing his hypocrisy, expressed in his further exploitation of his position and the law via the singular 'unwonted putting on' he delivers to the provost (IV.ii.94, 102–4). Forced into an impromptu rewriting of his script, the Friar-Duke must jeopardise his disguise (IV.ii.167). His costume, his 'coat, integrity [and] persuasion', had worked with Isabella and Marianna (III.ii.166). However, it does not convince the conscientious provost to swap impenitent Barnardine's head for Claudio's. Here, the Friar-Duke seems to have prepared for a plot twist. But his need to resort to plan B by invoking the signs of the Duke – his hand and seal – to divulge the absent Duke's imminent 'return' stretch the credence of his play-acting almost to breaking point (IV.ii.168). For theatregoers, I suggest that our knowledge of the dissonance between this outcome and the Duke's earlier confidence in the efficacy of his (already equivocal) scheme to 'scale' the deputy adds to our existing uncertainty about the Duke as both actor and playwright in the *theatrum mundi.*

When Barnardine, perhaps *Measure*'s most colourful character, insists that he 'will not consent to die this day, that's certain', the role of Friar-Duke and his script both appear to have reached their limits (IV.iii.47–8). Like Lucio, Barnardine is Shakespeare's creation independent of his sources. In his comic obstinacy, Barnardine shows no reverence for the religious persona before him, declaring that he 'will not die today for any man's persuasion' (IV.iii.51). In R. S. White's pithy phrase, he 'refuses to die simply to expedite the plot'.[93] To Barnardine, the Friar-Duke is merely one of 'any man', a point with which Shakespeare's play appears to agree. While the 'reprobate' probably would not make the distinction, *Measure* immediately lays emphasis on the Friar-Duke's status as a man, far removed from any transcendent authority such as the biblical God who has appointed the day of every person's death, as Job 14: 5 states (IV.iii.65). As a frail human actor and playwright, the Friar-Duke finds himself constrained by the very role he had put on to further his purposes. A friar (and a Duke) know that it is 'damnable' for Barnardine if he is 'transport[ed]' into the next life 'unprepared, unmeet for death' (IV.iii.58–60).

The Friar-Duke has written himself into a corner. We can sense his relief – 'Oh 'tis an accident that heaven provides' – when the provost presents him with a fix: Ragozine's head (IV.iii.68). Momentarily, the Friar-Duke situates himself as an indigent recipient of mercy from the divine playwright. But he does not dwell on the thought. Instead, he seemingly interprets this divinely orchestrated contingency as a prompt to immediately resume control over the action in his world. This time, he does this as he transitions his own role as an actor. From covert spectatorship as the Friar-Duke, he becomes the visible sovereign, the returning Duke who will preside over Angelo's public downfall 'by cold gradation and well-balanced form' and 'make [Isabella] heavenly comforts of despair / When it is least expected' (but not before lying to her about Claudio's death) (IV.iii.91, 101–2).

The Duke's 'plot' (as he puts it to Friar Peter while attired '*in his own robes*') appears to follow the trajectory of the disguised-ruler play: the Duke will reassert his authority as he unveils his identity (IV.v.2, oSD). However, it is difficult for *Measure*'s audience to forget that to this point the Friar-Duke's plotting (the bed-trick, the substitution of Barnardine for Claudio) had been foiled. The Duke himself is unfazed, staging his reassumption of power at the city gates, and arranging trumpeters to announce his return (IV.iii.123, IV.iv.4, IV.v.9, IV.vi.12, 14). To early moderns, this emphasis on both the meeting at the gates and the sound of the trumpets may well have turned their thoughts in two directions: the Royal Entry of James I to London on 15 March 1604 (as Gibbons notes) and biblical imagery depicting the eschatological king and judge.[94] The latter appears in two biblical books with which early modern English men and women were especially familiar: Psalms (Chapter 24) and Revelation. In Revelation 5, the author establishes that the future triumph of good over evil, announced by seven trumpet blasts across Chapters 8 to 11, is guaranteed by a past event – Christ's crucifixion, symbolised by a fragile 'Lambe [appearing] as though he had bene killed' (verse 6). The Geneva Bible glosses this verse as a 'vision [that] confirmeth the power of our Lord Iesus'. This is a paradox: sovereignty forged from seeming weakness.

Measure's Duke's staging of his return with echoes of England's Christian prince, the heavenly king's lieutenant, as well as the divine king himself, indicates that the Duke understands himself as a divine analogue. But if God is at once self-denying and all-powerful, the Duke's self-interpretation seems far from the mark. His actions and the events so far have aroused suspicion about his motivation and cast doubt over his authority. In *Measure*'s final single-scene act, the Duke's controlling theatricality continues on the stage he sets up as the scene of Angelo's judgement. As we watch, we also judge – not so much Angelo, but rather the Duke, especially when he enacts mercy in the semblance of divine mercy; mercy, seemingly, in the place of justice.

'Mercy is not itself that oft looks so'

For most of *Measure*'s long final act, mercy seems far from the Duke's mind. Instead, he leads his audience (both on and off the stage) to believe that open justice is foremost on his agenda. To *Measure*'s audience, the irony in the Duke's dissembling greeting of Angelo and Escalus is palpable: 'we hear / Such goodness of your justice' (V.i.5–6). The obvious doubleness of the Duke's next words seems to send the play's audience an even more pronounced knowing wink about his intentions: Angelo's 'desert speaks loud', and the Duke 'should wrong it / To lock it in the wards of covert bosom / When it deserves' to be engraved in brass – remembered in perpetuity (V.i.9–13).

'Desert' and 'deserving' are intrinsic to an economy of merit and its intersections with justice. As the Duke brings together merit and justice with *Measure*'s preoccupation with sincerity – the coherence of inner and outer self – he heightens the expectation that Angelo's gross hypocrisy will soon be laid bare. With the returned play-writing Duke starring as the judge in this most public court scene which he has put on, Angelo will receive his due desserts. *Measure* sustains this anticipation for several hundred lines. Justice is the keynote as accusations are made and denied, witnesses brought forth and interrogated, reputations commended and soiled, and characters hauled to and from prison. We expect that Isabella will eventually receive the 'justice, justice, justice, justice' she demands (V.i.25).

Along the way, Lucio's inadvertent unhooding of the Friar-Duke certainly detracts from the sense of Vienna's playwright's mastery over this decisive point in his plot, that is, 'the striking self-revelation [he] presumably intended' as his city's disguised ruler (as Beatrice Groves puts it).[95] But the hurried recalibrations of his shocked subjects show that they are not diverted by the Duke's clumsy handling of his transformation from counsellor and confessor to sacral ruler and judge. Most significantly, Angelo confesses immediately, without waiting to hear the Duke's evidence against him (V.i.360–1). The unveiling of the Duke's dual presence as religious figure and disguised ruler convinces Angelo that the Duke, 'like power divine', has seen his 'passes' (his course of action) (V.i.362–3).[96] Asking for mercy does not seem an option in Angelo's mind. He perceives, desires perhaps, only one outcome: a simple equation of justice. 'Immediate sentence then, and sequent death, / Is all the grace I beg' (V.i.366–7).

Angelo's 'like power divine' captures his and his fellow characters' instinctive response to their ruler. In contrast, to this point *Measure* has given its audience plentiful reasons to both question the Duke's similarity to God as all-seeing spectator in his *theatrum mundi* and read him as an exposed actor and blinded interpreter who operates under the constraints of a common frailty. Moreover, the play has gone out of its way to emphasise that, as much as administering justice, offering mercy is integral to the ducal remit. In the Duke's much-quoted speech, which includes *Measure*'s only direct allusion to its biblically inspired title, he further accentuates his contrariety to the divine. He evokes mercy but reconfigures it as law and justice.

In sentencing Angelo, the Duke's thinking mirrors that of his disgraced deputy. Whereas in the sphere of private, interpersonal relations, the Duke obligates Isabella to forgive Angelo 'for Marianna's sake', his judgement in the public court pivots on retributive justice (V.i.396). Angelo will be sentenced 'as he adjudged' Claudio:

> The very mercy of the law cries out
> Most audible, even from his proper tongue:
> An Angelo for Claudio, death for death;
> Haste still pays haste, and leisure answers leisure;
> Like doth quit like, and measure still for measure.
>
> (V.i.396, 400–4)

'The very mercy of the law' is a curious construction. Tambling asks whether the law can be merciful, concluding that it cannot as law and mercy are antitheses. The law is not a container for mercy. As seen, the Reformers would disagree. Recollecting Calvin, charity, for him, is intrinsic to the Old Testament's judicial law and should inform all subsequent law making.[97] Indeed, contrary to the spirit of his words just quoted, *Measure*'s Duke had expressed a similar perspective when he instructed Angelo to 'enforce or qualify' Vienna's laws (I.i.65).

The problem is not the Duke's interleaving of mercy and law, but his subsequent explanation. Personified, 'the very mercy of the law' appears to allow no latitude for qualification – for mercy itself – as it voices the singular principle of retributive justice. 'An Angelo for Claudio, death for death': *quid pro quo*, the *lex talionis*. Groves points out that there is a certain mercy in the Old Testament's 'eye for eye, tooth for tooth' as a rule which ensured that victims could not demand more than commensurate recompense from offenders.[98] Notwithstanding, in Matthew's gospel, Christ famously reinterprets the *lex talionis*: 'an eye for an eye, & a tooth for a tooth' transforms into turning the other cheek (Matt. 5: 38–9). The Geneva Bible glosses this injunction as: 'Rather receiue double wrong, then reuenge thine owne griefs.' Offering the not-yet-smited cheek is a far cry from 'An Angelo for Claudio'. And it is the New Testament which the Duke intimates that he has in mind by concluding his string of parallel substitutions with a misapplication of the biblical text. As discussed, both the Bible and the English Protestant liturgy steer readers and listeners away from the Duke's interpretation of Christ's 'with the same measure that ye mete withal, shall other men mete to you' in Luke 6 as advocating exact, punitive justice. Instead, mercy patterned on divine mercy complicates and softens humans' judgements of one another.

There must be an element of irony in the Duke's appropriation of Christ's words. Claudio is not dead, and it is unlikely that anyone in *Measure*'s audience believes that the Duke will have Angelo put to death. Groves reads in the irony the Duke directing Isabella to hear Christ's 'new message of mercy' which is layered into his 'trite, rhyming moralizing'.[99] In contrast, to Thomas Fulton the Duke's irony equates to the evident 'dark irony' of Shakespeare's reference to 'measure for measure' in *3 Henry VI* in which Warwick perverts the biblical words, using them to back revenge. 'Measure for measure must be answerèd', Warwick agrees, after Richard had insisted that they 'revoke that doom of mercy' (II.vi.55, 46). The politics of *Measure*'s Duke, Fulton contends, reflects 'the Machiavellian Bible-stealing of these early villains'.[100] Groves's interpretation is, I feel, too optimistic, Fulton's too cynical.

What can be said is that, as Vienna's playwright, the Duke has scripted his rhyming, contradictory expansion of 'the very mercy of the law', inclusive of the biblical allusion, as the curtain-raiser to the second dramatic revelation in his scene: the other characters' discovery that Claudio is still alive. Whether, following this disclosure, the Duke's plan was to impart to Angelo measured retribution – the enactment of *quid pro quo* anticipated since the scene's opening – or, as Groves suggests, mercy, for a second time the Duke loses control of his plot just as a revelatory, crowning juncture approaches. The Duke's evocation of punitive justice, concluding in his theatrical 'away with him' (to the block), compels Marianna and Isabella to step forward (V.i.407–9). The two women manifest an understanding of 'measure for measure' which resonates with its source as they ask the Duke to indeed judge Angelo according to 'the very mercy of the law'.

Theatregoers would struggle to find evidence in Shakespeare's characterisation of Angelo to justify Marianna's unshakeable love for him. It is easier to follow the Duke – not by 'mock[ing]' Marianna 'with a husband', but because of her husband (V.i.410–11). But Angelo's want of appeal seems to be the point. As Marianna pleads for Angelo, *Measure*'s melody line can be clearly made out as she sets forth her way of seeing human nature and human relations. Marianna's reasoning picks up the thread of Isabella's earlier argument to Angelo. Isabella had urged the deputy to see Claudio as God saw him (Angelo). Both men are 'forfeit' when measured against the standard of divine law, yet not beyond the reach of the divine 'remedy' of mercy (II.ii.75–81).

When Marianna kneels before the Duke, she is not deluded about Angelo's shortcomings. She does not claim that her new husband deserves reprieve. Rather, having asserted that 'I crave no other [husband], nor no better man', Marianna gives the Duke a gentle lesson in the possibility of human metamorphosis, a lesson with distinct theological overtones:

> They say best men are moulded out of faults,
> And for the most become much more the better
> For being a little bad: so may my husband.
>
> (V.i.419, 432–4)

'A little bad' no doubt presents a sanitised version of Angelo. Yet on the whole, Marianna follows the grain of Isabella's earlier reasoning, acknowledging Angelo's common frailty – the idea he had ironically introduced into the play-world – with another word that recurs throughout *Measure*: 'faults'. Through her choice of the passive tense, Marianna reminds the Duke, not that men with faults can remake themselves, but that they can be made better (here, by an unknown hand). The subjunctive, 'may', shows that Marianna does not believe that Angelo has undergone this remoulding. He is not yet 'new made'. But he could be in the future, and mercy, a second chance, would (literally) keep alive the hope of possibility becoming actuality.

In refusing to be merciful, especially as Marianna begs Isabella's assistance, the Duke recapitulates the logic of justice he had written into the heart of this scene: 'Against all sense you do importune her. / Should she kneel down in mercy of this fact' (V.i.426–7). Asking the injured party to be merciful, the Duke argues, contravenes 'all sense' by undermining the economy of desert and justice. It is, of course, exact justice that Isabella had demanded at the scene's commencement, and the prospect that 'the corrupt deputy' would be 'scaled' had (at least in part) motivated her willing complicity in the problematic bed-trick. Isabella had believed the Duke's reasoning as they plotted Angelo's 'deceit' (III.ii.238–9, 241).

In her final speech, Isabella enacts a volte-face. Not only does she 'kneel down in mercy', but she also does more than Marianna asks – she speaks:

> Most bounteous sir,
> Look if it please you on this man condemned
> As if my brother lived. I partly think
> A due sincerity governed his deeds
> Till he did look on me. Since it is so,
> Let him not die.
>
> (V.i.427, 435–40)

The legal technicalities of Isabella's argument are outside my focus (and have been analysed and debated by others).[101]

My interest is the nature and signification of Isabella's appeal, the dramatic effect of which is amplified manyfold in performance. How do we read an action that is at once so magnanimous and so unsettling? In dropping to her knees and speaking on Angelo's behalf, Isabella risks her own humiliation, or perhaps better, her continued humiliation, given the role of madwoman which the Duke had made her play for much of this scene. Does the Duke rightly interpret her choice? Is it indeed 'against all sense' for Isabella personally, and also morally: mercy eliding justice? If so, why does the Duke follow his dismissal of her petition – 'Your suit's unprofitable. Stand up, I say' – with a seeming wholesale meting out of mercy (V.i.448)? The Duke does not call Angelo to account for his corruption of his public office; he does pardon Claudio, forgive Lucio, and perhaps most surprisingly, offer mercy to Barnardine (V.i.489, 484, 511, 477).

Before all of this, Isabella's action calls to mind the archetypal act of divine mercy: Christ's crucifixion, a juxtaposition that, I propose, throws some light on these questions. As noted, in Calvin's use of the *theatrum mundi* motif, Christ's crucifixion is the turning point in God's script of history – the moment that would definitively reveal his glory and goodness. Unexpectedly, the *mise en scène* comprises the '*eschafaud*': the 'stage' doubles as the 'scaffold'. Even more surprisingly, the divine protagonist appears in the role of 'divine Fool'.[102] Clothed in weakness and indignity, this deed lacks all appearance of glory and goodness. Yet, Calvin asserts, the 'glory of God [. . .] was neuer more excellent and euident' than on the cross. The cross 'made a wonderfull chaunge of things', reversing humanity's 'damnation' and ensuring the future repair of 'the whole worlde'.[103] An instrument of harsh justice, shame and humiliation became the instrument of divine mercy.

Calvin recognises that this is not a natural interpretation of Christ's crucifixion. 'The preaching of the crosse doe not agree with mans wit', Calvin affirms. This strange message can be 'embrace[d]' or 'disdaine[d]': it elicits antithetical hermeneutics.[104] Calvin alludes to 1 Corinthians 1 to make his point. In this passage, Paul's teaching on the divisiveness of the cross brings out the divergent ways of seeing it. To some people in the ancient world, the cross is 'a stumbling block [and] foolishness'; to others, it is 'the power of God, and the wisdom of God' (verses 23–4). Expositions such as the Elizabethan 'Homily or Sermon Concerning the Nativity and Birth of our Saviour Jesus Christ' foregrounded the hermeneutic implications of these verses for early modern English congregations. Paul's first group looked at Christ on the cross with disdain. 'They think it an absurd thing, and contrary to all reason', the Elizabethan homilist explains, 'that a Redeemer and Saviour of the whole World, should be [. . .] scorned, reviled, scourged, condemned, and last of all cruelly hanged.'[105]

The ancient disbelievers would have found themselves a modern ally in Nietzsche. I began this chapter with Nietzsche's intriguing quotation about mercy and justice. Nietzsche was, of course, vociferous in his hostility towards Christian renderings of mercy. In *The Antichrist*, Nietzsche quotes from 1 Corinthians 1: 20–8, which begins, 'Hath not God made foolish the wisdom of this world?', and includes the earlier-quoted verses that identify the cross as pivotal to this reversal. Nietzsche denounces Paul's words as 'a first-rate document for the psychology of every chandala morality', or 'slave morality' as he terms it in *On the Genealogy of Morals*.[106] To Nietzsche, there is nothing more perverse than the '"holy cross"': 'that ghastly paradox of a "God on the cross", that mystery of an unimaginable ultimate cruelty and self-crucifixion of God *for the salvation of man*'. The cross seals the 'triumph' of '*ressentiment*'. For Nietzsche, the French *ressentiment* captures the 'vengefulness' of '"the slaves" or "the mob" or "the herd"' over '"the masters"'. This 'slave morality' overturns 'all *nobler* ideals' by identifying the 'good' not with the 'powerful', the 'beautiful', the 'happy', but with the 'poor, impotent, lowly [. . .] suffering, deprived, sick, ugly'.[107]

As Garrett Green observes, Nietzsche's enmity to Christianity comes from him 'really hear[ing]' and 'taking seriously' the truth claims at its heart. Nietzsche understood that the Christian gospel, centred on the cross, undoes hierarchies structured by the 'virtue' of 'natural' power: 'the creditor sacrifices himself for his debtor, out of love (can one credit that?)'.[108] But Nietzsche's interpretation of what he heard as *ressentiment*, as slave morality is, in Green's words, 'wrongly turned'. Nietzsche separates and opposes power and weakness; Christian thinkers from Paul to the Reformers contend that power is conveyed through weakness.[109] For the Elizabethan homilist, the cross is powerful for those who 'look' to it through the eyes of embracing faith – who 'look to be saved'.[110] This hermeneutic, what could be called, to employ Green's phrasing, a 'properly Christian hermeneutic of the cross', rightly turns (so to speak) Paul's 'dualities' in 1 Corinthians 1, recognising weakness as power and folly as wisdom – power and wisdom that effect 'redemption' (verse 30).[111]

There are evident resonances between Isabella's and Christ's performances of mercy. The 'upside-downness' of both engender hermeneutic perplexity for observers, immediate and more distant. Both acts turn on the willing, humiliating, self-denial of the 'creditor', that is, a turning away from self-realisation which seems unnatural and contrary to reason. Nietzsche indicts the cross as the symbol 'of the most subterranean conspiracy that ever existed – against health, beauty, whatever has turned out well, courage, spirit, *graciousness* of the soul, *against life itself*'.[112] Similarly, Isabella's actions can be seen as self-demeaning – an evisceration of the self. As briefly outlined, the argument against Nietzsche's view of Christ's crucifixion is that the philosopher's hermeneutic of disdain prevents him from seeing the duality inherent to the significance of the cross: glory and goodness, the powerful assertion of life achieved through seemingly senseless loss of self. What about Isabella's self-denying gesture of mercy? This is where the analogy breaks down. For there is no equivalent promise in Isabella's kneeling and speech for Angelo's liberation, no evidence that her actions contain within them the power to change anything. The Duke's rebuff and order to stand silences her, just as Angelo had done.

Still, while the Duke denies Isabella the ability to affect his judgement (possibly so that she does not upstage the climax of his theatre), according to a hermeneutic of the cross, her decision to embody mercy to secure Angelo's freedom (perhaps paradoxically) strongly affirms her agency as an interpreting self. Further, Isabella's physical and speech acts serve as a point of contrast that critiques the Duke's subsequent problematic acts of mercy. Here, I return to previously trodden territory, to the connections between divine activity, human identity and human agency set forth by the Reformers and sketched out by Isabella herself. Drawing together the thoughts of Calvin and Luther (and also Jüngel), Gregor argues that 'if true self-understanding of the self depends on true understanding of God', then the cross, as the means to knowing God, is key to self-knowledge. Knowledge of oneself mediated by a hermeneutic of the cross is 'ontologically disruptive': it overturns 'our understanding of what it is to *be*'. The cross displaces an 'ontology of self-justification' with an 'ontology of justification by faith' as people who look with faith to the cross interpret themselves as saved not by their own activity and merit, but Christ's. A hermeneutic of the cross decentres the self and gives it a new 'cruciform' identity. Then, having been remade by divine love (as Nietzsche quizzically describes the motivation behind Christ's crucifixion), the cruciform self becomes 'an agent' of that same love, as the twentieth-century theologian and German resister Dietrich Bonhoeffer observes. An ontology of justification by faith gives the self agency that enacts a 'being-there for others'.[113]

The arena of justice is, for Calvin, one locale in which cruciform selves justified by faith exercise their agency. In this hermeneutical situation, Christians can choose to 'doe good', specifically 'to them that doe them wrong'. Calvin is not arguing against Christians using legal processes. But he does insist that revenge should not govern the mind of the injured Christian, nor the Christian court.[114] Understanding that the temporal life involves 'the bearing of a continuall crosse' and taking on Christ's attitude of 'abhorr[ing] from desire of recompensing like for like' enables Christians to not 'seeke eye for eye, tooth for tooth, as the Pharisees taught their Disciples to desire reuenge'. Instead, they can 'forgiue and of their owne accord pardone' offences committed against them. Indeed, Christians may choose to give up their right to obtain justice if the process enflames their hatred for the other. How does one respond to being wronged? 'Charitie', Calvin concludes, is the determining principle in all matters of law and justice. Most emphatically, and disconcertingly, Calvin asserts that vengefulness and lovelessness together completely invert the character of justice seeking: it becomes 'uniust and wicked'.[115]

In asking the Duke to be 'bounteous' towards Angelo, Isabella chooses to be merciful towards the man she wanted to bring to justice, to view him through a perspective reminiscent of a hermeneutic of the cross. In this action, mercy does not elide justice. Rather, although she possesses almost no social or political power, Isabella shows that she does have the agency to allow justice to overcome itself as mercy in her own bearing. Charity rather than revenge rings through Isabella's words as she asks the Duke not to view Angelo through the lens of the egregious injustice they all thought he had committed, but rather as a frail person who had caught himself out with his own lust (V.i.436–40). *Measure* has offered significant clues that encourage its audience to see Isabella's own frailty. But her last words leave the impression that she is truly seeking to be merciful: to enact for Angelo what she asked of him.

The Duke's authoritative pronouncements of mercy, on the other hand, do little to dispel the doubts about him, suspicion which only deepened when he expounded the 'very mercy of the law' as like for like. His wresting back control from Isabella over the action within Vienna's *theatrum mundi* and the script that unfolds feels too much like the machinations of an incurved self bent on self-realisation. R. S. White describes (aptly, I think) *Measure*'s final minutes as the Duke's '*coup de théâtre* which will reveal himself in the adopted role of saviour'.[116] In his own script's climax, the Duke centres himself as 'saviour' while the characters whom he 'saves' make up the supporting cast, indeed his almost silent supporting cast. As has been widely noted, Lucio is the only other character who speaks amid the Duke's rapid-fire pardoning and marrying off of characters. Despite escaping hanging, the fantastic's voice is the (somewhat comical) lone protest against a form of mercy that appears to him as punishment: 'Marrying a punk, my lord, is pressing to death, whipping, and hanging!' (V.i.514–5). Compared with the tension generated as Isabella knelt and spoke for Angelo, the Duke's apportioning of mercy is anti-climactic, weighed down with the disbelief of those watching him from within and outside the play-world. *Measure*'s ending is formally, but not emotionally, comic.

The Duke's demotion in *Measure*'s more recent critical history is, I believe, well-founded. *Measure* leaves its audience feeling troubled about the Duke, offering no relief valve for our suspicion as he ends the play doing what we have seen him do throughout: 'bypass [. . .] the volition of those involved in his theater' (in Beckwith's words).[117] But as I have shown, the play resists easy transferences of this reading of and response to the Duke either to God or the Reformers' theology of grace encapsulated in the doctrine of justification by faith. At *Measure*'s conclusion, Shakespeare leaves open the door for playgoers and actors playing Isabella to imagine the character refusing the Duke's marriage proposal. This is quite possibly a final instance of the playwright inviting audiences to question his character's resemblance to 'power divine', even as he depicts the Duke trying to impose his will on those around him. Vienna's Duke is as mortal, as frail, as his subjects. Further, as seen, the Reformers' thinking about grace and justification and a hermeneutic of the cross offers a contemporary critique of the Duke's frailty manifest in his centring of himself. He is turned in upon himself and blinded as an actor, spectator and playwright in Vienna's *theatrum mundi*, a mode of being that affects how he sees and judges himself, others and mercy itself.

Despite the Duke's instrumentalisation of mercy at *Measure*'s dénouement, belief in mercy has, nevertheless, been the play's mainspring. More specifically, onwards from its title, *Measure* signals that the mercy inseparable from the application of the law in Vienna is patterned on a theology of mercy that refuses to make merit – human action – a condition of a person's receipt of divine saving grace. He 'which is the top of judgement' does not 'judge you as you are', Isabella reminds Angelo (II.ii.78–9). We can agree with Isabella, I think, when she parallels the gratuitousness of divine mercy towards fallen human beings with the mercy she asks Angelo to extend to Claudio. It takes Isabella's unexpected plea for the undeserving Angelo to bring to the fore the 'fundamental strangeness and alien quality' (to return to Gadamer) of the Reformers' concept of salvation. Free mercy engenders unease by completely undermining humans' instinctive striving for self-justification and our 'natural expectations' that merit should be met with reward, blame with punishment.[118]

Leaving aside the question of the motivation behind the Duke's heavy-handed parcelling out of pardons, the unearned and unqualified 'mercy' he gives Barnardine is as perplexing as Isabella's treatment of Angelo (V.i.477). In both acts we see images of justification by faith alone playing out to its logical conclusion. These disconcerting representations of mercy take us to the heart of hermeneutics and the human hermeneutic condition. The experience of being brought face to face with the 'paradoxical message of faith' exemplifies the claim of hermeneutics: that is, that understanding takes place when we 'let [. . .] something be said to us' as frail interpreting selves. Especially when it comes to gratuitous mercy, we need the voice of others to guide us towards clear-sightedness, as the logic of mercy 'is directed against *any* natural understanding of human nature'.[119]

Challenging as it is, an understanding of mercy is, it seems to me, worth seeking. As we sit as spectators of *Measure*'s characters and judge these fictional others, the play makes us conscious of our frequent acts of judging the others we see within our own *theatrum mundi*. *Measure* questions the frame of reference we bring to bear upon our seeing. 'Measure for measure' and its meaning within the biblical story rang in the ears of the play's first audiences. Theirs was a culture influenced by teaching which urged the interpreting self towards charitable judgement of others in light of one's own frailty and blindness, one's own need for unmerited mercy. Nevertheless, it was difficult to hold mercy and justice in tension and not yield to the human tendency to be a 'seuere censor' of others.[120] How much more is this the case today? With 'man, proud man' understood above all else as a self-determining, self-justifying, disengaged free agent planted even more immovably at the centre of all relations and all things, free mercy, it seems, is far from this self's sight-line, from how we see ourselves, other selves and justice. None of this should dispel our wariness of *Measure*'s Duke. But perhaps it helps us understand our own unease with the play's representation of mercy.

Notes

1. Thomas Heywood, *An Apology for Actors* (London: Nicholas Okes, 1612), Aa4r.
2. John E. Booty (ed.), *The Book of Common Prayer 1559: The Elizabethan Prayer Book* (Charlottesville: The University of Virginia Press, 1976, reissued 2005), 182.
3. Friedrich Nietzsche, *On the Genealogy of Morals*, ed. Walter Kaufmann, trans. Walter Kaufmann and R. J. Hollingdale (New York: Vintage Books, 1967), 73. Italics original.
4. See Nietzsche, *On the Genealogy of Morals*, 73n1, for a discussion of the complexity of 'aufhebend' – here translated as 'overcoming', but which has a semantic range that includes 'pick up', 'cancel', 'preserve' and 'keep', and which is translated as 'self-destruction' in Friedrich Nietzsche, *The Genealogy of Morals: A Polemic*, ed. Oscar Levy, trans. Horace B. Samuel (Edinburgh: T. N. Foulis, 1913), 83.
5. Thomas Fulton, 'Shakespeare's Everyman: *Measure for Measure* and English Fundamentalism', *Journal of Medieval and Early Modern Studies* 40, no. 1 (2010): 133.
6. Fulton, 'Shakespeare's Everyman', 119; Louise Schleiner, 'Providential Improvisation in Measure for Measure,' *PMLA* 97, no. 2 (1982): 227.
7. Booty, *The Book of Common Prayer 1559*, 182. The parallel verse in Matthew 7: 5 uses 'clearly'.
8. Hans-Georg Gadamer, 'Hermeneutics as a Theoretical and Practical Task', in *The Gadamer Reader: A Boquet of the Later Writings*, ed. and trans. Richard E. Palmer (Evanston, IL: Northwestern University Press, 2007), 258.
9. Ibid. 258.
10. Hans-Georg Gadamer, *The Relevance of the Beautiful and Other Essays*, ed. Robert Bernasconi, trans. Nicholas Walker (Cambridge: Cambridge University Press, 1986), 149.
11. Brian Gregor, *A Philosophical Anthropology of the Cross: The Cruciform Self* (Bloomington: Indiana University Press, 2013), 44.
12. Charles Taylor, *Sources of the Self: The Making of the Modern Identity* (Cambridge, MA: Harvard University Press, 1989),

82, 187; Ruth Abbey, 'Charles Taylor: *Sources of the Self*', in *Central Works of Philosophy. Volume 5, The Twentieth Century: Quine and After*, ed. John Shand (Chesham: Acumen, 2006), 278.

13. Peter Holbrook, *Shakespeare's Individualism* (Cambridge: Cambridge University Press, 2010), 23.
14. Sarah Beckwith, *Shakespeare and the Grammar of Forgiveness* (Ithaca, NY: Cornell University Press, 2011), 143–4, 80.
15. Devin Byker, 'Bent Speech and Borrowed Selves: Substitutionary Logic and Intercessory Acts in *Measure for Measure*', *Journal of Medieval and Early Modern Studies* 46, no. 2 (2016): 406, 421. On 'precise', see, for example, Fulton: 'Shakespeare's Everyman', 135, 46n77; Maurice Hunt, 'Being Precise in Measure for Measure', *Renascence* 58, no. 4 (2006): 243–4; Beatrice Groves, *Texts and Traditions: Religion in Shakespeare 1592–1604* (Oxford: Oxford University Press, 2007), 156.
16. Byker, 'Bent Speech', 408–10, 426–8, 413, 412, 415.
17. Ibid. 413, 412, 415, 427–8.
18. James I, King of England, *Basilikon dōron. Or His Maiesties Instructions to his dearest sonne, Henry the Prince* (Edinburgh: Robert Walde-graue, 1603), image 13v.
19. Beckwith, *Shakespeare and the Grammar of Forgiveness*, 73, 80, 76, 60.
20. Robert N. Watson, 'Introduction,' in *Measure for Measure*, ed. A. R. Braunmuller and Robert N. Watson, Arden Shakespeare Third Series (London: Bloomsbury, 2020), 1, 57.
21. Debora K. Shuger, *Political Theologies in Shakespeare's England: The Sacred and the State in Measure for Measure* (New York: Palgrave, 2001), 132, 131, 54, 47.
22. See also Julia Brett, '"Grace Is Grace, Despite of All the Controversy": *Measure for Measure*, Christian Allegory, and the Sacerdotal Duke', *Ben Jonson Journal* 6 (1999); Benedict J. Whalen, 'Private Conscience, Public Reform, and Disguised Rule in *The Malcontent* and *Measure for Measure*', *Ben Jonson Journal* 21, no. 1 (2014).
23. See, for example, Fulton, 'Shakespeare's Everyman'; Jonathan Goossen, '"'Tis set down so in heaven, but not in earth": Reconsidering Political Theology in Shakespeare's "Measure

for Measure"', *Christianity & Literature* 61, no. 2 (2012). Both Kenneth Graham and Jennifer Rust briefly summarise other critics who follow this line of thought. Kenneth Graham, 'The Reformation of Manners and the Grace of the Reformation: *Measure for Measure*'s Disciplinary Mingle-Mangle', *Religion & Literature* 49, no. 3 (2017): 167; Jennifer R. Rust, 'Religious and Political Impasses in *Measure for Measure*', in *The Cambridge Companion to Shakespeare and Religion*, ed. Hannibal Hamlin (Cambridge: Cambridge University Press, 2019), 187.

24. Jeremy Tambling, 'Law and Will in *Measure for Measure*', *Essays in Criticism* 59, no. 3 (2009): 207.
25. Gerald L. Bruns, *Hermeneutics Ancient and Modern* (New Haven, CT: Yale University Press, 1992), 158.
26. Belden C. Lane, 'Spirituality as the Performance of Desire: Calvin on the World as a Theatre of God's Glory', *Spiritus: A Journal of Christian Spirituality* 1, no. 1 (2001): 1; Björn Quiring, 'Introduction', in *'If Then the World, a Theatre Present . . .': Revisions of the Theatrum Mundi Metaphor in Early Modern England*, ed. Björn Quiring (Berlin: De Gruyter, 2014), 1–5.
27. Robert White, '*Theatrum mundi*: the Theatre Metaphor in Calvin', *Australian Journal of French Studies* 31, no. 3 (1994): 322n3, 311, 318–9.
28. Jean Calvin, *A Commentary Vpon the Prophecie of Isaiah*, trans. C. C. (London: Felix Kyngston, 1609), 410, 668; Jean Calvin, *The holy Gospel of Iesus Christ, according to Iohn, with the Commentary of M. Iohn Caluine*, trans. Christopher Fetherstone, in *A Harmonie Vpon the Three Euangelists, Matthew, Mark and Luke [. . .] Whereunto Is Also Added a Commentarie Vpon the Euangelist S. Iohn* (London: Thomas Dawson, 1584), 321.
29. Calvin, *A Commentary Vpon the Prophecie of Isaiah*, 582.
30. White, '*Theatrum mundi*', 314.
31. Calvin, *A Commentary Vpon the Prophecie of Isaiah*, 582.
32. Gadamer, 'Hermeneutics as a Theoretical and Practical Task', 258.
33. White, '*Theatrum mundi*', 314.

34. *OED Online*, s.v. 'hypocrisy, n.'; Robert Bolton, *A Discourse About the State of True Happinesse* (London: Felix Kyngston, 1611), 30.
35. Lucia Nigri and Naya Tsentourou, 'Introduction', in *Forms of Hypocrisy in Early Modern England*, ed. Lucia Nigri and Naya Tsentourou (New York: Routledge, 2018), 4.
36. Alec Ryrie, *Being Protestant in Reformation Britain* (Oxford: Oxford University Press, 2013), 104–5; Lucia Nigri, 'Religious Hypocrisy in Performance: Roman Catholicism and The London Stage', in *Forms of Hypocrisy in Early Modern England*, ed. Lucia Nigri and Naya Tsentourou (New York: Routledge, 2018), 57; John Jeffries Martin, *Myths of Renaissance Individualism* (New York: Palgrave Macmillan, 2004), 113. See Chapter 6 of Martin for an account of the development of this concern.
37. Jane Taylor, 'Of Hypocrisy: "Wherein the Action and Utterance of the Stage, Bar, and Pulpit are Distinctly Consider'd"', in *Performing the Secular: Religion, Representation, and Politics*, ed. Milija Gluhovic and Jisha Menon (London: Palgrave Macmillan, 2017), 36.
38. Jennifer Clement, *Reading Humility in Early Modern England* (Farnham: Ashgate, 2015), 44; White, '*Theatrum mundi*', 316.
39. Eberhard Jüngel, *Theological Essays*, ed. and trans. John B. Webster, vol. 2 (Edinburgh: T&T Clark, 1995), 219.
40. Ibid. 221–2.
41. Ibid. 222; Martin Luther, *Lectures on Romans*, ed. Hilton C. Oswald, trans. Walter G. Tillmans and Jacob A. O. Preus (Saint Louis, MI: Concordia Publishing House, 1972), 245, 291, 313, 345, 351, 513.
42. Jüngel, *Theological Essays*, 222.
43. Graham reads *Measure*'s characters as 'nominally Protestant and Catholic'. 'The Reformation of Manners', 163. Brian Gibbons, 'Introduction', in *Measure for Measure,* ed. Brian Gibbons (Cambridge: Cambridge University Press, 2006), 2; David Scott Kastan, *A Will to Believe: Shakespeare and Religion* (Oxford: Oxford University Press, 2014), 74. Stacy Magedanz argues that

Isabella's characterisation adheres to 'the model of an Anabaptist morality'. 'Public Justice and Private Mercy in *Measure for Measure*', *SEL: Studies in English Literature, 1500–1900* 44, no. 2 (2004): 321.

44. See Watson, 'Introduction', 67–81.
45. *OED Online*, s.v. 'remorse, n.5'. The *OED*'s most recent example of 'remorse' conveying this now obsolete meaning comes from 1700.
46. David Loades, *Tudor Government* (Oxford: Blackwell, 1997), 4.
47. James I, *Basilikon dōron*, image 2r.
48. Diarmaid MacCulloch, *Reformation: Europe's House Divided 1490–1700* (London: Penguin Books, 2004), 634–5. See also Peter Lake and Michael C. Questier, *The Antichrist's Lewd Hat: Protestants, Papists and Players in Post-Reformation England* (New Haven, CT: Yale University Press, 2002), 635–6.
49. B. J. Sokol and Mary Sokol, *Shakespeare's Legal Language: A Dictionary* (London: Bloomsbury Academic, 2000), 252–3. Aristotle's 'synesis' and Gadamer's hermeneutic application of it, discussed in Chapter 3, comes to mind.
50. Jean Calvin, *The Institution of Christian Religion*, trans. Thomas Norton (London: Arnold Hatfield, 1599), 2.8.8.
51. Ibid. 2.8.8; 4.20.15.
52. Ibid. 4.20.15–16.
53. The notion of equity and its application in early modern legal contexts have been much discussed and debated in analyses of *Measure*. See John C. Higgins, 'Justice, Mercy, and Dialectical Genres in "Measure for Measure" and "Promos and Cassandra"', *English Literary Renaissance* 42, no. 2 (2012); Magedanz, 'Public Justice', 327–8; Shuger, *Political Theologies*, 72–101; Sokol and Sokol, 'Shakespeare's Legal Language', 112–17; Eric V. Spencer, 'Scaling the Deputy: Equity and Mercy in *Measure for Measure*', *Philosophy and Literature* 36, no. 1 (2012).
54. Calvin, *The Institution of Christian Religion*, 2.7.7.
55. Ibid. 2.7.3, 7.
56. Ibid. 2.7.1, 2, 5, 7.

57. Ibid. 2.7.5.
58. Ibid. 2.7.4, 8.
59. Ibid. 2.7.8.
60. Calvin, *The holy Gospel of Iesus Christ [. . .] Iohn*, 321.
61. Jüngel, *Theological Essays*, 237. Italics original.
62. Beckwith, *Shakespeare and the Grammar of Forgiveness*, 48; *The Canons and Decrees of the Sacred and Ecumenical Council of Trent, Celebrated under the Sovereign Pontiffs, Paul III, Julius III and Pius IV*, trans. James Waterworth (London: C. Dolman, 1848), Canon IX.
63. Jüngel, *Theological Essays*, 237–8, 229.
64. Beckwith, *Shakespeare and the Grammar of Forgiveness*, 49.
65. Martin Luther, 'Disputation against Scholastic Theology', trans. Harold J. Grimm, in *Career of the Reformer I*, ed. Harold J. Grimm (Philadelphia: Muhlenberg Press, 1957), 12.
66. Calvin, *A Commentary Vpon the Prophecie of Isaiah*, 582.
67. Jean Calvin, *A Harmonie composed and made of three Euangelistes, Matthew, Marke and Luke, with the Commentaries of Iohn Caluine*, trans. E.P., in *A Harmonie Vpon the Three Euangelists*, 209.
68. Ibid. 210.
69. Tambling, 'Law and Will', 190, 204–5. Tambling's focus is Matthew 7, rather than Luke 6.
70. Calvin, *A Commentary Vpon the Prophecie of Isaiah*, 368.
71. Bolton, *A Discourse*, 30, 34; See also Ryrie, *Being Protestant*, 105.
72. Musa Gurnis, '"Most Ignorant of What He's Most Assured": The Hermeneutics of Predestination in *Measure for Measure*', *Shakespeare Studies* 42 (2014): 154.
73. Gurnis, '"Most Ignorant"', 152–3. See Gervase Babington, *A Profitable Exposition of the Lords Prayer*, (London: Thomas Orwin, 1588), 232; William Burton, *An Exposition of the Lords Prayer* (London: The widdow Orwin, 1594), 127.
74. Calvin, *The Institution of Christian Religion*, 2.3.1.
75. Martin Luther, *A Commentarie of M. Doctor Martin Luther Vpon the Epistle of S. Paul to the Galathians* (London: Thomas Vautroullier, 1575), image 261.

76. *OED Online*, s.v. 'temper, n.'.
77. Ryrie, *Being Protestant*, 104.
78. Ibid. 107.
79. Calvin, *The Institution of Christian Religion*, 3.3.5.
80. *Measure for Measure*, ed. Brian Gibbons, II.iv.16–17n.
81. Enno Ruge, 'Having a Good Time at the Theatre of the World: Amusement, Antitheatricality and the Calvinist Use of the *Theatrum Mundi* Metaphor in Early Modern England', in *'If Then the World, a Theatre Present . . .': Revisions of the Theatrum Mundi Metaphor in Early Modern England*, ed. Björn Quiring (Berlin: De Gruyter, 2014), 27.
82. Stephen Cohen, 'From Mistress to Master: Political Transition and Formal Conflict in "Measure for Measure"', *Criticism* 41, no. 4 (1999): 438; Groves, *Texts and Traditions*, 167–71.
83. Ruge, 'Having a Good Time', 29–30.
84. Calvin, *The Institution of Christian Religion*, 1.5.7.
85. These sources are Cinthio's *Hecatommithi* (1565) and George Whetstone's *Promos and Cassandra* (1578).
86. Shuger, *Political Theologies*, 97–8.
87. Beckwith, *Shakespeare and the Grammar of Forgiveness*, 60, 73.
88. Quiring, 'Introduction', 4–5; Sir Walter Raleigh, *The History of the World*, ed. C. A. Patrides (London: Macmillan, 1971), 70.
89. Ford Lewis Battles, 'God Was Accommodating Himself to Human Capacity', *Interpretation* 31 (1977): 32–3, 21.
90. Verna A. Foster, *The Name and Nature of Tragicomedy* (2004; repr. Abingdon: Routledge, 2016), 61–2; Marliss C. Desens, *The Bed-Trick in English Renaissance Drama: Explorations in Gender, Sexuality, and Power* (Newark: University of Delaware Press, 1994), 11. Peggy Muñoz Simonds presents brief examples of uses of the device in biblical, medieval and classical literature. 'Overlooked Sources of the Bed Trick', *Shakespeare Quarterly* 34, no. 4 (1983).
91. Karen J. Cunningham, 'The Shakespearean Legal Imaginary', in *The Shakespearean World*, ed. Jill L. Levenson and Robert Ormsby (London: Routledge, 2017), 630; *Measure for Measure*, ed. A. R. Braunmuller and Robert N. Watson, III.i.218n.

92. *OED Online*, s.v. 'scale, v.1'. The *OED* cites the Duke's words. *Measure for Measure*, ed. A. R. Braunmuller and Robert N. Watson, III.i.256n.
93. R. S. White, *Let Wonder Seem Familiar: Endings in Shakespeare's Romance Vision* (New Jersey: Humanities Press, 1985), 75.
94. *Measure for Measure*, ed. A. R. Braunmuller and Robert N. Watson, IV.v.9n. See Psalm 24 and Revelation 8–11.
95. Groves, *Texts and Traditions*, 171.
96. *Measure for Measure*, ed. Gibbons, V.i.363n.
97. Tambling, 'Law and Will', 190; Calvin, *The Institution of Christian Religion*, 4.20.15–16.
98. Groves, *Texts and Traditions*, 182.
99. Ibid. 182–3.
100. Fulton, 'Shakespeare's Everyman', 134.
101. See Byker, 'Bent Speech', 426–7; Cohen, 'From Mistress to Master', 452–3; Goossen, '"'Tis set down so"', 234–5; Maurice Hunt, 'Vincentio's Selves in *Measure for Measure*', *College Literature* 46, no. 3 (2019); Spencer, 'Scaling the Deputy', 176–7.
102. White, '*Theatrum mundi*', 315.
103. Calvin, *The holy Gospel of Iesus Christ [. . .] Iohn*, 321.
104. Calvin, *The Institution of Christian Religion*, 2.6.1.
105. *Certain Sermons or Homilies Appointed to Be Read in Churches in the Time of Queen Elizabeth* (London: George Wells, Abel Swall and George Pawlett, 1687), 426.
106. Friedrich Nietzsche, *The Portable Nietzsche*, trans. Walter Kaufmann (Harmondsworth: Penguin Books, 1967), 624; Nietzsche, *On the Genealogy of Morals*, 36.
107. Nietzsche, *On the Genealogy of Morals*, 34–7. Italics original.
108. Garrett Green, *Theology, Hermeneutics, and Imagination: The Crisis of Interpretation at the End of Modernity* (Cambridge: Cambridge University Press, 2000), 113, 138, 132; Nietzsche, *On the Genealogy of Morals*, 92.
109. Green, *Theology, Hermeneutics, and Imagination*, 131–2, 38.
110. *Certain Sermons or Homilies*, 426.
111. Green, *Theology, Hermeneutics, and Imagination*, 131.

112. Nietzsche, *Portable Nietzsche*, 655–6. Italics original.
113. Gregor, *A Philosophical Anthropology of the Cross*, 16, 44–5, 80, 44, 9–10, 125, 99. Italics original.
114. Calvin, *The Institution of Christian Religion*, 4.20.20, 19.
115. Ibid. 4.20.20, 21.
116. White, '*Let Wonder Seem Familiar*', 76. Italics original.
117. Beckwith, *Shakespeare and the Grammar of Forgiveness*, 80.
118. Gadamer, *The Relevance of the Beautiful*, 149.
119. Ibid. 149.
120. Calvin, *A Harmonie composed and made of three Euangelistes*, 209.

CHAPTER 5

ALL'S WELL THAT ENDS WELL? KNOWING IN PART

For now we se through a glasse darkely: but then shal we se face to face. Now I knowe in parte: but then shal I knowe euen as I am knowen. And now abideth faith, hope & loue, euen these thre: but the chiefest of these is loue.

Saint Paul, 1 Corinthians 13: 12–13

Ignoramus [means that] we don't know but there exists something which we don't know. And the fact that we don't know it doesn't mean that it doesn't exist.

Hans-Georg Gadamer, Interview with Jens Zimmermann, 13 March 2002[1]

No longer imminent, the End is immanent. So that it is not merely the remnant of time that has eschatological import; the whole of history, and the progress of the individual life, have it also.

Frank Kermode, *The Sense of an Ending*[2]

In *All's Well That Ends Well*, 'the end is immanent' from its opening as its mourning-attired characters enter the stage discussing death. Of course, for theatregoers, the play's end is immanent even before it begins. Through his proverbial and metatheatrical title, Shakespeare positions his audience to adopt an end-oriented hermeneutic. We read *All's Well*'s characters and plot in view of the comic and romantic resolution that its title signals. Does Shakespeare's play achieve this end? By its ambiguous dénouement, 'we don't know'. Gadamer phrases an apt response for us.

Ends absorbed the attention of many people in Shakespeare's Protestant England. Theology, specifically the Christian doctrine of last things – eschatology – informed this preoccupation. Eschatology shapes a way of reading for the interpreting self and a way of reading the interpreting self that incorporates epistemological, interpersonal, ethical and psychological dimensions of human being. The doctrine permeates *All's Well*'s end-oriented hermeneutic. Act 2, scene 4 offers a glimpse of how eschatological ideas may have inflected people's day-to-day reading of 'the progress of an individual life' (to borrow Frank Kermode's phrase). The fool Lavatch jestingly describes the Countess as 'very well indeed, but for two things. [. . .] One, that she's not in heaven, whither God send her quickly! The other, that she's in earth, from whence God send her quickly!' (II.iv.8–12). Lavatch's play on the motif of 'wellness' reflects the surplus of meaning available when viewing human existence through an eschatological lens. An eschatological hermeneutic interprets the condition of the (believing) self as simultaneously well and not well, a twofold state of being that ensues in individuals' ongoing experience of belief interpolated with doubt. This dialectic of belief and doubt runs through *All's Well* and, I suggest, also elucidates the response the play engenders in its audience.

Eschatology encompasses death, bodily resurrection, judgement, heaven and hell, and the eschaton. History climaxes with the eschaton, the age in which God gives fallen human beings the eternal salvation he promises in Scripture (a promise coupled, of course, with warnings about eternal damnation). In eschatological thought, ends – the close of a life or of the world – double as beginnings: gateways to a transcendent 'then' (to employ Paul's language in 1 Corinthians 13). For Paul, above all else, complete interpersonal knowing, especially knowledge of the divine other, will distinguish this future: 'then shal I knowe euen as I am knowen'. Thinking about and anticipating this felicitous end was, Patrick O'Banion demonstrates, 'ordinary and normative' for early modern English people. As Hannibal Hamlin and Stephen Marche both note, eschatological texts proliferated in a culture which was, in Cynthia Marshall's description, 'saturated with eschatological concerns' across personal and political spheres of thought and action.[3] For Shakespeare and his contemporaries, the last things framed interpretations of self and society in ways that infused human being in this world – every moment of a life, all of history – with 'eschatological import'.[4] Marshall stresses that it is 'nearly impossible' to imagine that the playwright ignored his culture's engrossment with this belief.[5]

All's Well exemplifies this influence. In addition to the eschatologically resonant experiential dialectic of belief and doubt threaded through the play, figures, symbols and patterns that function as signposts of the eschaton in theological discourse feature in Shakespeare's narrative. Specifically, miracles, marriage (and wedding rings) and pilgrimage are key turning points in *All's Well*'s plot. More broadly, both romantic comedy and eschatology are oriented towards or, perhaps better, oriented by the future. Both the literary and the theological narrative modes share an optimism about the experience of transcendence, culminating in marriage, which this future will usher in. All will be well.

However, as critics have often discussed, *All's Well*'s end is anything but decidedly 'well'. *All's Well*'s dénouement provokes doubt about its status as a romantic comedy by yielding ambivalent, fragmentary knowledge. Shakespeare leaves his audience questioning whether his play ironises or accomplishes the realisation of its title. Can we read a transcendent future of happiness and harmony from the equivocal language and tense interactions in *All's Well*'s final scene? Indeed, theatregoers' experience of their own epistemological finitude is not confined to this final scene. *All's Well* also keeps us in two minds, and sometimes in the dark, at other seemingly critical moments in the plot, an experience we have in common with most of the characters. Shakespeare situates both us and them as interpreting selves trying to make sense out of limited or conflicting knowledge. Gadamer's '*ignoramus*', acknowledging one's 'non-knowing', that I have reached the limits of what I can assert with certainty, gives expression to the predicament of characters and audience alike until and especially at *All's Well*'s end.[6]

Importantly, for Gadamer, reaching the point of saying 'we don't know' does not take the self down the path of (interpretive) nihilism. Rather, in his later thought (in keeping with the 'religious turn' in his hermeneutics) Gadamer posited that people's very consciousness of their limitations gives rise to, rather than precludes, an awareness that 'something greater and more mysterious than ourselves' exists beyond our unknowing.[7] Finitude occasions and thus coexists with an experience of transcendence, a 'desire' for which, Gadamer insists, 'our European thought contains [and which] is secretly present everywhere'.[8] As noted by Jens Zimmermann (whose work on Gadamer and transcendence I draw on in this chapter), to Gadamer this notion is not 'mere philosophical speculation'; rather, it describes real experiences affecting people's minds and emotions. More specifically, Gadamer figures the interpreting self's concurrent sensibility of finitude and transcendence as a 'religious feeling': 'it must have the power of religious conviction'.[9]

Gadamer insists that this 'religious experience' – '*ignoramus*' – is empty of 'positive content'.[10] However, although he avoids making the link, there are notable analogues between the state of being he delineates and Christian eschatology's (content rich) representations of believers' interconnected epistemological and relational condition in this world. Paul is (again) paradigmatic. The apostle anticipates a 'then' when he will know fully and be fully known. But within the confines of this world, he experiences only a shadowy foretaste of this future completeness: 'now I knowe in parte'. Now, he and his readers 'se through a glasse darkely'. In his interpretation of this verse, Jean Calvin asserts that Paul 'declareth that that thing which is infinite, cannot be comprehended by our small capacitie, and narrow compasse'.[11] The 'infinite' shows up humans' finitude. At the same time, similar to Gadamer's account of the self's experience when (an unknown) transcendence frames one's (not) knowing, Protestant eschatology maps the self in relation to the infinite.

For the Reformers, the disjunction between 'now' and 'then' necessitates that the temporal experience of the interpreting self will include both belief and doubt. This dialectical experience is perhaps best described as a sensibility of simultaneously '*having* and *not-having*'. Or, as *All's Well*'s clown puts it, of being both well and not well. 'Having and not-having' is T. F. Torrance's description of the principal dynamic at work in Martin Luther's eschatology. For Luther, justification by grace through faith alone, the cornerstone Reformation doctrine tied to his name, ensured that, in the present day, believing selves 'have' salvation. They are 'already-saved', as Grace Tiffany aptly phrases it. 'We must by all means believe for a certainty that we are in a state of grace, that we are pleasing to God for the sake of Christ', Luther writes.[12] Now, a Christian 'possesses a righteousness which is *real*'.[13] The end is immanent.

Luther's conception of Christian certainty highlights a significant point of divergence between early modern Protestant and Roman Catholic eschatology. Ending well, ensuring one's own and one's loved ones' salvation in the next life, was a priority of this life for people on both sides of the Reformation divide. However, they disagreed over the question of when the eschaton, the culmination of temporal history, begins. As Torrance explains, Roman Catholic thinkers located this moment 'beyond' history.[14] It is imminent, not immanent. The Reformers disagreed, a parting of ways rooted in the pivotal Reformation conflict over how one is justified before God and thus attains eternal salvation. Luther, Calvin and their fellow Reformers were adamant that, in this life, having faith (alone) in Christ's justifying of sinners through his historical death and resurrection assured one of salvation in the next life. In this Protestant schema of history, the end had already commenced with the first coming of Christ, the incarnate Word. At that time, Christ inaugurated the era of the eschaton and since that moment 'all history [is] moving under the impact of God's Word towards its goal': the eschaton's consummation when Christ returns.[15] But even before that final end, in God's eyes, 'already-saved' believers are righteous.

However, as this righteousness is not 'fully *realized*' until the future climax of the eschaton, sin, in Luther's words, 'is still clinging to our flesh during this life'.[16] Sin's persisting influence means that Christians undergo occasions of 'a conflict of conscience', that is, the dread that one does not have salvation because one cannot rid oneself of sin. Luther could speak of times when this sense rendered the afterlife a personally fearful prospect.[17] Now, sin muddies believers' assurance of their salvation:

> If we believed for a certainty that we are in a state of grace [. . .] then we would be truly happy and thankful to God [. . .] But because we experience the opposite feeling, namely, fear, doubt, sorrow, etc., we do not dare believe this for a certainty.[18]

Similarly, Calvin, in a single sentence, juxtaposes certainty and doubt: 'But truely, when we teach that faith ought to be certaine and assured, we do not imagine such a certaintie as is touched with no doubting, nor such an assuredness as is assailed with no carefulnesse [anxiety].' This coincidence of confidence and anxiety means that 'the faithfull haue a perpetuall strife with their owne distrustfulnesse'.[19] In this life, doubt is never far from belief. Arthur Dent, the English Puritan preacher and author, goes further in his bestselling 'dialogue': *The Plaine Mans Path-way to Heauen* (1601). Through his mouthpiece, Theologus, 'a Divine', Dent argues that doubt is a necessary sign of belief: 'hee, that neuer doubted, neuer beleeued'. Somewhat confusingly, for early modern English Protestants, doubt about one's fitness for salvation could, as Karen Bruhn observes, 'be interpreted as a sign of faith'.[20]

To Calvin, the interplay of human finitude – of knowing in part – and the temporal dialectic inherent in eschatology is a key to Christians' 'perpetuall strife'. With echoes of 1 Corinthians 13, Calvin opposes present hearing to future seeing. Now, because people only hear about and do not yet see the future 'brightnesse, ioie, felicitie, and glorie' promised them, this knowledge is 'most farre remooued from our sense, and remaine[s] as it were wrapped in darke speeches' until the day when they see God 'face to face'.[21] Until then, believers will experience belief mixed with doubt, psychological highs and lows borne of partial knowledge of the joyful, transcendent end that is immanent, yet not fully realised.

I drew on the opposition of belief and doubt in the previous chapter to argue that *Measure for Measure* evokes both: belief in its representation of mercy and doubt about the Duke, with whom enactments of mercy are closely associated. Not surprisingly (given the resonances between the two dramas), Shakespeare also works this layering of belief over doubt, doubt over belief, into the texture of *All's Well*. Indeed, the play draws on this language of belief and doubt when, in Act 1, the Countess states that her intuition that

Helen, the play's central character, loves the Countess's son Bertram 'hung so tottering in the balance that I could neither believe nor misdoubt' (I.iii.121–2).

As the character upon whom *All's Well*'s comedic end depends, Helen is the fulcrum of the play. Helen drives the key events of marriage, miracles and pilgrimage, pivotal points in *All's Well*'s plot which keep before theatregoers the possibility of its characters' future experiences of an everlasting end that will be 'sweet' (V.iii.331). As she does so, she invites belief from within and outside the play-world. The eschatological hermeneutic foregrounded by Helen's association with signposts of the eschaton centres her as the play-world's interpretive focal point. Despite their limited knowledge, reading Helen is exigent for the other characters. As they make judgements about Helen, an eschatological hermeneutic reminiscent of the Reformers' thinking sifts these characters' responses by connecting belief in Helen to astute self-understanding and (especially) virtuous action, and doubt about Helen to the antitheses of such right-mindedness (in every sense of the word).

By situating the beginning of the ultimate end in this life, the Reformers not only drew attention to how the believing self's partial knowledge of this end gives rise to the twofold experience of belief and doubt. They also connected such knowledge to ethics, that is, the question of how one should be with and towards others, including the divine other, in the present time. The answer lies in the trio of faith, hope and love with which Paul famously concludes 1 Corinthians 13. Faith, hope and, above all, love 'abideth' even though, or better because, the apostle only knows in part. These theological virtues pattern individuals' living as they journey towards heaven. Knowing, if only in part, about the transcendent future gives shape to people's actions in this temporal world.

The Reformers' connection of eschatology and ethics finds some parallels in Gadamer's assertion that ethics is integral to the knowing subject's experience of transcendence. For Gadamer, the voice of the other is one way in which interpreting selves encounter transcendence at the limits of one's own knowing. 'The meaning of our finitude', according to Gadamer, is 'our awareness of being delimited by the other' and 'the only way not to succumb to our finitude is to open oneself up to the other, to listen to the Thou in front of us.'[22] Opening oneself up, listening to the transcendent other is, for Gadamer, 'ethical virtue as enactment', a manifestation of 'an ontology of *being-toward*'. So too is humans framing their interpretations of others' words with the recognition that they do so within a context comprising both their finitude and the existence of knowledge in excess of their own.[23] Paul and the Reformers might well identify an ontology of being-toward and the virtuous interpretive posture it animates as expressions of faith, hope and love.

'Virtue' and 'virtuous' resound throughout *All's Well*. The play frequently turns its audience's attention to its characters' ethos as readers of self, of others and of their circumstances, and especially links its characters' virtue (or want of it) to their interpretation of Helen. Most believe in Helen, except Bertram who, before and after he becomes her husband, doubts. More emphatically, he refuses to believe. This disparity between Bertram's and others' responses to Helen contributes to the play's variegated mood and the mixed reactions it elicits. Yet, Helen herself is as responsible for these effects as other characters' readings of her. Helen signals beyond her world, but she does not transcend it. Rather, she too is bounded by the shortcomings of human being in the 'now'.

Just as it does with her fellow characters, an eschatological hermeneutic weighs Helen's accounts of herself and her actions. Indeed, Shakespeare sets up his audience to attend to Helen's inner life more than any other character's, directing us to query her 'intents' in ways that prompt suspicion of her

(I.i.225, I.iii.215, III.iv.21, IV.iv.3). *All's Well*'s most famous lines are spoken by a minor character: 'The web of our life is of a mingled yarn, good and ill together' (IV.iii.68–9). Lord E. has Bertram in mind, but for audiences his sentiment could also apply to Helen. Audiences know more about Helen than her fellow characters, and this knowledge serves to bring out the conflicting, contradictory sides of her character. Having said that, there are crucial moments when we do not have the knowledge we need to understand Helen, when 'we don't know'. To his play's end, Shakespeare both complicates his protagonist's character and withholds critical knowledge about her. As he does so, he suspends his audience 'tottering in the balance' between believing in Helen and the intimations of transcendence and possibility she embodies, and misdoubting her.

Helen is *All's Well*'s interpretive locus, but she is not its moral plumb line. The play's cast of older characters (the Countess, the King, Lafeu and the Widow of Florence, as well as the deceased Count of Roussillon and Gérard de Narbonne, Helen's father) fulfil that function. From its first scene, *All's Well* distinguishes between this group and the younger characters (especially Helen, Bertram and Paroles), prioritising the elders' voices and ways of being. The Countess and her cohort are very much unlike the older 'blocking characters' (as Jane Freeman describes them) found in several Shakespearean comedies. *A Midsummer Night's Dream*'s Egeus and *Much Ado About Nothing*'s Leonato are cases in point.[24] For the most part, *All's Well*'s older characters enact eschatologically shaped virtue – faith, hope and love – especially in their believing readings of and consequent being-toward, indeed being-for, the younger characters.[25] Before showing how *All's Well*'s elders reify belief and virtue, the configuration of (Protestant) eschatology and ethics informing my reading of these characters' reading requires some teasing apart.

'Love all, trust a few'

At face value, the prominence throughout *All's Well* of language and imagery readily associated with Roman Catholic theology – virtue, goodness, pilgrimage and so forth – suggests that the play rings truer with a Catholic account of salvation than the Protestant narrative I invoke. This is the perspective of David Beauregard, for whom a 'Roman Catholic theology of grace pervades the play at every level'. Beauregard links virtue and pilgrimage to notions of meritorious and penitential action, that is, to the thinking of sixteenth-century Roman Catholic theologians who followed Thomas Aquinas in asserting that humans can contribute to their future salvation.[26] The eschatologically oriented pronouncement of the sixth session of the Council of Trent (1547) represents this position: 'life eternal is to be proposed to those working well unto the end, and hoping in God, both as a grace mercifully promised [. . .] and as a reward [. . .] to be faithfully rendered to their good works and merits'. As Beauregard notes, one can hear strains of Shakespeare's title in these words.[27]

Joshua Avery is 'in partial agreement with Beauregard', arguing that while *All's Well* swings between a more pessimistic (Protestant) and a more optimistic (Catholic) anthropology, it ultimately favours the latter. Specifically, the play reflects the Catholic emphases on the role of human volition in matters of ethics and salvation (even after the Fall) found in the theology of Aquinas, Thomas More and Desiderius Erasmus. As such, for Avery, the play's affirmation of the mutual operations of 'divine and human agencies' leaves open the possibility that Helen may have miraculously effected a comic end.[28] In the only expansive exploration of *All's Well* and eschatology that I know about, Freeman's reading of the play also aligns closely with Roman Catholic theology, especially Catholicism's view of the last things. Shakespeare, according to Freeman, 'expresses the belief that a person can only "end well" through a combination of human effort and divine grace'.[29] Although Freeman does not explicitly make the connection, mainstream early modern Catholics would have heartily concurred. Imagining beyond *All's Well*'s dénouement (as I also do), Freeman proposes that the play's characters' eternal fates depend upon both 'continued human effort, and the grace of God': they must 'live well enough to die well'.[30]

The Protestant teaching which Shakespeare and his contemporaries received also stressed that virtue and goodness should mark Christians' behaviour. However, the Reformers also insisted that such actions do not advance one's prospects of salvation. Their perspective on pilgrimage is paradigmatic of their ethics. Undoubtedly, as Beauregard points out, Catholic practice stands behind *All's Well*'s Helen's identification of herself as undertaking the famous pilgrimage to the shrine of St James in Santiago de Compostela (in northwestern Spain) '*barefoot* [. . .] *with sainted vow my faults to have amended*' (III.iv.4–7).[31] Within a Catholic schema of salvation, the votive pilgrimage was a good work that could, in part, undo the effects of pilgrims' 'faults'. However, as Tiffany shows, the literature of sixteenth-century England indicates that, although they were still popular, physical pilgrimages were no longer primarily viewed as acts of spiritual self-justification. Instead, by Shakespeare's time the pilgrimage had evolved in at least three ways. First, actual pilgrimages were increasingly secularised, morphing into tourism or 'erotic adventure'; second, the concept of journeying, once reserved for the religious pilgrimage, broadened to incorporate a range of reasons for travel; and third, Protestants, following the early Church Fathers (including Tertullian and Augustine), metaphorised the pilgrimage by 'interioriz[ing]' it. The first two reconfigurations underlie Tiffany's contention that *All's Well*'s Helen is driven by carnal, not spiritual, intent. Under the guise of Saint Jacques's pilgrim, her goal is achieving 'the erotic purposes sacred to romantic comedy'.[32]

My primary interest is the relevance to *All's Well* of Protestantism's figurative use of pilgrimage. Unsurprisingly, the Reformers vehemently opposed votive pilgrimages. Calvin, for instance, does not mince his words when he writes that 'God abhorreth nothing more than fained worshippings' and gives as an example people who 'take vpon them vowed pilgrimages to holier places, and sometime either to go all their iourney on foote, or with their body halfe naked, that by their wearines the more merite might be gotten'.[33] For Beauregard, Helen's seemingly contrary attitude, shown in her taking up the persona of the penitential pilgrim, is evidence of *All's Well*'s (and Shakespeare's) Catholic leanings. Yet, as Tiffany notes, while denying that pilgrimage (or any human work) could contribute meritoriously to people's salvation, Calvin and his fellow Protestants did not discard the concept of pilgrimage.[34] Instead, they regularly put it to use as an eschatological metaphor, shedding its associations with acts of exceptional piety, and bringing it into line with their views about every believer's shared condition of 'having and not-having'.

To the Reformers, any person who is 'already-saved' is a pilgrim. All who are justified by faith are on a life-long 'iourney through a strange country, by which they trauell toward the kingdome of heauen'.[35] Tiffany posits that early modern Protestantism relocated this heavenward sojourn 'to an inward place'.[36] No doubt the spiritual experience which Calvin and company (and Tertullian and Augustine before them) allegorised by drawing upon the notion of pilgrimage begins and continues (until death and heaven) within individual believers' hearts and minds. Nevertheless, the Reformers also emphasised that pilgrims' teleologically directed interior journeys reconfigure relations outside the self. To the Reformers, eschatology has ethical implications. The transcendent end towards which pilgrims are headed has a bearing upon their character and conduct in the here and now. One might say that an eschatological hermeneutic inspires a being-toward and being-for the other.

Book Three, Chapter 7 of Calvin's *Institutes* illustrates the interconnections between the Reformers' eschatology and ethics. The chapter's topic is self-denial: 'the forsaking of ourselues'. At the heart of the chapter, Calvin embeds the statement that Christ 'teacheth that we must trauell as men being from home in this world, that the heauenly inheritance be not lost or fall away from vs'. Calvin figures those who forsake themselves, believers, as pilgrims journeying to their ultimate home in heaven.[37] At first glance, it may appear that Calvin here fits the caricature of 'champion of "inner worldly asceticism"' associated with him since the time of Ernst Troeltsch and Max Weber (as Raymond Kemp Anderson notes). But a closer look shows that Calvin understands self-denial not as a withdrawal from the world, but a forsaking of 'seeking for power and fauour of men [. . .] and all desire of worldly glorie'. How is this divesting of self-interest practised? By 'look[ing] vpon God in all things'.[38] This divine perspective has interpersonal implications. For Calvin, it produces humility that admits one's own failings and tendency to play them down coupled with a reverencing of others and recognition of one's contrary inclination to exaggerate their failings. At the juncture of humility and reverence (familiar themes in the Reformers' writings), Calvin envisages neighbourly kindness, whose only limit is 'measured by the rule of charitie', by love.[39]

Love, the greatest of the theological virtues, governs the mode of being-in-the-world of pilgrims as they 'do [their] dutie in seeking the profite of [their] neighbour'.[40] Such self-giving love in this world also adumbrates pilgrims' interpersonal relations in their promised destination. As Max Stackhouse observes, this presence of future realities in the substance of present-day actions differentiates the 'ethical teleology' of Christian eschatology from that of other religions and 'most philosophy'. Whereas Christian and most other eschatologies agree that people make decisions about how we live now on the basis of what we hope to attain in the future ('such as wealth, peace, happiness, and a just society'), Christian eschatology argues for a 'theology of history' in which the influence is bidirectional. Because 'a promised, more ultimate, futural good has, in Jesus Christ, broken into the present', the transcendent into the immanent, this future offers a model for Christians' lives now. For them, this future is 'imagined and anticipated ethically'.[41] This was the thinking of Calvin and his fellow Reformers, for whom Christians should (to employ Anderson's germane phrase) 'live proleptically into' their future life.[42]

Calvin does not romanticise this proleptic living. Instead, he acknowledges that 'nothing is more hard than [. . .] to giue ourselues to God and our brethren'.[43] Self-renunciating love is hard because, to return us to the earlier discussion, in this world, Christians do not yet experience the full knowledge of God and reality, nor freedom from sin. To love now, they require faith and hope – the other theological virtues. In Calvin's eschatology, faith and hope are inseparable: 'Faith beleeueth that eternall life is giuen vs, hope looketh that it be one day revealed. Faith is the foundation whereupon hope resteth, hope nourisheth and sustaineth faith.'[44] Together, faith and hope are, for the Reformers, the twin temporal interpretive lenses through which to read divine promises about a future 'day' that will open into the transcendent beyond.

What about the relationship of faith and hope to love? This Calvin explains as he denounces as 'mere madnesse' the idea which he attributes to Peter Lombard and other medieval scholastic theologians, that is, 'that charitie is before faith and hope'. Rather, 'it is faith onely that first engendreth charitie in vs', Calvin argues.[45] An eschatological hermeneutic comprising faith and hope, a believing hermeneutic, enables self-denying love. Yet, if there is 'nothing more hard' than ceding love of self for love of neighbour, the Reformers also did not underestimate the difficulties of embodying faith and hope. As I have touched upon, Calvin recognised the predicament of believing while 'assailed' by doubt and anxiety.[46] The heaven-bound pilgrim should expect to journey along a rocky path. Or, to follow *All's Well*'s clown, who alludes to Christ's metaphor in Matthew 7: 13–14, heaven is reached via 'the way narrowe that leadeth vnto life' (not the 'broad waye that leadeth to destruction') (IV.v.49–51).

Helen is *All's Well*'s literal pilgrim. However, it is the play's older cohort whose virtuous characters and conduct – their being-toward-the-other – more closely resemble the Reformers' descriptions of the life of those travelling on the narrow way. *All's Well*'s elders show themselves to be the 'true travellers' that Paroles, according to Lafeu, is not (II.iii.259). On the whole, it is possible to read these older characters as illustrative of what it might look like to apply an eschatological hermeneutic of faith and hope in one's interpretations of and interactions with others. At critical moments, *All's Well*'s contingent of wise, appealing older characters responds to the young in ways which call to mind self-denying love.

The older characters introduce an eschatological hermeneutic into the play-world when they draw the younger characters' attention to the finished lives of Gérard de Narbonne and the Count of Roussillon. Viewed from their ends, both men's past virtuous lives function as models of virtue in the present. Gérard was 'famous' for his 'excellent' medical skill (I.i.24, 26). But to the Countess, his 'dispositions', especially his 'honesty' (that is, his virtue) were also noteworthy (I.i.38, 43). The King is even more laudatory as he holds up the former Count of Roussillon to the Count's son, expressing the hope that Bertram will 'inherit' his father's 'moral parts' (I.ii.21–2). The King's portrait of his deceased friend reveals a pattern of life characterised by humility and reverencing of others, the very qualities that, for Calvin, display pilgrims' proleptic living. These attributes also show that the older Count was an estimable courtier (I.ii.36). Yet, despite his high status, the Count did not assert his superiority over those 'who were below him' (I.ii.41). Instead, 'he used [them] as creatures of another place', affording them dignity by 'bow[ing] his eminent top to their low ranks' (I.ii.42–3). Through this self-effacing reversal, the Count raised up others even as he humbled himself through accepting their praise (I.ii.44–5).

The Count's humility and generosity were especially evident at the end of his life, as expressed in his own 'plausive [commendable] words' that the King evokes:

> 'Let me not live', quoth he,
> 'After my flame lacks oil, to be the snuff
> Of younger spirits.'
>
> (I.ii.58–60)[47]

At his life's end, humility framed the Count's reading of himself. He acknowledged his own finitude and found meaning in lives beyond his own. His concern was that he did not stifle the flourishing of the next generation. This was not because he idealised them. The Count was fully aware of the flightiness of the young (I.ii.61–3). Nonetheless, he willingly overlooked their faults, seeing in them promise, a future stretching beyond his own end. It could be said that the Count had faith and hope in this future, despite not knowing if those upon whom it depends will change their ways. This openness to possibility allowed the Count to both assess his own place in history without hubris and interpret others with charity.

As the play progresses, the interactions of *All's Well*'s older characters with the young suggest that these elders share the deceased Count's embrace of an eschatological hermeneutic. Through their proleptic living, *All's Well*'s elders offer glimpses into a future reality whose chief characteristic is love. In addition, these elders join the King in urging the younger characters to follow after the modes of reading and being-in-the-world of the fathers whose lives could be read from their ends. The Countess had also directed Bertram to

> succeed thy father
> In manners, as in shape. Thy blood and virtue
> Contend for empire in thee, and thy goodness
> Share with thy birthright.
>
> (I.i.59–62)

'Blood' may refer to Bertram's inheritance from his noble father, or to the young Count's physical appetite. Either way, the Countess figures a battle within her son. Either the father's blood and virtue are struggling to influence the not yet virtuous son, or virtue is at war with Bertram's baser drives. Victory, from the Countess's perspective, will be declared when Bertram exhibits his father's 'manners'. Like the King in his panegyric of the former Count, the Countess has in mind her late husband's charitable behaviour, rather than his courtly decorum. For Bertram to succeed his father, he must 'love all' and 'do wrong to none' (I.i.62–3).

The King and the Countess associate the young Count's moral development with his ability to read and imitate a life reminiscent of the Reformers' spiritual pilgrim: a life lived in the light of both its own end and what might come after this end. Helen, too, receives instruction to model her life on her father's. The Countess has 'hopes of [Helen's] good', specially that 'education' will develop the 'dispositions she inherits' from her father (I.i.37–9). 'Good' here, like 'blood' above, could take on dual meanings. The Countess hopes that Helen will be 'virtuous' as her father was; and she has this hope that Helen will read and follow Gérard's finished life for her own good (I.i.40). Lafeu bluntly echoes the Countess: 'You must hold the credit of your father' (I.i.77–8). To *All's Well*'s elders, how Helen and Bertram read the transcendent voices which the elders have brought into the present, the voices of those who saw themselves and others from the perspective of the end, matters now.

Both characters show themselves to be problematic readers, and thus provoke doubt about them from other characters and *All's Well*'s audience. (This is especially true of Bertram.) But while there are clear resemblances between Helen and Bertram, their dissimilarities are probably more significant to the question of how the play's interpreters make sense of it, especially its end. The affinities between Helen and immanent signs of a transcendent, auspicious future situate her as the character whom all must read and believe in. *All's Well* cues its audience to not only judge Helen, but to also judge other characters for their responses to her. Yet, both the knowledge about Helen which the play reveals to us and the knowledge it denies us complicates our own belief: our belief in Helen and in *All's Well* as a romantic comedy. From its first scene, the play problematises our understanding of Helen.

'My intents are fixed'

All's Well introduces audiences to Helen via the Countess's and Lafeu's interpretations of her, especially her 'tears' (I.i.45). Both elders assume the Countess's praise of Gérard subjects Helen (again) to 'the tyranny of her sorrows' (I.i.48). Via two contrasting soliloquies in which Helen offers dissonant accounts of her own subjectivity, theatregoers soon realise just how far the Countess and Lafeu are from the truth. In the first soliloquy, Helen immediately discloses that she cries tears of longing, not grief.

> I think not on my father,
> [. . .]
> I have forgot him. My imagination
> Carries no favour in't but Bertram's.
>
> (I.i.79–83)

This is an abrupt change of tone (to say the least). In an instant, Helen dispels the elegiac, serious mood of the play's opening moments. As Shakespeare opens a window onto Helen's affective life, he creates the expectation for theatregoers that they are viewing a romance and establishes desire as a significant theme in his play. Helen employs that most familiar of Petrarchan conceits to adorn her unattainable lover. Bertram is 'a bright particular star' who 'is so above me' that only 'in his bright radiance and collateral light / Must I be comforted, not in his sphere' (I.i.86–9). As Kaara Peterson observes, Helen speaks from 'the masculine rhetorical position' of the Petrarchan persona to articulate what Shakespeare's intended audience would have recognised as 'wholly female-inflected' desire.[48] In Helen's clichéd mapping of the cosmos, it is impossible for her and Bertram's orbits of existence to intersect. Now, with Bertram 'gone', Helen resolves that her 'idolatrous fancy / Must sanctify his relics' (I.i.97–8). True to Petrarchan form, Helen vows to worship her beloved (using contentious language associated with contemporary religious polemics over the practice proscribed in the Thirty-Nine Articles: the 'worshippyng and adoration' 'of reliques').[49]

How do we read Helen's idealism and obsession? Other characters offer some guidance. When Rinaldo tells the Countess of his overhearing Helen's communication 'to herself', he goes to great lengths to represent the hyperbolic tenor of Helen's soliloquy. 'Fortune' 'was no goddess', 'Love no god', and 'Dian no queen of the virgins' while the social disparity between her and Bertram made it impossible for Helen to realise her love (I.iii.109–14). Suggestive of, to use Katherine Duncan-Jones's term, the 'anti-Petrarchan' aspects of Shakespeare's sonnets, Rinaldo's account implicitly (and gently) mocks Helen.[50] The Countess offers a more direct interpretation, founded on personal experience:

> Even so it was with me when I was young.
> If ever we are nature's, these are ours: this thorn
> Doth to our rose of youth rightly belong,
> Our blood to us, this to our blood is born.
>
> (I.iii.125–8)

The Countess uses the same image of blood as she did when urging Bertram to emulate his virtuous father by either acting in step with his 'blood' – his family line – or opposi-tely, resisting his 'blood' – his sexual appetite – in favour of virtue. Here, the Countess appears to have the latter in mind. To her, 'blood' is basic to 'nature', to having blood. But being natural does not mean that, when 'impressed in youth', 'love's strong passion' is benign for the self (I.iii.130). Rather, to the Countess, it is a 'thorn', the grievous, but necessary, counterpart of 'our rose of youth'. The benefit of hindsight allows her to view her own youthful captivation by eros as 'faults' which, at the time, she and her generation could not recognise: 'we thought them none' (I.iii.132). Empathy born of the ability to reflect upon her own past softens the Countess's interpretation of Helen. Nevertheless, the Countess is wary, and as one of *All's Well*'s sages her commentary mutes the play's perspective on love and desire. Compared with Shakespeare's earlier romantic comedies, *All's Well* is more sober, less sentimental.

The Countess's sketch of her younger self maps Helen's self-portrait in her first soliloquy as the lowly 'hind' that 'must die for love' of her elusive 'lion': afflicted, passive, helpless (I.i.91–2). But there is another side to Helen. Before theatre-goers observe the Countess's reading of her, we witness that other side. When Paroles interrupts her first soliloquy, Helen morphs from lovelorn, passive idealist into earthy, agile realist, making use of double entendres to banter knowingly about virginity and sex: 'Is there no military policy how virgins might blow up men?' (I.i.121–2). It is this spirited voice that we hear in Helen's second soliloquy, immediately after Paroles's prosaic leave-taking: 'Get thee a good husband, and use him as he uses thee' (I.i.210–11). Echoing Helen's emphasis on female agency, Paroles figures her as actively pursuing a marriage partner with whom, given the associations of 'use' with sex in *All's Well*, she will possess equal power in her future marriage bed.[51] Paroles's bawdy mock instruction to Helen is of course poles apart from the elders' earlier words of guidance. Moreover, as *All's Well* unfolds, Helen's assessment of Paroles as a 'notorious liar', 'great way fool' and 'solely a coward' proves true (I.i.100–1).

Nonetheless, Paroles's words do adumbrate a fair portion of the ensuing action as Helen sets her face toward the end of getting herself a husband, hinting at how she will do this in her second soliloquy. As with her first, there is a quasi-religious dynamic running through Helen's depiction of herself and her situation. In keeping with the transformation in her demeanour, in this second soliloquy all agents at play align behind what she had earlier defined as 'Th'ambition in my love' and despaired of realising (I.i.90). Helen speaks this second soliloquy in rhyming couplets, a marked contrast to the prose of her conversation with Paroles and her use of blank verse in her previous soliloquy. This different verse form conveys a heightened sense of activity, of the immanence of a transcendent force at work – through Helen and for Helen:

> Our remedies oft in ourselves do lie
> Which we ascribe to heaven. The fated sky
> Gives us free scope, only doth backward pull
> Our slow designs when we ourselves are dull.
> What power is it which mounts my love so high,
> That makes me see, and cannot feed mine eye?
> [. . .]
> Who ever strove
> To show her merit that did miss her love?
> The King's disease – my project may deceive me,
> But my intents are fixed and will not leave me.
> (I.i.212–25)

Whereas in Helen's first soliloquy, the heavens had been distant, housing her 'bright particular star', 'heaven' is now her co-agent. And while in her initial cosmic schema Bertram was central and unreachable, Helen now centres herself, confident that the 'power' directing her desire will also secure its satisfaction. Helen's upbeat tone manifests possibility, a form of faith, one could say. As Cynthia Lewis suggests, this faith is 'in the future' and 'in herself'.[52] Helen believes that her 'remedies' empower her to chart her own destiny.

In a way, the positive energy galvanising Helen's faith orients theatregoers towards their own version of this faith – to believing that *All's Well* will prove a satisfying romantic comedy with Helen as its heroine. At the same time, the language Shakespeare gives his character to detail her faith also stops us being swept up in Helen's 'project'. Helen's rhetoric introduces a note of doubt: doubt about her. There is the explicitly religious idiom which she draws on. Words such as 'fated' and 'merit' may have jarred in early modern ears. 'Fated' calls to mind pagan notions of fatalism that, to the dismay of Protestant teachers, retained a hold in post-Reformation English culture.[53] If Helen is associating the transcendent 'power' behind her faith in herself and a future with Bertram with fate, rather than a more personal entity akin to the Christian God, some in *All's Well*'s intended audience may have both nodded agreement with her sentiment and had an inkling that they shouldn't.

As seen throughout this book, 'merit' was an especially inflammatory word in a Reformation context. Helen articulates a parallel equation to the Catholic position on salvation. To Helen, 'her love' is the reward for 'her merit'. Of course, romance is not redemption. Nevertheless, Helen's reference to her merit absorbs some of the religious disquiet and controversy of Shakespeare's time. Should one person's merit prevail upon another person's affections in an analogous way to the Catholic Church's assertion that merit contributes to making one deserving of God's grace and love? This question is especially pointed because of the display of merit Helen has in mind. Travelling to Paris to heal the to-date-incurable King with the objective of gaining Bertram seems downright calculating (to continue the mathematical metaphor).

Other less overtly religious language compounds this impression of Helen's method as equivocal. 'Our slow designs' and 'my project', Helen's images of her idea to turn miracle into marriage, suggest scheming and self-interest. Helen's 'faith' seems a shadow of the future facing faith (and hope) that motivates selfless love, the faith intrinsic to the eschatological hermeneutic adopted by *All's Well*'s wiser interpreting selves. Some commentators argue that Helen's words and characterisation call to mind a very different ideology. Richard Levin points out the echoes of 'Machiavellian plotting' in 'design'. Similarly, Peterson reads Helen as developing into 'a Machiavellian-styled pragmatist', controlled by her desire and willing to be as manipulative as needs be to satisfy that desire.[54] Whether or not we would go as far as Levin and Peterson, Shakespeare certainly invites *All's Well*'s audience to feel some discomfort about his character's motives. Indeed, Helen herself directs attention to her inner psyche as she grounds her proposed action in her 'intents'.

'Intent' is a prominent word in *All's Well*. The Countess interrogates Helen's intents. Having eventually wrought from Helen a verbose (twenty-six line) 'confession' that she loves Bertram, the Countess is not taken in by her interlocuter's melodramatic assurances that she will not pursue her love object, that she 'seeks not to find that her search implies, / But riddle-like lives sweetly where she dies' (I.iii.188, 191, 213–14). When Helen finally draws breath, the Countess cuts straight to the point, unmasking the disingenuity of the younger woman's claims to restraint and helplessness: 'Had you not lately an intent – speak truly – / To go to Paris?' (I.iii.215–16). Helen's explanation focuses solely on the pathos of the King's 'desperate languishings' and her 'remedy' for them, found among her father's 'prescriptions / Of rare and proved effects' (I.iii.226, 225, 118–19). It turns out that Helen has not entirely forgotten her father. But it seems telling that she is more concerned to make use of his mystical prescriptions than enact his 'virtuous qualities' (I.i.40). Meanwhile, the savvy Countess asks again: 'This was your motive for Paris, was it? Speak' (I.iii.228). Like *All's Well*'s audience, the alert, possibly stern Countess fixes her interpretive energies on Helen's intent. Our – the Countess's and the audience's – mutual insight into Helen's inner life gives *All's Well*'s interpreters cause to doubt Helen and to feel uncertain about whether her 'project', her means to her own ends, can end well, even if she gets what she wants.

Be that as it may, these very means and ends also indicate yet another side to Helen. As significant turning points in *All's Well*'s plot, the events of miracle and marriage suggest the possibility of a propitious end. This familiar dramatic, generic code contains echoes of Protestant eschatology in which miracle and marriage function as signs in this finite world. Miracle and marriage fuel faith and hope as they point to the transcendent next world. On miracles, Calvin contends that being 'heedfull [. . .] to the miracles which throughout all the coasts of the world do offer themselues to our eyes' makes it less difficult to believe in the ultimate miracle of one's future eternal bodily resurrection: the crucial element of the eschaton. He cites biblical examples of miraculous 'likenesse[s] of the resurrection' as compass points for belief. Life sprouting from a seed sown to die (Paul's analogy in 1 Corinthians 15), the healing of the famous Old Testament figures of David and Job when both felt close to death, the nation of Israel's return from the desolation of exile – all such events are, for Calvin, foretastes of the final resurrection.[55]

As with such 'miracles', the Reformers also interpreted marriage as having eschatological significance. As noted in Chapter 3, Shakespeare's intended audience was likely acquainted with the idea of marriage as a theological sign.

In *The Book of Common Prayer* (1559), 'The Form of Solemnization of Matrimony' opens by describing marriage as betokening 'the mystical union that is betwixt Christ and his church'.[56] The analogy references the frequent biblical use of marriage as a metaphor for the loving relationship which God (or Christ) – the 'bridegroom' – establishes with his 'bride': Israel in the Old Testament, the church in the New Testament. But while the spiritual betrothal takes place in the 'now', believers' earthly experience of the 'mystical union' is anticipatory. They look forward to its consummation 'then', at their bodily resurrection to eternal life. As the Geneva Bible's gloss to Revelation 19 explains: 'God made Christ the bridgrome of his Church at the beginning, and at the last day it shalbe fully accomplished when we shal be ioyned with our head.' In 'The Freedom of a Christian', Luther individualises the analogy. Christ's 'bride' is the 'believing soul'. 'By the wedding ring of faith [Christ] shares in the sins, death, and pains of hell which are his bride's' and endows her with 'eternal righteousness, life, and salvation.'[57]

Viewed through an eschatological interpretive frame, miracle and marriage signal belief. Helen's proposed 'cure' of the King who is otherwise 'rendered lost' bears a 'likeness' (to repurpose Calvin) to the promised future bodily resurrection (I.iii.226–7). There are also resonances of the eschatological symbolism of marriage, especially as Helen makes her desired marriage contingent upon the success of her 'remedy' (I.iii.225). Helen's readings (or lack thereof) of her father, herself, Bertram and the 'King's disease' are problematic. But her centrality to the occurrences of the miraculous (or that which seems miraculous) and marriage in *All's Well* also elicits judgements of the other characters from within and outside the play-world. These judgements hinge upon the characters' reading of Helen as not only a transcendent other, but as an other who points to something greater than them all. In the face of their limited knowledge, the characters' responses of belief or doubt to both Helen's announcement of her 'project', and its favourable outcome, holds up a mirror to these characters' own moral condition as interpreting selves. Or, as Gadamer might express it, these characters should acknowledge their own limitations and open themselves up to Helen.[58]

'A showing of a heavenly effect in an earthly actor'

I start with the Countess. Upon uncovering Helen's 'motive for Paris', the Countess could have proved a roadblock to the younger woman. Instead, she relates to Helen in the same way that the old Count had treated 'younger spirits', allowing the younger woman to present her case. In another turnaround, Helen claims that 'there's something' in Gérard's 'good receipt' which points to a supernatural hand at work in her plan and backs this assertion by banking her life on its success (I.iii.239–45). 'Dost thou believe't?' the older woman asks the younger, and upon receiving the reply 'Ay, madam, knowingly', also believes (I.iii.246–7). Empowering Helen to leave for the King's court, the Countess will 'stay at home / And pray God's blessing into thy attempt', with the further assurance that 'what I can help thee to, thou shalt not miss' (I.iii.250–3). Loving action, a kind of being-for-the-other, follows from the Countess's believing interpretation of Helen, her openness to transcendence.

Lafeu demonstrates the same receptivity by also believing in Helen. He takes upon himself the mission of convincing the King to imitate his belief. To do so, Lafeu figures Helen as one who can effect a likeness of the resurrection for the King: 'I have seen a medicine / That's able to breathe life into a stone', 'whose simple touch / Is powerful to araise King Pippen' (II.i.70–1, 73–4). By depicting her as 'a medicine', Helen, Lafeu intimates, is not only physician, but also the physic. As frequently noted, the notion that Helen embodies her cure, along with the suggestiveness of 'araise', contribute to the sexual undercurrent at play as the scene is set for Helen's miracle.[59] So too does Lafeu's somewhat unexpected snapshot of his role: 'I am Cressid's uncle, / That dare leave two together. Fare you well' (II.i.95–6). Helen also employs a sexually knowing vocabulary as she takes over from Lafeu as the King's persuader. As Barbara Howard Traister points out, Helen ties the outcome of her intervention to her 'sexual reputation'.[60] If she fails, she knows she will be disgraced, subjected to 'Tax of impudence, / A strumpet's boldness, a divulged shame' (II.i.168–9).

Shakespeare weaves together sensual and spiritual at this decisive point in the plot, as he often does in *All's Well*. Here, my reading of this interplay differs from that of Tiffany, for whom the 'erotic overtones of the King's cure' empties Helen's 'miracle [. . .] of Reformation-era theological significance'.[61] In contrast, I suggest that we can discern significant eschatological notes in the evocative materiality of Helen's miracle, and that these notes also sound throughout the discourse around the miracle. As Lafeu and (eventually) the King express their belief in Helen, they underline her effect on their senses. Lafeu believes because he has 'seen a medicine', perhaps Helen putting on a 'public medicine show', as Kent Lehnhof suggests.[62] Seeing places an accent on the body, thus on the erotic. Lafeu also emphasises what he hears: 'I have spoke / With one that [. . .] hath amazed me' (II.i.80–2). The lord draws attention to the power of Helen's speech acts, linking her words to his belief. This movement from hearing to believing has a theological counterpart in the Reformers' eschatology. As discussed, it is by hearing God's speech act – Scripture – that (according to the Reformers) people place their faith in his promissory words about his future, miraculous raising of them, as inflected with doubt as this faith may be.

Helen's words, specifically, words associating her with the supernatural, also (eventually) convince the King to 'trust' her (II.i.204). Initially, the King is sceptical – he will not 'be so credulous of cure' (II.i.11). Given that the finest physicians could not cure him, Helen's offer is 'a senseless help' (II.i.115–17, 122). The King's refusal of Helen's aid rests on what he sees as their discrepant knowledge: 'what at full I know, thou knowst no part; / I knowing all my peril, thou no art' (II.i.130–1). The sceptical King dismisses Helen. Yet, even as he does so with words that convey misdoubt, he adopts a new mode of speech in these final lines. As with Helen's second soliloquy, the King's switch from blank verse to rhyming couplets signals a different mood that hints at 'the intervention of divine power', as Russell Fraser puts it. As he reaches the limits of his knowledge, the King appears to experience something akin to Gadamer's 'religious feeling'.[63]

Helen seems to sense this shift, taking up the King's register and, in concert with the religious feeling it appears to manifest, an explicitly religious vocabulary, to try again: 'He that of greatest works is finisher / Oft does them by the weakest minister' (II.i.134–5). To support her case, Helen adduces multiple biblical allusions. Most familiarly, she alludes to Moses' parting of the Red Sea after he had reluctantly accepted the role as mediator of God's rescue of Israel (II.i.136–9).[64] Like the biblical God who acted through, indeed despite, unlikely, impotent human vessels, a higher power can 'remedy' 'where hope is coldest' (II.i.133, 142). In a way, Helen asks the King to direct his faith towards this power: 'Of heaven, not me, make an experiment' (II.i.152). At the same time, she concludes by reminding the King that she will play a part in her proposed remedy: 'But know I think, and think I know most sure, / My art is not past power, nor you past cure' (II.i.156–7).

The content and register of Helen's words position her and her 'art' at the meeting point of the supernatural and the natural, conveying possibility and hope. Having insisted 'I must not hear thee', the King, it seems, cannot help but take notice (II.i.143). He is mesmerised, enchanted even.

After refusing to engage across many lines of dialogue, the King opens himself up to listening to her as he finally asks a question: 'Art thou so confident?' (II.i.157). When Helen pledges her life as her 'certainty and confidence' (as she did with the Countess), she wins him over (II.i.167). The King agrees that Helen's words originate from a divine source (II.i.173–4). Helen's words animate his faith: 'More should I question thee, and more I must, / Though more to know could not be more to trust' (II.i.203–4). In a reversal of his previous contention, the King now professes that Helen is the holder of knowledge. He only knows in part. But he knows enough to 'trust'.

All's Well's audience do not see Helen cure the King. Instead, we hear Lafeu's interpretation of it as he converses with Paroles and Bertram. The King's healing defies those who 'say miracles are past', demonstrating, as per the title of a broadside ballad conveniently at hand, 'A showing of a heavenly effect in an earthly actor' (II.iii.1, 23–4). As he did by describing Helen as 'a medicine', in reporting the sensation (as though he were composing a ballad for public circulation) Lafeu foregrounds both miracle and miracle worker. The most important person in France has escaped 'sure death', but he must share centre stage with his 'preserver' (II.iii.18, 48). The two enter the scene in tandem, quite possibly dancing – a mode of arrival that signals affinity and parity. The King further affirms Helen's newly elevated status by, first, positioning her at his side, and then investing her with the 'power to choose' a titled husband (II.iii.48, 57).

This entwining of Helen and her miracle with her anticipated marriage brings to mind the eschatological dimension of marriage in which temporal marriage gestures to the perfect, eternal relationship between resurrected believers and God. The King offers Helen's raising of him as the rationale which obligates Bertram (or any of the young lords) to marry her (II.iii.108–11). 'Heaven hath through me restored the King to health', Helen explains, and the King spells out the implications: 'Who shuns thy love shuns all his love in me' (II.iii.63, 73). As God's agent, Helen is no longer a mere commoner. Each lord must read her accordingly, believing that her miracle has transformed her into a desirable spouse. All do, except Bertram.

Bertram alone refuses this reading, expressing disbelief by disjoining miracle and marriage. Although he 'know'st' the miracle Helen 'has done for' the King, he 'never hope[s] to know why [he] should marry' the miracle worker (II.iii.108–10). To some commentators, Bertram has a point. Traister, for instance, implies that we should feel some pity for Bertram as he 'should not be forced to marry against [his] will'.[65] Nevertheless, by preferencing the play-world's elders' perspectives of Bertram, Shakespeare directs his audience to view his response as a misreading of the situation. First, before Helen makes her choice, we witness Lafeu's comic misunderstanding. As Helen declines the first four young lords, Lafeu, out of earshot of the main event, interprets her refusal of each in the reverse: 'An they were sons of mine, I'd have them whipped' (II.iii.86–7). Here, the old lord's judgement is awry. But it echoes sharply when Bertram reveals that he is out of step with his companions, and the King.

Bertram does not hide the reason for his resistance: 'She had her breeding at my father's charge. / A poor physician's daughter my wife?' (II.iii.114–15). Having asked for the liberty to employ 'the help of mine own eyes' in the matter of marriage, Bertram reveals that he sees Helen as little more than a household pet (II.iii.108). Unlike the other young lords (and the elders), Bertram does not engage with Helen. He does not open himself up to hearing her voice and instead addresses himself only to the King. We may have felt inclined to pity Bertram, but he is not really a sympathetic character. Or, in the terms of the play, and as the King none too subtly implies, he is not a virtuous character: '"A poor physician's daughter" – thou dislik'st / Of virtue for the name. But do not so' (II.iii.123–4). Quoting Bertram's words back to him emphasises the fallaciousness of his resolution to cast off virtue in favour of status. Even more pointedly, the King argues via a memorable image of disease and turgidity that a name without virtue is injurious to the self: 'Where great additions swell's, and virtue none, / It is a dropsied honour' (II.iii.127–8).[66] Honours are healthy for the self only 'when rather from our acts we them derive / Than our foregoers' (a person's inherited noble name) (II.iii.135–7).

To drum his point into Bertram's mind, the King turns to the end of life, to an eschatological perspective that exposes the false ties between rank and honour. In the early modern graveyard, only those who had been well off enough could afford gravestones or, more ostentatiously, tombs.[67] On these markers of now absent bodies, 'honour', the King claims, is everywhere wrongly attributed, entirely nominal. This 'mere word' has become 'a slave debauched on every tomb, on every grave / A lying trophy', whitewashing over lives which manifested anything but virtue (II.iii.137–9). Meanwhile, 'honour' 'is dumb' where it should be loudest: written over 'honoured bones' housed in 'dust and damned oblivion' – the bones of the poor (II.iii.139–41). Ralph Houlbrooke cites Thomas Parnell's description of these anonymous graves (in 'A Night-Piece on Death', 1721): 'with bended osier bound / That nameless heave the crumbled ground'.[68] The King's suggestion that 'honour' should be redistributed post-mortem to the 'nameless' represents a radical overturning of social hierarchies and an affront to Bertram.

To this point, the King adopts a restrained, even-handed rhetoric, seeking to reason his ward into belief. However, when Bertram remains unyielding, the King gets personal, and pugnacious. On his part, the King's 'honour's at the stake' and he will exert his authority to restore it (II.iii.149–50). Demeaning Bertram as a 'proud scornful boy', the King orders him to 'obey our will, which travails in thy good' (II.iii.150–1, 158). Bertram is the antithesis of the Reformers' 'already-saved' pilgrims, whose faith and hope in their eternal heavenly destination loosens their grip on their desire for worldly recognition.[69] Bertram must look again at himself and his world, to 'believe not thy disdain' and to instead transfer his disbelief from the King and Helen to himself (II.iii.159). The command comes with a punishment. If Bertram disobeys, the King will 'throw [him] from my care forever'; Bertram will feel the full force of the King's 'revenge and hate' (II.iii.162, 165).

Ironically (of course) Bertram's self-understanding and defiance presents a challenge to the King's own honour that piques him into exposing an authoritarian, punitive streak in his character. The King does not come away from this exchange without fault; he is not the perfect model of virtue. Nonetheless, underneath his hot temper and harsh language, it appears that the King's threat amounts to nothing more than leaving Bertram to his own devices. Under the institution of wardship established by the Court of Wards and Liveries (in operation from 1540 to 1660), guardians could decide who their wards married (and control their wards' assets). As Terry Reilly describes, guardians abused this situation for financial gain as the first of many exploitative practices which, from the end of the sixteenth century, gathered increasing opposition against the Court and the institution of wardship.[70] But patronising and flawed as *All's Well*'s King may be, he is hardly exploiting his guardianship. Bertram wants to step outside his wardship arrangement. With the implication that Bertram will undo himself because of his 'youth and ignorance', the King warns that Bertram's self-propulsion towards his own downfall is exactly the situation to which he will abandon his ward (II.iii.164). Moreover, calling to mind Lafeu's testimony to the King's benevolence in *All's Well*'s opening lines, the King maintains that he has Bertram's 'good' in mind (II.iii.158).

Even as Bertram sourly agrees to the match, his sarcastic tone signals his refusal to modify his view of either himself or Helen:

> I find that she, which late
> Was in my nobler thoughts most base, is now
> The praised of the King
>
> (II.iii.170–2)

All's Well's midpoint wedding dispels any lingering belief that the play will resolve into a regulation romantic comedy. Egged on by the equally self-absorbed, superficial Paroles to believe that 'the King has done you wrong', the obdurate groom defies the King twice over. He flees from his marriage (without consummating it) to the forbidden Florentine battlefield (II.iii.299; II.i.27). Further reinforcing his want of virtue, Bertram also obliges Helen to act as his courier: 'I have sent you a daughter-in-law. She hath recovered the King, and undone me. I have wedded her, not bedded her, and sworn to make the "not" eternal' (III.ii.19–22). The Countess's response re-sounds the reactions of the King and Lafeu, encapsulating the doubt Bertram has attracted to himself. With an obvious echo of the play's title, and Lavatch's eschatologically modulated play on 'well' and 'not well' a few scenes earlier, the Countess pronounces her verdict on Bertram's actions: 'This is not well, rash and unbridled boy' (III.ii.28).

Bertram has misinterpreted himself and others. 'By the misprizing of a maid too virtuous / For the contempt of empire', he has disregarded both his dependence on the King and the virtuous King's wish to benefit him (III.ii.31–2, 29). Yet, even as Bertram consciously turns his back on virtue, marriage and the anticipation of happiness which together adumbrate the eschatological hermeneutic often applied by *All's Well*'s elders, he unknowingly invites an eschatological reading of his unwanted union. In his letter to his mother, the pun on 'not'/ 'knot', and its juxtaposition with 'eternal' evokes the archetypal 'marriage' of Christ and his church, and the complete reconciliation and unmitigated joy this union represents. Bertram's definitive language should close off possibility; instead, his words work a thread of hope into the fabric of the play.

The Countess is not the only recipient of Bertram's epistolary exertions. He also blasts Helen with what he thinks is a watertight repudiation: 'When thou canst get the ring upon my finger, which never shall come off, and show me a child begotten of thy body that I am father to, then call me husband. But in such a "then" I write a "never"' (III.ii.57–60). Once more, an eschatological hermeneutic challenges what Bertram presents as certain. By calling attention to a future 'then' and to the ring that, as Luther figures it, represents faith in this 'then', Bertram again unwittingly hints at the trajectory and ultimate signification of marriage. As they simultaneously communicate impossibility and possibility, his words engender both despondency and hope, a dual response which Helen embodies.

Helen's first words after reading Bertram's letter suggest despair: 'This is a dreadful sentence' (III.ii.61). But *All's Well*'s movement towards the end of romance and comedy anticipated by its title – towards possibility and transcendence – relies upon Helen maintaining, and enacting, faith and hope. In many ways, this is what she does as her actions advance the play to its final reunion scene, and in so doing incline theatregoers towards belief. Nevertheless, Helen's morally ambiguous methods and, more than her actions themselves, the disorienting, patchy knowledge about these actions received by *All's Well*'s audience, further riddle possibility with uncertainty, belief with doubt.

'The web of our life is of a mingled yarn'

Until Bertram's churlish dismissal of Helen, reducing her from wife to messenger, *All's Well*'s audience feel that we know her. At least Helen's contradictions are mostly apparent to us. Why does Helen end up in Paris, her father's curative script in hand? Her soliloquies, together with other characters' interrogations and interpretations of her, point to a knot of romantic desire, mixed motives and, by dint of her eschatological signification, less tangible transcendent forces at work. Although we cannot reconcile these conflicting sides of Helen's identity as they surface across the play's early acts, we are clued in to them, and can map them simultaneously, dissonantly, onto her actions. Now, as Helen embarks on another journey, it seems that Shakespeare has hit reset and repeat on the sequence of soliloquy, interpretation and arrival. But this time, as its plot progresses, *All's Well* increasingly distances its audience from its protagonist's psyche, opening up ever-widening fissures in our knowledge of her.

Realising that 'we don't know' (Gadamer's phrase is again apt) comes as somewhat of a surprise for theatregoers. Our awareness of our unknowing follows fast after we are once more seemingly immersed in the workings of Helen's inner self. With Helen's (and the play's) return to Roussillon, she is again in soliloquy, and again giving voice to her devotion to Bertram. However, on this occasion Helen frames her relation to him very differently. In her first soliloquy, Helen had portrayed herself as helpless for want of Bertram: she 'must die for love' (I.i.92). Now, it is Bertram who is indigent, his death which Helen envisages. Not only so, but she also figures herself as the agent responsible for both Bertram's grim fate and his rescue from it. Reacting to Bertram's declaration that 'Till I have no wife, I have nothing in France', Helen blames herself for driving him from home and 'expos[ing] / Those tender limbs of thine to the [. . .] / none-sparing war' (III.ii.100, 103–6). To save Bertram by facilitating his homecoming she 'will be gone' (III.ii.123). Her action and intent are full of eschatological resonance, reminiscent as they are of Christ's self-denying acts which paved the way for people to journey to their heavenly home.

Are we being shown yet another side to Helen? Melodramatic tone aside, her willingness to leave her own home so that Bertram can return to it does seem to 'hint at self-sacrifice', as Michael Shurgot puts it.[71] Has Helen incorporated an ethical mode of being-for-the-other into her perspective of Bertram? Certainly, charity more than eros appears to motivate Helen's second departure from Roussillon. Her next communication, her farewell epistolary sonnet to the Countess, as well as the Countess's reaction to it, indicate similarly. Helen links her self-imposed exile from Roussillon to her supposed renunciation of her 'project'. Confessing the 'ambitious love [which] hath so in me offended', Helen will atone for her 'faults' with devoted prayer for Bertram as Saint Jacques' pilgrim (III.iv.5, 7, 10–11). There is no doubt an element of irony in Helen's choice to communicate her decision as a sonnet, evocative as the poetic form is of idealised sensual love and its torments. Helen declares that she will forgo her desire for Bertram while gesturing back to her earlier outpourings of youthful passion, associating her 'flight' with the contrasting subject positions and aspirations of both Petrarchan lover and self-denying pilgrim.

In her response, the Countess again draws attention to Helen's intents. This time, the Countess reads only the restorative possibilities of love (rather than the double-edged impulsiveness of youthful passion) off the pages of the other's letter (III.iv.21). Picking up on Helen's spiritual discourse, the Countess reframes the import of Helen's self-described religious endeavour by redistributing both blame and esteem. The Countess twice criticises her son as an 'unworthy husband', while emphasising Helen's 'worth' (III.iv.26, 31). It is squarely on Bertram's shoulders that the Countess puts the burden of responsibility for the newly-weds' estrangement. As she does so, she suggests that her son's actions have eschatological repercussions. Bertram

cannot thrive
Unless her prayers, whom heaven delights to hear
And loves to grant, reprieve him from the wrath
Of greatest justice.

(III.iv.26–9)

Bertram's end is contingent upon Helen's invocations on his behalf. For the Countess, this is not necessarily a hopeless state of affairs. She has faith in the efficacy of Helen's prayers, and moreover, in Helen herself. The Elizabethan 'Homily on Prayer' urges listeners to be continually in prayer, encouraging them that 'for [Christ's] sake [. . .] God hath promised to hear our Prayer, so he will truly perform it'.[72] The echoes of the homilist's language in the Countess's words suggest parallels between Helen and the homily's addressees. More than this, the Countess's image of the particular joy which God experiences when he hears Helen's voice hints at a further analogy: that Helen occupies an intercessory role between Bertram and heaven akin to Christ's present role (in the epoch between his past ascension and future return) as the sole intercessor between humanity and God the Father. As the homilist states, Christ stands behind God's promised attentiveness to humans' prayers. Because he made salvation possible through his redemptive crucifixion, Christ is now 'at the right hand of God the Father, and there liveth for ever to make Intercession for us'.[73]

As Gossett and Wilcox note, the Countess's 'whom' is ambiguous, implying that Helen herself, not just her prayers, is close to the divine ear.[74] The Countess may be suggesting that she believes Helen has Christ-like intercessory powers. Calvin assures his readers that they can 'boldly come to [God in prayer] trusting that we haue such an intercessor', that is, Christ.[75] Helen, it seems, animates in the Countess a form of faith and hope not unlike this trust. Her knowledge that Helen is praying for Bertram inspires the Countess to appeal to him to hasten home. Moreover, the Countess has the 'hope' that Helen, 'hearing so much, will speed her foot again, / Led hither by pure love' (III.iv.36–8). The Countess hopes for the newly-weds' happy reunion at home, and she expresses faith that love will bring about this unlikely end.

In Helen's own report, her 'ambitious love' had proved self-defeating. But in the place of 'ambitious love', the Countess identifies the presence of a different quality of love: 'pure love'. 'Pure love' encompasses the spiritual and secular strains of Helen's sonnet. Doubtless, the phrase signifies both romantic love and altruistic, self-giving love. The latter is consonant with the language around Helen's proposed pilgrimage, including the Countess's implied correlation of Helen and Christ. Unsurprisingly, the phrase 'pure love' is frequently found in early modern theological texts. Martin Luther and William Tyndale, for instance, each connect eschatology and ethics as they contend that 'pure loue', rather than divine reward or self-promotion, should motivate the virtuous actions of people who trust in God's grace alone (rather than their works) for their salvation.[76]

The Countess of course does not say if her understanding of pure love and its workings comes from this theological mould. Notwithstanding, the structure of this short scene – Helen's sonnet followed by the Countess's response – certainly suggests that the interplay of Helen's announcement that she will forfeit her own comfort to 'free' Bertram from 'death and danger', and the Countess's lofty view of her young gentlewoman inspire the Countess's hope in the reparative influence of pure love (III.iv.17, 15). The Countess's interpretation of Helen's words and Helen herself casts a faint gleam of optimism over the play. Love undiluted by self-interest may return Helen to Roussillon, and with her *All's Well* narrative back onto the track of romance.

Yet, just as theatregoers may feel ourselves drawn to this way of reading Helen and her actions, Shakespeare causes us to think again by obfuscating our understanding of his protagonist. From within the palace of Roussillon, Helen, in soliloquy, had sketched out a rough map of her intents, locating herself and Bertram on journeys that would distance them from one another. As Bertram transits home from Florence, Helen's route as a self-denying, remorseful pilgrim, she tells the Countess, will take her 'far' – far from Roussillon and even further from Florence (III.iv.10). Santiago de Compostela lies roughly due west of Roussillon, Florence due east.

The question of why, in the very next scene, Shakespeare transports his audience to Florence to join Helen supposedly 'bound', as she tells the Florentine Widow, for 'Saint Jacques le Grand' is one of the most frequent talking points about his play (III.v.33). For Jean Howard, Helen has arrived in Florence by her own design and never intended to go to Spain. Maurice Hunt, in contrast, argues that Helen appears in Bertram's locale by dint of 'the working of the mysterious natural magnetism' that draws them together.[77] Our knowledge of Helen as a complex, equivocal character suggests that either of these divergent interpretations (and indeed holding them in tension) is possible. One word captures the ambiguous nature of Helen's journey: 'pretence'. A few scenes later, Lord G. reports that Helen had 'some two months since fled' Roussillon, her 'pretence' being 'a pilgrimage to Saint Jacques le Grand' (IV.iii.45–7). While today 'pretence' invites an exclusively negative judgement of the character by signalling dissimulation and affectation, to early modern theatregoers 'pretence' also conveyed the more neutral idea (now obsolete) of intention or purpose.[78] Did Helen set out to deceive or simply to undertake a pilgrimage? Does ambitious love or pure love impel her to Florence?

As Shakespeare continues to interest his audience in understanding and judging Helen, the decisive point of difference from *All's Well*'s earlier scenes is that her internal self is now opaque to us. The play has brought us, in Gadamerian terms, to a point of 'non-knowing' about Helen.[79] Her soliloquy leads us to believe that we are privy to her intentions. So too does her sonnet-letter. It is noteworthy, however, that the knowledge which the letter yields is obtained at second hand, mediated by Rinaldo's reading of it and the Countess's interpretation (a distancing effect more noticeable in performance than on the page). When she seemingly detours from her travel plans, Helen problematises our confidence in both what we think we know about her and in her as the source of that knowledge. We do witness the Countess's hopeful interpretation of both Helen's epistle and the future, founded upon her faith in Helen and in love. But here also, Helen's subsequent actions may well overlay our prior reading of the Countess's perspective with doubt. Perhaps on this occasion the Countess has not been as attuned to Helen's 'pretence', her understanding skewed by her affection for, indeed her near veneration of, the other.

Long after we receive confirmation of Helen's abode in Florence, *All's Well* presents its audience with a further account of her journey (IV.iii.53). Lord G. reports the perplexing detail that Helen 'accomplished' her pilgrimage, 'intelligence' the soldiers attained from 'her own letters' (IV.iii.48, 58, 53). Even more astonishing is the news that, at Saint Jacques's shrine, Helen 'in fine, made a groan of her last breath, and now she sings in heaven' (IV.iii.50–1). If the baffling nature of this revelation itself does not prompt *All's Well*'s audience to query it, the play does this for us via Lord E.'s immediate inquiry: 'How is this justified?' (IV.iii.52). The reply that 'to the point of her death' Helen had authored this information about her, confirmed by one final letter by the rector at Saint Jacques after her 'death', is not reassuring (IV.iii.53–7).

This time, theatregoers do not hear Helen's actual words read by their recipient. The 'intelligence' we receive is now third-hand, and instead of 'mak[ing] her story true', as Lord G. asserts, her purported letters deepen our suspicion (IV. iii.54). Our knowledge that Helen has not died potentially discredits everything she says and writes (and reportedly writes) about her journey and the intents which took her from Roussillon to Florence. Again, we ask why. Why has Helen circulated misleading information about herself? The character herself offers no clues, and indeed makes only one fleeting, enigmatic mention of her 'death' to the Widow and Diana (IV.iv.10–11). As the play takes us further and further away from Helen's consciousness, any attempt to understand what underlies her intents becomes mere conjecture. Perhaps our best approach is to admit that 'we don't know'.

We do know, however, that Helen has come up with a new 'plot' (III.vii.44). Like *Measure*'s Duke (possibly a foreboding comparison), Helen lands on the bed-trick as her solution. Bertram wants to sleep with Diana; Diana will agree, but it is Helen who will 'fill the time' (III.vii.33). Unlike *Measure*'s Duke, Helen is both 'plotter' and actor. Further, without revisiting the ways that Shakespeare problematises *Measure*'s Duke's version of this controversial dramatic convention, another difference between the two plays stands out. *All's Well* presents no obvious crisis which Helen must resolve. No one's life is (ostensibly) at stake. Indeed, Helen had recently signalled in both her soliloquy and sonnet-letter that she thought she could protect Bertram's life by leaving him be, not by sleeping with him. Once more, the play turns our interpretive energies towards trying to understand Helen's motive. But as she successfully persuades the Widow to allow Diana to participate in her plan, their dialogue does not readily illuminate Helen's reason for proposing the bed-trick, revolving instead around justifying what it is.

All three characters recognise that the act is double-edged. The Widow boils down the bed-trick to a pithy paradox: it is 'deceit so lawful' (III.vii.38). Helen is more expansive. Her plot

> Is wicked meaning in a lawful deed,
> And lawful meaning in a wicked act,
> Where both not sin, and yet a sinful fact.
>
> (III.vii.45–7)

Emphasising the cold reality of Helen's marital status, which makes sleeping with her own husband 'lawful', over the instinct that it is 'wicked' to gull him into the act is not an emotionally compelling argument. As Peterson observes, Helen's 'machinations', culminating with the bed-trick, 'seem to generate particular distaste' from *All's Well*'s readers.[80] However, it is worth noting that the play not only weighs 'lawful' against 'wicked', but also 'lawful' against 'unlawful'. Twice, other characters use 'unlawful' to describe Bertram's desire to seduce Diana (III.v.69, IV.iii.25–6). While Helen's intents become increasingly difficult to decode, the motivation behind Bertram's intents towards Diana seems palpable. Once more, *All's Well* neutralises its audience's sympathy for Bertram by foregrounding his disreputable character, his lack of virtue. Within the play-world, the consensus is that Bertram has stepped outside both legal and moral boundaries, a reading of his objective which appears to offer Diana a valid reason for colluding in Helen's plot: 'I think't no sin / To cozen him that would unjustly win' (IV.ii.75–6).

The bed-trick is 'no sin'. Strictly speaking. Nevertheless, we cannot easily let Helen off the hook. She may not be sinning, but it feels as though she is, which may be what she means by 'sinful fact' (III.vii.47). As Helen Wilcox notes, the religious vocabulary the three female characters employ to rationalise the act points to the contemporary, and pessimistic, theological account of human being woven into the play's 'lament for human weakness and folly'. Reflective of this tone, Lord G. uses language evocative of the idea of original sin as he attributes Bertram's desire to 'flesh his will in the spoil of [Diana's] honour' to all people's ruinous condition: 'Now, God delay our rebellion! As we are ourselves, what things are we!' (IV.iii.15, 18–19).[81] 'As we are ourselves' is an image of postlapsarian humanity 'not supported by God's grace', as Fraser puts it.[82] To dispel any misconception that the tone of 'what things are we' is anything but regretful, Lord E. immediately glosses his brother's exclamation by spelling out that humans, collectively, are 'merely our own traitors' (IV.iii.20). Helen is no exception. In a way, she betrays herself through her use of theologically charged language to explain and justify her scheme. Her repetition of 'sin' and 'wicked' as she asserts its defensibility has the effect of associating Helen's bed-trick with human fallenness, thus inducing doubt about her. Indeed, the scene primes its audience to doubt, opening mid-conversation with Helen's acknowledgement to the Widow that 'if you misdoubt me' Helen must abandon her plot (III.vii.1–3).

All the same, while the 'wicked act' is problematic, suggestive of the corruptive impact of the Fall and original sin, it is nevertheless also a 'lawful deed'. Moreover, within a theological frame of meaning, it evokes the eschaton. The sexual consummation of human marriages figures the eschatological moment when the 'already-saved' will know perfectly and completely: when they see God 'face to face' and 'human weakness and folly' is a thing of the past. 'Mak[ing] her marriage "real"' is, in Howard's opinion, Helen's goal from the moment she reads Bertram's 'dreadful sentence'. She 'journey[s] and schem[es]' to satisfy his seemingly impossible demands – obtain my ring, show me my child – to the end of calling him 'husband' (III.ii.57–61).[83] Although this reading seems to offer an overly definite account of Helen's motivation and actions, I take Howard's point that the bed-trick fulfils Bertram's stipulations. In Protestant theology, without sex, Helen and Bertram are, in Daniel Swift's words, 'only half-married'.[84] Helen's method is distasteful, but it does actualise their marriage, and it does so on Bertram's terms.

Further, the juxtaposition of the eschatological associations of marriage with the theological imagery of human fallenness implied in other characters' readings of Bertram hints that Helen's plot might possibly benefit him. This spiritual dynamic reflects the Countess's (perhaps too optimistic) belief that Helen, through her prayers, could turn around Bertram's 'not well' condition (III.ii.28). Significantly, while 'misdoubt' is an evident motif informing the predominant mood of Helen's dialogue with the Widow, belief is also explicitly spoken of and enacted in the scene. 'I should believe you' is the Widow's response to Helen's request that she give her 'trust the count he is my husband' (III.vii.12, 8). Through her conditional 'should', the Widow acknowledges the possibility of believing Helen, but her disinclination to do so. However, when Helen presents a 'purse of gold' to 'buy your friendly help', shows her knowledge of Bertram's ancestral ring and elaborates upon her 'lawful' plot to secure it, the Widow 'yields' (III.vii.14–15, 22–36). Certainly, the Widow's own motives are mixed, and she mirrors Helen's calculating approach as she seeks to secure Diana's marriage with Helen's gold. Nonetheless, while showing the Widow's pragmatism, the scene also traces her burgeoning belief as she reads and understands Helen and her plot to seal her marriage. As Helen recognises, both she and her plot rely on the Widow's belief. Again, an elder's belief frames the play's action.

Indeed, *All's Well*'s plot, its trajectory towards the comedic end anticipated by its title, also hinges on the Widow's belief in Helen. The play continues to both centre Helen as the play-world's critical focal point of belief and stoke its audience's doubt about her. This tension engendered by the discordances in Helen's characterisation has become even more pronounced as our insight into her interior life dims. But not knowing does not mean that we do not want to know. In occluding knowing, Shakespeare makes understanding Helen more urgent for his audience, a circumstance that in turn heightens our awareness of our hermeneutic condition. As *All's Well* nears its end, the pressing concern for both the characters and the audience is whether it is possible to believe, more specifically, to have faith and hope in a bright future, when one only knows in part.

'Win me to believe'

After the offstage 'deceit so lawful' of Bertram, and the onstage execution of a parallel 'plot' – the hoodwinking of Paroles, which undoes and crushes him, exposing him as a 'braggart' – *All's Well*'s mood modulates again (IV.iii.314–16, 325, 327). It lightens, at least temporarily. The characters' believing postures, it seems, contribute significantly to this shift. Helen believes in her 'intents' (there's that word again), and that she can 'perfect' them (IV.iv.4). She journeys once more – from Florence to 'Marseilles' – on the understanding that this is the King's current locale. This time Helen has company: the Widow and Diana. Helen is confident that, with the King as her 'surety' and 'heaven aiding', they can mirror Bertram's itinerary as he 'hies him home' (IV.iv.3, 12). Having removed herself from Roussillon to supposedly free Bertram to return, Helen evidently now thinks that there is room at home for them both.

This turn of events may again arouse the audience's suspicion. The Widow and Diana, on the other hand, have shed their doubts. Like the Countess before them, they commit themselves in solidarity with Helen's intents. The Widow assures Helen that 'You never had a servant to whose trust / Your business was more welcome' (IV.iv.15–16). 'Servant' intimates both subordination and, given the use of the title in religious contexts, the Widow's devotion to Helen.[85] Similarly, when Helen forewarns Diana that she 'yet must suffer / Something in my behalf', Diana's response verges on religious veneration: 'I am yours / Upon your will to suffer' (IV.iv.29–30). Helen also evokes a spiritual discourse. Reminiscent of her second soliloquy, she expresses a type of faith, assuring her companions that 'heaven' has arranged the moving parts of the actions, circumstances and wills of human agents to financially secure the 'husband' – and with him the hope of safekeeping and happiness – she and Diana each desire or need (IV.iv.18–21). Providence meets the marketplace. It is a worldly redemption which Helen promises. But she locates its realisation in a more otherworldly, transcendent source.

Suffering is most immediately on the women's horizon, but after that 'with the word the time will bring on summer' (IV. iv.31). Fraser observes that '[i]t is hard not to feel that there are deeper intimations here, and that "the word" is analogous in power to Holy Writ'.[86] More particularly, Helen's auspicious forecast of the action of 'the word' recalls the Reformers' eschatology in which the Word of God advances history forward to the ultimate telos. Within the play-world, 'the word' will initiate time's movement towards a comparable end marked by new life and rebirth: 'Briars shall have leaves as well as thorns, / And be as sweet as sharp' (IV.iv.32–3). Helen affirms her believing posture by enfolding herself and her companions into the mystical, hope inspiring activity of the word and progress of time: 'We must away. / Our wagon is prepared, and time revives us' (IV.iv.33–4).

In addition, Shakespeare draws his audience towards belief: belief in both his comedy and his heroine as she gives voice to the play's title: 'All's well that ends well; still the fine's the crown. / Whate'er the course, the end is the renown' (IV. iv.35–6). The play appears to at once signal that it is back on track to reach its expected dénouement and that Helen has taken up the elders' advice to adopt an eschatological hermeneutic that views 'all' through the perspective of 'the end'. Helen is again key to others' embrace of a believing mode of reading – on this occasion through her own embodiment of this interpretive stance. As though to emphasise both the play's and its protagonist's future oriented outlooks, two scenes later Helen is again the conduit through which *All's Well*'s end is made immanent within its narrative via a repetition of its title. The King is not in Marseilles as thought. Whereas this news deflates the Widow, Helen remains hopeful: 'All's well that ends well yet, / Though time seem so adverse and means unfit' (V.i.24–6). Her optimism and the sense of anticipation it may arouse in theatregoers is, it seems, justified. The King is not in Marseilles because he is in Roussillon – the necessary setting for a happy ending (V.i.28).

At *All's Well*'s conclusion, it is possible to read irony back into Helen's incantation-like articulations of the play's title. However, when first spoken to chart the characters' convergence on Roussillon, the tone of Helen's words does not come across as ironic. Rather, it reflects the elevated register of earlier passages in which Shakespeare's lexical choices associate Helen and her intents with the presence and operation of an other, supernatural power within the play-world, a force that overlays major onto minor key – belief onto doubt, possibility onto uncertainty. Onwards from her arrival in Florence, Helen's inner life has become increasingly inscrutable. Knowledge of the psychological impetuses behind her actions is again withheld from *All's Well*'s audience as she (again) journeys home. What we are shown instead is Helen's pivotal, symbolic even, role as the character who signposts a future beyond the present-day 'thorns' and drives the play's action towards this end.

Even Helen's 'supposed' death moves the play closer to the romantic *finis* not accomplished by her own mid-drama marriage. Death is, of course, a key event of the eschaton. Death simultaneously shuts the door to this world and its 'thorns', and opens another door to 'summer' – to new life in the next world. Helen's 'death' is rich with eschatological implications. It is the catalyst for Bertram's homecoming, a cause and effect mentioned by several characters, including Bertram himself (IV.iii.39–78, 85–6; IV.iv.10–12; IV.v.67–8). Further, Helen's 'death' sparks an abundance of charitable readings by the play's elders. Their postures toward others gesture to the self-giving love that will characterise all relationships at the eschaton's consummation. Perhaps surprisingly, the main recipients of this largesse are Paroles and Bertram – thus far, the objects of the elders' censure.

After Paroles's gulling leaves him humbled and destitute, he seeks Lafeu's succour to support his new status as a fool (V.ii.25–6; IV.iii.329). With obvious theological overtones, the indigent man suggests that it 'lies in' his superior 'to bring me in some grace, for you did bring me out' (V.ii.44–5). Lafeu was the first to expose Paroles's pretentious self-interpretations: 'my good window of lattice [. . .] I look through thee' (II.iii.213–5). Now, the lord grasps that the reborn fool is obligating him to imitate 'the office of God'; and he does: 'you shall eat' (V.ii.46, 51). Similarly, the Countess reverses her earlier determination to 'wash [Bertram's] name out of my blood' (III.ii.68). Mercy overturns this judgement as the Countess asks the King to read Bertram's 'folly' kindly (V.iii.3, 5–8). Like the Countess, the King willingly lets go of the past in favour of a reading of the young Count expressive of the eternally restorative pattern of divine grace. 'I have forgiven and forgotten all / Though my revenges were high bent upon him', the King assures the Countess, before declaring that he and Bertram 'are reconciled' (V.iii.9–10, 21). 'The time is fair again', the King pronounces upon Bertram's return to Roussillon (V.iii.36). The characters are ostensibly on the threshold of Helen's hoped for 'summer', a turn precipitated by her 'death' and the elders' virtuous, eschatologically inflected mode of reading which Helen's death set in motion.

Two features of *All's Well*'s final scene frustrate the play's realisation of this turn: Bertram's want of virtue and the characters' unknowing. The entanglement of the two ensure that discord and confusion fill the final scene, rather than the anticipated harmony and resolution. An earlier description of Bertram looms over his subsequent actions and influence upon *All's Well*'s plot. The Countess had written him a letter in which 'every word' was laden with Helen's 'worth' and the Countess's 'greatest grief' (III.iv.31–2). As Bertram sleeps with Helen, thinking that she is Diana, Lord E. reports that on 'reading' his mother's letter, Bertram 'changed almost into another man' (IV.iii.3–4). 'Almost' is one of the pivotal modifiers overshadowing the interactions in *All's Well*'s last scene. The play's audience would take significant steps towards resolving the dilemma of whether the play ends well if Bertram could dispel the moral suspicion he has attracted to himself throughout the play. 'Almost' carries much weight, and the sense of foreboding it conveys proves true as details of past exchanges of rings surface, confirming that Bertram is unchanged. He is still the problematic 'man' we have known him to be.

When Bertram presents a ring as an 'amorous token' confirming his intention to marry Lafeu's daughter Maudlin, the reintroduction of this eschatological sign should mark the closure of the past and dawn of the romantic future, actualised in 'our widower's second marriage' (V.iii.68, 70). Instead, the ring gives rise to hermeneutic perplexity and interpersonal schism. Lafeu and the King recognise it as Helen's ring, given to her by the King who reveals that he instructed her to 'never put it from her finger', except in two circumstances: she could give it to Bertram 'in bed' or send it to the King 'upon her great disaster' to summon his 'help' (V.iii.109–12, 85). As Helen plotted her way to the first scenario, the conversations between herself and the Widow, and Diana and Bertram had centred, not on this ring, but on Bertram's ancestral ring – part of his 'dreadful sentence'.

The many lines of dialogue about Bertram's ring means that it is easy to miss a crucial thread of Helen's plan – the presence of 'another ring' (Helen's), whose introduction is as brief as discussion of Bertram's ring is long. Having eventually persuaded him to give her his ring, Diana tells Bertram that 'on your finger in the night I'll put / another ring', a ring that 'may token to the future our past deeds' (IV.ii.61–3). As Bertram reveals his possession of Helen's ring, it seems that it has performed its function. This is now 'the future', and the ring is indeed a 'token', attesting not to a later day and Bertram's marriage to Maudlin, but to his 'past deed' and its polysemic significations.

The play's audience may read the ring as something akin to a message from Helen to the King, indicating that in the one act she followed both his directives: she is both invoking the King's aid and signalling that she has been in bed with Bertram. As insiders to Helen's 'plot', we can decode this message. The King himself amplifies theatregoers' expectations that he can help, that he will believe and make things right for Helen (and all) through his description of his, now Helen's, ring's extraordinary, talismanic powers. Helen's ring, the King claims, contains more 'science' (knowledge) in it than 'Plutus', the god of riches who, like an alchemist with his 'multiplying medicine', can produce an ever-increasing supply of gold from common metals (V.iii.101–4).[87] For *All's Well*'s audience, the ring could emblematise promise and possibility, adverse circumstances transformed into gold – if the King believes.

In contrast, the problem of the ring's recent history prevents the play's characters from entertaining such a hopeful interpretation. While the ring embodies the potential to turn the plot towards a happy end, its appearance dampens the onstage mood. Bertram's display of the ring brings to the fore his unknowing, perhaps even his wilful unknowing, as well as the dubiety of his moral conduct. Five times, he pits himself against the King, Lafeu and the Countess (as well as the audience) by insisting that Helen never owned nor saw the ring (V.iii.80, 88, 92, 112, 124–7). The knowledge Bertram thinks he has – that he acquired the ring during his 'past deed' – incites him to the self-protective measure of impeding others' efforts to uncover the truth. The outlandish story he comes up with to explain his possession of the ring wins Bertram no friends from either his onstage or offstage audience (V.iii.92–101). To *All's Well*'s audience, Bertram damns himself twice over. On one hand, he deliberately misrepresents himself as morally upright – the antithesis of what he (and we) know the ring signifies about him. On another, as his vanity intersects with his ignorance, Bertram unwittingly mocks himself. The woman he thinks he charmed and lured to bed had emphatically declared in soliloquy that there was a fat chance of this ever occurring: 'I'll lie with him / when I am buried' (IV.ii.72–3). It is the wife he does not want who solely desires him, her bed which he occupied.

Meanwhile, the King may expound the ring's alchemical qualities, but the more Bertram insists that Helen never owned it, the more the King believes that a sinister act explains its rematerialising: 'Thou didst hate her deadly, / And she is dead' (V.iii.112, 117–8). Like a reversal of the alchemist's craft, the scene of reconciliation rapidly transforms into a trial scene – sublime gold into the dunghill of human corruption. In his own reasoning, the King's knowledge of Bertram's prior attitude and actions towards Helen – 'my fore-past proofs' – justifies his 'fears' and accusation (V.iii.120–2). The King may have 'forgiven', but he has not 'forgotten all' (V.iii.9). Of course, he also misreads the knowledge which the ring holds about both Helen and Bertram. As the latter insolently challenges the King's accusation, he inadvertently pinpoints their mutual want of understanding. The King has as much hope of 'prov[ing] / This ring was ever hers', Bertram contends, as he has of 'prov[ing] that I husbanded her bed in Florence, / Where yet she never was' (V.iii.124–7). Although the King can indeed verify the first side of the comparison, the other is necessarily inscrutable, despite the meaning he himself had inscribed into the ring. Nevertheless, Bertram's display of self-promoting mendacity shows that the King's misgivings about him are not unwarranted. Bertram's return has undone the believing, optimistic mood occasioned by the elders' posture of reconciliatory grace toward him in his absence.

Diana's introduction sharpens the scrutiny of Bertram while also compounding her fellow characters' sense of disorientation. Presenting the version of events which Bertram refuses to confess, Diana urges her hearers to 'not believe him' (V.iii.191). When she produces his ancestral ring, the Countess is convinced: 'This is his wife: That ring's a thousand proofs' (V.iii.198–9). Like the King, the Countess rightly misdoubts Bertram. But rather than afford the certainty expected of 'a thousand proofs', this second ring further accentuates the characters' epistemological finitude and accompanying confusion. The sense of disarray and disharmony climaxes when Diana claims ownership of the first ring (Helen's), then contradicts herself across many responses: 'It was not given me, nor I did not buy it', and so forth (V.iii.267–74). Helen's ring was already the site of hotly contested truth claims and shared ignorance. It is now even more so.

Diana's equivocation continues as she connects Bertram's bounded, flawed understanding and his moral condition – his 'lack' of 'virtue' (V.iii.222). The ensuing paradox renders her response to the King's 'Wherefore hast thou accused him all this while?' incomprehensible to all within the play-world:

> Because he's guilty, and he is not guilty.
> He knows I am no maid, and he'll swear to'it.
> I'll swear I am a maid, and he knows not.
>
> (V.iii.286–9)

To theatregoers, Diana is elucidating the truth about the bifurcating effect of Helen's bed-trick. Bertram does not know that he is 'not guilty'; but he does know, as Diana twice iterates, that he is 'guilty' (V.iii.296, 298). In the courtroom of his own heart, Bertram would convict himself on two counts: erroneously for his actions; rightly for his intentions. As this sense is necessarily veiled to the King, he directs his own accusation of improper behaviour, more precisely, of improper speech, at Diana: 'she does abuse our ears' (V.iii.292). Of course, unlike Bertram's motive for lying, misleading others is not Diana's endgame. Instead, her equivocation serves as the build-up to her articulation of a final, climactic paradox – her 'riddle: one that's dead is quick' – and the revelation of the 'meaning' that, she implies, will resolve all unknowing (V.iii.301–2).

As Helen enters the scene 'quick' (both alive and pregnant) the overriding question in *All's Well*'s last moments is if this 'meaning' has its intended effect. Does belief prevail over doubt? Helen's seemingly miraculous reappearance to those who thought her dead suggests that belief is germane. As with her healing of the King, Helen's own quasi-resurrection is eschatologically allusive. It is, as Wilcox observes, especially evocative of Christ's resurrection – the event 'vpon which the resurrection of vs all is founded', as Calvin puts it.[88] Calvin affirms the difficulty of believing in this future, in a next world when bodies that 'haue beene consumed with rottenesse, shall at their appointed time rise vp againe', and points to Christ's resurrection as one of Scripture's 'helpes'. The Reformer urges his readers to interpret Christ's past resurrection as the divine 'pledge' that they will experience the promised future restoration of their own degenerating bodies.[89] Analogously, Helen's 'resurrection' invites a believing reading of what she betokens for the future for those gathered around her: a happily ever after in which all will be well. Is this the miracle that will make real the marriage central to the actualisation of this joy? In Helen's words, will her status metamorphose from being 'but the shadow of a wife', 'the name' only – as she anxiously figures herself – to becoming 'the thing' (V.iii.305–6)?

Such another turn pivots on Bertram believing. His initial reaction suggests he does: 'Both, both. O, pardon!' (V.iii.306). Helen is both 'name' and 'thing' – his real wife. Summer's sunshine is palpable as Helen's 'resurrection' seems to bring about the rebirth the Countess's letter could not effect in Bertram. This is the third time Bertram asks for 'pardon'. Previously, his words had been either patently insincere or laced with self-interest (II.iii.167–8; V.iii.36–7). This time, however, Bertram's compact acknowledgement of his guilt – 'O, pardon!' – seems genuine. Whether he directs his words to the King (again) or to Helen, it is undoubtedly her voice, her presence which elicits his response. In turn, Bertram cues Helen to extend the soft, reconciliatory mood. Her 'O my good lord, when I was like this maid / I found you wondrous kind' indicates that she thinks she has been believed (V.iii.307–8).

If Shakespeare had ended his play at this romantic high point, his audience may well have left the theatre also believing: believing that the playwright had delivered on the promise embedded in his title. But in giving Helen more to say, Shakespeare re-evokes uncertainty and doubt, on and off his stage. Reading Helen continues to be an exigent activity, and Helen remains a complicated character to read (and, as an aside, to play).[90] Helen elicits both faith and unease from other characters and the audience. This situation saddles this collective of interpreting selves with the responsibility of determining if the play ends well.

Again, Helen's own questionable reading practices muddy others' reading of her. As she fudges Bertram's conditions for calling him husband, exchanging 'show me a child' with the unprovable 'are by me with child' and then declares 'this is done' – she has his ring and bears his child – *All's Well*'s audience may again experience nagging reservations about how she has masterminded her way to achieving her 'project' (III.ii.58, V.iii.311). We may indeed have more reasons than Helen's fellow characters to feel disquiet. Our knowledge that Helen manufactured her death (without knowing why she did it) distances us somewhat from the characters' initial wonder generated by her simulated resurrection, captured in the King's 'Is't real that I see?' and Bertram's swift

'Both, both' (V.iii.304, 306). The characters' astonishment (again) brings to mind Gadamer's rendering of interpreting selves as having a 'genuine' taste of transcendence when we arrive at the point of not knowing, an experience that has 'the power of religious conviction'.[91] As Helen stands before the assembly of characters, the dramatic moment is imbued with the sense that the extraordinary, compelling experience Gadamer describes is at this juncture their experience. The characters cannot account for Helen's presence (at least for now). But her being incomprehensibly there alerts them to the existence of 'something greater and more mysterious', something beyond themselves.[92]

In contrast, we can trace the characters' response to Helen's sleight of hand – to her skill as a dramatist, one might say. The onstage wonderment she evokes finds parallels in the sentiments of Shakespeare's audience in the reunion scenes of his late romances – as, for instance, *The Winter's Tale*'s Hermione transforms from insensate statue to a 'warm', embracing and speaking, individual (V.iii.109). But *All's Well*'s audience knows both too much and too little about Helen for this play to have that effect. Here, I disagree with Traister, who reasons that 'if Helen is virtuous, and audiences do not doubt that she is, the child is Bertram's'.[93] We do doubt, it seems; and we believe. Rather than tethering Helen's child's paternity (and indeed the fact of her pregnancy) to her estimable moral condition, *All's Well*, I suggest, positions its audience to continue straddling belief and doubt. The glimpses of romance, of comic possibility and transcendence at the horizon of the play's action call for trust in Helen's claims about the realisation of a marriage and an imminent new life, even as we feel less sure about characterising her as 'virtuous'.

Upon hearing Helen's claim that she has 'doubly won' him, Bertram doubts – moments after professing belief (V.iii.312). His eyes may have been on Helen as he asked for pardon. But they rapidly swivel to the King to whom Bertram appeals with his escape clause. Nothing less than everlasting romance is at stake as he yokes a promise of happily ever after to a demand for proof of that about which only Helen will ever be certain: 'If she, my liege, can make me know this clearly, / I'll love her dearly, ever, ever dearly' (V.iii.313–14). It is difficult to blame Bertram for introducing another condition. Nevertheless, his much commented upon 'if', eloquently described by Kiernan Ryan as a 'potent slip of a word', carries the illocutionary potential to act as a mood flattener and genre spoiler.[94] 'If' gives rise to uncertainty as it proleptically brings the end beyond *All's Well*'s end into the present. 'Now', characters and audience 'don't know' whether that future 'then' will be 'well' for all in Roussillon.

Added to the inherent inconclusiveness of Helen's evidence, the play's stress on virtue implies that Bertram's character, clouded again by his very recent, very public, problematic conduct also contributes to this unknowing. As it is difficult to imagine how Helen will 'make' him 'know this clearly', reconciliation and resolution also turn on how Bertram reads Helen. To take up his use of conditional language, he could choose to follow the play's elders and adopt an eschatological hermeneutic characterised by faith, hope and love. While only knowing in part, belief and virtue – a being-toward-, or even being-for-, the other – could frame his response to Helen and embolden him to 'love her dearly'. But given his track record, those reading Bertram may well doubt. 'If' looms as the potential wrecking ball which will undo *All's Well*'s comic aspirations, especially as Bertram's 'if' echoes four more times across the play's final lines.

All the same, 'if' is not 'no'. 'If' is conditional, but also open-ended. 'If', we might say, is 'we don't know' in shorthand, an acknowledgement of one's non-knowing. Or perhaps 'if' expresses the sometimes faltering faith of the pilgrim straining to 'se through a glasse darkely'. And if both Christian eschatology and philosophical hermeneutics (following Gadamer) are to be believed, knowing in part, not knowing, situates the self in the borderlands, in a place open to the presence, the immanence, of that which transcends the self, and indeed this world. Throughout *All's Well*, the play's characters, it seems, have often found themselves in that place. The many occasions of unknowing, and accompanying shadow of woe, have been met with an experience of transcendence which gestures to knowledge beyond their finitude and animates hope. More precisely, *All's Well*'s characters' taste of transcendence has not been via an immaterial force, but in the voice, the face, the actions of an other – Helen. Bertram's 'if' – his precondition for romance, which doubles as a metonym for his own finitude – includes Helen: 'If she'. 'If she' is not the same as promising to 'listen to the Thou in front of him' (we return to Gadamer).[95] Bertram is facing the King, not Helen. But his phrasing does leave ajar the possibility that, beyond the play's end, he may hear Helen's voice and embody virtue in his actions towards her and her, their, child.

If he does, Bertram will (finally) 'succeed' his father (I.i.59). Moreover, he will align himself with everyone else in his community whose belief in Helen and ethical reading of and being-toward others (including Helen herself) bear a resemblance to the Reformers' 'already-saved' pilgrims who 'anticipate ethically' their future life.[96] *All's Well*'s foregrounding of the presence of this circle of characters after Bertram's 'if she', and the brisk warp and woof of conversation between them, offer some cause for hope that the precarious relationship (and future family) of the problematic Count and complex Helen will be enfolded into this community. Helen's 'if' sounds ominous: 'If it appear not plain, and prove untrue, / Deadly divorce step between me and you' (V.iii.315–16).[97] At the same time, she had twice previously staked her life on her ability to enact the miraculous, and had delivered. Once again, Helen appears unconcerned, directing her final expression of affection not to Bertram, but to the Countess (V.iii.317). The intergenerational interactions continue as Lafeu reminds Paroles that he has a 'home' as his fool, and the King (perhaps problematically) offers to underwrite Diana's marriage to the husband of her choice 'if' she 'be'st yet a fresh uncropped flower' (V.iii.320, 324).[98]

All may be well, for all; and it may not. 'If' balances belief and misdoubt. This state of ambiguity is made even more emphatic by the King's addition of the equally equivocal 'seems' to 'if' as he recasts the title of the play to (almost) conclude it: 'All yet seems well, and if it end so meet / The bitter past, more welcome is the sweet' (V.iii.330–1). Uncertainty, knowing in part, has not resolved into full knowledge. In adumbrating the possibility of 'sweetness', the King articulates the outermost limits of what he – and we – can claim to know. His necessary indefiniteness leaves theatregoers where Shakespeare has located us for pretty much the duration of his play – in a hermeneutic situation that brings out our own epistemological finitude as the narrative holds out the possibility, but never achieves the realisation, of the conclusive happiness and joy which we expect from a romantic comedy. 'We don't know.'

Through *All's Well*'s title, Shakespeare had engendered for his audience a consciousness of our hermeneutic relation to his play. It is fitting that *All's Well* concludes by turning over the final interpretive act to us. In the Epilogue, the King becomes actor-'beggar' who trains the spotlight away from the stage onto the play's audience and our reading of the play. Now that 'the play is done', are we 'content' tottering between believing and doubting, as the actor-beggar asks us to be (Epilogue, 1, 3)? For many in Shakespeare's intended audience, this duality captured their ongoing existential tension as they read their lives through an eschatological hermeneutic, anticipating, but not yet experiencing, a consummate beyond when they 'shal [. . .] knowe euen as [they are] knowen'. To repurpose Gadamer, it could be said that this eschatological hermeneutic is expressive of the 'desire for transcendence [. . .] present everywhere' across early modern England's theologically full culture.[99]

In many ways, the hermeneutical situation into which *All's Well*'s King turned actor-beggar speaks today would be unrecognisable to the playwright and his contemporaries. We may insist on this distinction. Nonetheless, it may be that *All's Well* opens us to the possibility that we still have a 'desire for transcendence', even if this desire is only 'secretly present'.[100] Shakespeare's play interests us in what lies beyond its characters' and our knowing, while orientating our interpretive experience of it within a hermeneutic that accommodates possibility. 'We don't know' may not be the end for the modern interpreting self. In our present climate, such an adumbration of possibility, possibility whose centre of gravity lies beyond the self, could well be too 'strange' (to recall Gadamer), too distant and theological.[101] Yet, it seems to me that every day in so many corners of modern culture we catch glimpses of a striving to know and a desire to be known. Our obsession with celebrity, social media platforms brimming over with self-expression and the increasing prominence of loneliness as a topic of public interest come immediately to mind. We don't know, but perhaps *All's Well* has shown us that we just might want to know, and be known.

Notes

1. Jens Zimmermann, 'Ignoramus: Gadamer's "Religious Turn"', *Symposium* 6, no. 2 (2002): 211.
2. Frank Kermode, *The Sense of an Ending: Studies in the Theory of Fiction with a New Epilogue* (Oxford: Oxford University Press, 2000), 25.
3. Patrick J. O'Banion, 'The Pastoral Use of the Book of Revelation in Late Tudor England', *The Journal of Ecclesiastical History* 57, no. 4 (2006): 710; Hannibal Hamlin, *The Bible in Shakespeare* (Oxford: Oxford University Press, 2013), 275–6; Stephen

Marche, 'John Webster and the Dead: Reading *The Duchess of Malfi*'s Eschatology', *Renaissance and Reformation* 28, no. 2 (2004): 84; Cynthia Marshall, *Last Things and Last Plays: Shakespearean Eschatology* (Carbondale: Southern Illinois University Press, 1991), 115. For a discussion of the theo-political application of eschatology in Elizabethan England, see Avihu Zakai, 'Reformation, History, and Eschatology in English Protestantism', *History and Theory* 26, no. 3 (1987): 300–18.

4. Kermode, *The Sense of an Ending*, 25.
5. Marshall, *Last Things*, 2.
6. Zimmermann, 'Ignoramus', 208.
7. Ibid. 205, 207, 208.
8. Hans-Georg Gadamer, *Die Lektion des Jahrhunderts* (Münster: Lit Verlag, 2002), 139, quoted in and trans. Jens Zimmermann, 'The Ethics of Philosophical Hermeneutics and the Challenge of Religious Transcendence', *Philosophy Today* 51 (2007): 57n22.
9. Zimmermann, 'Ignoramus', 209, 205, 209.
10. Ibid. 208.
11. Jean Calvin, *The Institution of Christian Religion*, trans. Thomas Norton (London: Arnold Hatfield, 1599), 3.2.20.
12. Thomas F. Torrance, *Kingdom and Church* (Edinburgh: Oliver and Boyd, 1956), 15. Italics original; Grace Tiffany, *Love's Pilgrimage* (Newark: University of Delaware Press, 2006), 35; Martin Luther, *Lectures on Galatians 1535: Chapters 1–4*, ed. Jaroslav Pelikan and Walter A. Hansen, trans. Jaroslav Pelikan (Saint Louis: Concordia Publishing House, 1963), 377–8.
13. Torrance, *Kingdom and Church*, 14. Italics original.
14. Ibid. 2–3.
15. Ibid. 4.
16. Ibid. Italics original. Luther, *Lectures on Galatians 1535: Chapters 1–4*, 132–3.
17. Martin Luther, *Lectures on Galatians 1535: Chapters 5–6*, trans. Jaroslav Pelikan, in *Lectures on Galatians 1535: Chapters 5–6; Lectures on Galatians 1519: Chapters 1–6*, ed. Jaroslav Pelikan and Walter A. Hansen, trans. Jaroslav Pelikan (Saint Louis, MI: Concordia Publishing House, 1964), 21; Torrance, *Kingdom and Church*, 71–2.

18. Luther, *Lectures on Galatians 1535: Chapters 1–4*, 379.
19. Calvin, *The Institution of Christian Religion*, 3.2.17.
20. Arthur Dent, *The Plaine Mans Path-Way to Heauen*, 6th ed. (London: Robert Dexter, 1603), 1, 242; Karen Bruhn, '"Sinne Unfoulded": Time, Election, and Disbelief Among the Godly in Late Sixteenth- and Early Seventeenth-Century England', *Church History* 77, no. 3 (2008): 580.
21. Calvin, *The Institution of Christian Religion*, 3.25.10.
22. Gadamer, *Die Lektion*, 33, quoted in Zimmermann, 'The Ethics of Philosophical Hermeneutics', 50.
23. Zimmermann, 'Ignoramus', 212; Zimmermann, 'Ethics of Philosophical Hermeneutics', 50. Italics original.
24. Jane Freeman, 'Life-Long Learning in Shakespeare's *All's Well That Ends Well*', *Renascence* 56, no. 2 (2004): 74.
25. Zimmermann contrasts Gadamer's 'being-toward-the-other' with Emmanuel Levinas's 'being-for-the-other'. Zimmermann, 'Ethics of Philosophical Hermeneutics', 53. See also Gerald L. Bruns, 'On the Coherence of Hermeneutics and Ethics: An Essay on Gadamer and Levinas', in *Gadamer's Repercussions: Reconsidering Philosophical Hermeneutics*, ed. Bruce Krajewski (Berkeley: University of California Press, 2004), especially p. 39.
26. David N. Beauregard, '"Inspired Merit': Shakespeare's Theology of Grace in *All's Well That Ends Well*', *Renascence* 51, no. 4 (1999): 234, 224–6, 229.
27. *The Canons and Decrees of the Sacred and Ecumenical Council of Trent, Celebrated under the Sovereign Pontiffs, Paul III, Julius III and Pius IV*, trans. James Waterworth (London: C. Dolman, 1848), 42–3; Beauregard, '"Inspired Merit"', 229.
28. Joshua Avery, 'Faith in the Unseen: Helena's Sacramental Vision in *All's Well That Ends Well*', *Renascence* 69, no. 1 (2017): 33–4, 43, 35, 45–6.
29. Freeman, 'Life-Long Learning', 69.
30. Ibid. 81.
31. Beauregard, '"Inspired Merit"', 231.
32. Tiffany, *Love's Pilgrimage*, 15, 23, 20, 21, 24, 33, 34–5, 36, 97.
33. Calvin, *The Institution of Christian Religion*, 4.13.7.

34. Beauregard, '"Inspired Merit"', 231–2; Tiffany, *Love's Pilgrimage*, 33.
35. Calvin, *The Institution of Christian Religion*, 3.10.1.
36. Tiffany, *Love's Pilgrimage*, 34.
37. Calvin, *The Institution of Christian Religion*, 3.7.T , 3.7.3; McNeill's edition explicitly uses 'pilgrims'. John T. McNeill (ed.), *Calvin: Institutes of the Christian Religion*, trans. Ford Lewis Battles, 2 vols (Philadelphia: Westminster Press, 1960), 3.7.3.
38. Raymond Kemp Anderson, 'Corporate Selfhood and "Meditatio Vitae Futurae": How Necessary Is Eschatology for Christian Ethics?', *Journal of the Society of Christian Ethics* 23, no. 1 (2003): 26, 44; Calvin, *The Institution of Christian Religion*, 3.7.2.
39. Calvin, *The Institution of Christian Religion*, 3.7.4, 7.
40. Ibid. 3.7.5.
41. Max L. Stackhouse, 'Ethics and Eschatology', in *The Oxford Handbook of Eschatology*, ed. Jerry L. Walls (Oxford: Oxford University Press, 2007), 553.
42. Anderson, 'Corporate Selfhood', 32.
43. Calvin, *The Institution of Christian Religion*, 3.7.3.
44. Ibid. 3.2.42.
45. Ibid. 3.2.41.
46. Ibid. 3.2.17.
47. *OED Online*, s.v. 'plausive, adj.', cites this line.
48. Kaara L. Peterson, 'The Ring's the Thing: Elizabeth I's Virgin Knot and *All's Well That Ends Well*', *Studies in Philology* 113, no. 1 (2016): 107.
49. *Articles, whereupon it was agreed by the Archbishoppes and Bishoppes of both prouinces, and the whole cleargie, in the Conuocation holden at London in the yere of our Lorde God 1562* (London: Richarde Iugge and Iohn Cawood, 1571), article 22.
50. Katherine Duncan-Jones, 'Introduction', in *Shakespeare's Sonnets*, ed. Katherine Duncan-Jones, Arden Shakespeare Third Series (London: Bloomsbury, 2010), 45.
51. *All's Well That Ends Well*, ed. Suzanne Gossett and Helen Wilcox, Arden Shakespeare Third Series (London: Bloomsbury, 2019), I.ii.211n.

52. Cynthia Lewis, '"Derived Honesty and Achieved Goodness": Doctrines of Grace in *All's Well That Ends Well*', *Renaissance and Reformation* 14, no. 2 (1990): 156.
53. Alexandra Walsham, *Providence in Early Modern England* (Oxford: Oxford University Press, 2001), 20–2.
54. Richard A. Levin, 'Did Helena Have a Renaissance?', *English Studies* 87, no. 1 (2006): 30; Peterson, 'The Ring's the Thing', 107.
55. Calvin, *The Institution of Christian Religion*, 3.25.4.
56. John E. Booty (ed.), *The Book of Common Prayer 1559: The Elizabethan Prayer Book* (Charlottesville: The University of Virginia Press, 1976, reissued 2005), 290.
57. Martin Luther, 'The Freedom of a Christian', trans. W. A. Lambert, rev. Harold J. Grimm, in *Career of the Reformer I*, ed. Harold J. Grimm (Philadelphia: Muhlenberg Press, 1957), 352.
58. Gadamer, *Die Lektion*, 33, quoted in Zimmermann, 'The Ethics of Philosophical Hermeneutics', 50.
59. See Tiffany, *Love's Pilgrimage*, 7; Catherine Field, '"Sweet Practicer, thy Physic I will try": Helena and her "Good Receipt" in *All's Well, That Ends Well*', in *All's Well That Ends Well: New Critical Essays*, ed. Gary Waller (New York: Routledge, 2007), 202.
60. Barbara Howard Traister, '"Doctor She": Healing and Sex in *All's Well That Ends Well*', in *A Companion to Shakespeare's Works, Volume IV: The Poems, Problem Comedies, Late Plays*, ed. Richard Dutton and Jean E. Howard (Blackwell Publishing, 2005), 337.
61. Tiffany, *Love's Pilgrimage*, 96.
62. Kent R. Lehnhof, 'Performing Woman: Female Theatricality in *All's Well, That Ends Well*', in *All's Well That Ends Well: New Critical Essays*, ed. Gary Waller (New York: Routledge, 2007), 114.
63. *All's Well That Ends Well*, ed. Russell Fraser, The New Cambridge Shakespeare (Cambridge: Cambridge University Press, 2003), II.i.126–206n; Zimmermann, 'Ignoramus', 205, 208.
64. See Matthew 11: 25, 1 Corinthians 1: 27, Exodus 17: 6 and Exodus 14: 21 for the biblical allusions. *All's Well That Ends Well*, ed. Fraser, 2.1.134–5n, 135–6n, 136n, 137n.

65. Traister, '"Doctor She"', 344.
66. *OED Online*, s.v. 'dropsied, adj.'.
67. Ralph A. Houlbrooke, *Death, Religion, and the Family in England, 1480–1750* (Oxford: Oxford University Press, 1998), 366.
68. Ibid. 366.
69. Calvin, *The Institution of Christian Religion*, 3.7.2.
70. Terry Reilly, '*All's Well, That Ends Well* and the 1604 Controversy Concerning the Court of Wards and Liveries', in *All's Well That Ends Well: New Critical Essays*, ed. Gary Waller (New York: Routledge, 2007), 210–12.
71. Michael W. Shurgot, 'Bertram's Scar and Courts of Healing in *All's Well That Ends Well*,' *Shakespeare Bulletin* 37, no. 3 (2019): 397.
72. *Certain Sermons Or Homilies Appointed to be Read in Churches in the Time of Queen Elizabeth* (London: George Wells, Abel Swall and George Pawlett, 1687), 345.
73. Ibid. 344.
74. *All's Well That Ends Well*, ed. Gossett and Wilcox, III.iv.27n.
75. Calvin, *The Institution of Christian Religion*, 3.20.17.
76. Martin Luther, 'A Sermon of D. Martin Lvther, of the Svmme of Christian Life', trans. W.G., in *Special and Chosen Sermons of D. Martin Lvther* (London: Thomas Vautroullier, 1578), 188–90; William Tyndale, 'The parable of the wicked Mammon', in *The whole workes of W. Tyndall, Iohn Frith, and Doct. Barnes, three worthy martyrs, and principall teachers of this Churche of England* (London: Iohn Daye, 1573), 70.
77. Jean E. Howard, 'Female Agency in *All's Well That Ends Well*', *Journal of the Australasian Universities Language and Literature Association* 106 (2006): 51; Maurice Hunt, 'Helena and the Reformation Problem of Merit in *All's Well That Ends Well*', in *Shakespeare and the Culture of Christianity in Early Modern England*, ed. Dennis Taylor and David N. Beauregard (New York: Fordham University Press, 2003), 351. See p. 362n20 for a selection of opposing critical opinions.
78. *All's Well That Ends Well*, ed. Gossett and Wilcox, IV.iii.46n; *OED Online*, s.v. 'pretence, n.'.
79. Zimmermann, 'Ignoramus', 208.
80. Peterson, 'The Ring's the Thing', 106.

81. Helen Wilcox, 'Shakespeare's Miracle Play? Religion in *All's Well That Ends Well*', in *All's Well That Ends Well: New Critical Essays*, ed. Gary Waller (New York: Routledge, 2007), 150.
82. *All's Well That Ends Well*, ed. Fraser, IV.iii.17n.
83. Howard, 'Female Agency', 51.
84. Daniel Swift, *Shakespeare's Common Prayers: The Book of Common Prayer and the Elizabethan Age* (Oxford: Oxford University Press, 2012), 81.
85. *OED Online*, s.v. 'servant, n.'.
86. *All's Well That Ends Well*, ed. Fraser, IV.iv.31n.
87. *All's Well That Ends Well*, ed. Gossett and Wilcox, V.iii.102n, 103n.
88. Wilcox, 'Shakespeare's Miracle Play?', 151.
89. Calvin, *The Institution of Christian Religion*, 3.25.3.
90. Thanks to John Severn for this thought about playing Helen.
91. Zimmermann, 'Ignoramus', 209.
92. Ibid. 209.
93. Traister, '"Doctor She"', 343.
94. Kiernan Ryan, '"Where Hope Is Coldest": *All's Well That Ends Well*', in *Spiritual Shakespeares*, ed. Ewan Fernie (London: Routledge, 2005), 48.
95. Gadamer, *Die Lektion*, 33, quoted in Zimmermann, 'The Ethics of Philosophical Hermeneutics', 50.
96. Stackhouse, 'Ethics and Eschatology', 553.
97. Russell Fraser interprets 'deadly divorce' as 'divorcing death'. *All's Well That Ends Well*, ed. Fraser, V.iii.308n.
98. On the King's offer to Diana, see David Scott Kastan, '*All's Well That Ends Well* and the Limits of Comedy', *ELH* 52, no. 3 (1985): 580.
99. Gadamer, *Die Lektion*, 139, quoted in Zimmermann, 'The Ethics of Philosophical Hermeneutics', 57n22.
100. Ibid. 57n22.
101. Hans-Georg Gadamer, *Truth and Method*, trans. Joel Weinsheimer and Donald G. Marshall, 2nd, rev. ed. (London: Continuum, 2004), 295.

EPILOGUE

> The meaning of 'belonging' – i.e., the element of tradition in our historical-hermeneutical activity – is fulfilled in the commonality of fundamental, enabling prejudices.
>
> Hans-Georg Gadamer, *Truth and Method*[1]

> You, in the first place, touch upon justification by faith, the first and keenest subject of controversy between us. [. . .] you very maliciously stir up prejudice against us, alleging that by attributing everything to faith, we leave no room for works.
>
> Jean Calvin, 'Calvin's reply to Sadoleto', 1539[2]

Wherever we have religious differences, the problem of prejudice, it seems, rears its head. In the later years of the 1530s, Protestant Geneva was in the midst of much turmoil, due in large part to the conflict that arose between the civil authorities and Calvin and his fellow Reformer Guillaume Farel. Cardinal Jacopo Sadoleto (then Bishop of Carpentras in southern France) saw the in-fighting as an opportunity to weaken Protestantism's grip on Geneva. In March 1539, Sadoleto wrote to the city's magistrates and citizens, seeking to persuade them to return to Rome. At the time, Calvin was living in Strasbourg, having been expelled from Geneva (along with Farel) almost a year earlier. Nevertheless, the powers that be decided that Calvin was the person most able to respond to Sadoleto.[3] He did, after some persuasion.

Calvin identifies 'the first and keenest subject of controversy' between himself and Sadoleto as justification by faith, the critical issue which had impelled Luther's full-blooded challenge of the church that had, until then, been his haven. In his letter to the Genevans, Sadoleto paints the Reformers as 'inventors of novelties' on the pressing question of how a person is justified before God and thus attains eternal salvation. That is, if the Fall ruptured the divine-human relationship, by what mechanism can fallen human beings once more know and be known by God? Reflective of Rome's theological position, the Bishop contends that divine grace, Christ's crucifixion specifically, is the basis of 'the first access which we have to God; but it is not enough'. One must also contribute a pious mind and a willingness to do 'whatever is agreeable' to God. In contrast, according to Sadoleto, the Reformers' doctrine of faith alone promoted 'a mere credulity and confidence in God' that excluded 'charity and the other duties of a Christian mind'.[4]

A Protestant perspective on salvation, one could say, robs humans of agency as knowing, moral beings. Calvin begs to differ. While, as he puts it, 'we deny that good works have any share in justification', he also insists that 'we claim full authority for them [good works] in the lives of the righteous'. Christ not only gifts 'lost sinners' with justification, but he also empowers the wills and actions of these rescued, now righteous people, 'train[ing] them by His Spirit into obedience to His will'. By (mis)representing the Reformers as eliding moral responsibility in their framing of selfhood, Sadoleto, Calvin remonstrates, was 'very maliciously stir[ring] up prejudice against us'.[5]

Of course, accusations of prejudice cut many ways. A few years before Sadoleto and Calvin's dispute, William Tyndale and Thomas More also exchanged heated treatises. Each writer repudiated the other's reading of a decisive word found in the Greek New Testament: '*metanoia*'. Should *metanoia* be translated as 'repentance' or 'penance'? This philological question mattered deeply. It was, like most matters of religious contention at the time, caught up in the pivotal controversies about divine grace and human salvation. In the teaching of the medieval church, 'penance' was the catch-all term for the threefold actions of contrition of the heart, confession of the mouth and satisfaction of works a person must perform to receive forgiveness of sins (via priestly absolution). At the Council of Trent, penance was officially recognised as a sacrament. Tyndale argues that penance was devised by the 'doctours preachers', whereas 'the scripture knoweth not of' the doctrine. Instead, for Tyndale, 'repentance' captures the Bible's stress on God's forgiveness of fallen humans apart from any works, including works associated with penance: 'The greke hath Metanoia and metanoite / repentaunce and repente / or forthynkynge and forthynke. [. . .] So now the scripture sayeth repent or let yt forthynke you and come and beleue the gospell [. . .] and so shall all be forgeuen you.'[6]

Matthew 3: 1–2 in Tyndale's translation of the New Testament (1525) evinces his interconnected linguistic and theological convictions: 'In those days John the Baptist came & preached in the wilderness of Jury [Judea], saying, Repent, the kyngdome of heauen is at hande.'[7] Contra Tyndale, the first Catholic vernacular New Testament, published at Rheims in 1582, uses 'Doe penance' in the place of 'repent'. More railed against 'Tyndale's prejudicial translation' (to employ James Simpson's phrase).[8] To More, penance is an essential sacrament, one 'whyche Tyndale goeth about to destroye'. Tyndale 'purposely mysse translate[d] Crystes holy gospell', More alleges, because 'he wolde not that any man sholde do true penaunce wyth puttynge hymselfe to any payne for hys owne synnes'. Tyndale undermined the authority of Rome by influencing his readers to 'dysobaye the doctryne of Crystes catholyque chyrch'.[9]

Is humanity's fallen condition so dire (cue original sin) that a person does not have the capacity to put himself 'to any payne for hys owne synnnes' and cooperate with God for his own (and others') salvation? Does justification by grace through faith alone absolve individuals from moral action and responsibility? Is the church the definitive source of authority on these and other significant doctrinal sticking points? As I hope I have shown in this book, the responses of Calvin, Tyndale and their fellow Reformers to these questions informed a (re-)configuring of human subjectivity. Their provocative doctrines of *sola scriptura* and the priesthood of all believers situated human beings hermeneutically in relation to truth. *Sola scriptura* and universal priesthood contributed significantly to the emergence of the figure of the self who knows by way of interpretation.

More specifically, the identity and self-understanding of this interpreting self centres on her reflexive reading of God, that is, on her knowing of God and being known by him. One becomes oneself and comes to know oneself dialogically, in relation to personal, transcendent others, beginning with the divine other. This way of being (reprising Gadamer) 'really risks itself'.[10] The Reformers' account of God's salvation of finite, fallible – fallen – humanity emphasises that knowing is both vital to human being and, because people are fallen, largely beyond our control. One receives the interpersonal knowledge that underwrites self-understanding (and all understanding) as a gift – a condition of knowing that decentres, but does not diminish, the interpreting self. Indeed, according to the Reformers, being known by a (the) transcendent other assures individuals of their worth.

On one hand, people already known by God do not need to strive for recognition by proving that they merit justification. On the other hand, being known means being recognised as a responsible moral agent who enacts one's own personhood by recognising that of others. But, importantly, one's status before God is independent of one's moral performance. The gift of divine recognition does not – cannot – rest on a calculation of human value that equates moral agency with full responsibility for one's reading of and actions towards others – more to the point, full responsibility for one's inevitably flawed (fallen) reading and actions.

This complex model of human being – at once 'familiar' and 'strange' to us (to repurpose Gadamer) – echoes in diverse ways through the vexed hermeneutical situations which Shakespeare stages in his problem plays (and at least the other plays I have touched on throughout this book).[11] By attending to these allusions and associations, I hope to have shown how activating theological concepts that framed narratives of selfhood in Shakespeare's theologically full world sheds new light on his plays and the question of how they speak to the stories we moderns tell ourselves about who we are and why we matter. 'We understand in a *different way*.' (As discussed, Gadamer's phrasing captures the 'hermeneutic work' of this book.)[12]

Here, I return to the notion of prejudice. Protestant hermeneutics, one could say, offers modern interpreters 'productive prejudices that enable understanding' of the factors at play as (recalling Bruns) Shakespeare's characters inhabit all manner of given hermeneutical situations.[13] The interpreting self who has come into view challenges what Michael Davies describes as 'a prejudice that has long encircled Protestantism [. . .]: its alleged incompatibility with the magnanimous human imagination', while cutting across prevailing conceptions of selfhood often brought into conversation with Shakespeare – narratives of autonomous self-realisation, for instance, or of exchange and desert.[14]

Undoubtedly, Gadamer's positive correlation of prejudice and understanding requires immediate clarification, given our present-day use of the term to name the opposite of (interpersonal) understanding, indeed, a refusal to seek to understand (other people). However, Gadamer reminds his readers that it was not until the Enlightenment that 'prejudice' took on this solely 'negative connotation familiar today'. As Gadamer memorably phrases it, 'the fundamental prejudice of the Enlightenment is the prejudice against prejudice itself, which denies tradition its power'. To Gadamer, 'prejudice against prejudice' captures the 'essence' of the Enlightenment project. By making human reason the 'ultimate source of authority', the Enlightenment significantly downplayed human beings' historicity and finitude, that is, that 'we are always situated within traditions'.[15] But for Gadamer, this very situatedness of an interpreter of a 'text' – be it a traditionary text, another person, or indeed oneself – is a requisite of understanding. This is where his notion of enabling prejudices comes into play.

Gadamer associates prejudices with traditions. Few people nowadays would disagree. But, contrary to the Enlightenment verdict that prejudices forged by traditions are always 'false' or 'unfounded' judgements, Gadamer employs the broader, more neutral pre-Enlightenment sense of prejudice as 'a judgment [. . .] rendered before all the elements that determine a situation have been finally examined'. For Gadamer, prejudices are inherent to individuals' hermeneutic experiences and understanding of texts. Because an interpreter's tradition inflected prejudgements '*constitute the historical reality of his being*', they accompany him into every hermeneutic situation. Crucially, while one's prejudices can direct an interpreter down a path of misunderstanding, they can also be 'legitimate' and 'true' – 'there are justified prejudices productive of knowledge'. In addition, even as prejudgements come packaged with the traditions to which one 'belong[s]', interpreters can also, according to Gadamer, 'acquire [. . .] a connection with the tradition from which a text speaks'.[16] Be they innate or acquired, our prejudices – prejudgements – inevitably modulate our hermeneutic being-in-the-world.

Moreover, and perhaps more importantly, finite interpreting selves need prejudices if we are to attain any understanding. As Monica Vilhauer explains, for Gadamer (and Heidegger), one's prejudices 'have the positive function of making understanding possible. They are the provisional or anticipatory judgments that are initially projected' into a hermeneutic situation, kickstarting, so to speak, the interpreting self's journey towards understanding.[17] Gadamer unequivocally spells out why humans need prejudices: 'Since the human intellect is too weak to manage without prejudices, it is at least fortunate to have been educated with true prejudices.' It is noteworthy that this sentence follows immediately after Gadamer distinguishes the German Enlightenment from the parallel cultural developments in eighteenth-century England and France. Germany (unlike England and France) did not take the 'prejudice against prejudices [. . .] to the extremes of free thinking and atheism', but instead 'recognized the "true prejudices" of the Christian religion'.[18]

As the preceding discussion strongly suggests, Gadamer takes a mostly unfavourable stance against the Enlightenment. All the same, his insistence of the importance of Immanuel Kant to his own work points to the (inevitable) presence of the German Enlightenment in Gadamer's intellectual heritage.[19] Certainly, and to the point, we need not pin down the contribution of the German Enlightenment's softening of its European counterparts' 'anti-religious polemic' to affirm that Gadamer clearly 'developed a lifelong interest in theology'.[20] This interest bears out in the evident influence of Christian thought on his philosophical account of human understanding. In particular, as seen throughout this book, Gadamer locates his hermeneutics, with its emphasis on interpretation as ontology, within a tradition whose origin story includes the Reformers' theology.

Shakespeare, no doubt, belongs to this tradition. As seen, his plays frequently gesture to it. (Of course, he also belongs to other traditions.) The influence of philosophical hermeneutics in the modern West also links modern society to the full sweep of ideas which underlie Gadamer's rendering of the interpreting self. But even as we in the modern West have kept Shakespeare and his works close to the heart of contemporary culture, we have mostly lost connection with the theological line of this tradition to which he and we mutually belong. What difference might it make if readers of Shakespeare, with his help, (re)acquire some knowledge of the 'prejudices' about humans as knowing subjects that were highly meaningful in his world?

Such a renewed (and necessarily recontextualised) familiarity could introduce a 'different way' of seeing oneself and one another into a public square that is today riven with conflict and prejudice. Here, I (of course) employ 'prejudice' only in the negative sense of the term – as an interpretation of others which disavows their personhood. Most people, I'm guessing, would prefer to live in societies that place a high value on their citizens' recognition of one another. Yet it seems that the modern sphere of public opinion feeds on and feeds hermeneutic reflexes which work against tolerant, robust community life. In politics and interpersonal relations, we experience, for instance, the powerful imperative of self-aggrandisement playing out over and over to its logical, atomising end. Similarly, our collective impulse to shun responsibility (individual and corporate) – repentance in a more theological register – has also proved corrosive. A trigger-happy propensity to blame or shame others leaves very little airtime for alternate, disruptive discourses, most relevantly, explorations of the possible relevance in our day of the hermeneutical tradition which finds expression in Shakespeare's plays. The notion that all people share in the fallen human condition suggests, for instance, that individuals and groups ought to be wary of their self-interpretations while also framing their reading of others with empathy. More than that, the theology of grace or (otherwise put) gift offers modern selves and societies a reparative, reversing mode of being and acting towards others that holds out the possibility of hope for bounded people and fractured societies.

I end on this last implication, on the note of hope that sounds faintly in the problem plays and peals more distinctly in the late romances which *All's Well*, in particular, anticipates. In the final scene of *The Winter's Tale*, Leontes expresses to Paulina the thought that is likely on the minds of his fellow characters and theatregoers alike: 'Thou hast found mine [spouse] / But how is to be questioned' (V.iii.139–40). As in so many of the dramatic hermeneutic situations discussed in this book, Shakespeare engenders for his audience a deep consciousness of the human hermeneutic condition. On this occasion, however, his characters' need to know does not riddle the possibility of hope with doubt. Indeed, their awareness of their finitude contributes to the strong sense of hope that builds throughout the scene. Remorse fills Leontes' mind as he comes face to face with Hermione's 'statue':

> I am ashamed. [. . .]
> O royal piece!
> There's magic in thy majesty, which has
> My evils conjured to remembrance.
>
> (V.iii.37–40)

Sixteen years of 'sorrow' cannot undo Leontes' past actions or their effects (V.iii.49, 52). Not that his contrition has been pointless. Without it, Leontes would have remained the tyrant whom the oracle had named him to be (III.ii.133).

But now, repentance having reached the limit of what it can accomplish, Paulina asks Leontes to adopt a new posture: 'It is required / You do awake your faith.' (V.iii.94–5).

Faith is the apposite, the only, response to the gift Leontes and the whole community are about to receive – the gift of a returned life and restored relationships, of knowing and being known; a gift they could not have procured for themselves. Paulina and Hermione are the immediate sources of this gift. But the numerous allusions to magic, to the gods, to the oracle, and to the characters' wonder and amazement all suggest the behind-the-scenes workings of transcendent forces, and that the sum total of each character 'demand[ing] and answer[ing] to his part' as they come together will add up to more than the cumulation of sixteen years of human action (V.iii.154). This sense of transcendence complements, enables perhaps, the characters' openness towards knowing, indeed, their openness towards receiving understanding as a gift that, in turn, knits them together as a renewed community.

Theirs is a subjectivity that affords hope, a way of being which finds resemblance in Rowan Williams's description of 'an attitude to the world that acknowledges that there is more to anything and anyone I encounter than I can manage or understand'.[21] I take this quotation from Williams's argument for the contribution theology can make today to the cultivation of 'genuine pluralism', which he defines as 'a social and political culture that is consistently against coercion and institutionalized inequality, and is committed to serious public debate about common good'.[22] Williams contends, one could say, for theology as a prejudice productive of an understanding of how we might live together. For Williams, the public role of theology begins with the perspective on human subjectivity it offers – specifically, 'the sense that human beings are limited and dependent'. Such self-understanding (perhaps paradoxically) empowers individuals to loosen their hold on the 'fiction' that we control ourselves and the world, 'a letting-go [which] opens up the possibility of taking responsibility for meaningful action, action that announces the presence of the fundamental *giving* on which the world rests and entails also taking responsibility for the other'.[23] Self-understanding opens the door for gift and hence hope.

It is not surprising that Williams accords self-understanding (personal and corporate) a critical role in the constructive pluralism he envisages. He and we (in the West) belong to a tradition animated by the desire to understand what it is to be human. As our generation continues this hermeneutic endeavour, it is Shakespeare's stories to which we so often turn to illuminate our own, Shakespeare's voice whom we still welcome into our troubled public square and our debates about who we are and just what the common good might be. I have shown how bringing the Reformers' thinking about these questions into dialogue with Shakespeare provides interpreters with a complex and rich (and sometimes different) way of understanding his plays and their representations of selfhood. And it may also be that, together, Shakespeare and the Reformers offer us the opportunity to attain a fresh understanding of ourselves – to understand in a different way.

Notes

1. Hans-Georg Gadamer, *Truth and Method*, trans. Joel Weinsheimer and Donald G. Marshall, 2nd, rev. ed. (London: Continuum, 2004), 295.
2. John C. Olin (ed.), *A Reformation Debate: Sadoleto's Letter to the Genevans and Calvin's Reply*, 2nd ed. (New York: Fordham University Press, 2000), 60.
3. Ibid. 1–20.
4. Ibid. 29.
5. Ibid. 60–2.
6. William Tyndale, *An answere vnto Sir Thomas Mores dialoge made by Willyam Tindale* (Antwerp: S. Cock, 1531), xi–xii.
7. *The New Testament*, trans. W. Tyndale (London: John Day & Wylliam Seres, 1550).

8. James Simpson, *Burning to Read: English Fundamentalism and Its Reformation Opponents* (Cambridge, MA: The Belknap Press of Harvard University Press, 2007), 75.
9. Sir Thomas More, *The co[n]futacyon of Tyndales answere made by syr Thomas More knyght lorde chau[n]cellour of Englonde* (London: Wyllyam Rastell, 1532), xxix, image 3, xxiii, image 4.
10. Gadamer, *Truth and Method*, 328.
11. Ibid. 295.
12. Ibid. 296, 295. Italics original.
13. Ibid. 295; Gerald L. Bruns, *Hermeneutics Ancient and Modern* (New Haven, CT: Yale University Press, 1992), 158.
14. Michael Davies, 'Introduction: Shakespeare and Protestantism', *Shakespeare* 5, no. 1 (2009): 6.
15. Gadamer, *Truth and Method*, 272–3, 274, 283.
16. Ibid. 273, 272, 278, 295, 278, 275, 280, 295. Italics original.
17. Monica Vilhauer, *Gadamer's Ethics of Play: Hermeneutics and the Other* (Lanham, MD: Lexington Books, 2010), 52.
18. Gadamer, *Truth and Method*, 274–5.
19. Robert Dostal, 'Gadamer, Kant, and the Enlightenment', *Research in Phenomenology* 46, no. 3 (2016): 337–48.
20. 'Forum: The German Enlightenment', *German History* 35, no. 4 (2017): 593; Jens Zimmermann, 'Gadamer's Century: Life, Times, and Works', in Theodore George and Gert-Jan van der Heiden (eds), *The Gadamerian Mind* (London: Routledge, 2021), 13–14.
21. Rowan Williams, *Faith in the Public Square* (London: Bloomsbury Publishing, 2012), 5.
22. Ibid. 95–6.
23. Ibid. 4, 6. Italics original.

BIBLIOGRAPHY

Abbey, Ruth. 'Charles Taylor: *Sources of the Self*'. In *Central Works of Philosophy. Volume 5, the Twentieth Century: Quine and After*, edited by John Shand, 268–90. Chesham: Acumen, 2006.

Abbot, George. *An Exposition Vpon the Prophet Ionah*. London: Richard Field, 1600.

Anderson, Raymond Kemp. 'Corporate Selfhood and "Meditatio Vitae Futurae": How Necessary Is Eschatology for Christian Ethics?'. *Journal of the Society of Christian Ethics* 23, no. 1 (2003): 21–46.

Aristotle. *Poetics*. Edited by Anthony Kenny. Oxford: Oxford University Press, 2013.

Articles, whereupon it was agreed by the Archbishoppes and Bishoppes of both prouinces, and the whole cleargie, in the Conuocation holden at London in the yere of our Lorde God 1562. Poules Churchyard, London: Richarde Iugge and Iohn Cawood, 1571.

Atkinson, James. 'Introduction: To the Christian Nobility of the German Nation Concerning the Reform of the Christian Estate'. In *The Christian in Society I*, edited by James Atkinson, 117–21. Luther's Works, vol. 44. Philadelphia: Fortress Press, 1966.

Saint Augustine. *The City of God, Books I–VII*. Translated by Gerald G. Walsh, Demetrius B. Zema and Étienne Gilson. The Fathers of the Church, vol. 8. Washington, DC: Catholic University of America Press, 1950.

———. *The City of God, Books VIII–XVI.* Translated by Gerald G. Walsh and Grace Monahan. The Fathers of the Church, vol. 14. Washington, DC: Catholic University of America Press, 1952.

Avery, Joshua. 'Faith in the Unseen: Helena's Sacramental Vision in *All's Well That Ends Well*'. *Renascence* 69, no. 1 (2017): 33–48.

Babington, Gervase. *A Profitable Exposition of the Lords Prayer.* London: Thomas Orwin, 1588.

Barfoot, C. C. 'Troilus and Cressida: "Praise Us as We Are Tasted"'. *Shakespeare Quarterly* 39, no. 1 (1988): 45–57.

Battles, Ford Lewis. 'God Was Accommodating Himself to Human Capacity'. *Interpretation* 31 (1977): 19–38.

Beauregard, David N. '"Inspired Merit": Shakespeare's Theology of Grace in *All's Well That Ends Well*'. *Renascence* 51, no. 4 (1999): 218–39.

Beckwith, Sarah. *Shakespeare and the Grammar of Forgiveness.* Ithaca, NY: Cornell University Press, 2011.

Belsey, Catherine. *Shakespeare and the Loss of Eden: The Construction of Family Values in Early Modern Culture.* Basingstoke: Macmillan, 1999.

Berry, Lloyd E. 'Introduction to the Facsimile Edition'. In *The Geneva Bible: 1560 Edition.* Peabody, MA: Hendrickson Publishers, 2007.

Bevington, David. '"Instructed by the Antiquary Times": Shakespeare's Sources'. In *Troilus and Cressida*, edited by David Bevington, 375–97. Arden Shakespeare Third Series. London: Bloomsbury, 1998.

———. 'Introduction'. In *Troilus and Cressida*, edited by David Bevington, 1–117. Arden Shakespeare Third Series. London: Bloomsbury, 1998.

Blocher, Henri. *Original Sin: Illuminating the Riddle.* Downers Grove, IL: InterVarsity Press, 1997.

Boas, Frederick S. *Shakespeare and His Predecessors.* New York: C. Scribner's Sons, 1896.

Bolton, Robert. *A Discourse About the State of True Happinesse.* London: Felix Kyngston, 1611.

Booty, John E. (ed.). *The Book of Common Prayer 1559: The Elizabethan Prayer Book*. Charlottesville: The University of Virginia Press, 1976, reissued 2005.

Brett, Julia. '"Grace Is Grace, Despite of All the Controversy": *Measure for Measure*, Christian Allegory, and the Sacerdotal Duke'. *Ben Jonson Journal* 6 (1999): 189–207.

Brown, K. A. 'Courtly Love'. In *The Princeton Encyclopedia of Poetry and Poetics: Fourth Edition*, edited by Roland Greene, Stephen Cushman, Clare Cavanagh, Jahan Ramazani and Paul Rouzer, 311–12. Princeton: Princeton University Press, 2012.

Bruhn, Karen. '"Sinne Unfoulded": Time, Election, and Disbelief among the Godly in Late Sixteenth- and Early Seventeenth-Century England'. *Church History* 77, no. 3 (2008): 574–95.

Bruns, Gerald L. *Hermeneutics Ancient and Modern*. New Haven, CT: Yale University Press, 1992.

———. 'On the Coherence of Hermeneutics and Ethics: An Essay on Gadamer and Levinas'. In *Gadamer's Repercussions: Reconsidering Philosophical Hermeneutics*, edited by Bruce Krajewski. Berkeley: University of California Press, 2004.

Bullinger, Heinrich. *A Hvndred Sermons vpō the Apocalips of Iesu Christ*. Translated by John Daus. London: Iohn Day, 1561.

Burrow, Colin. 'Shakespeare and Epic'. In *Epic Performances from the Middle Ages into the Twenty–First Century*, edited by Fiona Macintosh, Justine McConnell, Stephen Harrison and Claire Kenward, 31–45. Oxford: Oxford University Press, 2018.

Burton, William. *An Exposition of the Lords Prayer*. London: The widdow Orwin, 1594.

Byker, Devin. 'Bent Speech and Borrowed Selves: Substitutionary Logic and Intercessory Acts in *Measure for Measure*'. *Journal of Medieval and Early Modern Studies* 46, no. 2 (2016): 405–32.

Calvin, Jean/John. *A Commentarie of Iohn Caluine, vpon the first booke of Moses called Genesis*. Translated by Thomas Tymme. London: Thomas Dawson, 1578.

———. *A Commentarie vpon the Epistle of Saint Paul to the Romanes, written in Latine by M. Iohn Caluin*. Translated by Christopher Rosdell. London: Thomas Dawson, 1583.

———. *Commentary on Corinthians – Volume 1*. Translated by Rev. John Pringle. Grand Rapids, MI: Christian Classics Ethereal Library, 1848.

———. *A Commentary Vpon the Prophecie of Isaiah*. Translated by C. C. London: Felix Kyngston, 1609.

———. *A Harmonie composed and made of three Euangelistes, Matthew, Marke and Luke, with the Commentaries of Iohn Caluine*. Translated by E. P. In *A Harmonie Vpon the Three Euangelists, Matthew, Mark and Luke [. . .] Whereunto Is Also Added a Commentarie Vpon the Euangelist S. Iohn*. London: Thomas Dawson, 1584.

———. *The holy Gospel of Iesus Christ, according to Iohn, with the Commentary of M. Iohn Caluine*. Translated by Christopher Fetherstone. In *A Harmonie Vpon the Three Euangelists, Matthew, Mark and Luke [. . .] Whereunto Is Also Added a Commentarie Vpon the Euangelist S. Iohn*. London: Thomas Dawson, 1584.

———. *The Institution of Christian Religion*. Translated by Thomas Norton. London: Arnold Hatfield, 1599.

———. *Tracts Containing Treatises on the Sacraments, Catechism of the Church of Geneva, Forms of Prayer, and Confessions of Faith*. Translated by Henry Beveridge. 3 vols. Vol. 2. Edinburgh: The Calvin Translation Society, 1849.

Campbell, Gordon. *Bible: The Story of the King James Version, 1611–2011*. Oxford: Oxford University Press, 2010.

The Canons and Decrees of the Sacred and Ecumenical Council of Trent, Celebrated under the Sovereign Pontiffs, Paul III, Julius III and Pius IV. Translated by James Waterworth. London: C. Dolman, 1848.

Certain Sermons or Homilies Appointed to Be Read in Churches in the Time of Queen Elizabeth. London: George Wells, Abel Swall and George Pawlett, 1687.

Charnes, Linda. '"So Unsecret to Ourselves": Notorious Identity and the Material Subject in Shakespeare's Troilus and Cressida'. *Shakespeare Quarterly* 40, no. 4 (1989): 413–40.

Chaucer, Geoffrey. *Troilus and Criseyde*. Edited by Barry A. Windeatt. London: Routledge, 1991.

Clement, Jennifer. *Reading Humility in Early Modern England*. Farnham: Ashgate, 2015.

Cohen, Stephen. 'From Mistress to Master: Political Transition and Formal Conflict in "Measure for Measure"'. *Criticism* 41, no. 4 (1999): 431–64.

Cole, Douglas. 'Myth and Anti–Myth: The Case of Troilus and Cressida'. *Shakespeare Quarterly* 31, no. 1 (1980): 76–84.

Colie, Rosalie L. *The Resources of Kind: Genre-Theory in the Renaissance*. Edited by Barbara K. Lewalski. Berkeley: University of California Press, 1973.

Cooper, Helen. *Shakespeare and the Medieval World*. London: Bloomsbury Publishing, 2012.

Cooper, Thomas. *Thesavrvs Lingvae Romanae & Britannicae*. Londini: Henry Denham, 1578.

Cousins, A. D. 'Shakespeare's Hamlet 1.2.153'. *The Explicator* 62, no. 1 (2003): 5–7.

Cox, John D. 'Shakespeare's Religious and Moral Thinking: Skepticism or Suspicion?'. *Religion & Literature* 36, no. 1 (2004): 39–66.

Cranmer, Thomas. 'A Prologue or Preface'. In *The Byble in Englishe that is, the olde and new Testament, after the translacion appoynted to bee read in the Churches*. London: Edwarde Whitchurche, 1549.

Crocker, Holly A. *The Matter of Virtue: Women's Ethical Action from Chaucer to Shakespeare*. Philadelphia: University of Pennsylvania Press, 2019.

Cummings, Brian. *The Literary Culture of the Reformation: Grammar and Grace*. Oxford: Oxford University Press, 2002.

———. *Mortal Thoughts: Religion, Secularity and Identity in Shakespeare and Early Modern Culture*. Oxford: Oxford University Press, 2013.

———. 'The Protestant and Catholic Reformations'. In *The Oxford Handbook of English Literature and Theology*, edited by Andrew Hass, David Jasper and Elisabeth Jay, 79–96. Oxford: Oxford University Press, 2007.

———. 'Religion'. In *The Oxford Handbook of Shakespeare*, edited by Arthur F. Kinney, 663–79. Oxford: Oxford University Press, 2012.

Cunningham, Karen J. 'The Shakespearean Legal Imaginary'. In *The Shakespearean World*, edited by Jill L. Levenson and Robert Ormsby, 622–36. London: Routledge, 2017.

Dabbs, Thomas. 'Paul's Cross and the Dramatic Echoes of Early-Elizabethan Print'. In *Paul's Cross and the Culture of Persuasion in England, 1520–1640*, edited by Torrance Kirby and P. G. Stanwood, 223–44. Boston: Brill, 2014.

Daniel, David P. 'Luther on the Church'. In *The Oxford Handbook of Martin Luther's Theology*, edited by Robert Kolb, Irene Dingel and L'ubomír Batka, 333–52. Oxford: Oxford University Press, 2014.

Daniell, David. 'Shakespeare and the Protestant Mind'. *Shakespeare Survey* 54 (2001): 1–12.

Davies, Michael. 'Introduction: Shakespeare and Protestantism'. *Shakespeare* 5, no. 1 (2009): 1–17.

Dawson, Anthony B. 'Appendix: Sources of the Play'. In *Troilus and Cressida*, edited by Anthony B. Dawson. The New Cambridge Shakespeare, 267–75. Cambridge: Cambridge University Press, 2017.

———. 'Introduction'. In *Troilus and Cressida*, edited by Anthony B. Dawson. The New Cambridge Shakespeare, 1–80. Cambridge: Cambridge University Press, 2017.

Dawson, Anthony B. and Paul Yachnin. *The Culture of Playgoing in Shakespeare's England*. Cambridge: Cambridge University Press, 2001.

De Grazia, Margreta. 'When Did Hamlet Become Modern?' *Textual Practice* 17, no. 3 (2003): 485–503.

Demetriou, Tania and Tanya Pollard. 'Homer and Greek Tragedy in early modern England's theatres: an introduction'. *Classical Receptions Journal* 9, no. 1 (2016): 1–35.

Dent, Arthur. *The Plaine Mans Path-Way to Heauen*. 6th ed. London: Robert Dexter, 1603.

Desens, Marliss C. *The Bed-Trick in English Renaissance Drama: Explorations in Gender, Sexuality, and Power*. Newark: University of Delaware Press, 1994.

Diehl, Huston. 'Religion and Shakespearean Tragedy'. In *The Cambridge Companion to Shakespearean Tragedy*, edited by

Claire McEachern, 86–102. Cambridge: Cambridge University Press, 2003.

Dixon, Leif. *Practical Predestinarians in England c. 1590–1640*. Farnham: Ashgate, 2014.

Dostal, Robert. 'Gadamer, Kant, and the Enlightenment'. *Research in Phenomenology* 46, no. 3 (2016): 337–48.

Duncan-Jones, Katherine. 'Introduction'. In *Shakespeare's Sonnets*, edited by Katherine Duncan-Jones. Arden Shakespeare Third Series, 1–106. London: Bloomsbury, 2010.

Edwards, Philip. 'Apendix 1: Textual Analysis'. In *Hamlet, Prince of Denmark*, edited by Philip Edwards. The New Cambridge Shakespeare, 253–77. Cambridge: Cambridge University Press, 2019.

Erasmus, Desiderius. 'De Libero Arbitrio'. Edited by E. Gordon Rupp and A. N. Marlow. Translated by E. Gordon Rupp. In *Luther and Erasmus: Free Will and Salvation*, edited by E. Gordon Rupp and Philip S. Watson, 33–97. Philadelphia: Westminster Press, 1969.

———. 'The Handbook of the Christian Soldier: *Enchiridion militis christiani*'. Translated by Charles Fantazzi. In *Spiritualia*, edited by John W. O'Malley, 1–127. The Collected Works of Erasmus, vol. 66. Toronto: University of Toronto Press, 1988.

Fernie, Ewan. 'Shakespeare and the Prospect of Presentism'. *Shakespeare Survey* 58 (2005): 169–84.

Field, Catherine. '"Sweet Practicer, thy Physic I will try": Helena and her "Good Receipt" in *All's Well, That Ends Well*'. In *All's Well That Ends Well: New Critical Essays*, edited by Gary Waller, 194–208. New York: Routledge, 2007.

Fisch, Harold. *The Biblical Presence in Shakespeare, Milton, and Blake: A Comparative Study*. Oxford: Oxford University Press, 1999.

Fischer, Robert H. 'Introduction to Volume 37'. In *Word and Sacrament III*, edited by Robert H. Fischer. Luther's Works, vol. 37. Philadelphia: Muhlenberg Press, 1961.

'Forum: The German Enlightenment'. *German History* 35, no. 4 (2017): 588–602.

Foster, Verna A. *The Name and Nature of Tragicomedy*. Abindgon: Routledge, 2016. First published by Ashgate Publishing, 2004.

Foxe, John. *A Sermon of Christ Crucified, Preached at Paules Crosse*. London: Iohn Daye, 1570.

Freeman, Jane. 'Life-Long Learning in Shakespeare's *All's Well That Ends Well*'. *Renascence* 56, no. 2 (2004): 67–85.

Fuller, Thomas. *The History of the Worthies of England*. London: J. G. W. L. and W. G., 1662.

Fulton, Thomas. 'Shakespeare's Everyman: *Measure for Measure* and English Fundamentalism'. *Journal of Medieval and Early Modern Studies* 40, no. 1 (2010): 119–47.

Fulton, Thomas and Kristen Poole (eds). *The Bible on the Shakespearean Stage: Cultures of Interpretation in Reformation England*. Cambridge: Cambridge University Press, 2018.

———. 'Introduction: Popular Hermeneutics in Shakespeare's London'. In *The Bible on the Shakespearean Stage: Cultures of Interpretation in Reformation England*, edited by Thomas Fulton and Kristen Poole, 1–14. Cambridge: Cambridge University Press, 2018.

Gadamer, Hans-Georg. 'Hermeneutics as a Theoretical and Practical Task'. Edited and translated by Richard E. Palmer. In *The Gadamer Reader: A Boquet of the Later Writings*, 246–65. Evanston, IL: Northwestern University Press, 2007.

———. 'Hermeneutics as Practical Philosophy'. Edited and translated by Richard E. Palmer. In *The Gadamer Reader: A Boquet of the Later Writings*, 227–45. Evanston, IL: Northwestern University Press, 2007.

———. *Philosophical Hermeneutics*. Edited and translated by David E. Linge. Berkeley: University of California Press, 1976.

———. *The Relevance of the Beautiful and Other Essays*. Edited by Robert Bernasconi. Translated by Nicholas Walker. Cambridge: Cambridge University Press, 1986.

———. *Truth and Method*. Translated by Joel Weinsheimer and Donald G. Marshall. 2nd, rev. ed. London: Continuum, 2004.

Gardiner, Stephen. *A declaration of suche true articles as George Ioye hath gone about to confute as false*. London: Iohannes Herforde, 1546.

George, Timothy. 'Reading the Bible with the Reformers'. *First Things* 211 (2011): 27–33.

Gerrish, Brian. 'Luther and the Reformed Eucharist: What Luther Said, or Might Have Said, About Calvin'. *Seminary Ridge Review* 10, no. 2 (2008): 5–19.

Gibbons, Brian. 'Introduction'. In *Measure for Measure*, edited by Brian Gibbons, 1–83. The New Cambridge Shakespeare. Cambridge: Cambridge University Press, 2006.

Gillies, John. 'Calvinism as Tragedy in the English Revenge Play'. *Shakespeare* 11, no. 4 (2015): 362–87.

———. 'The Question of Original Sin in *Hamlet*'. *Shakespeare Quarterly* 64, no. 4 (2013): 396–424.

Goossen, Jonathan. '"'Tis Set Down So in Heaven, but Not in Earth": Reconsidering Political Theology in Shakespeare's 'Measure for Measure'". *Christianity & Literature* 61, no. 2 (2012): 217–39.

Grady, Hugh. *Shakespeare's Universal Wolf: Studies in Early Modern Reification*. Oxford: Oxford University Press, 1996.

Graham, Kenneth. 'The Reformation of Manners and the Grace of the Reformation: *Measure for Measure*'s Disciplinary Mingle-Mangle'. *Religion & Literature* 49, no. 3 (2017): 162–71.

Green, Garrett. *Theology, Hermeneutics, and Imagination: The Crisis of Interpretation at the End of Modernity*. Cambridge: Cambridge University Press, 2000.

Gregor, Brian. *A Philosophical Anthropology of the Cross: The Cruciform Self*. Bloomington: Indiana University Press, 2013.

Gregory, Brad S. *The Unintended Reformation: How a Religious Revolution Secularized Society*. Cambridge, MA: The Belknap Press of Harvard University Press, 2012.

Grondin, Jean. *Introduction to Philosophical Hermeneutics*. Translated by Joel Weinsheimer. New Haven, CT: Yale University Press, 1994.

Groves, Beatrice. *Texts and Traditions: Religion in Shakespeare 1592–1604*. Oxford: Oxford University Press, 2007.

Guarini, Giovanni Battista. 'The Compendium of Tragicomic Poetry'. Edited and translated by Allan H. Gilbert. In *Literary Criticism: Plato to Dryden*, 504–33. Detroit: Wayne State University Press, 1962.

Gundlach, Bradley J. 'Augustine of Hippo'. In *Evangelical Dictionary of Theology*, edited by Walter A. Elwell, 121–4. Grand Rapids, MI: Baker Academic, 2001.

Gurnis, Musa. '"Most Ignorant of What He's Most Assured": The Hermeneutics of Predestination in *Measure for Measure*'. *Shakespeare Studies* 42 (2014): 141–69.

Hackel, Heidi Brayman. 'The "Great Variety" of Readers'. In *A Companion to Shakespeare*, edited by David Scott Kastan, 139–57. Malden, MA: Blackwell Publishers, 1999.

Hamlin, Hannibal. *The Bible in Shakespeare*. Oxford: Oxford University Press, 2013.

Hammill, Graham and Julia Reinhard Lupton. 'Sovereigns, Citizens, and Saints: Political Theology and Renaissance Literature'. *Religion & Literature* 38, no. 3 (2006): 1–11.

Harding, Vanessa. 'Families and Households in Early Modern London, c. 1550–1640'. In *The Oxford Handbook of the Age of Shakespeare*, edited by Malcolm Smuts, 596–615. Oxford: Oxford University Press, 2016.

Harrison, Peter. 'The Bible and the Emergence of Modern Science'. *Science & Christian Belief* 18, no. 2 (2006): 115–32.

———. *The Fall of Man and the Foundations of Science*. Cambridge: Cambridge University Press, 2007.

———. 'Philosophy and the Crisis of Religion'. In *The Cambridge Companion to Renaissance Philosophy*, edited by James Hankins, 234–49. Cambridge: Cambridge University Press, 2007.

Helm, Paul. *John Calvin's Ideas*. Oxford: Oxford University Press, 2004.

Herrmann, Erik. 'Luther's Absorption of Medieval Biblical Interpretation and his Use of the Church Fathers'. In *The Oxford Handbook of Martin Luther's Theology*, edited by Robert Kolb, Irene Dingel and L'ubomír Batka, 71–90. Oxford: Oxford University Press, 2014.

Heywood, Thomas. *An Apology for Actors*. London: Nicholas Okes, 1612.

Higgins, John C. 'Justice, Mercy, and Dialectical Genres in "Measure for Measure" and "Promos and Cassandra"'. *English Literary Renaissance* 42, no. 2 (2012): 258–93.

Hillman, David. 'The Worst Case of Knowing the Other? Stanley Cavell and Troilus and Cressida'. *Philosophy and Literature* 32, no. 1 (2008): 74–86.

Hirschfeld, Heather. 'Hamlet's "First Corse": Repetition, Trauma, and the Displacement of Redemptive Typology'. *Shakespeare Quarterly* 54, no. 4 (2003): 424–48.

Holbrook, Peter. *Shakespeare's Individualism*. Cambridge: Cambridge University Press, 2010.

Holder, R. Ward. 'Revelation and Scripture'. In *T&T Clark Companion to Reformation Theology*, edited by David M. Whitford, 32–56. London: Bloomsbury, 2012.

Holderness, Graham. '"The Single and Peculiar Life": Hamlet's Heart and the Early Modern Subject'. *Shakespeare Survey* 62 (2009): 296–307.

Homer. *Seauen Bookes of the Iliades of Homere, Prince of Poets*. Translated by George Chapman. London: Iohn Windet, 1598.

Hooker, Richard. *The Ecclesiastical Polity and Other Works*, vol. 3. London: Holdsworth and Ball 1830.

———. *A Learned Sermon of the Natvre of Pride*. Oxford: Ioseph Barnes, 1612.

Houlbrooke, Ralph A. *Death, Religion, and the Family in England, 1480–1750*. Oxford: Oxford University Press, 1998.

Howard, Jean E. 'Female Agency in *All's Well That Ends Well*'. *Journal of the Australasian Universities Language and Literature Association* 106 (2006): 43–60.

———. 'Shakespeare and Genre'. In *A Companion to Shakespeare*, edited by David Scott Kastan, 297–310. Malden, MA: Blackwell Publishers, 1999.

Hunt, Arnold. 'The Lord's Supper in Early Modern England'. *Past & Present*, no. 161 (1998): 39–83.

Hunt, Maurice. 'Being Precise in Measure for Measure'. *Renascence* 58, no. 4 (2006): 242–67.

———. 'Helena and the Reformation Problem of Merit in *All's Well That Ends Well*'. In *Shakespeare and the Culture of Christianity in Early Modern England*, edited by Dennis Taylor and David N. Beauregard, 336–68. New York: Fordham University Press, 2003.

———. 'Shakespeare's *Troilus and Cressida* and Christian Epistemology'. *Christianity and Literature* 42, no. 2 (1993): 243–60.

———. 'Vincentio's Selves in *Measure for Measure*'. *College Literature* 46, no. 3 (2019): 684–711.

Jackson, Ken and Arthur F. Marotti. 'The Turn to Religion in Early Modern English Studies'. *Criticism* 46, no. 1 (2004): 167–90.

James, Heather. 'Shakespeare's Classical Plays'. In *The New Cambridge Companion to Shakespeare*, edited by Margreta De Grazia and Stanley Wells, 153–68. Cambridge: Cambridge University Press, 2010.

———. *Shakespeare's Troy*. Cambridge: Cambridge University Press, 1997.

James I, King of England. *Basilikon dōron. Or His Maiesties Instructions to his dearest sonne, Henry the Prince*. Edinburgh: Robert Walde-graue, 1603.

Jamieson, Michael. 'The Problem Plays, 1920–1970: A Retrospective'. In *Aspects of Shakespeare's 'Problem Plays'*, edited by Kenneth Muir and Stanley Wells, 126–35. Cambridge: Cambridge University Press, 1982.

Jensen, Michael. '"Simply" Reading the Geneva Bible: The Geneva Bible and Its Readers'. *Literature & Theology* 9, no. 1 (1995): 30–45.

Jüngel, Eberhard. *Theological Essays*. Edited and translated by John B. Webster. Vol. 2. Edinburgh: T&T Clark, 1995.

Karant-Nunn, Susan C. 'Reformation Society, Women and the Family'. In *Reformation World*, edited by Andrew Pettegree, 433–60. London: Routledge, 2000.

Kastan, David Scott. '*All's Well That Ends Well* and the Limits of Comedy'. *ELH* 52, no. 3 (1985): 575–89.

———. *A Will to Believe: Shakespeare and Religion*. Oxford: Oxford University Press, 2014.

Kaula, David. '"Mad Idolatry" in Shakespeare's *Troilus and Cressida*'. *Texas Studies in Literature and Language* 15 (1973): 25–38.

Kenward, Claire. '"Of Arms and the Man": Thersites in Early Modern English Drama'. In *Epic Performances from the Middle Ages into the Twenty-First Century*, edited by Fiona

Macintosh, Justine McConnell, Stephen Harrison and Claire Kenward, 422–38. Oxford: Oxford University Press, 2018.

Kermode, Frank. '"Opinion" in *Troilus and Cressida*'. *Critical Quarterly* 54, no. 1 (2012): 88–102.

———. *The Sense of an Ending: Studies in the Theory of Fiction with a New Epilogue*. Oxford: Oxford University Press, 2000.

Kerrigan, John. 'Shakespeare, Oaths and Vows'. In *Proceedings of the British Academy Volume 167, 2009 Lectures*, edited by Ron Johnston, 61–89. Oxford: Oxford University Press, 2011.

Kirby, W. J. Torrance. 'Stoic and Epicurean? Calvin's Dialectical Account of Providence in the *Institute*'. *International Journal of Systematic Theology* 5, no. 3 (2003): 309–22.

Kirsch, Arthur. 'The Bitter and the Sweet of Tragicomedy: Shakespeare's *All's Well That Ends Well* and Montaigne'. *Yale Review* 102, no. 2 (2014): 63–84.

Kristeller, Paul Oskar. 'Humanism'. In *The Cambridge History of Renaissance Philosophy*, edited by C. B. Schmitt, Quentin Skinner, Eckhard Kessler and Jill Kraye, 111–38. Cambridge: Cambridge University Press, 1988.

Lake, Peter and Michael C. Questier. *The Antichrist's Lewd Hat: Protestants, Papists and Players in Post-Reformation England*. New Haven, CT: Yale University Press, 2002.

Landau, Aaron. '"Let Me Not Burst in Ignorance": Skepticism and Anxiety in Hamlet'. *English Studies* 82, no. 3 (2001): 218–30.

Lander, Jesse M. 'Maimed Rites and Whirling Words in Hamlet'. In *The Bible on the Shakespearean Stage: Cultures of Interpretation in Reformation England*, edited by Thomas Fulton and Kristen Poole, 188–203. Cambridge: Cambridge University Press, 2018.

Lane, Belden C. 'Spirituality as the Performance of Desire: Calvin on the World as a Theatre of God's Glory'. *Spiritus: A Journal of Christian Spirituality* 1, no. 1 (2001): 1–30.

Leake, Richard. *Foure Sermons Preached and Publikely Taught by Richard Leake*. London: Felix Kingston, 1599.

Lehnhof, Kent R. 'Performing Woman: Female Theatricality in *All's Well, That Ends Well*'. In *All's Well That Ends Well: New Critical Essays*, edited by Gary Waller, 111–24. New York: Routledge, 2007.

Levin, Richard A. 'Did Helena Have a Renaissance?' *English Studies* 87, no. 1 (2006): 23–34.

Lewis, Cynthia. '"Derived Honesty and Achieved Goodness": Doctrines of Grace in *All's Well That Ends Well*'. *Renaissance and Reformation* 14, no. 2 (1990): 147–70.

Lewis, Rhodri. *Hamlet and the Vision of Darkness*. Princeton: Princeton University Press, 2017.

Litzenberger, Caroline. *The English Reformation and the Laity: Gloucestershire, 1540–1580*. Cambridge: Cambridge University Press, 1997.

Loades, David. *Tudor Government*. Oxford: Blackwell, 1997.

Lundin, Roger. 'Meeting at the Crossroads: Fiction, History, and Christian Understanding'. In *Hermeneutics at the Crossroads*, edited by Kevin J. Vanhoozer, James K. A. Smith and Bruce Ellis Benson, 133–49. Bloomington: Indiana University Press, 2006.

Lupton, Julia Reinhard. 'The Religious Turn (to Theory) in Shakespeare Studies'. *English Language Notes* 44, no. 1 (2006): 145–9.

———. *Thinking with Shakespeare: Essays on Politics and Life*. Chicago: The University of Chicago Press, 2011.

Luther, Martin. 'Answer to the Hyperchristian, Hyperspiritual, and Hyperlearned Book by Goat Emser in Leipzig – Including Some Thoughts Regarding His Companion, the Fool Murner'. Translated by Eric W. Gritsch and Ruth C. Gritsch. In *Church and Ministry 1*, edited by Eric W. Gritsch, 143–224. Luther's Works, vol. 39. Philadelphia: Fortress Press, 1970.

———. *A Commentarie of M. Doctor Martin Luther Vpon the Epistle of S. Paul to the Galathians*. London: Thomas Vautroullier, 1575.

———. 'De Servo Arbitrio'. Edited by Philip S. Watson and B. Drewery. Translated by Philip S. Watson. In *Luther and Erasmus: Free Will and Salvation*, edited by E. Gordon Rupp and Philip S. Watson, 99–334. Philadelphia: Westminster Press, 1969.

———. 'Disputation against Scholastic Theology'. Translated by Harold J. Grimm. In *Career of the Reformer I*, edited by Harold J. Grimm, 3–16. Luther's Works, vol. 31. Philadelphia: Muhlenberg Press, 1957.

———. 'Explanations of the Ninety–Five Theses'. Translated by Carl W. Folkemer. In *Career of the Reformer I*, edited by Harold J.

Grimm, 77–258. Luther's Works, vol. 31. Philadelphia: Muhlenberg Press, 1957.

———. 'The Freedom of a Christian'. Translated by W. A. Lambert. Revised by Harold J. Grimm. In *Career of the Reformer I*, edited by Harold J. Grimm, 333–82. Luther's Works, vol. 31. Philadelphia: Muhlenberg Press, 1957.

———. 'Heidelberg Disputation'. Translated by Harold J. Grimm. In *Career of the Reformer I*, edited by Harold J. Grimm, 39–70. Luther's Works, vol. 31. Philadelphia: Muhlenberg Press, 1957.

———. *Lectures on Galatians 1535: Chapters 1–4*. Edited by Jaroslav Pelikan and Walter A. Hansen. Translated by Jaroslav Pelikan. Luther's Works, vol. 26. Saint Louis, MI: Concordia Publishing House, 1963.

———. *Lectures on Galatians 1535: Chapters 5–6*. Translated by Jaroslav Pelikan. In *Lectures on Galatians 1535: Chapters 5–6; Lectures on Galatians 1519: Chapters 1–6*, edited by Jaroslav Pelikan and Walter A. Hansen, 1–149. Luther's Works, vol. 27. Saint Louis, MI: Concordia Publishing House, 1964.

———. *Lectures on Genesis: Chapters 1–5*. Edited by Jaroslav Pelikan. Translated by George V. Schick. Luther's Works, vol. 1. Saint Louis, MI: Concordia Publishing House, 1958.

———. *Lectures on Romans*. Edited by Hilton C. Oswald. Translated by Walter G. Tillmans and Jacob A. O. Preus. Luther's Works, vol. 25. Saint Louis, MI: Concordia Publishing House, 1972.

———. 'Preface to the Complete Edition of Luther's Latin Writings'. Translated by Lewis W. Spitz. In *Career of the Reformer IV*, edited by Lewis W. Spitz, 323–38. Luther's Works, vol. 34. Philadelphia: Muhlenberg Press, 1960.

———. 'A Sermon of D. Martin Lvther, of the Svmme of Christian Life'. Translated by W. G. In *Special and Chosen Sermons of D. Martin Lvther*, 182–212. London: Thomas Vautroullier, 1578.

———. *The Table Talk of Martin Luther*. Edited and translated by William Hazlitt. London: H. G. Bohn, 1857.

———. 'To the Christian Nobility of the German Nation Concerning the Reform of the Christian Estate'. Translated by Charles M. Jacobs. Revised by James Atkinson. In *The Christian in*

Society I, edited by James Atkinson, 123–217. Luther's Works, vol. 44. Philadelphia: Fortress Press, 1966.

MacCulloch, Diarmaid. *Reformation: Europe's House Divided 1490–1700*. London: Penguin Books, 2004.

McGrath, Alister E. *Christianity's Dangerous Idea: The Protestant Revolution – A History from the Sixteenth Century to the Twenty-First*. HarperCollins e-books, 2007.

———. *The Intellectual Origins of the European Reformation*. 2nd ed. Malden, MA: Blackwell, 2004.

———. *Iustitia Dei: A History of the Christian Doctrine of Justification*. 3rd ed. Cambridge: Cambridge University Press, 2005.

———. *Luther's Theology of the Cross*. Oxford: Blackwell, 1985.

———. *Reformation Thought: An Introduction*. 4th ed. Chichester: Wiley-Blackwell, 2012.

Mack, Maynard. 'The World of *Hamlet*'. *Yale Review* 41 (1952): 502–23.

McNeill, John T. (ed.). *Calvin: Institutes of the Christian Religion*. Translated by Ford Lewis Battles. 2 vols. Philadelphia: Westminster Press, 1960.

———. 'Introduction'. In *Calvin: Institutes of the Christian Religion*, edited by John T. McNeill, xxix–lxxi. Vol. 1. Philadelpia: Westminster Press, 1960.

Magedanz, Stacy. 'Public Justice and Private Mercy in *Measure for Measure*'. *SEL: Studies in English Literature, 1500–1900* 44, no. 2 (2004): 317–32.

Maguire, Laurie E. 'Performing Anger: The Anatomy of Abuse(s) in "Troilus and Cressida"'. *Renaissance Drama* 31 (2002): 153–83.

Maltby, Judith. 'Foreword'. In *The Book of Common Prayer 1559: The Elizabethan Prayer Book*, edited by John E. Booty, vii–ix. Charlottesville: The University of Virginia Press, 2005.

Manley, Lawrence. 'Literature and London'. In *The Cambridge History of Early Modern English Literature*, edited by David Loewenstein and Janel Mueller, 399–427. Cambridge: Cambridge University Press, 2002.

Marche, Stephen. 'John Webster and the Dead: Reading *The Duchess of Malfi*'s Eschatology'. *Renaissance and Reformation* 28, no. 2 (2004): 79–95.

Marlow, A. N. and B. Drewery. 'Introduction'. In *Luther and Erasmus: Free Will and Salvation*, edited by E. Gordon Rupp and Philip S. Watson, 1–32. Philadelphia: Westminster Press, 1969.

Marotti, Arthur F. and Ken Jackson. 'Religion, Secularity, and Shakespeare'. In *The Shakespearean World*, edited by Jill L. Levenson and Robert Ormsby, 542–56. Abingdon: Routledge, 2017.

Marshall, Cynthia. *Last Things and Last Plays: Shakespearean Eschatology*. Carbondale: Southern Illinois University Press, 1991.

Marshall, Peter. *Beliefs and the Dead in Reformation England*. Oxford: Oxford University Press, 2002.

———. 'Choosing Sides and Talking Religion in Shakespeare's England'. In *Shakespeare and Early Modern Religion*, edited by David Loewenstein and Michael Witmore, 40–56. Cambridge: Cambridge University Press, 2015.

———. '(Re)defining the English Reformation'. *Journal of British Studies* 48, no. 3 (2009): 564–86.

Martin, John Jeffries. *Myths of Renaissance Individualism*. New York: Palgrave Macmillan, 2004.

Matheson, Mark. '*Hamlet* and "a Matter Tender and Dangerous"'. *Shakespeare Quarterly* 46, no. 4 (1995): 383–97.

Milton, John. *Milton: Paradise Lost*. Edited by Alastair Fowler. 2nd ed. London: Routledge, 2007.

Miola, Robert S. 'Lesse Greeke? Homer in Jonson and Shakespeare'. *Ben Jonson Journal* 23, no. 1 (2016): 101–26.

———. 'Reading the Classics'. In *A Companion to Shakespeare*, edited by David Scott Kastan, 172–85. Malden, MA: Blackwell Publishers, 1999.

Molekamp, Femke. 'Using a Collection to Discover Reading Practices: The British Library Geneva Bibles and a History of Their Early Modern Readers'. *eBLJ*. (2006). <http://www.bl.uk/eblj/2006articles/pdf/article10.pdf>.

Montaigne, Michel Eyquem de. *Montaigne's Essays*. Translated by John Florio. Everyman's Library, vol. 2. London: Dent, 1965.

More, Sir Thomas. *The co[n]futacyon of Tyndales answere made by syr Thomas More knyght lorde chau[n]cellour of Englonde*. London: Wyllyam Rastell, 1532.

Muir, Kenneth. *The Sources of Shakespeare's Plays*. Abingdon: Routledge, 1977, repr. 2005.

Muller, Richard A. 'John Calvin and Later Calvinism'. In *The Cambridge Companion to Reformation Theology*, edited by David A. Bagchi and David C. Steinmetz, 130–49. Cambridge: Cambridge University Press, 2004.

Navitsky, Joseph. 'Scurrilous Jests and Retaliatory Abuse in Shakespeare's *Troilus and Cressida*'. *English Literary Renaissance* 42, no. 1 (2012): 3–31.

Neill, Michael. 'English Revenge Tragedy'. In *A Companion to Tragedy*, edited by Rebecca W. Bushnell, 328–50. Malden, MA: Blackwell, 2005.

———. 'Shakespeare's Tragedies'. In *The New Cambridge Companion to Shakespeare*, edited by Margreta De Grazia and Stanley Wells, 121–36. Cambridge: Cambridge University Press, 2010.

The New Testament. Translated by W. Tyndale. London: John Day & Wylliam Seres, 1550.

Nietzsche, Friedrich. *The Genealogy of Morals: A Polemic*. Translated by Horace B. Samuel. Vol. 13 of *The Complete Works of Friedrich Nietzsche*, edited by Oscar Levy. Edinburgh: T. N. Foulis, 1913.

———. *On the Genealogy of Morals*. Edited by Walter Kaufmann. Translated by Walter Kaufmann and R. J. Hollingdale. New York: Vintage Books, 1967.

———. *The Portable Nietzsche*. Translated by Walter Kaufmann. Harmondsworth: Penguin Books, 1967.

Nigri, Lucia. 'Religious Hypocrisy in Performance: Roman Catholicism and the London Stage'. In *Forms of Hypocrisy in Early Modern England*, edited by Lucia Nigri and Naya Tsentourou, 57–71. New York: Routledge, 2018.

Nigri, Lucia and Naya Tsentourou. 'Introduction'. In *Forms of Hypocrisy in Early Modern England*, edited by Lucia Nigri and Naya Tsentourou, 1–14. New York: Routledge, 2018.

Nordlund, Marcus. 'Pride and Self-Love in Shakespeare and Montaigne'. In *The Shakespearean International Yearbook 6: Special Section, Shakespeare and Montaigne Revisited*, edited by Graham Bradshaw, Tom Bishop and Peter Holbrook, 77–98. Aldershot: Ashgate, 2006.

O'Banion, Patrick J. 'The Pastoral Use of the Book of Revelation in Late Tudor England'. *The Journal of Ecclesiastical History* 57, no. 4 (2006): 693–710.

Olin, John C. (ed.). *A Reformation Debate: Sadoleto's Letter to the Genevans and Calvin's Reply*. 2nd ed. New York: Fordham University Press, 2000.

Perkins, William. *An Exposition of the Symbole or Creed of the Apostles*. Cambridge: Iohn Legatt, 1595.

Peterson, Kaara L. 'The Ring's the Thing: Elizabeth I's Virgin Knot and *All's Well That Ends Well*'. *Studies in Philology* 113, no. 1 (2016): 101–31.

Pettegree, Andrew. 'The Spread of Calvin's Thought'. In *The Cambridge Companion to John Calvin*, edited by Donald K. McKim, 207–24. Cambridge: Cambridge University Press, 2004.

Prosser, Eleanor. *Hamlet and Revenge*. Stanford: Stanford University Press, 1967.

Quiring, Björn. 'Introduction'. In *'If Then the World, a Theatre Present . . .': Revisions of the Theatrum Mundi Metaphor in Early Modern England*, edited by Björn Quiring, 1–24. Berlin: De Gruyter, 2014.

Raleigh, Sir Walter. *The History of the World*. Edited by C. A. Patrides. London: Macmillan, 1971.

Reilly, Terry. '*All's Well, That Ends Well* and the 1604 Controversy Concerning the Court of Wards and Liveries'. In *All's Well That Ends Well: New Critical Essays*, edited by Gary Waller, 209–20. New York: Routledge, 2007.

Robinson, Hastings (ed.). *Original Letters Relative to the English Reformation*, vol. 2. Cambridge: The University Press, 1846 and 1847.

Rogers, Jami. 'Cressida in Twenty–First Century Performance'. *Shakespeare* 10, no. 1 (2014): 56–71.

Ross, Emily. '"Words, Vows, Gifts, Tears and Love's Full Sacrifice": An Assessment of the Status of Troilus and Cressida's Relationship According to Customary Elizabethan Marriage Procedure'. *Shakespeare* 4, no. 4 (2008): 413–37.

Ruge, Enno. 'Having a Good Time at the Theatre of the World: Amusement, Antitheatricality and the Calvinist Use of the *Theatrum Mundi* Metaphor in Early Modern England'. In *'If Then the World, a Theatre Present . . .': Revisions of the Theatrum Mundi Metaphor in Early Modern England*, edited by Björn Quiring, 25–38. Berlin: De Gruyter, 2014.

Rust, Jennifer R. 'Religious and Political Impasses in *Measure for Measure*'. In *The Cambridge Companion to Shakespeare and Religion*, edited by Hannibal Hamlin, 184–99. Cambridge: Cambridge University Press, 2019.

Ryan, Kiernan. '"Where Hope Is Coldest": *All's Well That Ends Well*'. In *Spiritual Shakespeares*, edited by Ewan Fernie, 28–49. London: Routledge, 2005.

Ryrie, Alec. *Being Protestant in Reformation Britain*. Oxford: Oxford University Press, 2013.

Ryrie, Charles Caldwell. 'Depravity, Total'. In *Evangelical Dictionary of Theology*, edited by Walter A. Elwell, 337. Grand Rapids, MI: Baker Academic, 2001.

Schanzer, Ernest. *The Problem Plays of Shakespeare: A Study of Julius Caesar, Measure for Measure, Antony and Cleopatra*. London: Routledge and Kegan Paul, 1963.

Schleiner, Louise. 'Providential Improvisation in *Measure for Measure*'. *PMLA* 97, no. 2 (1982): 227–36.

Semler, L. E. 'A Proximate Prince: The Gooey Business of "Hamlet" Criticism'. *Sydney Studies in English* 32 (2006): 97–122.

Shaheen, Naseeb. 'Biblical Echoes in *Troilus and Cressida*'. *Notes and Queries* 43, no. 2 (1996): 160–62.

———. *Biblical References in Shakespeare's Plays*. Newark: University of Delaware Press, 1999.

Shakespeare, William. *All's Well That Ends Well*. Arden Shakespeare Third Series. Edited by Suzanne Gossett and Helen Wilcox. London: Bloomsbury, 2019.

———. *All's Well That Ends Well*. The New Cambridge Shakespeare. 2nd ed. Edited by Russell Fraser. Cambridge: Cambridge University Press, 2003.

———. *The Famous Historie of Troylus and Cresseid*. London: G. Eld, 1609.

———. *Hamlet (Second Quarto Text)*. Edited by Ann Thompson and Neil Taylor. Arden Shakespeare Third Series. London: A & C Black, 2006.

———. *Hamlet: The Texts of 1603 and 1623*. Edited by Ann Thompson and Neil Taylor. Arden Shakespeare Third Series. London: Cengage Learning, 2006.

———. *Measure for Measure*. Edited by Brian Gibbons. The New Cambridge Shakespeare. Cambridge: Cambridge University Press, 2006.

———. *Measure for Measure*. Edited by A. R. Braunmuller and Robert N. Watson. Arden Shakespeare Third Series. London: Bloomsbury, 2020.

———. *Much Ado About Nothing*. Edited by Claire McEachern. Arden Shakespeare Third Series. London: Bloomsbury, 2015.

———. *Troilus and Cressida*. Edited by David Bevington. Arden Shakespeare Third Series. London: Bloomsbury, 1998.

———. *Troilus and Cressida*. Edited by Anthony B. Dawson. The New Cambridge Shakespeare. 2nd ed. Cambridge: Cambridge University Press, 2017.

———. *William Shakespeare: The Complete Works*. Edited by John Jowett, William Montgomery, Gary Taylor and Stanley Wells. 2nd ed. Oxford: Oxford University Press, 2005.

Shuger, Debora K. *Political Theologies in Shakespeare's England: The Sacred and the State in Measure for Measure*. New York: Palgrave, 2001.

Shurgot, Michael W. 'Bertram's Scar and Courts of Healing in *All's Well That Ends Well*'. *Shakespeare Bulletin* 37, no. 3 (2019): 391–407.

Simonds, Peggy Muñoz. 'Overlooked Sources of the Bed Trick'. *Shakespeare Quarterly* 34, no. 4 (1983): 433–4.

Simpson, James. *Burning to Read: English Fundamentalism and Its Reformation Opponents*. Cambridge, MA: The Belknap Press of Harvard University Press, 2007.

Sinfield, Alan. 'Hamlet's Special Providence'. *Shakespeare Survey* 33 (1980): 89–97.

Slights, Camille. 'The Parallel Structure of *Troilus and Cressida*'. *Shakespeare Quarterly* 25, no. 1 (1974): 42–51.

Snyder, Susan. 'The Genres of Shakespeare's Plays'. In *The Cambridge Companion to Shakespeare*, edited by Margreta De Grazia and Stanley Wells, 83–98. Cambridge: Cambridge University Press, 2001.

———. 'Introduction'. In *All's Well That Ends Well*, edited by Susan Snyder, 1–65. Oxford: Oxford University Press, 1993.

Sokol, B. J. and Mary Sokol. *Shakespeare's Legal Language: A Dictionary*. London: Bloomsbury Academic, 2000.

Spencer, Eric V. 'Scaling the Deputy: Equity and Mercy in *Measure for Measure*'. *Philosophy and Literature* 36, no. 1 (2012): 166–82.

Stachniewski, John. *The Persecutory Imagination: English Puritanism and the Literature of Despair*. Oxford: Clarendon, 1991.

Stackhouse, Max L. 'Ethics and Eschatology'. In *The Oxford Handbook of Eschatology*, edited by Jerry L. Walls, 548–61. Oxford: Oxford University Press, 2007.

Steinmetz, David C. 'The Council of Trent'. In *The Cambridge Companion to Reformation Theology*, edited by David A. Bagchi and David C. Steinmetz, 233–47. Cambridge: Cambridge University Press, 2004.

———. 'The Theology of John Calvin'. In *The Cambridge Companion to Reformation Theology*, edited by David A. Bagchi and David C. Steinmetz, 113–29. Cambridge: Cambridge University Press, 2004.

Sterrett, Joseph. 'Confessing Claudius: sovereignty, fraternity and isolation at the heart of *Hamlet*'. *Textual Practice* 23, no. 5 (2009): 739–61.

Stiller, Nikki. *The Figure of Cressida in British and American Literature: Transformation of a Literary Type*. Lewiston, NY: The Edwin Mellen Press, 1990.

Swift, Daniel. *Shakespeare's Common Prayers: The Book of Common Prayer and the Elizabethan Age*. Oxford: Oxford University Press, 2012.

Tadmor, Naomi. 'The Bible in English Culture: The Age of Shakespeare'. In *The Oxford Handbook of the Age of Shakespeare*, edited by Malcolm Smuts, 384–97. Oxford: Oxford University Press, 2016.

Tambling, Jeremy. 'Law and Will in *Measure for Measure*'. *Essays in Criticism* 59, no. 3 (2009): 189–210.

Targoff, Ramie. 'The Performance of Prayer: Sincerity and Theatricality in Early Modern England'. *Representations* 60 (1997): 49–69.

Taylor, Charles. *Human Agency and Language: Philosophical Papers 1*. Cambridge: Cambridge University Press, 1985.

———. *Sources of the Self: The Making of the Modern Identity*. Cambridge, MA: Harvard University Press, 1989.

Taylor, Jane. 'Of Hypocrisy: "Wherein the Action and Utterance of the Stage, Bar, and Pulpit Are Distinctly Consider'd"'. In *Performing the Secular: Religion, Representation, and Politics*, edited by Milija Gluhovic and Jisha Menon, 25–53. London: Palgrave Macmillan, 2017.

Thiselton, Anthony C. 'Further Implications and the Paradigmatic Status of Promise as Communicative Action'. In *The Promise of Hermeneutics*, edited by Roger Lundin, Anthony C. Thiselton and Clarence Walhout, 209–39. Grand Rapids, MI: Wm. B. Eerdmans, 1999.

Tiffany, Grace. *Love's Pilgrimage*. Newark: University of Delaware Press, 2006.

———. 'Not Saying No: Female Self-Erasure in *Troilus and Cressida*'. *Texas Studies in Literature and Language* 35, no. 1 (1993): 44–56.

Torrance, Thomas F. *Kingdom and Church*. Edinburgh: Oliver and Boyd, 1956.

———. *The Hermeneutics of John Calvin*. Edinburgh: Scottish Academic Press, 1988.

Traister, Barbara Howard. '"Doctor She": Healing and Sex in *All's Well That Ends Well*'. In *A Companion to Shakespeare's Works, Volume IV: The Poems, Problem Comedies, Late Plays*, edited by Richard Dutton and Jean E. Howard, 333–47. Blackwell Publishing, 2005.

Trueman, Carl R. *Luther on the Christian Life: Cross and Freedom*. Wheaton, IL: Crossway, 2015.

Tyndale, William. *An answere vnto Sir Thomas Mores dialoge made by Willyam Tindale*. Antwerp: S. Cock, 1531.

———. *The obedie[n]ce of a Christen man and how Christe[n] rulers ought to governe*. Antwerp: J. Hoochstraten, 1528.

———. 'The parable of the wicked Mammon'. In *The whole workes of W. Tyndall, Iohn Frith, and Doct. Barnes, three worthy martyrs, and principall teachers of this Churche of England*, 59–96 London: Iohn Daye, 1573.

Vanhoozer, Kevin J. *Biblical Authority after Babel: Retrieving the Solas in the Spirit of Mere Protestant Christianity*. Grand Rapids, MI: Brazos Press, 2016.

———. 'Discourse on Matter: Hermeneutics and the "Miracle" of Understanding'. In *Hermeneutics at the Crossroads*, edited by Kevin J. Vanhoozer, James K. A. Smith, and Bruce Ellis Benson, 3–34. Bloomington: Indiana University Press, 2006.

———. *Is There a Meaning in This Text? The Bible, the Reader, and the Morality of Literary Knowledge*. Grand Rapids, MI: Zondervan, 1998.

———. *Remythologizing Theology: Divine Action, Passion, and Authorship*. Cambridge: Cambridge University Press, 2010.

Vilhauer, Monica. *Gadamer's Ethics of Play: Hermeneutics and the Other*. Lanham, MD: Lexington Books, 2010.

Vorster, Nico. 'Sola Scriptura and Western Hyperpluralism: A Critical Response to Brad Gregory's Unintended Reformation'. *Review of European Studies* 5, no. 1 (2013): 52–64.

Waddington, Raymond B. 'Lutheran Hamlet'. *English Language Notes* 27, no. 2 (1989): 27–42.

Walsham, Alexandra. *Providence in Early Modern England*. Oxford: Oxford University Press, 2001.

Watson, Elizabeth S. 'Old King, New King, Eclipsed Sons, and Abandoned Altars in *Hamlet*'. *The Sixteenth Century Journal* 35, no. 2 (2004): 475–91.

Watson, Robert N. 'Introduction'. In *Measure for Measure*, edited by A. R. Braunmuller and Robert N. Watson. Arden Shakespeare Third Series, 1–148. London: Bloomsbury, 2020.

Watt, Tessa. *Cheap Print and Popular Piety, 1550–1640*. Cambridge: Cambridge University Press, 1991.

Welsh, Alexander. *What Is Honor? A Question of Moral Imperatives*. New Haven, CT: Yale University Press, 2008.

Werrell, Ralph S. 'Reformation Conflict between Stephen Gardiner and Robert Barnes, Lent 1540'. In *Paul's Cross and the Culture of Persuasion in England, 1520–1640*, edited by Torrance Kirby and P. G. Stanwood, 129–39. Boston: Brill, 2014.

West, William N. 'Humanism and the Resistance to Theology'. In *The Return of Theory in Early Modern English Studies: Tarrying with the Subjunctive*, edited by Paul Cefalu and Bryan Reynolds, 167–91. Basingstoke: Palgrave MacMillan, 2011.

Westbrook, Vivienne. 'Versions of Paul'. In *A Companion to Paul in the Reformation*, edited by R. Ward Holder, 427–63. Leiden: Brill, 2009.

Whalen, Benedict J. 'Private Conscience, Public Reform, and Disguised Rule in *The Malcontent* and *Measure for Measure*'. *Ben Jonson Journal* 21, no. 1 (2014): 73–91.

Whitaker, William. *A Disputation on Holy Scripture, Against the Papists, Especially Bellarmine and Stapleton*. Translated and edited by William Fitzgerald. Cambridge: The University Press, 1849.

White, R. S. *Let Wonder Seem Familiar: Endings in Shakespeare's Romance Vision*. New Jersey: Humanities Press, 1985.

White, Robert. '*Theatrum mundi*: the Theatre Metaphor in Calvin'. *Australian Journal of French Studies* 31, no. 3 (1994): 309–25.

Wicks, Jared. 'Roman Reactions to Luther: The First Year (1518)'. *The Catholic Historical Review* 69, no. 4 (1983): 521–62.

Wilcox, Helen. 'Measuring up to Nebuchadnezzar: Biblical Presences in Shakespeare's Tragicomedies'. In *Early Modern Drama and the Bible: Contexts and Readings, 1570–1625*, edited by Adrian Streete, 48–67. New York: Palgrave Macmillan, 2012.

———. 'Shakespeare's Miracle Play? Religion in *All's Well That Ends Well*'. In *All's Well That Ends Well: New Critical Essays*, edited by Gary Waller, 140–54. New York: Routledge, 2007.

Williams, Rowan. *Faith in the Public Square*. London: Bloomsbury Publishing, 2012.

Wilson, Thomas. *The Arte of Rhetorique*. London: Ihon Kingston, 1560.

Windeatt, Barry. *Troilus and Criseyde*. Oxford: Clarendon Press, 1992.

Wither, George. *An A.B.C. For Layemen*. London: Robert Waldegraue, 1585.

Wolfe, Jessica. *Homer and the Question of Strife from Erasmus to Hobbes*. Toronto: University of Toronto Press, 2015.

Wriedt, Markus. 'Luther's Theology'. Translated by Katharina Gustavs. In *The Cambridge Companion to Martin Luther*, edited by Donald K. McKim, 86–119. Cambridge: Cambridge University Press, 2003.

Yachnin, Paul. 'Shakespeare's Problem Plays and the Drama of His Time: *Troilus and Cressida, All's Well That Ends Well, Measure for Measure*'. In *A Companion to Shakespeare's Works, Volume IV: The Poems, Problem Comedies, Late Plays*, edited by Richard Dutton and Jean E. Howard, 46–68. Oxford: Blackwell Publishing, 2005.

Zakai, Avihu. 'Reformation, History, and Eschatology in English Protestantism'. *History and Theory* 26, no. 3 (1987): 300–18.

Zamir, Tzachi (ed.). *Shakespeare's Hamlet: Philosophical Perspectives*. New York: Oxford University Press, 2018.

Zimmermann, Jens. 'The Ethics of Philosophical Hermeneutics and the Challenge of Religious Transcendence'. *Philosophy Today* 51 (2007): 50–9.

———. 'Gadamer's Century: Life, Times, and Works'. In *The Gadamerian Mind*, edited by Theodore George and Gert-Jan van der Heiden, 9–23. London: Routledge, 2021.

———. *Humanism and Religion: A Call for the Renewal of Western Culture*. Oxford: Oxford University Press, 2012.

———. 'Ignoramus: Gadamer's "Religious Turn"'. *Symposium* 6, no. 2 (2002): 203–17.

———. *Recovering Theological Hermeneutics: An Incarnational-Trinitarian Theory of Interpretation*. Grand Rapids, MI: Baker Academic, 2004.

Zwingli, Ulrich. 'On the Lord's Supper'. In *Zwingli and Bullinger*. Edited and translated by G. W. Bromiley, 185–238. London: SCM Press, 1953.

INDEX

Printed in the USA
CPSIA information can be obtained
at www.ICGtesting.com
LVHW052307310723
753641LV00019B/54